Month-By-Month
GARDENING
IN
PENNSYLVANIA

Month-By-Month
GARDENING
IN
PENNSYLVANIA

Liz Ball

COOL
SPRINGS
PRESS

Franklin, Tennessee

Ball, Liz.
        Month-by-month gardening in Pennsylvania / Liz Ball.
        p. cm.
        Includes bibliographical references (p.   ).
        ISBN 1-930604-50-5 (pbk. : alk. paper)
        1. Gardening--Pennsylvania I. Title.

SB453.2.P4 B36 2001
635'.09748--dc21

                                                    00-012742

Published by Cool Springs Press, a Division of Thomas Nelson, Inc.,
P.O. Box 141000, Nashville, Tennessee 37214.

First printing 2001

Printed in the United States of America
10 9 8 7 6 5 4 3

Horticultural Nomenclature Editor: Dr. Ken Tilt

On the Cover: Lilac; photographed by Alan Detrick

Visit the Thomas Nelson website at: www.ThomasNelson.com

DEDICATION

To the memory of Tugger, wonderful cat companion, who lived

out his allotted days in my garden.

ACKNOWLEDGEMENTS

I am indebted once again to my many horticultural friends in Pennsylvania who have
shared their knowledge and experiences with me over the years. I am most grateful, in particular,
to Charlotte Kidd and Bob Lollo for their able research, and to Rick Ray and
Charles O. Cresson for their patient support, loving advice, and expert editing services.
A special thank you, also, to Jane Alling at the McLean Library of the
Pennsylvania Horticultural Society for her speedy research.

Many thanks to Billie Brownell, Jan Keeling, and all the friendly, supportive staff at
Cool Springs Press for their help and understanding. Much appreciation to Dr. Ken Tilt for
the horticultural read. Finally, a special thank you to Louise Richter for giving me a
Spider Plant many, many years ago.

Contents

Contents

Introduction

"I have undertaken this work, and arranged the matter according to the seasons of the year, that the reader may have an easy reference to the particular business to be performed in every month."

Bernard M'Mahon, 1806
The American Gardener's Calendar

The idea of providing information about gardening and plant care in a monthly schedule is as practical and appropriate an approach to gardening for the 21st Century as it was for the 19th Century when Irishman Bernard M'Mahon arrived in the recently established United States of America. He settled in Pennsylvania—then, as now, Philadelphia was a center of horticultural activity and interest—and founded a successful seed and nursery business here. In 1806 he published *The American Gardener's Calendar,* a compendium of the most advanced horticultural knowledge of the day.

Much of the information came from England, where gardening had a long, established tradition, but M'Mahon modified and adapted it for climate and soil conditions here in the states. For the next fifty years and through eleven editions, his book was the best gardening resource available. It covered everything from kitchen gardens to fruit trees to flower gardening to landscape design. The calendar format, proving to be enormously useful, was imitated but not improved on for many years.

In the tradition of M'Mahon's book and in the shadow of his achievement, *Month-by-Month Gardening in Pennsylvania* provides a resource for contemporary gardeners and homeowners. Although the times have changed, technology has changed, and, sadly, the environment has changed, plants have not. Nor have people's interest in and enthusiasm for caring for them. There is still a season for all things, especially in the garden.

Benefits of a Gardening Schedule

Successful gardening involves being willing to make time when it is time to do certain tasks in the garden. Caring for plants is a team effort, and the other member of the team, Mother Nature, is extremely organized. If we are to have success, we must cooperate with her schedule, although experience teaches that it is not as rigid a schedule as it may seem. Over time, gardeners learn where there is flexibility and forgiveness in the rapid progression of the days that turn into weeks, turning into months, then seasons. There is some adaptability in the seemingly relentless parade of responsibilities and tasks. In the effort to keep up, we can learn a lot about our own ability to be flexible and forgiving.

Caring for plants is not rocket science. Most of the tasks are not difficult at all. The difficult part is the timing—knowing when to do them. It helps to understand how plants grow and how weather and soil work, to know how plants and animals interact, to learn how light and moisture affect everything. It helps to consult a book such as this one that outlines the main tasks involved in raising and growing all kinds of plants through the year.

Introduction

Consider this book a basic calendar, a playbook that will make you a better member of the gardening team.

Eventually you will write a garden calendar of your own. You will read a lot of reminders in this book of how valuable it is to keep a garden notebook or journal. Not only will recording information about your previous years' gardens help keep you organized, it will also save you time and energy by reminding you of past mistakes. Recalling through your notes both the great successes and the notable failures will help you learn and understand the dynamics of weather, soil, light, moisture, and plant behavior on your own property. The calendar of tasks that evolves from your experiences in your own garden will ultimately make your own personal book much more useful than this one could ever be.

How to Use This Book

This volume is intended to be a practical reference.

- Look at it when you are considering creating a garden or acquiring a new plant. It will help you anticipate and avoid problems and plan your work so you are not overwhelmed during the busy garden and yard care months. It is **not** intended to be a nag or a reproach about things left undone or unfinished.

- Consult it when you are planning changes in your landscape.

- Use it as a guideline for caring effectively for whatever plants you grow, including proper pruning times. If you have only a couple of houseplants, or just grow some tomatoes during the summer, it will help. If you are a non-gardening homeowner and your landscape consists of only some spring bulbs, a lawn, and a few trees and shrubs, it will help. If you are a beginning gardener, it will give you the confidence to try more plants. If you are an experienced gardener, it will inspire you to expand your gardening skills even further.

Other Resources

To get a fuller perspective on growing the groups of plants included in this book, consult the resource material in the back. There is a glossary of terms used in the text and the planting charts, and a list of award-winning trees and shrubs that are especially appropriate for Pennsylvania. There are lists of county extension agents, plant societies, horticultural organizations, and other information resources. This book is about time, about **when to** perform certain tasks in the yard and garden. For more detailed information on **how to** perform the specific tasks, consult books devoted to pruning, seed-starting, fertilizers, individual plant families, and design principles.

Gardening in Pennsylvania

Growing Plants in Pennsylvania

Homeowners and gardeners in Pennsylvania are fortunate. Situated between colder Northern states that have serious winters and shorter growing seasons and the warmer Southern states where winters are not cold enough to grow certain plants, we have the best of both worlds. Even though the state encompasses several hardiness zones, an overwhelming number of ornamental and edible plants grow well almost everywhere in Pennsylvania. Add to that the legacy of rich soil from the protective eastern hardwood forest that carpeted the state for eons, and the fairly generous rainfall throughout the seasons most years, and you have great conditions for gardening.

As it stretches from the Delaware River to Lake Erie, Pennsylvania's varied topography influences the climate across the state. Climatic variation is most obvious and significant in the winter months, when as you move westward as indicated by the USDA cold-hardiness zone map on p. 339, increasingly cooler conditions prevail. In other words, as you travel in a western direction, the dates of expected frost in the fall are earlier, while those of last frost in the spring are later. The differences between the zones are about two weeks (see Quick Facts, p. 339).

The warmest area of Pennsylvania is just south of Philadelphia, with mild zone-7 temperatures fostered by proximity to the Delaware River and the big city. Here, where the gently rolling Piedmont arises from the coastal plain, on a good day the climate resembles that of Virginia. West and north toward the Allegheny Mountains, the increasing elevation promotes a zone-6 climate marked by slightly chillier mornings and evenings and earlier fall frosts. As the mountains yield to the Allegheny Plateau and Pittsburgh, a zone-5 climate prevails, and even earlier frost cuts short the outdoor growing season. An awareness of the zone in which you garden will help you select plants that are appropriate to that climate.

Growing Plants in the Home Landscape

State or regional climate is only one factor that influences gardening success; in many cases it is not even the most important one. All gardening is local, quite local. It is the conditions that prevail on your particular property that have the most impact on plants. Specific elements such as the type of soil, the amount of light, the presence of wind, the frequency of rainfall, and even the incidence of visits by deer are most important. It is your job to choose plants that are suitable for these conditions. The more adapted plants are to their environment, the healthier they will be.

It is a rare property where the soil, light, and moisture conditions are uniform throughout. In every yard there are microclimates—small areas where conditions are modified by the presence of buildings, natural springs, walls, large trees, or rows of shrubs. Second-story balconies and roof-overhang environments are different from open lawn areas and growing beds near pavement. These special areas offer opportunities for fine-tuning plant choices so that an even wider palette of plants can be used. Get to know them by reading, asking experts, visiting gardens, joining plant societies, and mostly by experience and experimentation. All great gardeners will tell you about the huge number of plants they have inadvertently killed over the years as they learned which ones suited their yards.

Your plants are part of an unique ecosystem, a community of living things both animal and vegetable that interact in a mutual effort to survive and be healthy. Whether you are installing an entirely new landscape on an undeveloped property or maintaining and enhancing an existing garden, it is useful to consider the entire yard when planning and planting. Consider the variations and take advantage of them.

Gardening in Pennsylvania

Plant Names

Most plants are referred to in this book by their common names, with their botanical names appearing in parentheses for accurate identification. Like people, plants have two names—a formal one and an informal one. Because the formal name is scientific, it is in Latin—that way botanists and horticulturists anywhere in the world can be sure they are all talking about the same plant. The formal name has two parts: the first is the genus, which indicates the group of related plants it belongs to; the second is the species, the word often describing a particular feature the plant shares with other members of the group. For example, *Hydrangea macrophylla* is a member of the **Hydrangea** group of shrubs, and it is one of the large-leaved ones (*macrophylla* means "large leaves").

A plant usually has only one formal, scientific name, but it may have several common names. Like people's nicknames, plant common names vary depending on their source. Often limited to a specific region, these colorful, descriptive appellations may be deeply rooted in the history and experience of local gardeners. In some areas of Pennsylvania, our native *Amelan-chier laevis* is called **Juneberry** or **Serviceberry,** but in parts of eastern Pennsylvania it is usually called **Shadblow,** because it blooms about the time the shad are running in the Delaware River. Common names remain in our memories better than Latin ones, because they reflect the regional and local culture which we share. For that reason we tolerate the confusion that sometimes arises when two different plants have the same common name. While they are not normally capitalized, in this book we have capitalized the common names in order to make them stand out in the text.

General Gardening Techniques

Most of the people I know are never as organized as they want to be. I am always impressed, though, by the organization skills of the wonderful gardeners I know. At least in the gardening part of their lives, they are very focused and aware of tasks that need to be done. More important, they get them done. Even the busiest gardeners make caring for their plants a priority. I suspect this is why they are so successful.

A sense of what needs to be done for plants over the months of the year is fundamental to being organized. Familiarity with the rhythms of the seasons, and the concomitant needs of plants, both indoors and outdoors, helps gardeners anticipate their needs. For seasoned gardeners, this sense comes from years of experience and observation of plant and weather behavior in their yards and gardens. For others, it can come from a book such as this one.

Plants that have their needs met are happy and have relatively little stress. Plants without stress are vigorous and healthy. If they are not debilitated by the effort of coping with drought, poor soil, or insufficient light, their natural defense systems are at peak performance, and they are able to fend off pest and disease problems. The savvy gardener knows that healthy plants can largely take care of themselves. It is easier in the long run to learn what each plant prefers for soil, light, moisture, nutrients, and protection, and to see to it that it gets it. A proactive approach, working *with* plants, is far easier than a reactive one, working *against* pest, disease, and environmental assaults later in the game.

Make a Plan

Just as in real estate, location is (almost) everything. The first step in plant care is to plan an appropriate place for each plant in its new environment. To assure its happiness, provide a situation that emulates its natural environment as closely as possible. For example, most flowering bulbs prefer sun and well-drained soil.

1 Make a sketch showing existing plants.

2 Identify areas of best sun and shade.

3 Designate an area for a compost pile.

4 Identify potential or actual microclimates.

5 Note which areas are convenient to the hose.

6 Consider fencing needs.

7 Locate existing drainage patterns and utilities.

Choose Good Plants

Choose plants that are appropriate for the sites. Do not fall for a plant simply because it is trendy, on sale, or gorgeous. It is easier to choose plants to fit the conditions on the property than to try to change conditions to suit the plant. Aim to have lots of different kinds of plants—trees, shrubs, bulbs, herbs—and lots of varieties of each. The more diverse the plants on your property, the more hosts there will be for the beneficial organisms and insects that will protect plants from predators.

- Choose perennials appropriate for your hardiness zone.

- Choose disease-resistant plant varieties.

- Buy many diverse kinds of plants.

- Select varieties for your preferences in color, height, texture, and other qualities.

- Choose plants to solve landscape problems.

General Gardening Techniques

Improve the Soil

Before planting, make improving the soil on your property a priority. In many areas of Pennsylvania the soil has historically been rich and arable; strive to maintain it. Our role models are the Amish farmers in Lancaster County who have not only maintained the soil as their farmer forefathers found it, but have improved it over the generations so it is even better and more productive. Good soil reduces garden work because it provides plant nutrients and holds moisture. The cliché is true: Take care of the soil and it will take care of the plants.

- Maintain soil acidity. Test for pH.

- Do not dig or cultivate soil that is very wet or very dry.

- Avoid compacting the soil.

- Add organic matter to the soil every year.

- Avoid pesticides that kill beneficial organisms in the soil.

- Use slow-acting fertilizers that work with microbial life to help the soil deliver nutrients to plants.

- Protect the soil in the off-season with a layer of organic mulch or a cover crop.

Plant Properly

In recent years we have learned a lot more about plants. New technology has promoted an understanding of how roots work at the molecular level, and this has changed planting practices for some groups of plants, especially trees and shrubs.

1 Plant at the correct depth.

2 Plant at the correct time of year.

3 Choose the correct method for bare-root, container, or balled-and-burlapped plants.

4 Allow enough space for the mature size of the plant.

5 Provide follow-up care until the plant is established.

Water Thoughtfully

Even though Pennsylvania usually receives adequate rainfall over the year, the rain does not always fall at regular intervals, and supplemental watering is often necessary. This is especially true for lawns and vegetable crops in summer. Plants vary in their need for moisture, and soils vary in their ability to hold the moisture and make it available to plants. Water by hose, sprinkler, or drip irrigation.

- Water newly planted plants generously.

- Water only when scarce rainfall makes watering necessary.

- Water the soil rather than the plant.

- Water plants according to their individual needs.

- Water according to soil quality—the better the soil, the less often watering will be needed.

- Water lawns deeply but not often.

- Conserve water by mulching to reduce runoff and loss through evaporation.

Fertilize Judiciously

How and when to fertilize plants is easy to determine. *Why* we fertilize is a little more complicated to explain. Fertilizer is intended to feed the soil, thus it feeds plants only indirectly. In situations where the soil has been depleted of certain nutrients—primarily nitrogen, potassium, phosphorus—and they have not been replaced naturally by the annual cycle of decay of organic debris, the gardener must add them to the soil in the form of fertilizer. The action of microbial life in the soil along with soil temperature and moisture helps convert the nutrients in the fertilizer into a form that can be taken up by plant roots. Whether

General Gardening Techniques

that happens rapidly or slowly depends on whether or not the fertilizer, especially its nitrogen, is soluble in water. Depending on what the soil test reveals, you may need fertilizer that is complete (has all three major nutrients). Sometimes the soil test will show that all nutrients are present, but they are not in balance. Then you must use a special fertilizer that features a greater proportion of one or more nutrients.

- Maintain the correct soil pH to assure optimum effectiveness of fertilizer.

- Topdress beds and lawns with organic material every year.

- Use slow-acting fertilizers for long-term, consistent nutrition over many weeks.

- Lime lawns and beds to provide calcium and magnesium to the soil. A soil test report will indicate the correct amount of lime.

- Fertilize just before or during the growing season, not when plants are dormant.

- Fertilize soil where plants are heavy feeders.

Prune Purposefully

Pruning is a very important to plant health. When done properly at the correct time, it fosters thick growth and prolific blooming and fruiting. It can bring back a plant from old age, forestall disease, or create a hedge or an espalier work of art. When done improperly or at the wrong time, it can ruin the next bloom season or even kill a plant. Woody plants such as trees, shrubs, and vines are most often pruned to control their size, but pruning at the wrong time will actually stimulate plant growth.

- Always have a pruning goal, and time the procedure correctly.

- Keep pruner, lopper, saw, and mower blades sharp.

- Prune or pinch off injured and diseased plant parts promptly.

- Disinfect pruning equipment used on diseased plants.

- Move plants that need constant pruning (to control size) to a larger space.

- Prune to maintain the natural shape of the plant. Reserve shearing for plants that will be trained to be formal hedges or topiary.

Protect Vulnerable Plants

If plants are chosen, sited, and cared for correctly, most of the time they will be able to cope with environmental and pest problems—but because cultivated plants in a residential landscape are in an essentially contrived environment, they sometimes need some protection from the elements and natural enemies.

- Stake plants that are vulnerable to injury by wind, rain, people.

- Know which potential pest problems affect your plants.

- Observe and inspect plants regularly for pest problems.

- Treat serious plant problems as soon as possible.

- Shelter or spray foliage of plants exposed to harsh winter wind and sun.

- Fence out critters.

- Mulch plants to buffer soil-temperature extremes around their roots.

- Overwinter tender plants in frost-free areas.

- Acclimatize plants gradually to indoor or outdoor sites.

Gardening Notes

Annuals

Everyone loves annuals because they are reliable. It is no wonder that annuals are the type of flowering plant most commonly planted by non-gardeners and beginners who want to decorate their home landscapes, apartment balconies, and sunny windows; and that they are also found in the most elegant gardens of the most experienced gardeners. They offer so much for so little.

Dependable Annuals

Count on annuals to bloom with abandon. Once the weather warms up, there is no holding them back. In no time at all they will be spilling onto the walks, punctuating the border, climbing arbors, carpeting beds, hanging from the porch roof in baskets and windowboxes, and overflowing containers of all kinds in and around the yard. They are perfect for sustaining color in the yard during the pauses between the various bloom times of perennials.

Count on annuals for color, just about any color imaginable. With the exception of true black, there is probably an annual out there with the exact color you want. **Petunias, Geraniums, Salvias, Marigolds, Zinnias, Impatiens**—the list goes on and on. Reliable color means the yard has a consistent look all season long. It means it is even possible to match color trim on shutters, lampposts, and windowboxes!

Count on annuals to keep producing blooms all season long. They live only one season, and they make the most of that time. Under a biological imperative to produce as much seed as possible to assure future generations, annuals direct their energy to producing flowers. This means a steady supply of blooms for indoor arrangements and outdoor beauty. By the time frost arrives to end their lives, they have given their all.

Count on annuals for versatility. Whatever the landscape situation, there is probably an annual that will suit it. Need a ground cover planting? There are annuals that creep. Need a screen to block a view? Many annuals are vines and will climb rambunctiously over a fence or trellis. There are trailing annual plants for hanging from baskets, or for scrambling over an eyesore to hide it. Others provide fragrance, attract butterflies or hummingbirds, edge a bed, lighten a shady area, or provide interesting, colorful foliage.

Count on annuals to be easy to care for. Most are quite self-reliant, requiring very little care once established. If they are planted correctly in an appropriate place, they manage just fine with only some extra water during droughty periods, a fertilizer energy boost every so often, and perhaps pinching back for renewal during the dog days of summer. Annuals rarely have serious disease or insect problems. In the event that they are besieged, they are inexpensive enough that it is a simple matter to pull them up and replace them with new transplants.

Annuals

Count on most annuals to grow easily from seed. If planted indoors under lights ahead of the season, most types of annuals fairly burst from seed to sprout in their effort to start pleasing, and most are ridiculously easy to grow from seed right in the garden. If sown in early or mid-May, they will have time to sprout and mature into flowering plants for the season; they are never very far behind the homegrown or store-bought transplants that are put into the garden slightly later in May.

Planting Annuals

Annuals, by definition, live their entire lives from seed through youth to mature flowering and seed formation over the course of a single season. Inevitably, they die with the onset of cold and frost. Each spring brings new opportunities to try annuals of different types and new colors, as soon as they are available at the garden center as young plants for transplanting into garden beds and containers. Purchasing started plants makes it possible to acquire exactly the color and number of plants you need. For many, this is the easiest, most efficient way to grow annuals.

Among last year's annuals, however, there may have been some "hardy" types that can handle some chill. Tougher than the average annual, these plants release copious numbers of seeds as they die and dry up. Since these seeds are able to withstand winter weather and germinate on their own in the spring, a new crop is virtually assured. Leave these bonus plants in place and thin them as they grow, or transplant them to other places in the yard. Some examples of hardy annuals are **Spider Flower, Snapdragon, Four-o'-clock, Cosmos, Love-in-a-mist,** and **Pot Marigold.**

Sowing Seed

Growing annuals from seed is less expensive than buying transplants. If you do not want to invest in and master the equipment for indoor seed-starting (or simply cannot get your act together to start seeds when it is still wintry outside), wait and sow seed directly into the garden. This is the preferred method for those annuals that do not transplant well because they have taproots, or because they grow too fast after germinating indoors while spring makes up its mind to arrive. Young seedlings grown outdoors in the garden are immediately acclimated; they do not need hardening off.

Broadcasting the seeds creates an informal, natural look in a bed or border, along a wall or fence, or in a mini-meadow. Simply take a handful of seeds, and gently sprinkle them randomly over the prepared soil. If the seeds are particularly tiny, such as those of **Portulaca** or **Petunia,** mix them with a bit of coarse sand or vermiculite so they are easier to cast evenly over the area. Toss larger seeds such as **Nasturtium** freestyle, then poke them gently into the soil where they fall. Check to see if the package label says seeds must be covered with soil or left exposed to light.

Alternatively, you may choose to sow annual seeds in more formal rows. This is the most efficient way to plant if you are growing them for cutting, or if you want to fit them into a designed bed where several plants are in front of or behind them. Follow the directions on the seed packet.

Annuals for Pennsylvania

Common Name (Botanical Name)	Bloom Time Height	Type	Light Needs Water Needs	Start Seeds Indoors (or Direct-Sow) Degree of Difficulty
African Daisy (*Dimorphotheca* sp.)	Summer 12 inches	Tender	Sun Low	4 to 5 weeks before last frost Moderate
Alyssum, Sweet (*Lobularia maritima*)	Summer to fall 4 to 8 inches	Hardy	Sun Low	(Direct-sow outdoors) Easy
Baby's Breath (*Gypsophila elegans*)	Summer (2 to 3 weeks) 15 to 18 inches	Hardy	Sun Low	(Direct-sow into garden) Easy
Bachelor's Button (*Centaurea cyanus*)	Summer 12 to 30 inches	Hardy	Sun Low	(Direct-sow into garden) Easy
Begonia, Wax/ Fibrous Begonia (*Begonia semperflorens-cultorum* hybrids)	Later spring to early fall 6 to 12 inches	Half-hardy	Sun to shade Medium	8 to 12 weeks before last frost Difficult
Blanket Flower (*Gaillardia pulchella*)	Summer 24 to 30 inches	Hardy	Sun Low	4 to 6 weeks (or direct-sow fall/spring) Moderately easy
Browallia (*Browallia speciosa*)	Summer 9 to 10 inches	Half-hardy	Sun to part shade High	8 to 10 weeks before last frost Easy (may self-sow)
Busy Lizzie (*Impatiens wallerana*)	Late spring to fall 8 to 24 inches	Tender	Part shade to shade High	8 weeks before last frost Moderate
California Poppy (*Eschscholzia californica*)	Spring through summer 8 to 12 inches	Hardy	Sun Low	(Direct-sow in fall or early spring) Easy (may self-sow)
Candytuft, Globe (*Iberis umbellata*)	Summer 8 inches	Hardy	Sun Medium	(Direct-sow late fall or spring) Moderately easy
Cockscomb (*Celosia* sp.)	Summer through fall 6 to 12 inches	Half-hardy	Sun Low	4 to 6 weeks before last frost Moderately easy

Annuals for Pennsylvania

Common Name (Botanical Name)	Bloom Time Height	Type	Light Needs Water Needs	Start Seeds Indoors (or Direct-Sow) Degree of Difficulty
Coleus (*Solenostemon scutellarioides*)	Late spring to early fall 8 to 20 inches	Tender	Shade, sun for cultivars High	6 to 8 weeks before last frost Moderately easy
Corn Poppy (*Papaver rhoeas*)	Summer 18 inches	Hardy	Sun	(Direct-sow seeds fall/early spring) Easy
Cosmos (*Cosmos bipinnatus*)	Spring to early fall 24 to 60 inches	Half-hardy	Sun Low	6 to 8 weeks before last frost Easy
Cupflower (*Nierembergia hippomanica*)	Summer 6 to 15 inches	Half-hardy	Sun High	8 to 10 weeks before last frost Easy
Dusty Miller (*Senecio cineraria*)	Summer through fall 12 inches	Half-hardy	Sun Low	6 to 8 weeks before last frost Easy
Floss Flower (*Ageratum houstonianum*)	Summer 6 to 24 inches	Half-hardy	Sun, part shade Medium	6 to 10 weeks before last frost Easy
Forget-me-not (*Myosotis sylvatica*)	Spring 7 to 12 inches	Hardy	Sun High	4 to 6 weeks before last frost Easy
Four-o'-clock (*Mirabilis jalapa*)	Midsummer to fall 10 to 18 inches	Hardy	Sun Low	4 to 6 weeks before last frost Easy (may self-sow)
Geranium (*Pelargonium × hortorum*)	Summer 8 to 14 weeks	Tender	Sun to part shade High	10 to 12 weeks before last frost Easy
Globe Amaranth (*Gomphrena globosa*)	Late spring to early fall 8 to 30 inches	Half-hardy	Sun Low	6 to 8 weeks before last frost Easy
Gloriosa Daisy (*Rudbeckia hirta*)	Summer 24 to 30 inches	Tender	Sun Low	6 to 8 weeks before last frost Easy (may self-sow)

Annuals for Pennsylvania

Common Name (Botanical Name)	Bloom Time Height	Type	Light Needs Water Needs	Start Seeds Indoors (or Direct-Sow) Degree of Difficulty
Heliotrope (*Heliotropium arborescens*)	Summer to fall 15 (dwarf) to 48 inches	Tender	Sun to part shade Medium	10 to 12 weeks before last frost Easy
Johnny-Jump-Up (*Viola tricolor*)	Spring and fall 8 inches	Hardy	Sun, part shade Medium	12 weeks before last frost Easy (also self-sows)
Larkspur (*Consolida ambigua*)	Spring 18 to 36 inches	Hardy	Sun, part shade Medium	(Direct-sow outdoors fall or spring) Difficult
Love-in-a-mist (*Nigella damascena*)	Spring 12 to 18 inches	Hardy	Sun Low	(Direct-sow into garden) Moderately easy (self-sows)
Marigold (*Tagetes* sp.)	Summer, fall 8 to 36 inches	Tender	Sun	4 to 6 weeks before last frost Very easy
Medallion Flower (*Leucanthemum paludosum* syn. *Melampodium*)	Late spring to early fall 18 to 24 inches	Tender	Sun Low to medium	(Direct-sow into garden when weather warms) Easy
Mexican Sunflower (*Tithonia rotundifolia*)	Summer to fall 36 to 60 inches	Tender	Sun Medium	4 to 6 weeks before last frost Easy
Moss Rose (*Portulaca grandiflora*)	Summer to early fall 4 to 8 feet	Half-hardy	Sun Low	8 weeks before last frost (or direct-sow) Easy (also self-sows)
Nasturtium (*Tropaeolum majus*)	Summer and fall Creeps 8 to 12 feet	Half-hardy	Sun Low to medium	Direct-sow outdoors in garden Easy
Ornamental Cabbage and Kale (*Brassica oleracea*)	Fall to spring 8 to 14 inches	Hardy	Sun High	8 to 10 weeks before last frost in spring (or direct-sow) Moderately easy
Pansy (*Viola × wittrockiana*)	Fall, winter, spring 4 to 8 inches	Hardy	Sun, part shade Medium	12 weeks before last frost Easy

Annuals for Pennsylvania

Common Name (Botanical Name)	Bloom Time Height	Type	Light Needs Water Needs	Start Seeds Indoors (or Direct-Sow) Degree of Difficulty
Petunia (*Petunia × hybrida*)	Spring through summer 6 to 18 inches	Half-hardy	Sun Medium	10 to 12 weeks before last frost Moderate
Phlox, Annual (*Phlox drummondii*)	Summer To 18 inches	Half-hardy	Sun Medium	(Direct-sow into garden in spring) Easy
Pincushion Flower (*Scabiosa atropurpurea*)	Summer 20 to 24 inches	Half-hardy	Sun Medium	4 to 5 weeks before last frost Easy
Polka-Dot Plant (*Hypoestes phyllostachya*)	Summer 12 inches	Half-hardy	Sun to part shade Medium	6 to 8 weeks before last frost Moderate
Pot Marigold (*Calendula officinalis*)	Spring 18 to 25 inches; dwarf, 12 inches	Hardy	Sun, part shade Medium	6 to 8 weeks before last frost Easy
Red Salvia (*Salvia splendens*)	Summer 7 to 24 inches	Half-hardy	Sun Low	8 to 10 weeks before last frost Moderate
Snapdragon (*Antirrhinum majus*)	Spring to summer; fall 6 to 36 inches	Half-hardy	Sun, part shade Medium	12 weeks before last frost Easy
Spider Flower (*Cleome hasslerana*)	Summer through fall 3 to 5 feet	Hardy	Sun Low	4 to 6 weeks before last frost Moderately easy (also self-sows)
Statice (*Limonium sinuatum*)	Summer 30 inches	Half-hardy	Sun Low	8 to 12 weeks before last frost Moderately easy
Strawflower (*Helichrysum bracteatum* syn. *Bracteantha bracteata*)	Spring through fall 16 to 18 inches	Half-hardy	Sun Medium	6 to 8 weeks before last frost Easy
Sunflower (*Helianthus annuus*)	Summer 2 to 12 feet	Hardy	Sun Low	(Direct-sow into garden) Easy

Annuals for Pennsylvania

Common Name (Botanical Name)	Bloom Time Height	Type	Light Needs Water Needs	Start Seeds Indoors (or Direct-Sow) Degree of Difficulty
Sweet William (*Dianthus barbatus*)	Late summer 6 to 12 inches	Hardy	Sun Medium to low	10 weeks before last frost Moderately easy
Tobacco Flower (*Nicotiana alata*)	Summer To 5 feet	Tender	Sun, part shade Medium	6 to 8 weeks before last frost Moderately easy
Transvaal Daisy (*Gerbera jamesonii*)	Summer 12 to 24 inches	Half-hardy	Sun Medium	8 to 10 weeks before last frost Difficult (plant nursery-grown)
Treasure Flower (*Gazania* series)	Summer 8 to 11 inches	Half-hardy	Sun Low	4 to 6 weeks before last frost Moderately easy
Verbena (*Verbena × hybrida*)	Summer 10 to 20 inches	Half-hardy	Sun Low	8 to 10 weeks before last frost Moderately easy
Vinca/Madagascar Periwinkle (*Catharanthus roseus*)	Summer 4 to 18 inches	Tender	Sun to part shade Low	12 weeks before last frost Moderate
Wishbone Flower (*Torenia fournieri*)	Summer through fall 8 inches	Tender	Part shade to shade Medium	8 to 10 weeks before last frost Easy
Zinnia, Tall (*Zinnia elegans*)	Summer to fall To 36 inches	Half-hardy	Sun Low	5 to 7 weeks before last frost Easy

Planning

It's never too soon to begin planning this year's garden. The colorful seed and plant catalogs are piling up, begging for attention, and January is the perfect time to consult them. Most mail-order companies also have websites that offer lots of help for gardeners. Even if you do not buy annual flowering plants or seeds by mail, catalogs provide a wealth of information. They:

- highlight new varieties.

- provide cultural information.

- help you learn the names of plants, common and botanical.

- help you compare prices.

- provide cooking and storing information for vegetables, fruits, and herbs.

- suggest ways to use plants in your landscape.

Think about whether you will raise your own seedlings indoors or wait and buy transplants from the garden center. Probably you will end up doing both. While it is a bit early to actually start seeds, it is not too early to select and order them.

Order seed-starting supplies as well. Commercially designed equipment such as adjustable fluorescent lights and a heat mat produces sturdy, vigorous seedlings. Study the catalogs for various seed-starting systems that can make it much easier to produce young plants than does a makeshift arrangement on a windowsill.

Consult past garden journals or calendars to refresh your memory of the annuals that did best and looked best in your yard last year. Labels that you have (hopefully) kept will remind you of the specific varieties you chose.

In anticipation of planting seeds to raise your own seedlings, buy or build a sturdy, freestanding light table for seedlings. This can be put out of the way in a basement or unused room and will free up valuable counter space elsewhere.

1 Securely fasten a board onto already-assembled sawhorses, or convert an existing workbench to use as a shelf to hold trays (flats) of sown seeds. Surfaces that measure 4 feet long and 20 inches wide are roomy enough for several flats or small pots.

2 Erect lights over the shelf—install a frame to support one or two inexpensive shop lights that hold at least two 40-watt ordinary fluorescent tubes. If you suspend them on chains from hooks in the ceiling over a shelf or bench, they can be easily adjusted for height.

3 Arrange the light setup so that the lamps can be raised so they are always 2 to 3 inches above the stem tips of young seedlings as they grow over the months.

Planting

If you are propagating some annuals from last year by rooting stem cuttings taken in the fall, they should be well rooted by now. Pot up **Coleus, Geranium, Wax Begonia, Impatiens,** and others in

Freestanding Light Table

soilless mix with granular slow-acting fertilizer added. Expect those rooted in a glass of water to droop a bit until they adjust to a soil-like environment. You can tell they are established when they begin to develop new leaves.

Seeds of cool-season annuals that need a long head-start may need sowing indoors by the end of this month. Read the instructions on the seed packets. Most warm-season annuals will not go out into the garden until May, so wait awhile before sowing their seed indoors.

Care for Your Annuals

Planted rooted cuttings need lots of bright light in winter when daylight hours are limited. Put them in a bright window or under some fluorescent lights in the kitchen.

Watering

Periodically *check* newly potted rooted cuttings for moisture. If the house is warm and/or they are in clay pots, they will dry out quickly.

Fertilizing

If you added granular slow-acting fertilizer to the planting medium when you potted up the cuttings, there is no need to fertilize any more. If not, add some *very* dilute water-soluble (fast-acting) fertilizer to their water every two weeks or so. *Plants that are not blooming do not need much fertilizer.*

Grooming

As they stretch to reach the limited light from the window, indoor annuals develop leggy stems. *Pinch them back* to keep the plants compact. Put them under fluorescent lights if necessary.

Problem Solving

Indoor plants of all kinds are bothered by pest insects because the plants are under stress. New seedlings and young plants are extremely vulnerable. Typically the air is too dry from hot-air heat, there are drafts, and the light is insufficient because of the reduced number of daylight hours in early winter.

Whiteflies, aphids, scale, and mites—the big four—plague potted annual cuttings and annual plants brought indoors just as they do regular houseplants and outdoor plants.

- *Rinse* infested foliage and stems under the faucet to interrupt the insects' life cycle.

- *Pinch off* leaves that have scale if the plant can spare them; otherwise, scrape off the crusty bumps with a fingernail.

- *Spray* the plant thoroughly with light (superior) horticultural oil to handle major scale infestations.

Growing Smarter

There is time now to do things you will not have time for once the gardening season begins.

- Clean and sharpen tools.
- Paint the wooden handles of tools with a bright color so they are easily found in the garden.
- Check **Geraniums** that are overwintering bare-root in the dry basement.
- Catch up on journal entries.
- Read gardening books and magazines.
- Clean up empty containers stored indoors.

Planning

Finalize your decisions about which annuals you will purchase as seeds by mail. Some are best started indoors several weeks before last frost is expected in your area so they will have grown into young plants when it is safe to plant outdoors. Some seeds you will sow directly into the garden when the soil warms and dries. If you prefer to purchase annuals at the store, look for them in garden and home centers soon.

Many mail-order seed catalogs advertise commercially raised young annual or biennial plants for spring planting outdoors. If you plan to use them, get your order in early to be sure that the company will have your first choice. The young plants will be delivered at the appropriate planting time for your part of Pennsylvania.

Seeds of plants that do not mind cool weather, such as **Pansy** and **Calendula,** should be started indoors at least six weeks before last frost, so this is the month to plant them. Check the individual seed packets for specific timing according to where you live in Pennsylvania. Count backwards on the calendar from the last frost date in your region of Pennsylvania (see Appendix for frost dates).

Planting

If you did not plant **Pansies** in the garden last fall, look for young transplants now at your local garden or home center. If they have been kept in cool conditions at the store, they will be hardened off enough to go right into the ground as soon as it thaws. If it snows after you plant them, they will be okay.

Some biennials—plants that sprouted and developed leaves last season and will be flowering this season—may be visible in the garden if there is no snow cover. Look for clumps of **Forget-me-not** and **Money Plant.** If they are bunched together, you may want to *transplant* them to different locations when it is possible to work the soil in a month or two.

Sprouts from seeds sown indoors at the end of last month will need transplanting into larger pots by mid-month. Use regular soilless planting mix with slow-acting fertilizer, and repot.

It's time to set up a light stand if you are starting seeds indoors now (see January). Follow these steps to start seeds indoors under lights:

1 Fill wooden or plastic flats or peat pots with moistened soilless mix. Fine-grained soilless mixes labeled specifically for seed-starting are ideal, but not essential.

2 Following seed packet instructions, *sow* the seed in the flats. Some seeds must be covered with mix; others require exposure to light.

3 *Label* each flat or pot to keep track of what you are growing, as new sprouts look amazingly similar.

4 *Cover* the flats or pots with plastic wrap, or slip them into plastic bags to prevent the potting mix from drying out.

5 Attach the lights to a timer and set it so the plants receive 10 to 12 hours of bright light per day.

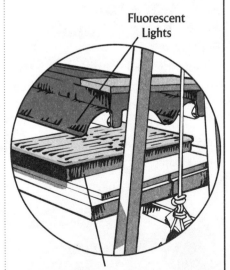

Fluorescent Lights

Seed-Starter Tray in 10x20" Flat Tray

6 *Optional* Set the flats or pots on a warming mat to promote faster germination.

Care for Your Annuals

If the rooted cuttings you took in the fall are not already potted, *pot* them as soon as substantial roots develop. To promote sturdy stems and a compact habit, *pinch* the stems of any that are getting leggy. (These pinchings might be rooted for even more plants!)

To care for indoor seedlings:

1 *Remove* any plastic covers from the new sprouts so that they avoid damping off. *Moisten* planting medium when it begins to dry out.

2 Adjust the lights periodically so that they are always about 2 inches above the growing plants.

3 To avoid a hopeless tangle of roots, separate seedlings in flats as soon as they develop true leaves (their second set). *Plant* them in individual pots in soilless medium.

Watering

Water young plants from rooted cuttings when the soil feels dry about 1 inch down. *Do not overwater.*

Keep seedlings moist, but not wet. *Water from below*, if possible.

Fertilizing

If you did not add slow-acting fertilizer to the potting medium of rooted cuttings, add some water-soluble fertilizer to the water every two weeks when you water them.

Seeds carry their own energy for early development, and sprouts will need no fertilizer for awhile. Delay fertilizing until you transplant the seedlings into individual containers. Add a granular, slow-acting fertilizer to the planting medium, or water gently with a *very* dilute liquid fertilizer every week or two.

Problem Solving

Aphids and whiteflies annoy young indoor annuals. They seem to come out of nowhere, but they are probably on nearby houseplants. *Spray* persistent pests on plant foliage with commercial insecticidal soap.

Damping off is the bane of seedlings. It is caused by a pathogen in the real soil base and is aggravated by overwet medium. Young seedlings will seem to be progress-

Growing Smarter

All-America Selections (AAS) is an independent, nonprofit organization that tests promising new varieties of annual flower and vegetable plants. Each year certain plants that show outstanding performance in trial gardens all across the country are selected as winners. They must demonstrate superior home-garden qualities when compared to existing varieties already on the market in North America. They must also meet criteria for introductions such as laboratory germination tests. Look for the AAS emblem on plant labels, seed packets, and catalog descriptions to ensure that you will be growing winning varieties. For more information, visit the AAS website: www.all-americaselections.org.

ing well, then suddenly their stems darken near the surface of the planting medium and they topple over. To prevent damping off:

* Use *soilless* planting medium. (It is sterile.)

* Water sprouts from below.

* Maintain light and humidity to avoid stressing new sprouts.

Planning

This is the month to start thinking seriously about beginning outdoor work in the yard and garden. While it is still too early to transplant most plants into cold, wet garden soil, some cold-loving annuals will start to appear at garden centers. **Pansies** and their **Johnny-Jump-Up** and **Viola** cousins can handle chill, and you can try planting them in windowboxes and containers filled with soilless mix.

Some of the seedlings you have raised may be outgrowing their indoor space, but it is too soon to transplant them directly into the garden. Consider setting up a "halfway house" or cold frame outdoors to help the young plants begin their transition to the cooler yard. Spending some time in this sort of sheltered nursery is a good way for them to "harden off"—to adjust to cool, outdoor conditions before they go into the ground.

Planting

Certain annuals can be sown directly into the garden this month even though it is still cold. **Sweet Peas** and **Corn Poppies** are good examples. Their seeds need chilly conditions for germination. Check seed packets for exact timing.

Sometime this month you can *sow* seeds indoors for those warm-weather-loving annuals that need six to eight weeks' lead time before they are old enough to go into the soil. Determine the date for the expected last frost in your area in Pennsylvania, and count back the number of weeks indicated on the seed packet. In the Philadelphia area, last frost is expected about April 20. Add two weeks or so to that for central Pennsylvania, and assume that last frost is a full month later (May 20) in the mountains. Consult your garden notebook or journal for previous years' dates.

If you haven't done so already, *transplant* into larger pots seedlings that were started last month. If there is no granular, slow-acting fertilizer incorporated into the potting mix, add some before potting. Otherwise, plan to water seedlings with a very dilute, fast-acting, water-soluble product at about half the strength suggested on the label.

Bring out **Geraniums** that were stored bare-root over the winter in the basement or attic. *Examine* them and *pot them up* if they are in good condition. Their stems should be green, even though their leaves are dried out. Use the usual soilless potting medium with slow-acting fertilizer mixed in.

Care for Your Annuals

Annuals established from rooted cuttings probably have been enjoying the increased daylight hours as spring approaches. They may need repotting into larger containers before it is safe to finally plant them outdoors.

Adjust fluorescent lights over young annuals grown indoors from seed to within 2 or 3 inches of the tops of the plants as they grow. This will keep the stems sturdy. You can tell the days are getting longer—there are more daylight hours—when you have to adjust the timer. If seedlings are growing on a windowsill, *rotate* them periodically so that light falls on every side, and this will keep them from leaning too much.

Research suggests that gently brushing tender tops of seedlings a couple of times a day with your fingertips or open hand helps them develop sturdy stems.

Watering

Use a houseplant water meter to be sure annuals grown from rooted cuttings do not dry out. While the central heating is still on, potting medium will dry out faster—especially in clay (terracotta) pots. Stick the probe down into the soil to where the roots are growing, and water if the meter indicates *dry*.

Keep seedlings moist, but do not soak the soil; it is okay if they dry out slightly between waterings. In fact, many annuals like to have a wet/dry cycle. If seedlings dry out very quickly, this signals that they need repotting into a larger pot. Its larger volume of planting medium will hold more moisture. Always water with tepid water, not water directly from the cold-water faucet.

Fertilizing

In the milder parts of the state, it may just be possible to get outside and start to work the soil by the end of this month. If it has dried out enough so it does not turn into a sticky ball when you grab a handful and squeeze, begin to *dig* the beds to loosen and aerate the soil in which you plan to plant annuals. To provide transplants with long-term, consistent nutrition, add granular slow-acting fertilizer to the soil as you work.

Grooming

The key to full, compact, bushy annuals is pinching the tips of their stems periodically as they mature

Growing Smarter

These are the advantages to growing annuals from seed indoors:

- It is less expensive.
- There's no need to wait until spring to garden.
- There are more varieties to choose from.
- You can experience the enjoyment of an indoor gardening activity.

These are the advantages to buying annuals as transplants:

- It saves time and energy.
- Professionally raised plants are dependably sturdy.
- You are able to choose just the number of plants you want.
- It is easier to select for color.

from seedlings to young transplants. This will stimulate them to generate more stems and foliage. Do this with plants purchased at the garden center as well, if they show a tendency to grow too lanky.

Problem Solving

Spider mites are often a problem on plants that have been under the stress of indoor living for months. If indoor annuals look a little "off," their foliage slightly mottled or speckled with yellow dots, inspect them. Spider mites are almost too small to see without a magnifying glass, but they cause pale stippling on the leaves, and sometimes they make a fine webbing on stems and leaves. *Wash* the plant foliage in tepid water from the faucet several times a week to remove and disrupt

the mites. Use insecticidal soap on stubborn infestations, following label directions.

Damping off remains a threat to new homegrown seedlings (see February).

The presence of **leggy stems** on seedlings is a condition usually caused by insufficient light. *Lower* the fluorescent lights to within 2 inches of the plant tops.

Pale, yellowed foliage indicates that seedlings or young potted annuals need some fertilizer.

Weeds, believe it or not, are likely to appear outdoors any time now in the spots you intend to plant annuals. *Pull them* or *cultivate the soil* to destroy them before planting new transplants in the garden bed. *Spread mulch* over the soil to discourage weed seeds from germinating.

APRIL

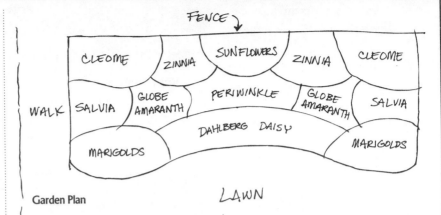

FENCE

CLEOME ZINNIA SUNFLOWERS ZINNIA CLEOME

WALK SALVIA GLOBE AMARANTH PERIWINKLE GLOBE AMARANTH SALVIA

DAHLBERG DAISY

MARIGOLDS MARIGOLDS

Garden Plan LAWN

Planning

Finally! Annual gardening goes outdoors by the end of this month. The danger of hard frost is past in all but the coldest areas of Pennsylvania. Spring is on the calendar, if not on the thermometer, and the switch to Eastern Daylight Saving Time shifts the increasing number of daylight hours to later in the day so there will be more time to garden after work.

Young annual plants are arriving daily at the garden center in a swirl of bright color. Think about trying a kind of annual you have never grown before. Notice which plants prefer sun and which do well in part shade so you will have the right plant for the right place in your landscape. While you are at the garden center, buy bags of soilless potting mix and granular, slow-acting fertilizer labeled for flowers. Other things on the shopping list: stakes, string, plant labels, journal or notebook for garden records, insecticidal soap, and light horticultural oil.

If you need an excuse to get outdoors, there's lots of work to be done:

- Clean up hanging containers, garden ornaments, and flower pots.

- Clean, repair, and refurbish birdhouses and feeders.

- Pick up sticks and other debris on planted beds.

- Reset and secure stones in walls and terraces that may have been moved by freeze-and-thaw cycles in the soil over the winter.

Planting

If they are not already going strong out in the garden, put out some **Pansies.** They are ideal for a ground cover planting among **Daffodils, Tulips,** and other bulbs. They also brighten windowboxes and planters.

Young plants that are waiting in a cold frame can come out to enjoy milder days. Be sure to vent the cold frame on days when there is strong sunshine so that plants do not cook while they wait their turn for planting in the garden. Prop open glass covers, or cut slits in plastic tunnels or covers.

Sow seeds of hardy annuals such as **Cleome, Cosmos, Four-o'-clocks, Portulaca,** and **Sweet Alyssum** directly on the soil in the area of the garden you want them to grow.

Care for Your Annuals

When the soil dries out a bit from spring rains, get outdoors and *clean up* any planting areas that were overlooked last fall. Pull out weeds and dead plants, and pick up winter debris. Do not disturb the soil in areas where you encouraged plants like **Cleome** (**Spider Flower**) and **Nigella** (**Love-in-a-mist**) to self-sow last fall: there will be new sprouts there soon.

By the end of the month, most seedlings raised indoors can be set outdoors daily for increasingly longer times to adjust to the weather. Bring them in at night until it is mild enough for planting. This "hardening off" process gets them used to the outdoors so they will experience less transplant stress when they are finally planted in the garden or in a decorative outdoor container. While they wait (a cold snap may delay planting for a week or two), some young plants may grow so large that they need repotting into larger pots.

Watering

April showers should keep **Pansies** and new seedlings outdoors moist and perky. If rain is not reliable, water areas where seeds are due to sprout or young sprouts have recently appeared. There is no need to water deeply; just *moisten* the soil down an inch or so. *Water* biennial plants such as **Money Plant** and **Forget-me-not** more deeply, since their root systems will have grown deeper. If they are mulched, they will not dry out as fast as seedlings and newly sprouted seeds.

Fertilizing

When the soil is dry enough to be easily worked, *prepare* annual beds. Dig and turn over shovelsful of soil to aerate it. Mix in some granular, slow-acting fertilizer while you're at it. This is also a good time to incorporate some organic material such as compost, chopped leaves, or mushroom soil into the beds if the soil is sandy or has a lot of clay; these amendments also improve soil fertility to some degree.

Grooming

Pinch back leggy stems of maturing seedlings and plants grown from potted rooted cuttings if necessary. This will make their stems more sturdy and their foliage denser.

Pick **Pansies** to enjoy indoors. This practice will encourage more new blossoms.

Problem Solving

Weeds are responding to spring weather, too. Cultivating the soil brings many weed seeds to the soil surface where they are exposed to the sun and begin to sprout. Watch

for young sprouts, and *pull* them as soon as they are large enough to grasp between thumb and forefinger. They will come up easily if the soil is moist.

Deer love to nibble on tender annuals. Protect planted beds and containers with spray repellent, or erect a barrier such as wire fencing.

Planning

Young annuals are available at the garden center in riotous abundance this month. Think about what you want to achieve with your plantings.

1 Choose tall varieties to screen unpleasant views or for privacy, to make a backdrop for other flowers, or for cutting.

2 Medium-height annuals anchor container plantings and fill in mixed borders.

3 Low-growers are ideal for ground covers, hanging baskets, and edges of planted beds.

Perhaps you would like to attract butterflies, hummingbirds, and/or beneficial insects to your garden. Study displays, and read plant labels and materials available at the garden center to learn which plants attract which wildlife. Red, tubular flowers are a sure thing for hummers.

This might be the year to try a fragrance garden or to grow annuals for drying for floral crafts. Select different sizes to create pleasing, balanced profiles for large container arrangements. Remember to purchase shade-lovers for beds and containers in shady areas.

Planting

Prepare planting beds and containers for transplants. In all but the coldest areas of the state (where frost is still a possibility as late as the third week of May), young plants that were displayed outdoors at the garden center probably can go right into the garden or hanging basket. Those that were grown indoors will need a few days of gradual exposure to the outdoors to adjust to the weather before you plant them permanently.

1 *Dig* a hole in prepared soil about the size of the container that the young transplant is in.

2 Slip the plant from its pot. If it sticks, rap the bottom of the pot with a trowel. (Sometimes young plants are potbound, their roots crowding the pot and protruding from the bottom. With your fingers or a small stick, gently *tease* tangled roots apart so they hang freely.) Slide the pot off the rootball.

3 Set the plant in its hole, making sure it is at the same depth it was in the pot.

4 Gently *firm* the soil over the roots and around the stem, and water well.

5 If there is no slow-acting, granular fertilizer in the soil, add water-soluble fertilizer to waterings after a few days, and afterward according to package label instructions.

Remember to *space* plants correctly so they will have enough room when they are mature. They will be growing all summer and may become too crowded. Most plant labels provide spacing information. Dainty, small-flowered plants make more of an impact when planted in groups of five or more; plant larger plants in groups of three.

Sow seeds for other annuals outdoors as soon as your area is safe from frost.

1 *Dig* the soil to loosen it, and remove lumps and debris to make a smooth seedbed.

2 Trace a shallow indentation in the soil with a pencil or your finger in a pattern that you prefer.

3 Dribble the seeds into the indentation, and cover with soil. (Some seeds need light to germinate, so read the seed packet carefully.) Pat the soil gently to encourage contact between soil and seed, then water.

Care for Your Annuals

Plant on a cloudy day or late in the day so new transplants will not suffer added stress from the sun while they cope with transplant shock.

If it is unseasonably warm, erect some temporary shade for them for a few days. An inch or two of organic mulching material such as chopped leaves over the bare soil around transplants will discourage weeds and help keep the soil moist and cool.

Keep the seedbed where you have planted annual seeds moist and free of debris.

Watering

Water new transplants immediately to settle the soil comfortably around their roots. If it does not rain for more than five days, check the soil moisture.

Annuals in containers in the sun will need watering more often, especially when it gets hotter. This is especially true if the containers are clay or terracotta.

Fertilizing

If you have already added granular slow-acting fertilizer to the soil when preparing the bed, do not fertilize again now. If you have not added fertilizer, add it to the soil as you plant each seedling according to the directions on the package label.

If you plan to water-in fast-acting fertilizer, which requires periodic feedings all summer, be conservative. Too much nitrogen too soon or too often promotes excessive tender growth, which attracts aphids and other pests.

Grooming

Snip off any broken stems or crushed leaves from store-bought transplants before you plant them out in the garden.

Sprouts of self-sown seeds from last season's **Cleome** or other notorious self-seeders will thickly carpet a bed. *Thin* them by pulling up most of the spindly seedlings, leaving a potentially sturdy seedling every few inches where you want them to grow. An alternative is to treat the site as a nursery bed: thin to encourage strong remaining seedlings, then *transplant* them to other areas of the garden.

Problem Solving

Weed problems will continue, because new weed seeds come to the surface and find light to germinate when the soil is disturbed by planting. *Pull* them as soon as possible. Mulching the soil when young annual transplant are 4 inches tall will cover weed seeds.

Deer and rabbits like tender new growth on young plants. *Spray* threatened annuals with repellent products as directed on the label until plants are older and tougher. Fences or wire barriers are the best deterrents.

Slugs show up very early in the season. Put out shallow plates of beer as traps in moist, shady areas where they might be a threat to tender young annuals.

Planning

Annuals really start to show their stuff this month as warm weather settles in. Take time to record in a journal or notebook information on which plants do best and look best as the season unfolds. Have a few transplants on hand to *replace* **Pansies** if hot weather causes them to peter out. Certain ephemeral perennial plants such as **Bleeding Heart, Virginia Bluebells,** and **Poppies** will die back and leave empty spaces in the garden that can be quickly filled with pots and baskets of annuals.

Decide if you want to encourage the resident biennials on your property. Those that are in their second season will be flowering and then forming seeds. If you want to limit the abundance and spread of **Forget-me-nots, Money Plant** (**Honesty**), **Hollyhocks, Sweet William,** and others, *pull up* the plants after they bloom and before they sow their seed.

Planting

In the coldest areas of the state it is now probably safe to *plant* warm-weather annuals outdoors in the ground or in containers. Elsewhere in Pennsylvania, it is warm enough for even the tropical plants to go out on the patio or into the garden. Although plants such as **Mandevilla,** certain **Hibiscus, Plumbago, Bougainvillea,** and others are perennials by nature, they are not hardy enough to survive winter months in regions where it actually gets cold. Treat them as you would annuals in containers or in the ground.

Seedlings from last year's self-sowers are probably large enough to transplant. If you want some to grow where they are, *thin* the group to allow space for them to grow comfortably to maturity. Either plant the seedlings that you remove while thinning elsewhere on the property, or plant them in pots to give away to friends and neighbors.

Care for Your Annuals

When young transplants or direct-sown seedlings reach about 4 inches tall and produce a second set of leaves (their true leaves), *spread* some organic material as a mulch over the bare soil between and around them. This will discourage weeds from competing with the young plants for soil moisture and nutrients. It will also prevent the soil from drying out too quickly.

By the end of the month, some tall annuals will need staking to prevent their collapse from wind or heavy rain. It is best to set stakes in the ground beside **Zinnias, American Marigolds, Cosmos, Larkspur,** and similar plants before they are at full height, when there is less risk of disturbing their roots. Tie plant stems loosely so there is room for them to grow thicker over the season.

Start picking flowers as they develop to enjoy indoors. This practice will also encourage sturdier stems and stimulate the production of more blooms.

Watering

Most annuals are shallow-rooted, preferring to spend their energy blooming rather than developing deep root systems. This means they experience dryness fairly quickly when rainfall is limited. When it gets hot, the soil dries out even faster. Watch for wilt that does not go away when the sun and heat abate. If annuals are not mulched, check their soil more often than you check mulched plants. Insert the probe of a houseplant water meter into the soil about 2 or 3 inches, and *water* if the meter registers toward the dry reading.

Water the soil, not the plants, if possible, to help discourage mildew on plant foliage. A leaky pipe drip irrigation system is the easiest way to do this. Otherwise, use a watering can or handheld hose. If an overhead sprinkler is the best option in your situation, run it at mid-morning so plant foliage will have time to dry off by dark. This will prevent wasted water through evaporation.

Fertilizing

If there is no granular, slow-acting fertilizer in the soil, *water-in* dilute fertilizer at intervals indicated on the package label. Because they bloom continuously, most annuals are heavy feeders, using up lots of nutrients from the soil over the season. *Sprinkle* more slow-acting fertilizer on the soil after six or eight weeks to give them a boost over the second part of the season.

Remember, annuals in containers are not in soil, so they depend entirely on slow-acting complete fertilizer in the potting mix or periodic fertilizer watering for their nutrition. A good way to deliver a quick boost of energy to annuals is to spray their foliage with a dilute kelp-based fertilizer.

Grooming

Some plants drop their dead blossoms, while others hold on to them. In addition to marring the appearance of the plants, decaying flowers promote the development of fungal infections. *Pinch off* faded blooms from large-flowered annuals such as **Petunia, Annual Phlox, Marigold,** and others to keep them looking attractive and to forestall possible mildew problems.

No matter how carefully you sow seeds directly into the garden, there are always more new sprouts than are desirable, and they are never spaced far enough apart. It is necessary to *thin* them as they grow into seedlings to ensure the remaining ones will have sufficient light and air to grow into healthy plants. This means the sacrifice of the excess seedlings: either *pull up* or *break off* the less vigorous, overcrowded ones.

Problem Solving

Since pest insects arrive in the garden before beneficial ones do, expect pest problems early in the season.

Aphids are the most common early arrivals, as they love tender, juicy young plants. These soft-bodied, pear-shaped insects cluster at the

Growing Smarter

While annuals are famous for their nonstop, richly colored blooms, some are most valuable in the garden for their foliage. Brightly colored, interestingly variegated, or unusually shaped foliage on a plant works wonders in planted beds and decorative containers. It is a simple matter to pinch off insignificant or inconspicuous flowers. Use them as fillers, color accents, or texture contrasts along with flowering annuals. Some examples of annual or tropical plants that feature foliage are:

- **Coleus**
- **Croton**
- **Dusty Miller**
- **Orach**
- **Taro**

new tips of stems and foliage and suck their juices. Handle them one of the following ways:

- *Pinch off* infested stem tips and discard them in the trash.

- *Wash* aphids off stems and foliage with a forceful water spray from the hose.

- *Spray* insecticidal soap or fine horticultural oil on the offenders according to label directions.

Planning

If you are growing certain annual flowers to be dried for floral crafts, plan to begin harvesting later this month, and then continue into fall as the various plants mature and produce perfect blooms. While many flowers are easily air-dried, some dry best in silica gel and/or borax and sand. Have these materials and appropriate equipment on hand to use the minute you can pick blemish-free, fresh blossoms.

Plan for the maintenance of the garden and planted containers while you are away on vacation. Arrange for someone to water container plants daily if it is very hot and dry. Gather the plants into one or two locations near the hose or water faucet to facilitate the job.

Planting

Get all remaining warm-season annuals out of their little market packs (which dry out so quickly) and in the ground as soon as possible. They are likely to be potbound, so take time to gently loosen their matted roots. Plant in the evening or on an overcast day to minimize stress from heat and sun while the young plants cope with transplant shock. *Water*, then *mulch* them well.

If you have not already done so, plant some **Sunflower** seeds, which will produce wonderful golden flowers in the fall. These days **Sunflowers** come in all kinds of colors and different heights, and some are pollenless and do not produce seeds. Check to make sure you are planting varieties that have the characteristics you desire.

Care for Your Annuals

Mulch the soil around transplants that are over 4 inches tall with an inch or so of some organic material such as chopped leaves or dried grass clippings. This will discourage weeds, block evaporation of moisture from the soil, reduce wasteful runoff from rain or watering, and cool the soil.

Stake tall plants such as **Sunflower, Larkspur, Hollyhock,** or **Castor Bean** to prevent their collapse from wind or heavy rain. Use sturdy, unobtrusive green or brown stakes that are a foot taller than the expected height of the plant. Insert them a foot into the soil next to the plants while they are still young, and tie plant stems with twine or other soft material—loop the tie around the plant stem, then loop it around the stake, tying it loosely so there is room for stem growth.

Pick more flowers to enjoy indoors. This practice stimulates plants to produce even more blooms.

Watering

Check the soil around annuals if there has been no rain for several days, or if the plants are wilting. Insert your finger or the probe of a houseplant water meter through the mulch and into the soil about 2 inches. If the soil is dry, water gently for several minutes so the water can penetrate to the shallow roots. If the soil is already wet, the wilting may be due to heat, in which case the leaves will perk up by evening. Overwatering is the problem if the leaves do not perk up in a few hours.

Fertilizing

The slow-acting fertilizer mixed into the soil at planting time is sufficient for most plants for six to ten weeks or more, depending on the product. Some prodigious bloomers might also appreciate a boost from a foliar spray of a kelp-based or other dilute liquid product. Spraying it directly on the foliage delivers the energy quickly and does not affect the soil. Do not overdo.

Too much nitrogen stimulates plants to produce lots of excess foliage, which attracts insects and disease. Also, excess nitrogen distracts the plants from producing flowers. Never fertilize a plant that is under stress from drought or extreme heat.

Grooming

By the end of the month, some annuals such as **Petunias** and **Impatiens** may develop thin, leggy stems. *Pinch back* each stem a few inches; this will promote bushiness by stimulating the development of fresh foliage and new flower buds. Plants in containers may need a trim, too. Do this before going on vacation and the plants will be blooming again with their new flush of growth when you return.

Spider Flowers (Cleome) will be stretching upward and developing seedpods along their elongating upper stems. If it is important to you to minimize reseeding, *pinch* or *snip off* these pods as they are ripening, before they dry, burst, and scatter their seeds. Cutting back the main stem encourages branching.

Leave the attractive seedpods on **Love-in-a-mist** (**Nigella**), as they add to the ornamental appearance of the plant. Cut them off when the plants finally finish flowering and the pods have dried to crispy capsules. The black seeds in the chambers of the capsule are easy to harvest and save, or to scatter for a repeat crop.

Problem Solving

Japanese beetles arrive around the Fourth of July in the warmest parts of the state, south of Philadelphia. They appear a week or two later elsewhere in Pennsylvania. *Check* the plants in your yard that they traditionally prefer (some Japanese beetle favorites are **Four-o'-clocks, Hollyhocks, Roses,** and **Zinnias**), and try to catch the earliest arrivals. If possible, patrol twice a day, and *handpick* them or knock them off leaves into a jar of soapy water. Avoid using pheromone traps, which are so effective they will attract beetles from the entire neighborhood to your yard. Use neem or a pyrethrum-based insecticide according to label directions if infestations are overwhelming.

Aphids and other common insect pests enjoy their glory days in July, when serious heat and possible drought will begin to stress plants, making them vulnerable to attack. In a healthy landscape, populations of beneficial insects such as ladybugs are now on the job and can control the pests.

Ladybug

Nymph

Pest problems may explode in a landscape that lacks diverse plants or one whose beneficials have been killed by frequent use of general insecticides that kill beneficials as well as pests. Try washing aphids and mites from plant surfaces with a strong water stream every day or two for a week or ten days. *Spray* foliage with hot pepper wax or insecticidal soap to deter stubborn pests.

Planning

While many favorite annuals are capable of blooming with gusto until frost, others tend to peter out by late August. Sometimes they just run out of steam; other times it is just the colors that seem tired. With the onset of fall, with its shorter days and golden light, it is time to *replace* them with plants that have a richer color palette. Sow seeds for seedlings early in this month, or plan to purchase young transplants as Labor Day approaches for fall replacements in beds and containers. Some possibilities are **Celosia, Marigolds, Red Salvia,** and others that feature rich golden, orange, and red harvest colors.

Plan to visit gardens while on vacation. Public gardens and arboreta in New England, the Midwest, and the South will feature lots of familiar annuals that grow well in Pennsylvania, as well as many you may not be familiar with. Visits to Florida, Southern California, the Caribbean, and other tropical places are an education in how to use tropical plants to advantage. What a great way to relax and enjoy the outdoors! Enjoy beauty, inspiration, and educational experiences at public gardens that will benefit the garden at home.

Planting

This month is really too hot and droughty to plant or transplant significant numbers of annual plants, so it is best to wait until after Labor Day. However, it is not a problem to *replace* the occasional dead or damaged annual in container arrangements. Sometimes a group of annuals in a bed dies out for some reason and needs replacing. Do this on an overcast day, or provide shade for new transplants. *Water* them well.

By mid-month, seeds planted to start young annual plants for the fall flower garden will be sprouting, if they have not already done so. When they are about 2 or 3 inches tall, *thin* them to the correct spacing, indicated on the seed packet.

Care for Your Annuals

Continue to *protect* plants from the elements. Heat stimulates the activity of the microbial life in organic mulch, which causes it to decompose faster than normal. Add material to the thinning mulch layer to maintain 2 or 3 inches of mulch over bare soil around annuals in the garden. The mulch will conserve water and cool the soil. As it decomposes, it enriches the soil.

If you intend to harvest their seeds for use as birdseed or food, cover the maturing heads of **Sunflowers** with garden fleece or cheesecloth to prevent the squirrels and finches from taking them. If they are too tall to reach, cut off the seedheads as soon as they start to mature, and put them in a dry space indoors for the seeds to ripen and dry.

If you do not mind if the animals get the seeds, allow them to dry on the plant, or pick the heads and let them dry on the ground in the sun. Pull up the drying stalks to keep the garden neat.

Watering

Watering is critical to getting plants through the heat and possible drought that is typical of this month. Most annuals positively love the sun and heat and can be counted on to soldier on during this stressful weather as long as they receive sufficient moisture. Those in containers need watering once or twice daily, especially if they are in the sun most of the time. Those in clay (terracotta) containers dry out fastest. At this point in the season, root systems take up more and more space in the container, leaving less room for the soil, which holds the moisture.

Beds of annuals that are not mulched will need watering more often than those that have a protective layer of chopped leaves or something similar over the soil to help it retain moisture.

Fertilizing

Do not feed plants that are coping with harsh heat and drought. *Water* them and help them through the stress first. As it decomposes, the protective mulch will provide some nutrition, as will the slow-acting fertilizer that was incorporated into the soil at planting time. Wait until the weather breaks, then *spray* their foliage with a diluted liquid fertilizer to give plants an energy boost.

Grooming

Pick flowers to enjoy as bouquets indoors or to dry for floral crafts. Groom plants by deadheading faded flowers, snipping off dead or injured stems and leaves.

Do not allow dried or rotted plant debris to lie in planting beds; this fosters disease problems.

Remember to allow some flowers to ripen and produce seeds to

Growing Smarter

The All-America Selections (AAS) organization sponsors display gardens and trial gardens filled with annual flowers and vegetables at many locations throughout the country.

Display Gardens in Pennsylvania are:

Temple University
Ambler Research Gardens
580 Meetinghouse Rd.
Ambler, PA 19002-3994

Rodale Research Center
611 Siegfiredale Rd.
Kutztown, PA 19530

Longwood Gardens
Route 1
Kennett Square, PA 19348

Trial Gardens in Pennsylvania are:

Pennsylvania State University
Department of Horticulture
101 Tyson Building
University Park, PA 16802

W. Atlee Burpee Co.
300 Park Avenue
Warminster, PA 18974

attract birds. Finches of all kinds love the seedheads of **Gloriosa Daisies** and many other annuals.

Problem Solving

Mildew is a problem during August. Some plants seem to be prone to developing the telltale gray coating on their foliage.

- Choose varieties of **Zinnia, Annual Phlox,** and **Garden Verbena** that are listed as mildew-resistant.

- Make sure plants are far enough apart so they can enjoy good air circulation.

- When you water, water the soil, not the foliage.

Mildew is unsightly but not life-threatening. It is best ignored on annual plants, which will be pulled up in a few weeks anyway.

Winds and heavy rains from August storms can be fierce, and sometimes there are brief hailstorms at this time of year. If you have not had a chance to do it so far this summer, *stake* tall plants such as **Zinnias, Castor Bean, Phlox,** and others that have grown very large by this time.

Planning

Contrary to popular belief, in much of Pennsylvania the end of the gardening season does not arrive this month. There are a few wonderful weeks of gardening weather ahead before the first light frost arrives at our north-central reaches. In the warmer areas around Philadelphia, there may be many weeks to enjoy gardening. As temperatures moderate from summer heat, get back out in the yard and enjoy the fresh flush of flowers. This is when annuals are much appreciated, because most are still going strong. Those in warm fall harvest colors of orange, yellow, and gold will light up the landscape for another month or six weeks.

Some "annual" plants that will need some attention soon are the tropical plants on the deck or patio. Although **Brugmansia, Mandevilla, Taro, Abutilon, Bougainvillea,** and others are actually perennial by nature, they are too tender to withstand Pennsylvania winters. Consider them annuals, and decide whether to allow the frost to kill them outdoors or to bring them indoors in pots and try to winter them over, either displayed as houseplants or stored in a cool, dark place.

While the impressions of your garden are fresh in your mind, make some notes in your garden journal or notebook.

- What annuals were most successful this summer?

- Are there areas where you did not plant annuals that you would like to plant with annuals next season?

- What problems did annual plants encounter this year, and how did you solve them?

- What changed in the yard over the season?

A gardener's landscape is very much like an artist's painting: it is never finished. You will always find places that can be improved with a little daub of color or a broad stroke of texture. Fortunately, there is always another season ahead, and there will always be another opportunity to improve the picture.

Planting

Replace tired summer annuals, and fill in bare spots that have developed in containers and garden beds over the season with fall-colored plants. *Plant* **Ornamental Cabbages** and **Kale** that are guaranteed to withstand light frost and increasingly chilly weather.

Richly hued **Marigolds** that have been growing on the property should continue to be fine for another month. Other annuals with warm seasonal colors will also make the transition. Some suggestions:

- **African Queen Impatiens**

- **Bright Lights Cosmos**

- **Celosia/Cockscomb**

- **Gazania**

- **Snapdragon**

- **New Guinea Impatiens 'Macarena'**

Care for Your Annuals

As soon as nighttime temperatures drop to about 55 degrees Fahrenheit, bring in those tropical plants that you intend to try to winter over as houseplants. Wash their stems and foliage well to remove dust and pest insects, then *spray* the foliage with hot pepper wax to forestall pest problems indoors.

There are three ways to overwinter favorite **Geraniums:**

1 **Treat them as houseplants.** Cut back their leggy stems, dig them up, pot them up in soilless mix with granular, slow-acting fertilizer mixed in, and bring them indoors.

2 **Propagate new plants.** Take stem cuttings to root in water

SEPTEMBER

or damp vermiculite. Plant the rooted cuttings in pots later in the fall or early winter, keeping them under bright lights to encourage sturdy stems and foliage. (**Impatiens, Coleus,** and **Begonia** also root easily in a glass of water on the windowsill.)

3 **Store them as dormant plants.** Dig up plants from the garden, or remove them from decorative containers. Knock the soil from the roots. Trim back the stems and hang them in a cool, dry cellar or storage area.

Watering

Continue to water annuals in containers and garden beds if rainfall is scarce. Annuals need less water as temperatures cool.

Fertilizing

There is no need to fertilize annual plants in garden beds at this time of year since the frost will soon kill them. Those brought in to overwinter as houseplants will need some granular, slow-acting fertilizer mixed into their soilless potting medium to give them consistent nutrition over the winter months.

Grooming

Pull up any annuals that are obviously exhausted or dead, and smooth mulch over the area for a neat appearance. Cut off any seedpods or capsules that develop on those annuals you do not want to self-sow seeds for next year. When first frost blackens the most tender annuals, *pull* them immediately.

Clip off broken or diseased stems from annuals promptly. *Pinch off* unsightly dead flowers or discolored leaves to keep them looking fresh and perky.

Problem Solving

Insect eggs, disease pathogens, and fungal spores nestle in the crevices of plant leaves and stems. They overwinter there, conveniently situated for next season. Pull up dead, decaying plants promptly, and *discard* them in the trash to prevent future pest and disease problems. (Healthy plants can go into the compost pile.)

Deer will make an appearance if they are in the area. *Spray* a repellent product on the remaining flowering annuals to prevent damage. Those in hanging baskets are usually safely out of reach.

Growing Smarter

Many Pennsylvania gardens are shaded by the large trees that grow so well in our state. Here are some annual flowers that tolerate some shade:

- **Beefsteak Plant** (*Perilla frutescens* '**Atropurpurea**')
- **Browallia** (*Browallia* **sp.**)
- **Coleus** (*Solenostemon scutellarioides*)
- **Impatiens** (*Impatiens wallerana*)
- **Nicotiana** (*Nicotiana alata*)
- **Periwinkle** (*Vinca major* '**Variegata**')
- **Polka-Dot Plant** (*Hypoestes phyllostachya*)
- **Wax Begonia** (*Begonia semperflorens*)
- **Wishbone Flower** (*Torenia fournieri*)

Many **weeds** develop seed this time of year. Continue to *pull* them wherever they appear—hopefully before their seeds dry and disperse. It is important to prevent them from going to seed so they do not come back to haunt next season.

Planning

In anticipation of the first light frost this month, bring in any remaining annuals that you want to keep over the winter. Because indoor space is usually limited and annuals are so inexpensive, most gardeners do not try to overwinter them but instead let them succumb to frost when it arrives. The most tender ones out in the open will turn black overnight with the first light frost. Others, with sturdier constitutions or located under the protection of a roof line, shrub, or tree, may carry on for weeks of delightful fall weather in the warmer parts of the state. When a hard frost finally hits, sometimes weeks later, they too will die.

Make a note of when first frost arrives. In most regions it is about the same time every year, give or take a week or two. In the coldest parts of the state it may arrive anytime after mid-September, although the benchmark date is September 30. In the warmer Philadelphia area, the first light frost may not arrive until the third week of October (see Appendix). Conditions vary within your own yard, too. The best way to determine if a light frost has occurred during the night is to check indicator plants. These are the tenderest annuals that are quite susceptible to even the lightest frost. **Impatiens** and **Nasturtiums** are two examples.

Some summer annuals that can handle light frost are **Marigolds, Snapdragons, Petunias, Portulaca,** and **Verbena.**

Planting

Put in fall plantings of **Ornamental Cabbage** and **Kale** to fill bare spots. These plants will withstand frosts until early winter when a hard frost comes along. (Do not leave them in the ground once they have been frozen, because they will smell just like rotten cabbage when they thaw.)

If you have not already done so, take stem cuttings from any favorite annuals that you wish to keep going indoors over the winter.

- *Remove* any flowers or buds and foliage that are within an inch of the cut ends.

- Either put the cut ends in a glass of water on the windowsill, or dip them in powdered rooting hormone from the garden center and insert them in a pot of moist vermiculite or seed-starting medium.

- *Cover* the container with a clear plastic bag to maintain humidity.

- When the stems in water develop tiny root fibers about an inch long, pot them up.

- In a couple of weeks, gently tug on the stems of those plants in the growing medium to ascertain whether they have roots. Then *pot them up.*

Any cuttings that you took last month will probably have developed roots by now. Pot them up in small containers filled with soilless medium and granular slow-acting fertilizer. *Water* well. After they adjust to the transplanting, set them where they can get maximum bright light.

Care for Your Annuals

Pull out annuals when they succumb to frost. *Clean up* rotting organic debris, and *cover* the bare soil with a 3- or 4-inch mulch of compost, chopped leaves, pine needles, or evergreen boughs to protect the soil over the winter.

Some self-sowers—**Cleome, Four-o'-clocks, Love-in-a-mist**—will leave lots of seeds behind on the soil.

- To *encourage* copious numbers of free seedlings next spring, disturb the soil as little as possible while removing the dead and dying plants.

- To *discourage* hosts of seedlings, rake up the remaining summer mulch and *replace* it with a fresh layer of chopped leaves or other material.

Watering

Water any annuals that are still going strong if rainfall is scarce. In cooler weather they do not require as much moisture as they did during the hot summer. If they are well mulched, they should be fine.

Grooming

Remember to collect seeds from any annuals you think you would like to grow again next year. Cut off the ripening seedheads prior to throwing the spent plants onto the compost pile or into the trash. Store the seeds tightly wrapped in a cool place, such as the back of the refrigerator or an unheated garage.

Reminder: Flowers and fruit grown from seeds can be very variable in color and size.

Clean up beds where annuals grew over the season. For a head start on next year, dig in some chopped leaves left by the mulching lawn mower during the last few mowings of grass covered by leaves fallen from nearby trees. The leaves will provide organic matter and condition the soil as earthworms go to work on them and they decompose. Then *mulch* the soil in the cultivated bed with more leaves, pine needles, straw, or some other organic material to protect it over the winter.

Problem Solving

Aphids, whiteflies, and spider mites manage to plague annuals that have been potted up and brought indoors to overwinter (**Coleus, Geranium, Impatiens, Wax Begonias**). To avoid bringing indoors any eggs and larvae with the plants, wash foliage with a forceful spray of tepid water to dislodge the pests while still outside. Then *spray* thoroughly with hot pepper wax or insecticidal soap. Plan to do this every month or so while the plants are indoors.

Insufficient light is a fact of life for summer annuals that are overwintering indoors. Place them in the brightest window or set up fluorescent lights for them. If you have a seed-starting table (see January or February), they can spend the darkest early winter days there until you need it for seed-starting early next year.

Growing Smarter

It has long been the routine in the South to plant **Pansies** in the fall. These cool-weather lovers do best down there when it is not hot summer. Only recently have **Pansies** become available up North for fall planting. What a great idea! They have an opportunity to grow strong root systems during the mild fall days when the weather suits them perfectly, and they are able to become well enough established to withstand winter cold and snow over the winter months. When winter wanes and hardy bulbs begin to bloom, the **Pansies** are ready to bloom, too. They are wonderful in beds of their own or interplanted with **Tulips, Daffodils,** or **Hyacinths.**

Continue to *pull* weeds from outdoor planting beds to prevent them from going to seed and causing problems next year.

Planning

With the advent of the first hard frost, the main season for growing annuals outdoors is over. It is a good time to rethink the garden. If you have really enjoyed this year's annuals, you may want to try more next year.

Think about a cutting garden as a possibility for next year. More a production garden than a display bed, the plot can be tucked in an out-of-the-way place and does not require the maintenance that a display garden does. *Plant* lots of annuals in easy-to-access rows for harvest and display indoors or for gifts. Grow some plants with interesting foliage, pods, or flowers that dry easily for floral crafts and dried arrangements.

Gather together all the paperwork that has accumulated from your gardening activities this past season. It is helpful to develop the habit of saving the labels from plants that you buy and grow each season. Try to find the seed packets and labels that came with your annuals, and store them with your garden notes. It's worth keeping the label information, which includes the name of the plant, a color picture, and information about its cultural requirements. The labels are a good place to start when planning and ordering next season's annual flowers.

Planting

As long as the ground remains unfrozen, it is still okay to plant **Pansies.** They will handle cold and snow just fine with a little protective mulch on their soil to buffer temperature extremes that might otherwise disturb the soil and heave them out of the ground.

Care for Your Annuals

Pull out the hardier annuals—including **Ornamental Kale** and **Cabbage**—that have finally succumbed to hard frost.

Mulch all bare soil and any young **Pansy** plants with a 2-inch layer of chopped leaves for winter protection.

Watering

Watch the soil of annuals that have been potted for indoor overwintering: it will dry out quickly if the heating system runs most of the time.

On the other hand, beware of overwatering and causing plants to rot. Use a houseplant water meter to determine whether the soil has actually begun to dry out before automatically pouring more water on plants. Until they resume blooming, they will not need as much water each time as they did outdoors.

Fertilizing

Annuals will stall when they are brought indoors. So will newly rooted and potted stem cuttings. They need a period of adjustment to the new, less-than-ideal conditions. Light deprivation due to shortened winter daylight hours will slow their growth, too. While they adjust, they can manage on the slow-acting granular fertilizer added to their soilless potting mix, and they will begin to bloom freely again in a few weeks.

NOVEMBER

Problem Solving

Aphid, mite, whitefly, and scale problems are likely to develop on indoor annuals because the plants are under stress. Daylight hours are reduced dramatically, heating systems dry out the air and cause hot blasts, and opening doors causes cold drafts. Under these circumstances, pest eggs hidden on the plant may hatch. To prevent problems, try to keep your plants as stress-free as possible by giving them strong light, adequate moisture, and even air temperatures. Rinse their foliage with tepid running water every so often, and follow up with a foliage spray of insecticidal soap, hot pepper wax, or similar repellent to stop problems before they develop.

Growing Smarter

While some gardeners avoid annuals that tend to self-sow, many welcome them to their gardens. Here are some that may appear year after year:

- **Snapdragon** (*Antirrhinum majus*)
- **Browallia** (*Browallia speciosa*)
- **Calendula** (*Calendula officinalis*)
- **Bachelor's Button** (*Centaurea officinalis*)
- **Cleome** (*Cleome hasslerana*)
- **Rocket Larkspur** (*Consolida ambigua*)
- **Cosmos** (*Cosmos bipinnatus*)
- **California Poppy** (*Eschscholzia californica*)
- **Impatiens** (*Impatiens wallerana*)
- **Morning Glory** (*Ipomoea sp.*)
- **Toadflax** (*Linaria maroccana*)
- **Sweet Alyssum** (*Lobularia maritima*)
- **Money Plant/Honesty** (*Lunaria annua*)
- **Four-o'-clock** (*Mirabilis jalapa*)
- **Bells of Ireland** (*Moluccella laevis*)
- **Forget-me-not** (*Myosotis sylvatica*)
- **Baby Blue Eyes** (*Nemphila menziesii*)
- **Corn Poppy** (*Papaver rhoeas*)
- **Love-in-a-mist** (*Nigella damascena*)
- **Moss Rose** (*Portulaca grandiflora*)
- **Wishbone Flower** (*Torenia fournieri*)
- **Johnny-Jump-Up** (*Viola tricolor*)

Planning

In the warmest parts of Pennsylvania the ground may not yet be frozen. Continue to enjoy **Ornamental Cabbage** and **Kale** until severe cold turns them mushy, then dig them up and *discard* them.

Make the final entries for the year in your garden notebook or journal. Record the dates of the arrival of the first frost and then the hard frost. This will be a useful reference for next year.

When the new seed and plant catalogs begin to arrive in the mail this month, put them aside until holiday festivities are over and you can give them your full attention. Clean up and inventory seed-starting supplies so you can order additional pots or soilless mix right after the new year.

Planting

To grow your own **Pansy** seedlings, *sow* seeds this month, and prepare to put the sprouts under lights when they appear (see January/ February on growing seedlings indoors). Pot seedlings individually when they grow large enough to handle.

Check stem cuttings that are in water or flats of moist vermiculite or perlite to see if rooting has started. *Pot up* those that have developed good root systems. Use soilless medium with some granular, slow-acting fertilizer mixed in. Set them under lights.

Watering

Water new sprouts and previously potted rooted cuttings when the soil feels dry.

Fertilizing

Add granular, slow-acting fertilizer to the potting mix for rooted stem cuttings and new seedlings. Hold off on other fertilizer until annuals begin to bloom well. Then *water-in* some very dilute fast-acting fertilizer every few weeks or as the label directs.

Grooming

When annual plants adjust to indoor life and begin to grow, they may stretch to get more light. *Pinch back* stems of **Begonia, Impatiens, Geranium,** and others to make more compact plants. Set them under artificial lights if necessary.

Pick up fallen leaves and other debris around plants to avoid disease problems.

Problem Solving

The trick to preventing serious pest and disease problems is to examine your annuals and other nearby plants frequently for signs that something is amiss. The sooner you notice and diagnose a problem, the easier it is to deal with. Things to look for:

- Ants crawling on stems and foliage

- Shiny, sticky coating on the leaves and pot rim

- Tender growing tips and new foliage that is twisted, discolored

- Fine webbing near the main stems and leaf stems

- Leaves pale or speckled

- Lower leaves turning yellow and dropping

- Stems discolored near the soil line

- Leaves yellowed except for dark-green veins

- Gray or white coating on the foliage

Bulbs, Corms, Rhizomes, & Tubers

It is likely that some variety of flowering bulb appears on almost everyone's list of top ten flower favorites, and **Tulips** and **Daffodils** rank highly among the public's all-time sentimental favorites. They are right up there with **Daisies** as the flowers most easily recognized by children and youth who have virtually no gardening experience or special knowledge of plants.

This familiarity suggests how thoroughly **Daffodils** and **Tulips** in particular and spring-flowering bulbs in general have pervaded our popular culture. And it's no wonder! Indoors in the winter, pots of forced **Tulips** or bouquets of cut **Daffodils** and **Tulips** anticipate the arrival of warm weather, promising yet another spring of beauty. Then these flowers bloom outdoors, appearing on the scene to a grateful world weary of winter. Their rich, cheery colors and distinctive shapes, emblematic of rebirth and renewal, decorate the outdoor landscape.

Bulbs for the Garden

It is no coincidence that many other varieties of flowering bulbs appear on home gardeners' lists of flower favorites as well. What else is easier to grow and care for? Stick them in the ground and they will do the rest. Bulbs offer enormous returns on a very small investment of time and effort. They also provide an opportunity to get double duty from planting areas, because they die back after blooming to make way for another wave of plants that can show off during a subsequent season.

Most new home gardeners' first bulb-growing experiences are with a few hardy spring-flowering bulbs such as **Tulips, Daffodils,** and **Hyacinths.** Success is virtually guaranteed because these bulbs are so self-reliant. Success often leads to experimentation with other hardy bulbs, including the wonderful minor bulbs such as **Crocus, Snowdrop,** and **Glory of the Snow.** In no time at all, a gardener will be eyeing the later-flowering bulbs such as **Lilies** and **Ornamental Onions** (**Alliums**), which beckon from garden center shelves. It is only a matter of time before the lure of growing fall-blooming **Sternbergia** and **Autumn Crocus** becomes irresistible.

You can always find interesting and unusual bulbs to grow. Choose **Fritillaria** or **Dogtooth Violets,** and tiny **Squill** or **Winter Aconites.** Go beyond traditional spring bloomers and try summer-blooming **Crocosmia** and fall-blooming **Italian Arum.** Then try those such as **Colchicum** that have two seasons— one to show off foliage, another to flower. Take advantage of the versatility of bulbs, and use them many different ways in the landscape. Naturalize **Snowdrops** or **Crocus** in the late-winter lawn. Plant **Anemones** and **Daffodils** as ground covers in woodland areas. Mix and match **Tulips** and **Grape Hyacinths** in beds or borders. Combine **Iris** and **Ornamental Onions.** Use **Dahlias** and **Lilies** in the summer flower border. And don't forget that many bulbs will grow in containers and, surprisingly, some will grow in water.

Types of Bulbs

The term "bulb" has a both a general and a specific meaning. For gardening purposes (and this chapter), it describes any plant that has special fleshy organs formed from underground modified stems that store energy in the form of carbohydrates. These organs come in several different forms.

Bulbs, Corms, Rhizomes, & Tubers

A **true bulb** is a distinctive kind of storage organ, one that has compressed within it a short stem, an already formed flower bud, and rings or layers of foliage around the bud that appear as scales on its outer surface. One way to see this kind of structure is to slice a cooking onion in half. Some true bulb examples are:

- **Amaryllis**
- **Hyacinth**
- **Lily**
- **Narcissus**
- **Tulip**

True Bulb

Another type of energy-storage organ is a **corm.** Resembling a thick, flat, brownish disk, it too is a compressed stem. A close look reveals a growing tip on one side; the other, even flatter side is where roots emerge after the corm is planted. There are no scales on the outer surface. Some examples of plants that grow from corms are:

- **Crocosmia**
- **Crocus**
- **Freesia**
- **Gladiolus**

Corm

Yet another form of energy-storage bulb is a **rhizome,** a swollen, fleshy length of modified stem that likes to lie horizontally in the soil. The roots grow along the bottom of its length, and shoots grow from the top, usually at one end. Some plants that grow from rhizomes are:

- **Bearded Iris**
- **Canna**
- **Waterlily**

Rhizome

Tubers are energy-storing mechanisms for some of the plants included in the general category of bulbs. They are essentially swollen, rounded stems covered with scale-like leaves and eyes, or growth buds. Stems and buds may grow from all sides of a tuber. Examples:

- **Caladium**
- **Jack-in-the-pulpit**
- **Lotus**
- **Orchid**
- **Potato,** ornamental or edible

Tuber

Growing Bulbs

You can see that the world of bulbs extends far beyond the traditional spring **Crocus, Daffodils,** and **Tulips.** In fact, there can be bulbs blooming in the garden through nine or ten months of the year. For the most part, these successive waves of colorful flowers and handsome foliage take very little care beyond routine watering, some fertilizer, and cleanup.

After the hardy bulbs bloom, die back, and then go dormant to ride out the hot season, tender summer bloomers sustain the colorful parade. Growing tender bulbs in the garden requires a bit more work because some of them need staking and deadheading as they grow and bloom over the long summer season. It also requires a bit more skill and knowledge if the intention is to keep them for the following summer. Because they cannot withstand winter weather in Pennsylvania, tender bulbs must be dug up to be stored over the winter. Another option is to leave them in the soil to freeze and die, then replace them the following spring.

Fall-blooming bulbs take over soon after Labor Day when the daylight hours begin to shrink and the evening temperatures begin to drop. Their flowers brighten the fading fall garden as they bloom among the falling leaves. As carefree as their spring counterparts, these hardy bulbs die back and go dormant again as temperatures fall and winter arrives.

Bulbs for Pennsylvania

Common Name (Botanical Name)	Hardiness	Type	Planting Time	Planting Depth	Bloom Time
Amaryllis (*Hippeastrum* sp.)	Tender	Bulb	Fall in pot	$2/3$ soil covered	Force for indoor winter bloom
Autumn Crocus (*Crocus speciosus*)	Hardy	Corm	Mid- to late October	4 to 6 inches	Mid to late October
Autumn Daffodil (*Sternbergia lutea*)	Hardy	Bulb	Late summer	4 to 6 inches	Late September to October; wintergreen foliage
Bearded Iris (*Iris germanica*)	Hardy	Rhizome	Late summer; fall	At soil surface, partly exposed	Flowers late May, early June; foliage all summer
Calla (*Zantedeschia* sp.)	Tender	Tuber	Late spring	3 to 4 inches	Early summer
Camass (*Camassia* sp.)	Hardy	Bulb	Fall	6 inches	May (tolerates, but does not require wet soil)
Canna (*Canna* × *generalis*)	Tender	Tuber	Late spring	3 to 4 inches	All summer (some grow in water, too)
Colchicum Meadow Saffron (*Colchicum* hybrids)	Hardy	Corm	Late summer to fall	6 inches	Leaves late winter to June; flowers September to October (poisonous)
Common Caladium (*Caladium bicolor*)	Tender	Tuber	Spring after last frost	3 to 4 inches	Grown for foliage; multicolored foliage all summer
Common Crocus Dutch Crocus (*Crocus vernus*)	Hardy	Corm	Fall	4 inches	March to April
Common Hyacinth (*Hyacinthus orientalis*)	Hardy	Bulb	Fall	6 inches	April (strongly fragrant)
Common Tulip (*Tulipa* hybrids)	Hardy	Bulb	Fall	8 to 12 inches	April or May
Crown Imperial (*Fritillaria imperialis*)	Hardy	Bulb	Fall; as soon as possible	6 inches	April (grows 3 to 4 feet tall)
Daffodil (*Narcissus* sp.)	Hardy	Bulb	Early fall	4 to 6 inches	Late March through April (naturalize easily)
Dahlia (*Dahlia* sp.)	Tender	Tuber	Late spring	4 to 6 inches	All summer (tall types need staking)
Dogtooth Violet (*Erythronium dens-canis*)	Hardy	Bulb	Fall	6 inches	April (shade garden)
Flowering Onion (*Allium* sp.)	Hardy	Bulb	Fall	2 to 3 inches	May to June

Bulbs for Pennsylvania

Common Name (Botanical Name)	Hardiness	Type	Planting Time	Planting Depth	Bloom Time
Garden Lily (*Lillium* sp. and hybrids)	Hardy	Bulb	Spring/fall	6 inches	Asiatic: late May to July; Trumpet: June and July; Oriental: July to September
Gladiola (*Gladiolus × hortulanus*)	Tender	Corm	Spring	2 to 3 inches	Mid- to late summer if planted at 2-week intervals (stake)
Glory of the Snow (*Chionodoxa* sp.)	Hardy	Bulb	Fall	3 to 4 inches	March to April; naturalizes as spring-season ground cover
Grape Hyacinth (*Muscari armeniacum*)	Hardy	Bulb	Fall	4 inches	Leaves in fall; flowers April to May
Greek Windflower (*Anemone blanda*)	Hardy	Rhizome	Fall	4 inches	March to April
Hardy Amaryllis Resurrection Lily, Naked Lily (*Lycoris squamigera*)	Hardy	Bulb	Fall	6 inches	Leaves in spring, die back; flowers in August (likes crowding)
Hardy Cyclamen (*Cyclamen coum*)	Hardy	Corm	Fall	Just below soil surface	February to April (likes dry shade)
Italian Arum (*Arum italicum* 'Pictum')	Hardy	Rhizome	Fall	3 to 4 inches	Spring flower, red berries summer; foliage in fall to spring
Reticulated Iris (*Iris reticulata*)	Hardy	Bulb	Fall	4 inches	March to early April
Siberian Squill (*Scilla sibirica*)	Hardy	Bulb	Fall	4 inches	March and April (naturalizes easily)
Snowdrop (*Galanthus nivalis*)	Hardy	Bulb	Fall	4 to 6 inches	Late February to March
Spring Star Flower (*Ipheion uniflorum*)	Hardy	Bulb	Fall	3 inches	April to early May; long bloom season; leaves appear in fall
Summer Snowflake (*Leucojum aestivum*)	Hardy	Bulb	Fall	6 inches	April; tolerates wet soil
Tuberose (*Polianthes tuberosa*)	Tender	Bulb	Early June	1 inch	Late summer, early fall (waxy white flowers are fragrant)
Tuberous Begonia (*Begonia × tuberhybrida*)	Tender	Tuber	Late spring	1 to 2 inches	All summer in ground or pots
Winter Aconite (*Eranthis* sp.)	Hardy	Rhizome	Fall	3 inches	February to March (likes deciduous shade)
Wood Hyacinth formerly **Endymion** (*Hyacinthoides* sp.)	Hardy	Bulb	Fall	4 to 6 inches	May

Hardy Bulb Bloom Sequence

Name	February	March	April	May	June	July	August	September	October	November
Autumn Daffodil								flower ●─────	●─────	
Camass			●── flower ──●							
Colchicum	┊───── foliage	┊─────	┊	┊	┊──●			fall flowering ●──	──●	
Crocus	●── spring flowering	──	──●							
Crown Imperial		●── flower ──●								
Cyclamen (Hederifolium)	┊───── foliage	┊	┊──●				flower ●──	──●	┊ foliage	┊
Daffodil		●── flower ──●								
Grape Hyacinth			●── flower ──●							
Hardy Amaryllis	┊───── foliage	┊──●				flower ●──	──●			
Hyacinth, Common			●── flower ──●							
Ipheion	┊ foliage	┊──●		●── flower				──●	┊ foliage	┊
Italian Arum	┊ foliage	┊──●		●──		fruit ●──	──●		┊ foliage	┊
Ornamental Onion				●── flower ──●						
Snowdrop	●── flower ──●									
Snowflake		●── flower ──●								
Squill		●── flower ──●								
Tulip			●── flower ──●							
Windflower		●── flower			──●					
Winter Aconite	●── flower ──●									
Wood Hyacinth				●── flower ──●						

51

Planning

The wonderful thing about bulbs, especially the hardy types, is that they are basically care-free: once you get them in the ground, they take care of themselves. Under cover of snow or winter mulch the hardy, spring-blooming ones are already stirring, preparing to emerge from dormancy. Those that are "true" bulbs, such as **Tulips,** have their entire flower structure fully formed in miniature, deep within each bulb. Because bulbs store the food the plant will need, (manufactured last spring as their foliage soaked up the sun's energy), they are virtually self-reliant. Last fall they developed root systems to sustain them, and shortly their internal calendars will signal the time for each type to begin to grow toward the soil surface.

Tender, summer-flowering bulbs have a different schedule because winter weather kills them in the soil. They are grown as annuals in our state, planted when the soil is warm, then pulled from the ground—for potting, storing, or discarding—when frost threatens in the fall. This month is a good time to study the colorful mail-order catalogs and select the bulbs you want to grow this summer. Even though you can't plant bulbs outdoors until late spring, you can get a head start by planting them in pots and start them growing indoors weeks before it is safe to plant outdoors.

It is not too late to force **Paperwhite Narcissus** bulbs indoors. They are still available in stores and need no chill period (see October for forcing steps).

New Year's Resolutions: To try at least one new type of bulb this year; to save package labels to help remember bulb names and varieties; to keep a garden journal.

Care for Your Bulbs

If you notice **Crocus** and **Daffodil** foliage emerging already, don't panic. In fact, don't do anything. There's no need to pile more mulch on the foliage for protection—just let it alone. Frost and snow might brown the tips a bit, but the bulbs will develop more foliage and will be fine (hardy bulbs have a lot of experience with winter weather).

What to do with a gift-planted **Amaryllis** bulb that has finished blooming? There are two choices—treat it as an annual plant and throw it away, or keep it for next year. To keep it for next year:

1 *Cut off* faded flowers and stems.

2 Allow the big straplike leaves to develop and soak up the sun in a bright window.

3 *Water* it as you would a house-plant to keep the soil moist, not overly wet.

4 *Fertilize* it with houseplant fertilizer if there is no granular, slow-acting fertilizer in its planting mix.

5 When nice weather arrives in the spring, put it outdoors in the light. Protect the drooping foliage from slug attack.

6 In the fall, bring it in, stop watering, and let the leaves die back so it can have a dormant period. Then *water* it to begin the bloom cycle once again.

If bulbs planted in pots last fall for forcing indoors have had a long enough chill period, you will notice that green shoots are starting to emerge. Each bulb will have developed lots of roots, which may be nudging the crowded bulbs up out of the soil or gravel a bit.

1 Move the pots into warmth gradually, beginning by putting them in an area that is about 45 degrees F for a few days, then into one that is closer to 60 degrees F. *Water* the bulbs when the planting mix is dry.

2 Place the bulb pots in a bright, sunny window as the buds swell. Avoid overheated rooms, which will cause the buds to bloom and fade very quickly.

Watering

If their soil dries out, keep watering pans of bulbs that need longer cool storage for forcing. Make sure the soil or gravel is never so soggy that the bulbs are immersed in water.

Fertilizing

Bulbs come packaged with fertilizer in the form of stored energy. Those that are potted for forced bloom will have enough to produce lovely blooms. If you later plant them in the ground, add granular, slow-acting fertilizer or bulb fertilizer to the soil at planting time.

Grooming

Improve the appearance of blooming potted bulbs by mulching their soil surface lightly with decorative gravel, colorful pebbles, sphagnum moss, nut shells, or some other attractive material. *Trim off* any withered foliage tips or blooms.

Problem Solving

Rot is sometimes a problem with bulbs potted for forcing. It destroys bulb roots in cool, soggy soil; if you find this destruction has occurred, *throw away* the bulbs. Always examine bulbs carefully for discolored, soft spots before planting them, and do not overwater.

Aphids and fungus gnats sometimes attack houseplants, including hardy bulbs blooming indoors. *Wash off* the aphids, or *spray* affected plants with commercial insecticidal soap. Flying gnats are more nuisance than danger. Their larvae in the soil go after plant roots, so *discard* the soil in the trash after the bulbs are finished blooming. Discard heavily infested bulbs as well.

Growing Smarter

Since January is the month of new beginnings, it is an appropriate time to begin a garden journal. Journaling is one of the easiest, fastest ways to become a better gardener. While it may seem as though jotting down notes every week or so takes extra time, it in fact saves time. By providing a history of past events and adventures in the garden, a journal reminds us of our successes and failures. Knowing what did not work helps prevent wasting more time, energy, and money trying it again. Recording the weather, noting what is blooming, listing new plants and their names, and making sketches of where plants are located gives gardeners a new perspective on their efforts.

A journal can be a bunch of notecards, a lined legal pad, a calendar, a computer file, or a lovely bound book–there are no rules. Keep it nearby–perhaps on top of the refrigerator, in the tool shed, or beside the bed–so you can make notes when you think of them. If keeping records for an entire garden seems to be too big an effort, why not start with just bulbs? Some things that you might keep track of are:

- Snow- and ice-storms
- The time when pots of **Crocus** for forcing were brought out
- Lessons learned from trying to force bulbs
- An order for new tender bulbs (quantity, price)
- Date of the first **Crocus, Snowdrop, Daffodil, Tulip** (and others)
- Where bulbs are planted on the property (a sketch)
- Dates of last hard frost and last light frost
- When you cleaned up all ripened foliage from hardy bulbs
- When you planted tender bulbs in the spring

Planning

Look for **Snowdrops** *and* **Winter Aconite** *anytime now; note when you see the first flower.* If you do not have any of these stalwart early bloomers, plan to purchase some late next summer to plant in the fall. When winter becomes tiresome, the appearance of these flowering bulbs is great encouragement.

If you have not already made a sketch of where hardy bulbs are planted in the yard, get ready to make one this spring as their bloom season unfolds. It will be useful for planting bulbs next fall and will also help with locating spots for tender bulbs later this spring. Think about planting foliage ground covers over bulb beds. **Ivy, Pachysandra, Liriope, Sweet Woodruff,** and others will cover unsightly ripening bulb foliage later this spring.

Plan where you will site tender, summer-blooming bulbs later this spring. (Don't forget that many also do well in containers.) Order any time now by mail—they will be sent to you at the appropriate time for your climate.

Shopping List: containers for summer bulbs, soilless potting mix

Planting

As soon as Pansies become available at the garden center, they can be planted where you have planted bulbs such as **Tulips, Hyacinths,** and **Daffodils. Calendulas** and **Forget-me-nots** are also cool-weather annuals that look really lovely when interplanted with hardy bulbs in special beds, in the garden, or in containers.

When **Snowdrops** are finished blooming and only their green foliage remains, they can be moved or thinned. If the ground is workable, take this opportunity before the season begins full force to ***transplant*** the little bulbs to new sites for next year. They are ideal for edging beds or naturalizing in woodland settings. Just *poke* them an inch or two into soft, moist soil with your finger. If you choose to plant them in the lawn, you will have to delay mowing that area until the foliage ripens and collapses six to eight weeks after bloom.

Care for Your Bulbs

The earliest bloomers of the hardy bulbs will be showing up any time now. In fact, if it has been a mild winter and they are planted near heat-retaining masonry walls, **Snowdrops, Crocus,** and even certain types of **Daffodils** may have already started to emerge through the mulch. Do not be concerned if a sudden freeze or snowstorm comes along; the bulbs will be fine. The mulch covering on the soil will help it stay chilly, which will slow the bulbs until it is late enough in the winter for them to emerge safely.

There is no need to remove the mulch layer over bulb beds unless it is thicker than 2 or 3 inches, or if the beds are mulched with evergreen boughs. In either of these situations, move the mulch aside, or discard the boughs toward the end of the month to allow the soil to warm gradually and make way for the emergence of bulb foliage.

Check stored tender bulbs such as **Cannas, Dahlias,** and **Gladiolas** from last year. *Discard* any that are mushy or dried out. Make sure the temperature in the room doesn't freeze. In another month or two it will be time to bring them out of storage to plant in pots for an early indoor start prior to planting out. It is not safe to put tender bulbs into the ground until late May or early June.

Colchicum foliage will appear this month. Difficult to miss in the garden bed, these wide, bright-green leaves eventually grow to 10 inches long. They will soak up the sun all spring, then gradually yellow and die back by June; do not cut them off until they have collapsed on the ground. You will have to wait until September to see the **Colchicum** blossoms.

Watering

Hardy bulbs planted out in the yard in mulched beds will not need watering even if winter rain and snow is limited. Those planted in windowboxes and planters outdoors aboveground may need watering. Make sure containers have drainage holes so excess water or melting snow can drain away.

Fertilizing

Sprinkle granular bulb fertilizer over the soil of beds of hardy bulbs now, so there will be time for the nutrients to soak down to the roots before bloom time. Broadcast it over the soil, then scratch it into the surface a bit.

Growing Smarter

There are lots of small bulbs that bloom literally and figuratively in the shadow of the more familiar, high-profile **Dutch Crocus, Common Tulips,** and **Daffodils.** Many of these are resistant to squirrels in areas of Pennsylvania. Some small bulbs:

- **Checkered Lily (***Fritillaria meleagris***)**
- **Dogtooth Violet (***Erythronium* 'Pagoda'**)**
- **Glory of the Snow (***Chionodoxa* sp.**)**
- **Snow Crocus (***Crocus tomasinianus***)**
- **Snowdrop (***Galanthus nivalis***)**
- **Snowflake (***Leucojum aestivum***)**
- **Squill (***Scilla sibirica***)**
- **Striped Squill (***Pushkinia scilloides***)**
- **Winter Aconite (***Eranthis hymenalis***)**
- **Wood Hyacinth (***Hyacinthoides* sp.**)**

Grooming

After hardy bulbs have bloomed out in the yard, it is important to allow their foliage to continue to grow. (*Clip off* the faded flowers of the larger types—**Tulips, Hyacinths,** and **Daffodils**—to direct their energy into manufacturing carbohydrates for energy rather than producing seeds.) Resist the temptation to neaten the foliage, even though it gets pretty unsightly as it ages and flops. Clean it up only after it is so limp it pulls away easily.

Problem Solving

Squirrels just love early **Crocuses**—probably because there are few fresh food alternatives, and **Crocuses** are fresh and tender. Fashion low covers from wire hardware cloth to lay over threatened **Crocus** beds to deter the critters. Soon squirrels will find other food, and later-blooming **Crocuses** are not as bothered by them.

Deer, if they are in the area, will be a problem for spring bulbs. They love **Crocus** and **Tulips.** Use the squirrel preventative mentioned above, or *spray* plants with repellent as directed on the product label.

MARCH

Planning

Spring-blooming bulbs begin their main show this month, and often the show coincides with Easter and other religious holidays. It is not surprising that the seasonal display in the yard is echoed or anticipated by the array of gift plants in florist and garden center windows.

Tulips and **Daffodils** are available in a dizzying array of types and varieties, and they also have varying bloom times. As you enjoy spring-blooming bulbs in your garden and elsewhere, think about planting more next fall. Many mail-order bulb companies will send out catalogs soon to invite you to order bulbs now when you are most enchanted by them. Read catalog information closely to determine which bulbs to order. Plan for continuing bloom from March through May by selecting and planting early-, mid-, and late-flowering varieties of your favorites. Even though you will not receive the bulbs until fall when it is planting time, the best time to choose is now when the flowers are on display in public and residential landscapes. Ordering bulbs ahead of time often saves money, too. See the bloom chart on p. 51.

The long, wide, straplike leaves you may notice in gardens this time of year belong to **Summer Amaryllis,** also called **Resurrection Lily.** They will die back and disappear soon. Look for **Amaryllis**-like flowers without foliage in the same places next August.

Shopping List: stakes, bulb fertilizer

Planting

Snowdrop blossoms have faded by now, and only the foliage persists. During the next month or so while the leaves are still green, *divide* overcrowded clumps of **Snowdrops** if the ground has thawed sufficiently. Having the foliage still attached to the bulbs is a real help.

1 Gently *dig up* masses of rooted **Snowdrop** bulbs, and shake away excess soil.

2 Tease apart individual bulbs, taking care not to tear the roots or break off the foliage.

3 *Discard* any bulbs that are damaged or diseased.

4 Replant some of the bulbs in the original spot, about 3 inches apart and 3 inches deep.

5 Give away the remainder, or replant them at a new site.

Plant cool-season annuals—**Forget-me-nots, Pansies, English Daisies**—as companion plants for spring-flowering hardy bulbs. They will soon appear at the garden center.

If you did not plant hardy bulbs last fall but would love to have some **Tulips** or **Daffodils** now, visit the garden center and purchase some potted ones that are just starting to show new foliage. Set each pot outdoors in the garden bed, either placing it on the soil or sinking it into the soil. An alternative is to remove the bulbs from the pot, taking care to keep the soil intact around the roots, and plant the entire clump in the garden bed.

Care for Your Bulbs

The earliest **Crocuses,** tiny **Snow Crocuses,** naturalize easily, often spreading into lawns. After they bloom, delay mowing the lawn to allow their foliage to ripen.

Pots of **Tulips, Daffodils, Hyacinths, Lilies,** and other forced bulbs are gifts that will keep on giving. Once they have bloomed and their foliage is allowed to age naturally in a sunny window, plant them outdoors. They will adjust to the outdoor schedule and bloom next year in the yard. In the case of **Amaryllis,** which is tender and will not winter over in the soil, set the pot of foliage outdoors for the summer. (See October for instructions for forcing blooms indoors.)

In a few weeks it will be time to take the tender bulbs out of winter storage. *Check* them this month to be sure they have not dried out.

Watering

Normal spring rainfall or melting snow should provide sufficient moisture for bulbs. If it has been a dry winter, *water* bulb beds after the ground has thawed.

Fertilizing

Bulbs, corms, rhizomes, and tubers are special structures in which plants store energy from the previous season, so these plants do not require spring fertilizing. If you wish to fertilize in spring to give them a boost, however, *spread* a bit of granular slow-acting or special bulb fertilizer over their soil; do this before they bloom so there will be time for rain to soak the fertilizer deep into the soil.

Common Tulips, including **Darwin** hybrids or **Cottage** types, are not always reliably perennial. They are not as strong their second year of bloom and weaken even more after that. Fertilizing them twice a year, in early spring and fall, helps to keep them stronger.

Growing Smarter

There are all kinds of **Daffodils,** also called **Narcissus,** and the various types bloom at different times throughout the spring. It is possible with a little forethought to have some blooming continuously in the yard for up to four months (see Bulbs for Pennsylvania chart).

- Small **Daffodils** that have reflexed petals (such as **'Peeping Tom'**) appear in March and April.
- The familiar large-cup and "trumpet" types such as **'King Alfred'** start the main April bloom time. They are followed by small-cup, double **Daffodils.** Some have fancy, split, frilly trumpets.
- Dainty nodding types that bear several flowers per stem are often fragrant; **Jonquils** and **Tazetta** varieties bloom in mid- to late April.
- **Poet's Narcissus** (*Poeticus* **'Actea'**), with tiny cups edged with red or orange, are among the latest to bloom. They appear in May.

Grooming

Pinching off the faded flowers of minor bulbs that carpet the ground such as **Squill, Anemone,** and **Snowdrops** is not necessary because they are fairly unobtrusive. In the garden setting it may help to pinch off faded blossoms of the large **Dutch Crocus** and **Grape Hyacinth** if they are very visible. *Snip or pinch off* faded **Narcissus, Tulip,** and **Hyacinth** flowers to improve the appearance of the plants while their leaves continue to grow. This also prevents their wasting energy on developing unnecessary seedpods. Do not cut back, tie, or otherwise disturb the foliage while it is still green; this interferes with its job of collecting sun for energy for next year.

Problem Solving

Deer are quite fond of hybrid **Tulips** and will nibble the blossoms from the tops of their stems. An entire bed of **Tulips** may disappear overnight. If deer are just occasional visitors to the yard, try spraying the **Tulips** with repellent, or *protect* them with cages of chicken wire while they are in bloom. If deer are a regular nuisance, either *fence* the property or grow **Narcissus** instead of **Tulips.**

Mice will nest in the same kinds of dark, cool places where tender bulbs are stored indoors over the winter. Keep an eye out for signs of their activity when you check the bulbs, and set traps if necessary. Take pains to block holes and cracks around doors, utility wires, and pipes.

Planning

The show goes on. Garden beds and borders that were brown and empty just a month ago are alive with colorful flowering bulbs this month. Bulb-planted areas are also becoming increasingly crowded with maturing foliage as the season progresses. Because it is necessary for the long-term health of hardy bulbs to allow the foliage to bask in the sun for as long as it takes for it to mature and die back, the appearance of the area where they are growing is always a concern. Take some time to evaluate the location of your plantings of **Narcissus, Tulips, Hyacinths, Ornamental Onions,** and others. If their foliage looks unsightly or obscures the developing perennial flowers that are currently emerging in the bed, it may be a good idea to transplant the bulbs to areas where the dying foliage will be less obtrusive:

- Plant bulbs in beds of evergreen ground covers such as **Ivy, Pachysandra, Vinca.**

- Plant bulbs among perennials that will emerge and leaf out just in time to mask ripening bulb foliage (examples: **Daylily, Hosta, Liriope**).

- Plant bulbs in beds by themselves for display or cutting so they can be screened from view by a fence when the bloom period is over.

Soon it will be time to plant tender bulbs. *Check* your garden journal or sketches to identify places that will be empty after spring bulb foliage dies back. These spots and those left by ephemeral spring perennial plants such as **Bleeding Heart** and **Virginia Bluebells** are perfect sites for pots and planters filled with summer-blooming bulbs.

Find an opportunity to visit a public garden or arboretum where spring bulbs are in full display. Not only is this a good way to enjoy those that you yourself do not grow, but you can also learn about unusual types from the plant labels.

Shopping List: potting mix, bulb fertilizer, watering can

Planting

Like **Snowdrops, Daffodils** can be divided while "green." Although they can go indefinitely without thinning, as they do when naturalized in a meadow or woodland setting, sometimes clumps become disproportionately large for a garden bed or border, and crowding may decrease the number of blooms. Rather than wait until fall when you may forget or cannot find them, do the job as soon as they finish blooming.

1 Carefully *dig* the clump of bulbs out of the ground so it is free of soil. Take care not to damage or break the foliage.

2 Gently brush excess soil from the bulbs, and separate them, teasing apart the tangled roots at the base of each large knobby bulb.

3 If a large bulb has developed several good-sized subsidiary bulbs with roots, you may choose to separate them from the mother bulb by breaking them apart, or you can plant them intact.

4 *Check* bulbs for injury or disease, and *discard* any that are dubious.

5 Replant some of the bulbs in the former location, 4 to 6 inches apart and about 6 inches deep. *Water* well.

6 *Plant* the remaining divisions elsewhere, or give them away. Smaller ones may not bloom for a year or two. They are perfect for naturalizing.

If you have stored **Tuberous Begonias** in pots, you can begin to nudge them out of dormancy by watering them and bringing them gradually into the warmth of the house. It is still too early for them to go outdoors.

Rather than wait until next month when the weather has warmed up significantly enough to plant tender bulbs outdoors in the yard, start them indoors now. Bring them out of winter storage, cull any injured or diseased, and divide those overgrown. *Plant* **Canna, Caladium, Dahlias,** and others in soilless potting medium with a bit of granular, slow-acting fertilizer mixed in. *Water* them, and set the pots in a bright room for a few weeks. They will be well sprouted when it is warm enough to plant them outdoors.

This is a good time to plant outdoors the hardy bulbs that you forced indoors back in January and February. Keep any remaining foliage intact, and plant as you would in the fall (see October for planting instructions).

Care for Your Bulbs

Later this month, *check* stored tender bulbs that you intend to plant outdoors next month. If you didn't sort them last fall, go through them now and *discard* any that look bad. Clean the soil off them, and remove desiccated pieces of root or sections of rhizome. *Divide* Dahlia tubers where they are linked, making sure each separate tuber for planting has an "eye," or growing

tip. Break off bulblets or cormlets from **Begonias** and **Gladiolas** to plant separately. They are too young to bloom this year; wait until late May to plant them outdoors.

Watering

If the April showers live up to their reputation, there will be no need to water bulb beds this month. Make sure the potted medium of tender bulbs is moist, but never soaking wet.

Fertilizing

If you want to fertilize hardy spring bulbs to help them develop good foliage, wait until after they bloom and you have clipped off the faded flowers. Do not overdo the fertilizing, because excess tender foliage attracts pest insects. If you can't get to it now, plan to fertilize in the early fall when you plant new bulbs—that is the most important time to fertilize.

Grooming

Cut off faded **Tulip** and **Daffodil** flowers as soon as they finish blooming and their petals drop. Cut back the stems to where the leaves begin, leaving as much foliage as possible.

Problem Solving

Rabbits as well as deer may be damaging your blooming **Tulips.** Soon they will become more interested in the young lettuce in the garden or some tender weeds in the lawn. *Spray* vulnerable **Tulips** with repellent, or put up a temporary barrier such as a wire cage to protect them.

Tulip fire (*Botrytis tulipae*) is a serious disease which attacks **Tulips** that have been growing in the same place for several years and deforms their flowers and bulbs. *Dig up and discard* affected bulbs, and do not plant **Tulips** in that soil for at least four years. The disease will die out on its own.

Planning

Danger of frost is past in Pennsylvania this month—early May in the Philadelphia area, late May up in the mountains. Finally the soil has dried out from April rains and is warm enough for planting tender, summer-blooming bulbs. When planting **Dahlias, Cannas,** and others in containers, remember that they will grow larger over the summer, and factor that into the design. By the end of the month the storage area for overwintered tender bulbs should be empty.

Continue to make notes about the areas in which ripening foliage of already-bloomed hardy bulbs is an eyesore. Think about ground covers or companion plants to plant now that will mask the foliage next year.

Not all summer-blooming bulbs are tender, requiring special winter storage; some types will overwinter in the soil in Pennsylvania. **Ornamental Onions** of various kinds will bloom this month along with the **Rhododendrons** and **Mountain Laurel. Hybrid Lilies** and **Crocosmia** foliage will appear as the weather becomes increasingly warm, and they will bloom in summer. Plan to plant more of these types if you feel you do not have time to plant tender summer bulbs every year.

Shopping List: potted tender bulbs, ground cover plants

Planting

This is a busy planting month.

- **Tuberous Begonias** overwintered in pots as houseplants may need repotting into larger containers. They can go outdoors into the garden in their pots or directly into the soil. Choose a shady spot that receives good air circulation, indirect or filtered light, and good soil that drains well.

- Finish planting out in the yard those gift plant bulbs from Easter that you do not intend to throw away (see August and September for planting instructions for hardy bulbs). The **Amaryllis** bulb should stay in its pot; set it in a bed or on the deck outdoors so its great foliage can enjoy the sun.

- *Plant* all your tender bulbs by the end of the month. If they have been started in pots and are already sprouted, *transplant* them into the garden or into decorative containers with other plants when the weather is dependably warm.

- *Plant* the first wave of **Gladiola** corms mid-month. To enjoy continuous blooms over the season, plant more corms every two weeks until July.

Care for Your Bulbs

Certain summer-blooming bulbs need support to prevent their collapse in heavy rain or wind. Support **Lilies** that will grow over 3 feet tall when they begin to gain some height. Insert a stake into the soil near each stem gently so it does not damage the bulb. Use green twine to loosely tie the stem to the stake. Do the same with **Dahlias** and **Gladiolas.** Make sure the stakes are shorter than the ultimate height of the plant so they are unobtrusive. Clumps of narrow **Crocosmia** foliage may need support. Set up stakes around the perimeter of the planting, then tie twine to them in a circle to hold them upright.

Watering

Water the soil where newly planted summer bulbs are located to make sure the soil settles around them properly. Those in pots will need closer attention for watering, because soilless potting medium tends to dry out faster than garden soil, especially when the weather gets hotter.

Fertilizing

Although bulbs, corms, tubers, and rhizomes store energy for the plant to use, plants benefit from nutrients in the soil as well. Some, such as **Dahlias** and **Begonias,** produce flowers all summer and welcome an extra ration of fertilizer to sustain strong growth. To enhance the fertility of your soil, *sprinkle* some slow-acting, granular, all-purpose fertilizer over the soil of bulb beds so the rain can soak it in. Mix it into the potting medium when planting or transplanting bulbs in containers. If the bulbs are already in containers, sprinkle the complete, slow-acting granular fertilizer over the surface of the planting mix.

Grooming

By month's end, the foliage of the earlier hardy bulbs will be yellowing and collapsing. Clean it up when it has ripened to the point that it easily detaches from the underground bulb when you tug on it.

Growing Smarter

Many summer bulbs are magnets for hummingbirds and butterflies. Their richly colored, often fragrant, blossoms entice visitors on the lookout for nectar and pollen. Watch your **Cannas, Crocosmias, Lilies,** and **Gladiolas** for hummingbirds. The trumpet shapes of these flowers are just what hummers like. The brilliant colors of **Dahlias** make them a favorite of butterflies, which also visit **Lilies, Crocosmia,** and **Gladiolas.**

Problem Solving

Insects crawling all over round, lilac-blue **Ornamental Onion** blossoms are beneficial! **Ornamental Onion** flowers are valuable allies in pest control because they support the tiny predator wasps, lacewings, and other insects that attack pest insects and their larvae throughout the garden.

Aphids and mites are potential problems for blooming bulbs, just as they are for other plants. Try washing off the clusters of insects at tender foliage tips and buds. If that doesn't work, *spray* them directly with insecticidal soap.

Fungal diseases may mar the foliage of certain bulbs. **Tuberous Begonias** sometimes develop mildew and leaf spot infections. The best defense is a good offense. Make sure they have good air circulation, and keep foliage dry. *Pinch off* infected leaves, and *clean up* fallen leaves promptly to arrest the spread of the fungus.

Weeds are easily controlled if you deal with them early before they get entrenched. *Pull or spot-treat* stubborn weeds with herbicide before the bulbs emerge from the soil. *Mulch* bare soil to discourage the growth of weeds.

JUNE

Planning

As spring turns into summer, you may find more bulb catalogs in your mailbox. This will give you an opportunity to order hardy bulbs for fall planting ahead of time, if you have not already done so. There are many advantages to pre-ordering fall bulbs in late spring:

- The bulbs you need are fresh in your mind from the bloom season just past.

- You can find and have first choice of the less common bulbs that are in limited supply.

- Mail-order firms often offer smaller-sized bulbs in bulk for naturalizing at an economical price.

- Pre-ordering usually earns a discount.

- Bulbs will be shipped at the end of the season when it is appropriate to plant them.

Remember the New Year's resolution about trying at least one new bulb this year? Study the photographs and information in the catalogs and choose something that looks interesting. Some suggestions: **Fritillaria, Colchicum, Dwarf Iris, Hardy Cyclamen, Snowflake.**

Shopping List: pre-ordered fall bulbs, garden stakes

Planting

Last call for transplanting into the ground those tender summer bulbs that were started in pots. Soon they will outgrow their pots and need larger ones if they are not planted. Time is also running out for thinning clumps of **Daffodils** and replanting the bulbs while their foliage is still attached to make it easier. You can dry and store the extra bulbs from the clumps until fall planting time, but why go to the trouble? *Plant* them in a new bed, under trees and shrubs, or naturalized in a woodland setting now, and the job is done.

Remember to put in another planting of **Gladiola** corms so there will be **Glads** in bloom when the first batch fades.

Care for Your Bulbs

Continue staking plants that need support. Some **Dahlias** grow very tall by midseason, and their brittle stems break quite easily. *Stake* **Gladiola** stems individually to prevent their heavy blossoms from flopping in heavy rains.

Watering

A sudden onset of heat and/or lack of rain later this month may require getting out the garden hose. Summer-blooming bulbs appreciate the water because they are in their major growth period. Those planted under trees may miss out on light rainfall because the canopy of new leaves blocks it. Those planted in pots and ornamental containers dry out quickly in the heat.

Hardy spring-blooming bulbs have finished their season and are going dormant to wait out the coming weeks of heat. Most prefer dry conditions during this time and do not need supplemental watering.

Fertilizing

The slow-acting granular fertilizer incorporated into bulb soil or potting medium is on the job now. If it is not in the potting mix, *water-in* very dilute liquid fertilizer every two weeks while the plants are blooming.

Grooming

Pick **Dahlias** and **Glads** for indoor display and to stimulate the plants to produce new blossoms. This also keeps them neat, improving the appearance of the yard and garden as well as the plants. *Pinch off* shabby leaves and faded flowers and stems of **Begonias.**

Problem Solving

Squirrels may go after bulbs in pots on the ground or patio and tip them over. Group the pots, or raise them from ground level to make them less accessible.

Growing Smarter

One of the great summer bulb success stories is **Lilies.** These summer bloomers are different from most of the other summer bloomers because they are tough enough to withstand real winters in the ground. They have lots of other virtues as well:

- Enormous variety of color
- Fragrance
- Varying heights
- Neat habit
- Formal look (yet they blend with other plants)
- Attract butterflies and hummingbirds
- Make excellent cut flowers

Slugs (snails without shells) are fond of **Tuberous Begonias.** Raise pots off the ground by setting them on other, overturned pots, bricks or decorative concrete "feet." *Sprinkle* diatomaceous earth (DE) over the soil around those planted in soil. This sharp material will discourage slugs from slithering over to the plant foliage.

Starting Caladiums

Planning

If it has been awhile since you recorded information in your garden journal or notebook, take some time this month—the halfway point of the calendar year—to catch up. Things that are worth noting:

- Major weather events such as late snowfall, late frost, early heat, spring drought

- Which hardy bulbs were a disappointment

- When the first blossoms of **Snowdrops, Iris, Daffodils, Crocus, Tulips, Ornamental Onions** appeared

- How the tender bulbs withstood winter storage

- If you thinned overgrown clumps of **Daffodils** or other flowers

- Things you intended to do, but didn't get to

- When you planted summer-blooming bulbs

- Any significant events in the landscape—large trees removed, construction, flooding

Shopping List: vases for cut flowers, floral preservative

Planting

Allow the bulbs acquired from thinning overgrown clumps of **Daffodils** and the early fall-blooming bulbs (**Colchicum, Sternbergia,** and **Fall Crocus**) to dry out and rest in a dark place with good air circulation until later next month. If you wait to plant them then, when the soil is not so warm, they will be less likely to suffer a disease.

Care for Your Bulbs

Finish staking tall **Dahlia** plants and others that may fall over in storms. Be careful not to poke or damage the tubers when inserting the stake into the soil near them.

Mulch any bare soil around summer bulbs with an inch or two of chopped leaves, dried grass clippings, or similar organic material. It will help prevent the soil from drying out, discourage weeds, and help condition the soil as it decomposes in the summer heat.

Watering

Water bulbs in pots if the weather is dry and/or hot. Make sure the pots are draining well so the planting medium does not get soggy. *Water* summer bulbs in the garden when it becomes necessary to water other plants.

Fertilizing

If you have used granular, slow-acting fertilizer when planting bulbs in containers or garden soil, there is no need to fertilize now, for the bulbs are getting gradual, consistent, uniform nutrition—the best kind. Soil covered by a protective organic mulch gains fertility over time as the mulch decomposes and microorganisms are introduced into the soil.

Grooming

Some **Dahlia** varieties are dwarf and grow to only 1 or 2 feet tall. The medium and tall varieties, however, reach from 3 to 8 feet tall. Strategic pinching will promote side branching and help keep these taller ones more compact. Begin the process by pinching out the center stem after there are a half-dozen leaves on the plant.

Remove faded **Begonia** blooms promptly to forestall disease. *Cut off* **Lily** flowers after all the blooms on a stem have faded. Leave the leaf-covered stem so the foliage can continue to soak up sun for energy that will be stored in the bulb for next season. In a month or six weeks, the stem and foliage will have dried sufficiently so they can be easily separated from the bulb deep in the soil. Cut stems, and *discard* them on the compost pile.

Problem Solving

Insects and diseases are more of a problem for tender, summer-blooming bulbs than they are for hardy spring bloomers. This is mainly because the insects and disease spores are not out and about in the chilly spring. They share a preference for warmth with the summer bloomers. Handle these problems as you would for any other garden plant.

1 Keep your summer bulb plants as happy and stress-free as possible by giving them proper moisture, nutrition, light, and air circulation.

2 Keep after weeds, which harbor pest insects and disease pathogens and compete with bulbs for nutrients and light.

3 Examine blooming bulbs regularly to discover problems early, before they become severe.

4 *Pinch or clip off* foliage, blossoms, or stems that are infested with bugs or fungus to reduce the problem and keep it from spreading. Remove them from the garden and put in the trash.

5 *Spray* affected plants with a strong water spray to dislodge insects. Treat severe infestations with insecticidal soap spray as directed on its label.

Growing Smarter

Like other plants, plants that grow from bulbs, tubers, corms, and rhizomes—collectively referred to as bulbs in this book—have multiple names. Only one is official, and that is the scientific, or botanical, name, which is in formal Latin and is recognized throughout the horticultural world. Other names for bulbs are informal, common names that change from region to region. *Erythronium* is called both **Dogtooth Violet** and **Troutlily.** *Lycoris* is called variously **Resurrection Lily, Magic Lily,** and **Naked Lady,** depending on who is talking. When buying bulbs, it is best to use their Latin name as listed in the catalog to be sure you get what you ask for.

Planning

Enjoy the **Resurrection Lilies** *that pop up in local yards and gardens.* Always a bit of a surprise, they seem to appear out of nowhere on tall stems without any foliage. In fact, their foliage bloomed back in the spring and died down in early summer. If you decide to plant some in your yard, put them among **Hostas,** which can provide some foliage for the charming bare-stemmed flowers.

Fall is a good time to renovate garden beds where the soil has lost its organic content over the years and become compacted. Plants may be overgrown, the bulbs crowded and tired. Take some time to improve the planting area when the weather cools a bit and before bulb-planting time.

1 *Dig up* existing plants and bulbs and set them aside, covered with newspaper and in the shade.

2 *Dig* deeply into the soil with a shovel and turn it over. *Remove* debris and stones, then add some peat moss, compost, or chopped leaves to provide organic material to help drainage.

3 Mix in some granular, slow-acting fertilizer as you break up clumps of soil and distribute the organic matter through it.

4 *Rake* the soil level, and then dig holes to replant perennials and bulbs in a pleasing arrangement. Take this opportunity to *divide* those that have become overgrown.

5 *Water* well, and *mulch* to prevent weed seeds that have been exposed to the light from germinating.

Shopping List: bulb planter, fertilizer, hardy bulbs

Planting

Early this month is a good time to move, or divide and replant, hardy bulbs that have been in the ground so long they have become densely crowded. Smaller blossoms or reduced blooming often signals overcrowding. If clumps of **Snowdrop** bulbs start to rise up from under the soil or if the centers of clumps of **Iris** are woody, it is time to dig up the clumps and separate the bulbs. *Discard* those that look diseased or damaged. *Replant* the healthy ones, with some space between them.

As soon as pre-ordered hardy bulbs arrive, start planting them. There are several ways to use bulbs in a residential landscape. One way is to *naturalize* them. This means the planting pattern is random and informal, as might be the case in nature, rather than making official planting beds according to a scheme; it is a good way to improve undeveloped or marginal areas of the yard.

Pop small **Crocus** and **Glory of the Snow** bulbs into an area of the lawn where the soil is damp and easy to penetrate, and next spring they will provide a scattering of color over the green lawn. *Plant* **Daffodils** in a woodland area where they will provide spots of cheery yellow before the leaves come out on the trees. Each year these bulbs will multiply, and the planting will become even more beautiful. Steps for a naturalized planting:

1 Naturalized bulbs do not need to be topsize, which is the most expensive. Use smaller, more economical bulbs that can be purchased in bulk.

2 *Scatter* the bulbs so they fall randomly over the area to be planted.

3 *Dig* a hole in the soil where each bulb has dropped, and plant the bulb at the correct depth.

4 *Fill* the hole with soil, and firm it gently.

5 *Water* the area if rain is not expected for awhile.

Care for Your Bulbs

Sometimes in summer the mulch layer decomposes and the soil surface dries out and shrinks, revealing piles of tiny bulbs such as **Snowdrops** or **Glory of the Snow** that are shallowly planted. They are dormant and do not mind the dry soil, but they should not be exposed to light and air for long. Poke them back a couple of inches into the soil. They may have surfaced because of crowding, so take this opportunity to *thin* the clump. Plant the excess bulbs elsewhere.

Watering

In heat and drought, container bulbs dry out fast! Be sure to check them every day. *Water* summer-blooming bulbs in the garden when all the plants need it.

Grooming

Continue to *deadhead* faded blossoms on **Dahlias** and other flowers that are still blooming. The stems of **Lilies** will probably be drying and the foliage turning yellow by now.

Growing Smarter

Planting time for hardy bulbs is not far away. If you buy bulbs at a store rather than through the mail, you will have an opportunity to examine them closely and select the best quality. How to tell the best? Growers generally grade bulbs by their size, sifting them through holes of various circumferences to sort them. Since the largest bulbs usually perform best–producing larger or more numerous blossoms– they are rated "tops" or topsize. They are usually the most expensive and are ideal for forcing indoors as specimen plants. Bulbs that are somewhat smaller are perfectly satisfactory for gardens and bedding designs. The smallest sizes, which are least expensive, are ideal for naturalizing. If they do not bloom the first year it does not matter, since they are planted randomly with lots of others. Check bulbs for firmness and plumpness. A touch of blue mold on the surface is not a problem; neither is a peeling tunic or dry skin on a bulb.

It is okay to cut off the stems at ground level, but do not try to pull them out of the soil, because you may pull up the bulb. If stems are crowded and a lot of them are thin and spindly, make a note to *dig up and divide* the **Lily** bulbs this fall.

Problem Solving

Deal with **annual weeds** before they mature and begin to set and spread seed. Pull them promptly. If they have rooted in a mulch layer, they will come up easily.

Mildew problems increase as humidity increases. Look for a telltale gray coating on foliage, especially on **Tuberous Begonias.** *Pinch off* any infected leaves, and set pots where plants have good air circulation. Spraying a sulfur-based fungicide on the healthy leaves may prevent the spread of the problem to them. *Repeat* sprays as new leaves emerge and open.

SEPTEMBER

Planning

Plan to plant all your hardy bulbs over the next few weeks as soon as you get them. They store better and more safely in the ground than in the garage, where they may be forgotten. Open the box they arrive in and spread out the packages of bulbs in a dry place so they will have some air circulation.

It really helps to chart where new bulbs are to go in the yard. If you have not done so already, sketch the layout of your existing beds and bulb plantings in your garden journal the best you can remember, and add the locations for the new plantings this year. Consider the height, bloom time, and color of each in the plan. Think about how their ripening foliage might be obscured by perennial plants such as **Pachysandra** or **Hostas,** which will emerge and grow next spring as bulb foliage dies back.

Spring-flowering bulbs need lots of sunshine, but that does not mean they cannot be planted under trees and in woodland situations. The leaves do not usually emerge on the trees until they have finished blooming and soaking up sun in their foliage and are ready to go dormant.

If you plan to have **Amaryllis** in bloom for Christmas, buy and *pot* the bulbs now to force their bloom for December (see October for information on forcing bulbs). The packaged planting kits include instructions and make lovely holiday gifts.

Shopping List: shallow pots for forcing bulbs, decorative gravel, Amaryllis bulb kits

Planting

Planting season for hardy bulbs begins as soon as you buy them at the store or they arrive in the mail. **Daffodil** bulbs need maximum time to develop roots before the ground freezes, so it is a good idea to plant them first. **Tulip** planting can be delayed until next month if you do not have time to plant all your bulbs now. **Tulips** do not need to root first, and they are less subject to disease if they can avoid sitting in warm ground.

Many years ago it was customary to plant bulbs in beds of their own. Carefully spaced in uniform rows for maximum effect, they were separate from other flowering plants, trees, and shrubs. While this "bedding" system of planting is still common for public sites such as parks, malls, corporate campuses, and other formal landscapes, it is less common in smaller contemporary home landscapes. Bedded bulb plantings look best in large, formal landscapes where there are expanses of lawn. To plant bulbs in formal beds:

1 *Dig* a trench in the soil at the correct depth for the type of bulb you are planting. Make it as wide and long as the intended bulb display area. Reserve the soil nearby.

2 *Level* the bottom of the trench, and position the bulbs pointed side up, spaced equidistant, exactly as you prefer.

3 *Sprinkle* some bulb fertilizer over the fill soil, and mix it in. Refill the trench, taking care not to disturb the bulbs. Never let fertilizer directly touch the bulbs.

4 *Firm* the soil gently over the bulbs, and water the bed well.

5 *Mulch* the area with 2 or 3 inches of wood chips or chopped leaves.

Because spring never comes soon enough outdoors, *pot* some bulbs to force early bloom indoors in January. Some, such as **Tulips, Grape Hyacinths,** or **Crocus,** need to have twelve to sixteen weeks of chill and then deeper cold for dormancy before they will bloom. To start the process, imitate these conditions by planting them in pots and storing them in the cold now (see

October). **Paper-white Narcissus** are the exception, as they will root and bloom without a chill period. Buy lots of bulbs and start some every few weeks as winter closes in.

Care for Your Bulbs

When digging or mulching, be especially careful in the areas you have planted **Colchicum** bulbs. Unaccompanied by foliage (which emerged last spring and then died back), these fragile-looking lilac crocus-shaped flowers will bloom this month.

Bring last year's potted **Amaryllis** indoors so it can have a dormant period of at least six to eight weeks. Withhold water so its foliage dies back, and set it in a cool, dark cellar. Any time after Thanksgiving, start watering it four to six weeks before desired bloom time.

Soon tender bulbs will face frost outdoors. Decide whether to treat them as annuals and leave them in the ground to succumb to winter, or to dig them up and store them in a cool, dark place where they will be safe from freezing.

Watering

If it is a dry fall, water tender bulb plants and newly planted bulbs. With only a few exceptions (some kinds of **Canna** and **Iris** actually prefer to grow in water gardens), bulbs prefer soil that drains well. If you notice that the water pools on the soil over bulbs and takes a couple of minutes or longer to soak into the soil, chances are the soil lacks good drainage. Make a note to correct this situation next summer.

Fertilizing

Fall is a good time to fertilize bulbs. Add granular, slow-acting all-purpose or bulb fertilizer to the fill soil when planting new bulbs. *Sprinkle* some over existing bulb beds if you have not fertilized other plants there already.

Problem Solving

Insects often come indoors on plants that were outside all season. When potting up tender bulbs to bring in as houseplants, *wash* stems and foliage with a strong water spray to remove eggs and larvae. *Spray* them with insecticidal soap, pepper wax, or light horticultural oil to control insect outbreaks.

Slugs like **Colchicum** flowers. *Sprinkle* diatomaceous earth (DE) over the soil around the fragile flower stems if there are signs of slugs. An alternative is to use the new, nontoxic slug baits that contain iron phosphate.

Disease on tender bulbs is best controlled at this point by discarding any bulbs that look suspicious when you dig them up for winter storage. Throw them in the trash, not the compost. Tender bulbs left in the ground will die and decompose.

Planning

While bulb planting is in full swing, do not forget to save the labels from bulb packages so you can remember which varieties you have. Store them in an envelope in the back of your garden journal with the sketch of the bulb locations in the yard.

It is time to set up a storage area for overwintering tender bulbs. The space should maintain about 45 to 55 degrees F and should be dry and rodent-proof. If you are storing other plants—tropical **Water Lilies,** rooted cuttings—you may need to install shelves or hooks for bags of bulbs. Unheated cellars and garages are often suitable, and so is an old refrigerator in good working order.

Shopping List: shelving, potting soil, bulb fertilizer

Planting

Continue to *plant* spring-blooming bulbs outdoors while the weather is relatively mild and the soil is easy to work. Plant large bulbs in groups or clusters of three, five, seven, or more. Smaller, or "minor" bulbs, such as **Crocus, Snowdrop, Squill,** and **Glory of the Snow,** look best when planted in large numbers. Their small blossoms make a stronger impact when they are in

patches of several dozen. Mix bulbs into beds of ground cover plants, or perennial borders; plant minor ones under trees whose shallow roots will not be disturbed by the shallow planting depth. To plant bulbs in the ground:

1. *Prepare* the soil in the planting area by digging and loosening it with a spade, and add organic matter to improve its drainage and fertility. Most bulbs require excellent drainage—if your soil is horrible clay, consider building raised bulb beds.

2. *Mix* some granular, slow-acting fertilizer into the soil as you dig.

3. With a narrow pointed trowel or bulb planter, *dig* a hole in the prepared soil as deep as the depth indicated on the packaging. If there are no instructions, the rule of thumb is that the hole depth should be about three times the height of the bulb. A bit deeper is not a problem. Space the holes as you desire.

4. *Set* the bulb in the hole, flat side down, pointed side up. The sides are easy to determine with **Tulips** and **Daffodils,** but with some bulbs or corms it may be more difficult. Just remember that it does not matter if they are planted upside down; the growing sprout will find its way.

5. *Fill* the hole with soil, and water well. Spread a mulch of chopped leaves or other organic material over the soil in the area after the ground freezes.

To plant bulbs in pots for forcing:

1. *Purchase* **Tulips, Crocus,** or **Daffodils** that are labeled good for forcing (certain varieties accept this process better than others).

2. *Fill* wide, relatively shallow containers with soilless potting mix, fine gravel, or coarse sand. Set the bulbs in the planting medium so their tips are slightly above the edge of the pot. Set them shoulder to shoulder (this is one time when it is okay to crowd the bulbs). Then *water*.

3. *Store* the pots in a cool (40 to 50 degrees F) place for several weeks so that roots can grow. Around Thanksgiving, put them where they will experience mild "winter" temperatures (35 to 40 degrees F) and have their dormant period. A cellar, unheated garage, outdoor cold frame, or old refrigerator will be fine.

4. In about sixteen weeks you will notice signs of green sprouting. *Bring* the pans out into a cool room where the bulbs will get light so they will think it is spring. When they are on the verge of blooming, *display*

them in the heated rooms where the family can see and enjoy them even though there may be snow outdoors.

Care for Your Bulbs

Last call to *dig up* tender **Dahlia** tubers, **Gladiola** corms, and other tender bulbs to store them for winter. This must be done after a light frost but before the ground freezes and they are impossible to dig up. Examine them after brushing off the soil, and *discard* any that are injured or diseased. Many bulbs, such as **Canna** and **Dahlias,** will have multiplied by developing offshoots, or new bulb segments. Either store the whole clump now and separate them next spring before planting, or cut them into separate bulbs now. After frost, when their tops have blackened and collapsed, you can *dig up* **Tuberous Begonia** corms to store indoors over the winter, or you might want to pot them up and use them as houseplants instead.

Mulch bulb beds only after the ground freezes so that rodents will not be tempted to nest in the area.

Watering

If it is a dry fall, *water* newly planted hardy bulbs and existing bulb beds. Even though you cannot see them, they are developing roots, and they need moisture.

Fertilizing

Add a granular, slow-acting fertilizer or a product formulated specifically for bulbs to the soil when planting. Never put the fertilizer in the bottom of the hole—it may burn the bulb root tissues if it touches them. *Sprinkle* it over the soil of established bulb beds. If you plant bulbs among shrubs and perennials you have already fertilized for the fall, they will benefit from that and no further fertilizing is necessary.

Problem Solving

Squirrels and other rodents are a real problem with bulbs other than those in the **Daffodil** family. They find them, even though they are underground, by smell. Do not leave packaging or litter from the bulbs where you plant them, and line planting holes with wire cages if necessary. Hardware cloth cages set on the soil over fall-blooming

Growing Smarter

If space in the yard is at a premium, you can plant bulbs in an outdoor container such as a windowbox, planter, or half-barrel that has drainage holes.

1 Fill it with soilless potting medium mixed with granular, slow-acting fertilizer.

2 Plant the bulbs at the correct depth, then fill up the container with the medium.

3 When mixing different varieties of bulbs, first plant the larger, taller ones in a deeper layer, then add some potting medium. Plant the smaller, shorter ones in a shallower layer at their correct depth.

4 Fill the rest of the container with potting medium, and water well.

5 Mulch the medium at the top of the container.

Crocus will protect the flowers from deer and rodents.

Weeds are fair game if air temperatures are still mild. To prevent them from returning next spring, *spray* stubborn perennial weeds with Roundup® while the bulbs are safely underground.

Planning

Potted bulbs from the florist or forcing kits for **Amaryllis** *or* **Paper-white Narcissus** *make great holiday and hostess gifts during November and December.* If purchasing commercially planted bulbs in pots, choose those that are barely sprouting; this way the recipient will have a longer time to enjoy their development and bloom.

Christmas Cyclamen (*Cyclamen persicum*) is a perfect holiday gift for all your friends. It likes bright light in a chilly place. This plant that grows from a corm has everything going for it:

- Fragrance

- Silver-mottled green, heart-shaped foliage

- Variety of flower colors—white, pink, red, lilac, salmon

- Charming butterfly-like flowers

- Very long bloom time

- Availability in mini-size and full-size 12-inch-wide plants

Check the garage, basement, mud room, or tool shed for any bulbs you may have overlooked and forgotten to plant. As long as the ground is not frozen, you can still plant them. *Better late than never* is the rule.

Shopping List: hardware cloth to thwart rodents, **Paper-white Narcissus** bulbs to force for the holidays

Planting

Hardy bulbs are better off in the ground than stored, so plant leftovers if you can. If the ground has frozen, you can plant them in an outdoor planter (see October), or pot them up for forcing indoors. Forced bulbs probably will not be finished with their dormant period until about the time their outdoor counterparts are blooming. After they bloom, plant them outdoors for their foliage to ripen and die back. They will be in place for sure for next spring.

Care for Your Bulbs

Fall-blooming hardy bulbs such as **Sternbergia, Colchicum,** and most **Autumn Crocus** have finished blooming by now. The faded blossoms that have collapsed on the ground can remain there, as they will decompose rapidly.

If you have not already mulched areas where you have planted bulbs, do so after the ground freezes, if you can (if your schedule permits you to do it only before the ground freezes, do it then). The mulch is not intended to prevent the ground from freezing; it just buffers soil temperatures during the winter to minimize the extremes of fluctuating temperatures. Alternate freezing and thawing sometimes causes the soil to heave shallow-planted bulbs to the surface. Spread 2 or 3 inches of chopped leaves or pine needles, or lay needled evergreen boughs over the bulb beds.

Watering

Start watering potted, dormant **Amaryllis** bulbs by Thanksgiving to start them growing for late-December holiday bloom. Do not keep their soil soaking wet.

If the soil is not yet frozen hard, use your houseplant water meter probe outdoors to check its moisture where you have planted bulbs if rain has been scarce. *Water* if necessary.

Use the water meter to check the soil moisture in the pots of bulbs stored for forcing. If they are out in a cold frame, they may have dried out.

If you have dug up and stored tender bulbs for the winter, make it a habit to *check* them periodically. Some need moist storage; while they must not be wet, they should be protected from drying out completely. Nesting them in damp sawdust, sphagnum moss, or shredded newspaper in ventilated bags usually does the job. Others, such as **Gladiolas, Tuberose,** and **Caladium,** need drier storage. Wrap them in paper or hang them in open netting. *Check* the instructions that accompany your bulb purchase for guidance.

Growing Smarter

Bulb-forcing vases are special glass vases with narrow necks and flaring tops. Available in many colors, they are designed to support a bare bulb so that its base where the roots emerge is just at water level. As they develop, the roots are visible through the glass. Bulb glasses are available in various sizes to accommodate bulbs as small as **Crocus** and as large as **Amaryllis.** The most common ones are for **Dutch Hyacinth**–just a single bulb will fill a room with fragrance.

Problem Solving

Once serious frost arrives, most potential problems with bulbs are past. Delaying mulching of bulb beds until the soil is hard forces rodents to nest elsewhere (they may choose evergreen ground cover plantings). When the ground is frozen, though, they will not be able to go after bulbs planted beneath **Pachysandra, English Ivy,** or **Spreading Juniper.**

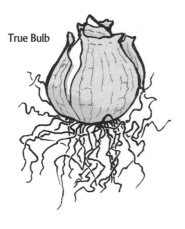

True Bulb

See page 48 for descriptions of each illustration shown here.

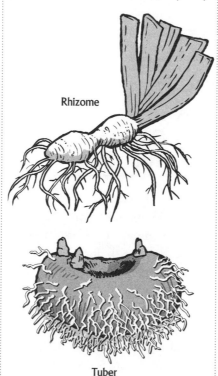

Rhizome

Tuber

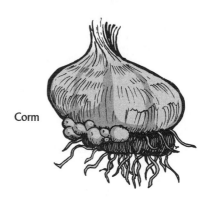

Corm

Planning

It seems as if **Amaryllis,** *especially red or red-and-white ones, have become an established winter holiday flower.* If you did not plant these large bulbs in pots and start watering them last month, they will not bloom in time for Christmas and New Year's. Fortunately, your local florist or garden-center people did plant and water last month, so **Amaryllis** timed to bloom in late December are available in stores for gifts and decorations at home. Purchase pre-potted ones that are just starting to send up their incredible tall stems so the entire process will be on display. Bulbs bought and potted up now can be started for display in February.

Do not be surprised to see that limp, green, grasslike foliage has appeared in the garden. This is the foliage of **Grape Hyacinths,** which often precedes the flowers by several months. It will survive through snow and ice just fine. **Sternbergia's** foliage emerges with its flowers in October and will remain all winter, even though the flowers die. It will eventually die back in spring.

Catalogs begin to arrive this month. Some mail-order companies specialize in bulbs, and others include bulbs in their line of annual and perennial plants and seeds. Put the catalogs aside in a pile to study and enjoy after the first of the year. Thinking about ordering some tender, summer-blooming bulbs will help the winter days pass faster.

Holiday Gift Shopping List: a book on growing bulbs, a bulb planter, **Paper-white Narcissus,** garden center gift certificate for tender bulbs this spring

Planting

If the ground is not frozen, you can *still* plant bulbs outdoors.

If you received an **Amaryllis** bulb planting kit as a gift, plant it and water it now for bloom in February. Maybe it will be blooming by Valentine's Day.

Care for Your Bulbs

Although December is not yet bitterly cold in most parts of the state, assume the worst and check pots of bulbs that you intend to force indoors in February. The planting medium of those stored outdoors in a cold frame or under straw or a tarp for their chill period may be dried out. Make sure their temperature is correct. Do not let the area where forced bulbs are stored to drop below 35 or 40 degrees F. If they freeze, they will turn to mush.

Watering

Moisten the sawdust, shredded paper, or sphagnum moss that tender bulbs are stored in for the winter season with a spritz of mist if they seem to be drying out. *Check* the bulbs again soon to be sure that this packaging stays damp without making the bulbs wet.

Bulbs that have been potted up for forcing need some moisture even in cold storage. *Check* the soil to be sure it hasn't dried out (one clue: the pots are lighter than normal when the soil is dried out). Do not overdo the watering, because too much moisture causes rot. It is important that the bulb pots have drainage holes.

Problem Solving

Mold is a threat to stored bulbs in overwet potting medium. *Remove* plastic covers from pots planted for forcing if condensation is collecting on their surfaces, and allow them to get better air circulation.

Herbs & Vegetables

There are lots of reasons people still grow some of their own food in this day and age of grand supermarkets and farm stands. It certainly isn't to save time and money. Purchasing all the necessary food gardening equipment, seeds, fertilizer, and pest-control products costs a lot more money than you would pay for a season's worth of vegetables at a local farm stand; and creating, planting, tending, and harvesting a garden takes a lot more time than any season's worth of food shopping.

Why Grow Food?

Why, then? Mostly because home-grown food tastes best. The very freshest vegetables and herbs have peak flavor. Fully ripened on the plant and freshly picked, backyard tomatoes have real flavor and more juice. Peppers are crisp with deeper flavor. Fresh basil or parsley picked minutes before it is used provides a whole new taste sensation.

And vegetables grown in the back-yard and picked just before they are eaten have much more nutritional value than fresh vegetables from the supermarket. Store-bought produce typically is picked before peak ripeness because it must spend many hours in transit. Then it sits on the store shelf for many more hours; then it sits in a home refrigerator. How can it possibly provide the nutrition of homegrown peas, corn, carrots, lettuce, and other crops?

Then there is convenience—vegetables and herbs growing in the yard means that fresh produce is just a few steps away. Add to that the assurance that there are no unknown pesticide residues in homegrown crops. Better taste, better nutrition, ready access, and control over pesticides make a compelling case for going to the trouble and expense of growing at least some food.

There are also the intangible delights of food gardening. There is always a heightened sense of well-being gained by physical exertion outdoors, of working to understand and harness the natural processes that are part of any kind of gardening. Somehow food gardening intensifies these feelings. Maybe it is because working the soil to produce food puts us in touch with the fundamental experiences of our ancestors in a time when these skills meant survival.

Ways to Grow Food

Food gardening is not an all-or-nothing thing. It no longer necessary to garden on the huge scale required to grow enough food to feed the family year-round. Besides, most of us have left behind the rural life and large properties. All the benefits of food gardening can still be enjoyed when done on a more modest scale.

- **Grow just for fun.** Grow plants in individual containers, or combine several—a **Tomato** plant, some **Basil,** and a **Pepper** plant—in a large container. When set conveniently on a sunny patio, roof, or balcony, they provide an opportunity to learn about how to grow the particular plants and to enjoy the rewards with little effort.

- **Set up a basic bed,** a small bed dedicated to a few summer vegetable and/or herb plants. Take the trouble to dig deeply and improve the soil. You may want to box it in with boards for a neater appearance. Planting just a few plants—two **Tomato** plants, two **Squash,** two **Peppers,** or whatever you like—yields substantial food, yet keeps the maintenance and harvesting chores to a minimum.

- **Set up a vertical bed.** Add a trellis to one side of the basic vegetable bed to take advantage of the airspace above it.

Herbs & Vegetables

Encourage **Tomato, Bean,** and **Cucumber** plants to climb. Then there will more space in the same basic bed to try **Eggplants, Carrots, Beets,** and others.

- **Extend the season** by adding some cool-weather crops to your repertoire. Start the growing season earlier with **Lettuce, Peas, Cabbage,** and **Broccoli.** Maybe even plant another round in late summer to grow in the cool fall weather. With the help of some protective plastic mulch and coverings, you can double productivity from the same basic bed.

- **Extend the garden.** If you find vegetable gardening satisfying, add another bed or two as space permits, or grow in both beds and containers. There is always a way to grow more herbs and vegetables.

Edibles Plus Ornamentals

The very latest trend is to incorporate food crops into the home landscape as part of the ornamental plantings. Take advantage of the wonderful colors and textures of modern varieties of food plants—purple basil; red rhubarb; red, yellow, and orange peppers; yellow and orange tomatoes; red cabbages; scarlet-flowered beans; pink eggplants; golden raspberries; and speckled watermelons. Celebrate the shapes—of pear tomatoes, skinny eggplants, softball zucchini, marble-sized tomatoes, and yard-long green beans.

It is possible to grow almost any food plant among shrubs or mixed in with flowers in a flower bed. Plants most commonly planted this way are **Tomatoes, Peppers, Lettuce, Parsley**, and **Basil.** They are annuals, just like **Petunias** and **Zinnias,** and are just as easy to grow. Pick up a few seedlings at the garden center when you shop for other plants and yard-care supplies.

The key to growing food crops among other landscape plants around the property is to provide enough light and space for them to grow to full size without disturbing the appearance of the landscape in general. Like traditional ornamental plants, each vegetable or herb variety has characteristic growing habits and soil needs. Tall, vining **Tomatoes** can form a green foliage backdrop. **Beans** can climb a trellis to screen a view. Take advantage of dwarf versions of **Peppers, Basil,** and others for small spaces. Use **Lettuce** varieties for edging. Plant a hedge of **Rosemary** or **Blueberry** shrubs. Do not forget to provide access to those plants for harvesting.

Combining veggies and herbs with traditional ornamental plants makes more efficient use of available space and light and increases the number of different crops you can grow. It maximizes production by extending the space for food crops.

Combining edible and ornamental plants also improves the health of the individual plants and the overall environment. As the diversity of plantings in all parts of the yard increases, so does the diversity of beneficial insects, the first line of defense against pest insect problems. In smaller yards, your food crops can be rotated more effectively when you blend lots of plant species in various ways. This blending practice confuses pest insects that prey on plants as well as disease pathogens that may lurk in the soil.

Take it in stages. Move gradually toward blending edibles and ornamentals:

1 First, add some flowers to the vegetable garden to test the concept.

2 Second, add flowering culinary herbs to flower beds and borders. They are at home anywhere.

3 Third, add a few vegetable plants to a flower bed or border and see how it looks.

4 Fourth, create a new garden using both food and ornamental plants. If that works, do it some more.

Culinary Herbs for Pennsylvania

Plant Name Spacing in Rows/ between Rows (inches)	Plant in Garden (in zone 6+)	Comment
Basil 12/18	May 15 to June 10	Sun. Available in purple, curly, dwarf versions. Plant some for pesto, tomatoes, spaghetti sauces.
Chives 6/20	March 15 to April 15	Sun. Onion substitute. Nice flowers, but flowers change the flavor. Can be brought inside in fall.
Cilantro-Coriander 6/20	March 15 to April 15	Same plant produces foliage (called **Cilantro**) and seeds (called **Coriander**). Used for 3,000 years in Chinese stir-fry. Staple of Mexican dishes.
Dill 12/24	March 15 to April 15	Needs sun and rich soil. Plant in succession for a supply all season.
Fennel 12/24	March 15 to April 15	Sun, well-limed soil. Grow away from other herbs. Use green version; bronze type is more ornamental than food crop.
Horseradish 24/24	March to April	Buy divisions the first time. You will cry when you grind this.
Mint 12/12	March 15 to April 15	Sun. Easier to buy plants; many kinds available. Grow in containers to prevent invasive spreading.
Oregano 12/12	March 15 to April 15	Sun. Easier to buy plants. There are several kinds.
Parsley 6/12	April 1 to May 1	Italian has strongest flavor. Curly and Italian types both like sun. Highly nutritious. Use fresh or dried. Try **'Forest Green'** and **'Banquet'**.
Rosemary 18/18	April 15 to May 15	Sun. Woody shrub. Buy started plants. Protect or bring inside for winter.
Sage 18/18	April 1 to May 15	Ornamental foliage in gray-green or multicolor. Sun or part sun. Favorite for pork, sausage, poultry, and cheese.
Salad Burnet 12/12	March to April	Full sun. Salad herb. Use in herb cheese, butters, and dips.
Savory, Summer 6/12	April 20 to May 15	Sun. Start in peat pots. Food seasoning with a peppery taste. Use on beans.
Savory, Winter 24/24	April 15 to May 15	Sun. Start indoors in peat pots. Food seasoning with a peppery taste. Use on beans.
Sorrel, French 12/12	April 1 to May 15	Sun. Sour taste. Cole slaw, mixed salads.
Sweet Cicely 12/18	March 15 to April 15	Shade or partial shade. Anise flavor, root divisions.
Sweet Marjoram 6/12	May 1 to May 31	Sun. Meats, salads, eggs, soups, sauces, vinegars, vegetables.
Tarragon 12/18	March 15 to April 15	Buy started plants. Sun to part sun. Licorice flavor.
Thyme 12/12	March 15 to April 15	Sun to part sun. Over 400 varieties; great ground cover.

+The Philadelphia area can plant everything one to two weeks earlier. Delay planting in the mountain areas across northern Pennsylvania about two weeks.

Vegetable Varieties for Pennsylvania

Plant	Variety/ Maturity in Days	Sow Seeds Indoors	Plant Seeds/ Plants Outdoors	Spacing in Rows/ between Rows (inches)	Comments
Asparagus	Jersey Centennial/ 360 to 720		March 15 to 30 (roots)	12 to 18/ 36 to 48	Buy disease-free plants. Male plants yield smaller stalks but have more of them.
	Jersey Giant/ 360 to 720		March 13 to 30 (roots)	12 to 18/ 36 to 48	
	Viking/ 360 to 720		March 13 to 30 (roots)	12 to 18/ 36 to 48	
Beans, Lima	Eastland/ 68		May 25 to June 15	3/24	
	Fordhook/242 Large Seeded/72		May 25 to June 15	3/24	Tender, sweet. Harvest just slightly undersized.
Beans, Pole	Kentucky Blue/63		May 15 to June 15	36/30	Trellis needed to support vines.
	Kentucky Wonder/65		May 25 to June 15	36/30	
Beans, Snap	Bush Blue Lake/56		May 15 to July 15	3/24	
	Bush Kentucky Wonder/55		May 15 to July 15	3/24	
	Derby/57		May 15 to July 15	3/24	
	Gator Green/55		May 15 to July 15	3/24	
	Gold Rush/50		May 15 to July 15	3/24	Milder flavor than green beans.
	Provider/50		May 15 to July 15	3/24	Multiple plantings over many weeks yield continuous harvest.
	Roma II/59		May 15 to July 15	3/24	Flat, Italian type.
	Royal Bungundy/58		May 15 to July 15	3/24	Pods turn green when cooked.
	Slenderette/53		May 15 to July 15	3/24	
	Tendercrop/53		May 15 to July 15	3/24	
Beans, Snap Yellow	Goldcrop/54		May 15 to July 15	3/23/24	Yellow beans also called wax beans

[+]The Philadelphia area can plant everything one to two weeks earlier. Delay planting in the mountain areas across northern Pennsylvania about two weeks.
[++]SE=sugar enhanced

Vegetable Varieties for Pennsylvania

Plant	Variety/ Maturity in Days	Sow Seeds Indoors	Plant Seeds/ Plants Outdoors	Spacing in Rows/ between Rows (inches)	Comments
Beans, Snap Yellow	Majestic/58		May 15 to July 15	3/24	
	Resist Cherokee/52		May 15 to July 15	3/24	
Beets	Burpee Golden/55		April 15 to July 10	1 to 3/ 12 to 18	Yellow, not red.
	Crosby Green Top/60		April 15 to July 10	1 to 3/ 12 to 18	A few **Beet** plants may go a long way with your family.
	Detroit Dark Red/63		April 15 to July 10	1 to 3/ 12 to 18	Old favorite.
	Red Ace/50		April 15 to July 10	1 to 3/ 12 to 18	
	Ruby Queen/55		April 15 to July 10	1 to 3/ 12 to 18	
Broccoli	Green Comet/55	March 1 to 31	April 10 to May 15 (plants)	24/30	Different varieties give different results depending on soil types—experiment!
	Green Valiant/66	March 1 to 31	April 10 to May 15 (plants)	24/30	
	Packman/48	March 1 to 31	April 10 to May 15 (plants)	24/30	
	Premium Crop/71	March 1 to 31	April 10 to May 15 (plants)	24/30	
	Southern Comet/55	March 1 to 31	April 10 to May 15 (plants)	24/30	
Brussels Sprouts	Jade Cross E/92	March 1 to 31	April 10 to May 15 (plants)	24/30	Harvest after the first frost.
	Prince Marvel/90	March 1 to 31	April 10 to May 15 (plants)	24/30	
Cabbage	Charmant/65	March 1 to 31	April 10 to May 15 (plants)	12/24	The shorter the maturity time, the smaller the head.
	Gourmet/70	March 1 to 31	April 10 to May 15 (plants)	12/24	
	Resist Golden Acre/64	March 1 to 31	April 10 to May 15 (plants)	12/24	
	Roundup/76	March 1 to 31	April 10 to May 15 (plants)	12/24	

[+]The Philadelphia area can plant everything one to two weeks earlier. Delay planting in the mountain areas across northern Pennsylvania about two weeks.
[++]SE=sugar enhanced

Vegetable Varieties for Pennsylvania

Plant	Variety/ Maturity in Days	Sow Seeds Indoors	Plant Seeds/ Plants Outdoors	Spacing in Rows/ between Rows (inches)	Comments
Cabbage	Stonehead/70	March 1 to 31	April 10 to May 15 (plants)	12/24	
Cabbage, Chinese	Blues Hybrid/57	April 1 to 15	July 1 to August 1 (seeds)	6/24	All love cool weather.
	Early Hybrid/60	April 1 to 15	July 1 to August 1 (seeds)	6/24	
	Jade Pagoda/68	April 1 to 15	July 1 to August 1 (seeds)	6/24	
	Joi Choi/45	April 1 to 15	May 15 to June 1 (plants)	6/24	Mild, slightly spicy flavor.
	Lei Choi/47	April 1 to 15	July 1 to August 1 (seeds)	6/24	
	Mei Qing Choy/45	April 1 to 15	May 15 to June 1 (plants)	6/24	
	Monument/80	April 1 to 15	July 1 to August 1 (seeds)	6/24	
	Prize Choi/50	April 1 to 15	July 1 to August 1 (seeds)	6/24	
Cabbage, Red	Perfect Ball/87	March 1 to 31	April 10 to May 15 (plants)	12/24	Pretty in salads. Good substitute for tomatoes.
	Ruby Red/75	March 1 to 31	April 10 to May 15 (plants)	12/24	
Cabbage, Savoy	Savoy Ace/78	March 1 to 31	April 10 to May 15 (plants)	12/24	Curly leaves. A nice change from traditional cabbage.
	Savoy King/82	March 1 to 31	April 10 to May 15 (plants)	12/24	
Carrots	Chantenay Types/70		April 15 to July 10	1 to 3/ 12 to 24	Homegrown tastes better.
	Danvers/72 to 75		April 15 to July 10	1 to 3/ 12 to 24	
	Nantes/68 to 70		April 15 to July 10	1 to 3/ 12 to 24	
	Napoli/58		April 15 to July 10	1 to 3/ 12 to 24	
	Pioneer/67		April 15 to July 10	1 to 3/ 12 to 24	
Cauliflower	Snow Crown/50	March 1 to 31	April 10 to May 15 (plants)	24/24	Cover heads with leaves to keep white.

+The Philadelphia area can plant everything one to two weeks earlier. Delay planting in the mountain areas across northern Pennsylvania about two weeks.
++SE=sugar enhanced

Vegetable Varieties for Pennsylvania

Plant	Variety/ Maturity in Days	Sow Seeds Indoors	Plant Seeds/ Plants Outdoors	Spacing in Rows/ between Rows (inches)	Comments
Cauliflower	Snowball/70	March 1 to 31	April 10 to May 15 (plants)	24/24	
	Violet Queen/65	March 1 to 31	April 10 to May 15 (plants)	24/24	
Celery	Florida 683/100	March 1 to 31	May 1 to June 1 (plants)	6 to 8/ 24 to 30	
	Golden Self-Blanching/115	March 1 to 31	May 1 to June 1 (plants)	6 to 8/ 24 to 30	
Collards	Blue Max/68		April 15 to May 1	12/24	Delicious if you like greens.
Corn, Bicolor	Bi Queen/92		April 20 to May 15	10/36	Bicolor corn has come a long way for better flavor.
	Harmony/73		April 20 to May 15	10/36	
	Seneca Dawn/69		April 20 to May 15	10/36	
	Sweet Sal/86		April 20 to May 15	10/36	
	Sweet Sue/88		April 20 to May 15	10/36	
	Tri-Sweet SE++/68		April 20 to May 15	10/36	
Corn, Pop	White Cloud/97		April 20 to May 15	10/36	Fun and easy.
	Yellow Hybrid/100		April 20 to May 15	10/36	
Corn, White	Alpine/79		April 20 to May 15	10/36	Some people prefer white to yellow.
	Quicksilver/75		April 20 to May 15	10/36	
	Seneca Starshine SE++/71		April 20 to May 15	10/36	
	Silver Queen/92		April 20 to May 15	10/36	Old favorite.
	Silverado/79		April 20 to May 15	10/36	Early. Good one.
Corn, Yellow	Bellringer/77		April 20 to May 15	10/36	Plant every two or three weeks for continuous harvest.

[+]The Philadelphia area can plant everything one to two weeks earlier. Delay planting in the mountain areas across northern Pennsylvania about two weeks.
[++]SE=sugar enhanced

Vegetable Varieties for Pennsylvania

Plant	Variety/ Maturity in Days	Sow Seeds Indoors	Plant Seeds/ Plants Outdoors	Spacing in Rows/ between Rows (inches)	Comments
Corn, Yellow	Bodacious/75		April 20 to May 15	10/36	
	Breeder's Choice/65		April 20 to May 15	10/36	
	Incredible SE++/84		April 20 to May 15	10/36	SE, sugar enhanced, means sweeter flavor.
	Miracle/81		April 20 to May 15	10/36	
	Seneca Horizon/64		April 20 to May 15	10/36	
	Sugar Buns SE++/73		April 20 to May 15	10/36	
	Sundance/69		April 20 to May 15	10/36	
	Tuxedo SE++/75		April 20 to May 15	10/36	
Cucumbers, Pickling	Calypso/52	March 20 to April 20	May 15 to June 15	48/36 (hills)	
	Picklebush/52	March 20 to April 20	May 15 to June 15	48/36 (hills)	These are good to eat raw, too.
	SMR 58/63	March 20 to April 20	May 15 to June 15	48/36 (hills)	
	Triple Mech/55	March 20 to April 20	May 15 to June 15	48/36 (hills)	
Cucumbers, Slicing	Burpless Hybrid/62	March 20 to April 20	May 15 to June 15	48/36 (hills)	For those who burp other varieties.
	Bush Champion/55	March 20 to April 20	May 15 to June 15	48/36 (hills)	
	Comet 86/60	March 20 to April 20	May 15 to June 15	48/36 (hills)	
	Dasher II/60	March 20 to April 20	May 15 to June 15	48/36 (hills)	
	Fanfare/63	March 20 to April 20	May 15 to June 15	48/36 (hills)	
	Marketmore 76/65	March 20 to April 20	May 15 to June 15	48/36 (hills)	A favorite.
	Palace King Hybrid/62	March 20 to April 20	May 15 to June 15	48/36 (hills)	

[+]The Philadelphia area can plant everything one to two weeks earlier. Delay planting in the mountain areas across northern Pennsylvania about two weeks.
[++]SE=sugar enhanced

Vegetable Varieties for Pennsylvania

Plant	Variety/ Maturity in Days	Sow Seeds Indoors	Plant Seeds/ Plants Outdoors	Spacing in Rows/ between Rows (inches)	Comments
Cucumbers, Slicing	Raider/52	March 20 to April 20	May 15 to June 15	48/36 (hills)	Bush varieties take less space.
	Salad Bush/57	March 20 to April 20	May 15 to June 15	48/36 (hills)	
	Sweet Slice/63	March 20 to April 20	May 15 to June 15	48/36 (hills)	
	Sweet Success/55	March 20 to April 20	May 15 to June 15	48/36 (hills)	
Eggplant	Classic/75	March 15 to 31	May 15 to June 15	24/24	Must be picked when skin is shiny.
	Dusky/68	March 15 to 31	May 15 to June 15	24/24	Very popular.
	Epic/64	March 15 to 31	May 15 to June 15	24/24	
	Ghostbuster/ 80	March 15 to 31	May 15 to June 15	24/24	White.
Endive	Salad King/97		April 1 and August 15	6/18	
Escarole	Florida Deep Heart/85		April 1 and August 15	6/18	Popular nationwide.
Garlic	Elephant/127		Plant in late September	3/12	Big fellow—mild.
	Extra Select Sets/100		Plant in late September	3/12	
	Italian/127		Plant in late September	3/12	
Kohlrabi	Purple Danube/51		April 1	4/24	Needs moisture.
Leeks	Broad London/130	April 15	May 15	6/18	
	Carina/150	April 15	May 15	6/18	
	Poncho/80	April 15	May 15	6/18	Mild, good in cream of leek soup.
Lettuce, Butterhead	Buttercrunch/ 64	March 1	April 1 and August 1	3/18	Butterhead is easier to grow than **Romaine** or **Head Lettuce.**
	Nancy/58	March 1	April 1 and August 1	3/18	
	Pirat/55	March 1	April 1 and August 1	3/18	

[+]The Philadelphia area can plant everything one to two weeks earlier. Delay planting in the mountain areas across northern Pennsylvania about two weeks.
[++]SE=sugar enhanced

Vegetable Varieties for Pennsylvania

Plant	Variety/ Maturity in Days	Sow Seeds Indoors	Plant Seeds/ Plants Outdoors	Spacing in Rows/ between Rows (inches)	Comments
Lettuce, Butterhead	Salad Bibb MTO/60	March 1	April 1 and August 1	3/18	
	Summer Bibb/65	March 1	April 1 and August 1	3/18	
	Waldmann's Dark Green/50	March 1	April 1 and August 1	3/18	
Lettuce, Head	Ithaca/75	March 1	April 1 to May 15	6/18	The best.
Lettuce, Leaf	Green Ice/45	March 1	April 1 and August 1	3/18	Pick outer leaves and plant keeps on growing.
	Cocarde/46	March 1	April 1 and August 1	3/18	
	Red Sails/45	March 1	April 1 and August 1	3/18	
	Red Salad Bowl/48	March 1	April 1 and August 1	3/18	Pretty in salads.
	Royal Oak Leaf/50	March 1	April 1 and August 1	3/18	Old favorite.
	Salad Bowl/45	March 1	April 1 and August 1	3/18	Matures earlier than other types.
Lettuce, Romaine	Green Towers/72	March 1	April 1 and August 1	3/18	
	Paris Island Cos/68	March 1	April 1 and August 1	3/18	Very popular and nutritious.
	Romance/50	March 1	April 1 and August 1	3/18	
	Rosalita/65	March 1	April 1 and August 1	3/18	
	Rouge D'Hiver/60	March 1	April 1 and August 1	3/18	
Onion Sets	Early Yellow Globe/96	February 1	April 1 to 30	2 to 3/8	Buy small sets and get more per pound—big and little sets grow same.
	Ebenezer/70	February 1	April 1 to 30	2 to 3/8	
	Southport Red Globe/110	February 1	April 1 to 30	2 to 3/8	

+The Philadelphia area can plant everything one to two weeks earlier. Delay planting in the mountain areas across northern Pennsylvania about two weeks.
++SE=sugar enhanced

Vegetable Varieties for Pennsylvania

Plant	Variety/ Maturity in Days	Sow Seeds Indoors	Plant Seeds/ Plants Outdoors	Spacing in Rows/ between Rows (inches)	Comments
Onion Transplants	Gambler/107	February 1	April 1 to 30	3 to 4/8	Plant close and pick every other one for spring onions—long maturity time.
	Ringmaker/118	February 1	April 1 to 30	3 to 4/8	Good for deep-frying.
	Spartan Banner 80/115	February 1	April 1 to 30	3 to 4/8	
	Sweet Burmuda/115	February 1	April 1 to 30	3 to 4/8	
	Sweet Sandwich/110	February 1	April 1 to 30	3 to 4/8	
	Sweet Spanish Types/125	February 1	April 1 to 30	3 to 4/8	
Parsnips	All American/ 110		April 15 to 30	3 to 4/ 18 to 24	Little may go a long way.
Peas, Edible Pod	Dwarf Grey Sugar/57		When ground can be worked	1/2 to 21/2	Tall **Peas** need support, dwarfs do not. All are good choices.
	Dwarf White Sugar/50		When ground can be worked	1/2 to 21/2	
	Mammoth Melting/68		When ground can be worked	1/2 to 21/2	Larger pods and taller plants.
	Snappy/63		When ground can be worked	1/2 to 21/2	
	Sugar Ann/58		When ground can be worked	1/2 to 21/2	
	Sugar Snap/72		When ground can be worked	1/2 to 21/2	
	Super Sugar/60		When ground can be worked	1/2 to 21/2	
Peas, Garden	Frosty/64		April 1 to May 15	1/2 to 21/2	
	Green Arrow/70		April 1 to May 15	1/2 to 21/2	Old but good variety.
	Knight/62		April 1 to May 15	1/2 to 21/2	
	Lincoln/66		April 1 to May 15	1/2 to 21/2	Old but good variety.

[+]The Philadelphia area can plant everything one to two weeks earlier. Delay planting in the mountain areas across northern Pennsylvania about two weeks.
[++]SE=sugar enhanced

Vegetable Varieties for Pennsylvania

Plant	Variety/Maturity in Days	Sow Seeds Indoors	Plant Seeds/Plants Outdoors	Spacing in Rows/between Rows (inches)	Comments
Peas, Garden	Novella II/68		April 1 to May 15	$1/2$ to $2^1/2$	
	Olympia/62		April 1 to May 15	$1/2$ to $2^1/2$	
	Sparkle/60		April 1 to May 15	$1/2$ to $2^1/2$	Hull **Peas** are good, but **Sugar Peas** are easier to prepare.
	Wando/68		April 1 to May 15	$1/2$ to $2^1/2$	Old but good variety.
Peppers, Bell	Ariane/66	March 15 to 31	May 15 to June 1 is best	18/30	Try different varieties—not all work well in all soils.
	Bell Boy/72	March 15 to 31	May 15 to June 1 is best	18/30	
	Flavor Fry/67	March 15 to 31	May 15 to June 1 is best	18/30	
	Green Boy/76	March 15 to 31	May 15 to June 1 is best	18/30	
	Gypsy/64	March 15 to 31	May 15 to June 1 is best	18/30	Very good for frying and as salad peppers.
	Jupiter Types/70	March 15 to 31	May 15 to June 1 is best	18/30	Popular.
	Lady Bell/74	March 15 to 31	May 15 to June 1 is best	18/30	
	Staddons Select/72	March 15 to 31	May 15 to June 1 is best	18/30	Very good—thick walls.
	Summer Sweet 860/86	March 15 to 31	May 15 to June 1 is best	18/30	
	Superset/65	March 15 to 31	May 15 to June 1 is best	18/30	
Peppers, Hot	Hungarian Wax/70	March 15 to 31	May 15 to June 1 is best	18/30	Check carefully, some are hotter than others.
	Jalepeno/75	March 15 to 31	May 15 to June 1 is best	18/30	
	Large Red Cherry/80	March 15 to 31	May 15 to June 1 is best	18/30	
	Mexibelle/74	March 15 to 31	May 15 to June 1 is best	18/30	The only hot **Bell Pepper.**
	Super Cayenne/70	March 15 to 31	May 15 to June 1 is best	18/30	

[+]The Philadelphia area can plant everything one to two weeks earlier. Delay planting in the mountain areas across northern Pennsylvania about two weeks.

[++]SE=sugar enhanced

Vegetable Varieties for Pennsylvania

Plant	Variety/ Maturity in Days	Sow Seeds Indoors	Plant Seeds/ Plants Outdoors	Spacing in Rows/ between Rows (inches)	Comments
Peppers, Hot	Super Chili/75	March 15 to 31	May 15 to June 1 is best	18/30	
	Surefire/65	March 15 to 31	May 15 to June 1 is best	18/30	
Peppers, Sweet	Italian Sweet/62	March 15 to 31	May 15 to June 1 is best	18/30	Not a **Bell Pepper** like Gypsy—thinner. Good for salad, frying.
	Super Red Pimento/70	March 15 to 31	May 15 to June 1 is best	18/30	Very sweet.
Potato	Carible		Early April	9 to 12/36	
	Irish Cobbler		Early April	9 to 12/36	
	Katahdin		Early April	9 to 12/36	
	Kennebec		Early April	9 to 12/36	
	Superior		Early April	9 to 12/36	
	Yukon Gold		Early April	9 to 12/36	Yellow flesh; great flavor!
Potato, Red	Dark Red Norland		Early April	9 to 12/36	
	Red Pontiac		Early April	9 to 12/36	Good flavor.
	Viking		Early April	9 to 12/36	
Pumpkins	Atlantic Giant/120	April 20	June 1 to 15	72/72 (hills)	Need large area for **Pumpkins;** bush types take less space. The earlier the maturity the smaller the pumpkin. Very large.
	Ghost Rider/115	April 20	June 1 to 15	72/72 (hills)	
	Howden's/115	April 20		72/72 (hills)	
	Prize Winner/120	April 20	June 1 to 15	72/72 (hills)	
	Small Sugar/100	April 20	June 1 to 15	72/72 (hills)	
	Spirit/95	April 20	June 1 to 15	72/72 (hills)	
	Spookie/115	April 20	June 1 to 15	72/72 (hills)	
	Thomas Halloween/110	April 20	June 1 to 15	72/72 (hills)	
	Triple Treat/110	April 20	June 1 to 15	72/72 (hills)	

[+]The Philadelphia area can plant everything one to two weeks earlier. Delay planting in the mountain areas across northern Pennsylvania about two weeks.
[++]SE=sugar enhanced

Vegetable Varieties for Pennsylvania

Plant	Variety/ Maturity in Days	Sow Seeds Indoors	Plant Seeds/ Plants Outdoors	Spacing in Rows/ between Rows (inches)	Comments
Radishes	Champion/26		April 1 to 30 and August 10 to September 1	1/12	
	Cherry Belle/22		April 1 to 30 and August 10 to September 1	1/12	Round types.
	Sparkler/25		April 1 to 30 and August 10 to September 1	1/12	
	White Icicle/28		April 1 to 30 and August 10 to September 1	1/12	Longer root.
Spinach	Melody/42		April 1 to May 1 and August 15 to 31	3/18	All are great for salads.
	Olympia/46		April 1 to May 1 and August 15 to 31	3/18	
	Tyee/39		April 1 to May 1 and August 15 to 31	3/18	
	Winter Bloomsdale/45		April 1 to May 1 and August 15 to 31	3/18	Plant in October for early spring crop.
Squash, Scalloped	Peter Pan/50	April 15	May 15 to June 15	36/36	Nice mild flavor.
	Sunburst/60	April 15	May 15 to June 15	36/36	Yellow skin.
Squash, Winter	Buttercup/105	April 15	May 15 to June 15	60/48	All winter squash are good.
	Cream of the Crop/82	April 15	May 15 to June 15	60/48	
	Delicata/100	April 15	May 15 to June 15	60/48	
	Early Butternut/85	April 15	May 15 to June 15	60/48	
	Golden Delicious/110	April 15	May 15 to June 15	60/48	
	Hubbard Types/120	April 15	May 15 to June 15	60/48	

[+]The Philadelphia area can plant everything one to two weeks earlier. Delay planting in the mountain areas across northern Pennsylvania about two weeks.
[++]SE=sugar enhanced

Vegetable Varieties for Pennsylvania

Plant	Variety/ Maturity in Days	Sow Seeds Indoors	Plant Seeds/ Plants Outdoors	Spacing in Rows/ between Rows (inches)	Comments
Squash, Winter	Royal Acorn/80	April 15	May 15 to June 15	60/48	
	Table Ace/70	April 15	May 15 to June 15	60/48	
	Table King Bush Acorn/80	April 15	May 15 to June 15	60/48	
	Table Queen Acorn/85	April 15	May 15 to June 15	60/48	
	Tivoli/100	April 15	May 15 to June 15	60/48	
	Waltham Butternut/85	April 15	May 15 to June 15	60/48	
Squash Yellow	Gold Rush/46	April 15	May 15 to June 15	Same as **Zucchini**	Milder than zucchini.
	Golden Zucchini/48	April 15	May 15 to June 15	Same as **Zucchini**	
	Seneca Prolific/51	April 15	May 15 to June 15	Same as **Zucchini**	
	Seneca Zucchini/48	April 15	May 15 to June 15	Same as **Zucchini**	
	Sundance/50	April 15	May 15 to June 15	Same as **Zucchini**	
Squash, Zucchini	Cocozelle/55	April 15	May 15 to June 15	72 (vine)	Small.
	Gourmet Globe/50	April 15	May 15 to June 15	72 (vine)	Round.
	Milano/50	April 15	May 15 to June 15	36 (bush)	
	Zucchini Elite/48	April 15	May 15 to June 15	36 (bush)	Very popular.
Sweet Potatoes	Centennial/100		June 1 (slips)	12/30	Don't grow the slips (potential for disease).
	Georgia Jet/100		June 1 (slips)	12/30	
	Jewel/100		June 1 (slips)	12/30	
Swiss Chard	Fordhook/55		April 15 to July 15	1 to 2/12	Good for salads.
	Rhubarb Chard/63		April 15 to July 15	1 to 2/12	Pretty color.

[+]The Philadelphia area can plant everything one to two weeks earlier. Delay planting in the mountain areas across northern Pennsylvania about two weeks.
[++]SE=sugar enhanced

Vegetable Varieties for Pennsylvania

Plant	Variety/ Maturity in Days	Sow Seeds Indoors	Plant Seeds/ Plants Outdoors	Spacing in Rows/ between Rows (inches)	Comments
Tomatoes, Cherry	Golden Nugget/56	April 7 to 20	May 15 to June 1	18/48	
	Sweet/100	April 7 to 20	May 15 to June 1	18/48	Excellent; small.
	Sweet Chelsa/64	April 7 to 20	May 15 to June 1	18/48	
	Sweet Million/58	April 7 to 20	May 15 to June 1	18/48	Extra sweet; very small.
Tomatoes, Early	Cold Set/65	April 7 to 20	May 15 to June 1	18/48 (staked)	
	Early Girl/55	April 7 to 20	May 15 to June 1	18/48 (staked)	
	Pixie Hybrid II/52	April 7 to 20	May 15 to June 1	18/48 (staked)	
Tomatoes, Early to Mid	Better Boy VFN/72	April 7 to 20	May 15 to June 1	18/48 (staked)	
	Celebrity/70	April 7 to 20	May 15 to June 1	18/48 (staked)	
Tomatoes, Main Season	Big Beef/73	April 7 to 20	May 15 to June 1	18/48 (staked)	
	Delicious/77	April 7 to 20	May 15 to June 1	36/36 (no stakes)	
	Floramerica/75	April 7 to 20	May 15 to June 1	36/36 (no stakes)	
	Mountain Delight/68	April 7 to 20	May 15 to June 1	18/48 (staked)	
	Mountain Pride/77	April 7 to 20	May 15 to June 1	36/36 (no stakes)	
	Supersonic/79	April 7 to 20	May 15 to June 1	36/36 (no stakes)	
Tomatoes, Paste	Heinz 1439/75	April 7 to 20	May 15 to June 1	18/48	
	Roma VF/75	April 7 to 20	May 15 to June 1	18/48	
Tomatoes, Yellow	Lemon Boy/72	April 7 to 20	May 15 to June 1	18/48	
	Sunray/72	April 7 to 20	May 15 to June 1	18/48	

[+]The Philadelphia area can plant everything one to two weeks earlier. Delay planting in the mountain areas across northern Pennsylvania about two weeks.
[++]SE=sugar enhanced

Vegetable Varieties for Pennsylvania

Plant	Variety/ Maturity in Days	Sow Seeds Indoors	Plant Seeds/ Plants Outdoors	Spacing in Rows/ between Rows (inches)	Comments
Turnips, Tops Only	All Top Hybrid/28		April 1 to 30	2 to 4/12 to 18	
	Shogoin/30		July 25 to August 5	2 to 4/12 to 18	
Turnips, Roots	Just Right/60		July 25 to August 5	2 to 4/12 to 18	
	Purple Top White Globe/58		July 25 to August 5	2 to 4/12 to 18	
Watermelon	Bush Baby II Hybrid/80	March 10 to 31	May 10 to 31	36/36 (bush)	Requires a large space to raise **Watermelons**.
	Crimson Sweet/87	March 10 to 31	May 10 to 31	36/36 (bush)	
	Golden Crow Hybrid/75	March 10 to 31	May 10 to 31	72/120 (vines)	
	Yellow Baby/72	March 10 to 31	May 10 to 31	72/120 (vines)	

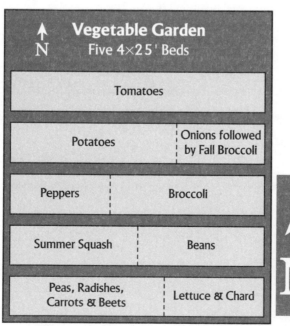

Vegetable Garden
Five 4×25' Beds

Tomatoes

Potatoes | Onions followed by Fall Broccoli

Peppers | Broccoli

Summer Squash | Beans

Peas, Radishes, Carrots & Beets | Lettuce & Chard

N

[+]The Philadelphia area can plant everything one to two weeks earlier. Delay planting in the mountain areas across northern Pennsylvania about two weeks.
[++]SE=sugar enhanced

Planning

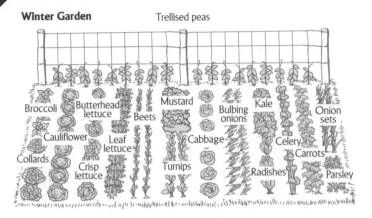

Winter Garden   Trellised peas

Broccoli — Butterhead lettuce — Beets — Mustard — Bulbing onions — Kale — Onion sets — Cauliflower — Leaf lettuce — Cabbage — Celery — Carrots — Collards — Crisp lettuce — Turnips — Radishes — Parsley

It's time to plan the vegetable garden. Whether it is a sketch on paper or a more formal scheme on a computer program, a plan assures space for all the varieties you want to grow. If you want to extend your garden season by starting cool-weather crops early in the spring and growing another planting of them in fall after the warm-weather crops have finished, you must make several garden plans.

If you already have a food garden, consult last year's plan to make sure you do not plant the same crop in the same place. *Rotation* of crops, even moving them a few feet, helps reduce pest insect and disease problems.

When starting a new food garden, design it first, then plan which crops will go where. Whether you will be planting in *traditional rows* or in *modern, boxed, raised beds:*

- Draw your garden to scale, orienting your rows or beds north and south to maximize the amount of sun they can receive, so that tall crops or those growing vertically on supports will not shade shorter ones.

- Incorporate vining plants into your garden design. **Cucumbers, Squash, Pole Beans,** and **Garden Peas** can all be supported by a fence on the periphery of the garden.

- Plan to *fence* the garden if there are numerous pest animals in the area. A relatively low fence will thwart rabbits, but groundhogs need a more substantial one (see November Problem Solving). A low-voltage electric fence will repel most pest animals.

- Allow at least 36 inches between rows in a traditional garden where a mechanized cultivator is used. For a modern boxed bed design, allow at least 24 inches for paths between the beds.

- New to food gardening? *Start small.* Preparing and planting a large area is an enormous amount of work. It takes a lot of knowledge to manage many different vegetable species.

- Think about where to locate herbs. Plant them among the vegetables, or put them in a bed of their own that is convenient to the kitchen.

Shopping List: fish emulsion or liquid seaweed fertilizer, mulch, fencing. Order seeds, and tools not found locally.

Planting

Grow mushrooms this month if there is a warm, dark space available in the house. Follow the directions on the label of a commercial planting kit.

It is not too early to begin browsing through mail-order plant and seed catalogs. New gardeners may have to purchase catalogs, but once you are on a mailing list they will arrive frequently, starting in December. Some suggestions:

- Don't place an order from the first seed catalog you receive. Other companies may have preferable varieties.

- Choose popular varieties for the main crop of each vegetable you grow, and experiment with one other that sounds interesting (see Planting Chart).

- *Check* records from previous years before ordering plants or seeds.

- Place your orders as early as possible. Some plants or seeds may be in limited supply.

Plant and Garden Care

The sun is moving higher in the sky each day, adding a minute or two of daylight and striking the cold frame more directly. Control heat buildup in the cold frame on sunny days if you are wintering over plants such as **Rosemary.** Ventilate gradually as the frost melts on the glass. Leave snow on the glass cover—it is good insulation. If there is no snow cover, *cover* the glass with a mat or old rug at night to buffer extreme nighttime temperatures.

If you plan an early-season garden in late February with cool-weather-loving crops such as **Broccoli** and **Lettuce,** buy black plastic mulch to warm the soil.

Rotate herb plants growing indoors on the windowsill so they can receive sun on all sides and grow uniformly. *Pinch back* leggy stems, and set plants about 2 inches below adjustable fluorescent lights.

Watering

If there has been no rain or snow for the past month or so, unmulched perennial herb and food plants overwintering in the herb garden may need watering. *Check* their soil.

Water herbs growing in pots indoors when the top inch or so of the soil is dry. Avoid overwatering.

Fertilizing

Be stingy when fertilizing herbs growing indoors. **Basil, Chives, Mint,** and others need nutrition to generate foliage, but too much nutrition causes rapid growth, which dilutes the flavor in the leaves.

Both seaweed (kelp)– and fish emulsion–based organic fertilizer products are excellent all-purpose fertilizers and "tonics" for indoor plants. They are loaded with stress-reducing trace minerals as well as the three major nutrients. Use as directed on the package label.

Grooming

- *Pinch off* any flowers that are on **Basil** and other herbs growing indoors. Flowering alters the flavor of the foliage.

- Keep pinching off herb foliage for use in the kitchen. Even if you do not intend to use it, pinch anyway to shape the plant and promote compactness and dense foliage.

Problem Solving

Aphids, mites, and whiteflies are the usual suspects on indoor plants. They target plants stressed by drafts, overheating, and dryness from indoor heating systems. *Spray* hot pepper wax or insecticidal soap on the pests on stems and both sides of the leaves. Spray the plant over a box or sink. Follow the directions on the product label, and repeat as needed.

Growing Smarter

If you are planting large quantities of any vegetable from seed, such as **Peas** or **Beans,** don't buy large numbers of small packs of seeds off the rack at the garden center. Bulk buying is often less expensive; order larger bags of seeds from a reputable mail-order seed company.

FEBRUARY

Planning

This is inventory month.

- *Check* your tools to see if any need to be repaired or replaced. Do you need some new tools, perhaps some that are ergonomically designed?

- *Check* supplies of pest- and disease-control products. Many organic products such as soaps and oils will keep on the shelf for several years. *Discard* containers of serious chemical products that have sat around for years, being sure to follow the instructions for disposal on the product label.

Think about why you grow herbs. Do you simply appreciate the plants as ornamentals and never use them in cooking? use them frequently in meals and for teas? value them as natural pest repellents in the garden? Your answers will influence how much space you devote to growing herbs rather than food crops. They will also influence your decisions on which ones to grow. Maybe it is time to get rid of the **Mint** that threatens to take over every year! Plant more **Basil** if you love pesto!

Shopping List: seeds, soilless potting mix; water-soluble (fast-acting) fertilizer, replacement tools, seed-starting equipment, fluorescent light units

Planting

It is still pretty bleak outdoors in most parts of Pennsylvania. Some diehard gardeners sprinkle **Spinach** seeds on the snow so that when it melts they will have a head start.

This is the month to start seeds indoors under lights for cool-weather crops, such as **Onions** and **Cabbage,** that go out into the garden as early as April. If you are new to gardening or have just a small garden, it is easier to buy young plants than to try to start them in the house.

Plant **Chives, Cilantro-Coriander, Dill, Fennel, Salad Burnet, Sage, Winter Savory, French Sorrel,** and **Thyme** seeds toward the end of the month. For best results, use commercial seed-starting equipment.

1 Fill seed-starter trays or individual peat pots with moist soilless seed-starting medium.

2 *Sow* seeds in rows in the trays, or individually in each pot or chamber, depending on the type of equipment. Cover them with a bit of the mix, and water lightly.

3 *Record* the name of the plant on labels (popsicle sticks work well) for each pot or larger container. Use a pen with moisture-resistant ink.

4 Gently cover the tray with plastic wrap or a plastic bag so the moisture is retained until sprouts emerge.

5 *Remove* the plastic wrapping and set fluorescent lights so they are 2 inches above the sprouts. Make the fixtures adjustable so they can be raised as the seedlings grow, to maintain the 2-inch distance.

6 *Water* seedlings from below with tepid water when the medium begins to dry out.

Many gardeners prefer to wait and buy commercially raised young plants rather than fuss with raising seedlings. Order them by mail for delivery at the correct time for planting, or wait until they are available at the local garden center.

Plant and Garden Care

- Keep an eye on seeds planted indoors so you can prevent them from drying out.

- When sprouts emerge, do not let them push against the plastic over them. *Remove* the plastic promptly.

- Gently *brush* your hand daily over the tops of growing seedlings, flexing their stems to help them grow strong.

Watering

When starting seeds indoors, make certain the medium is moist but not wet. As a general rule it is better to keep plants on the dry side, but do not let the seedlings wilt.

The easiest way to water established indoor herb and vegetable plants in pots is to take them to the sink and run tepid water on them. When all the water has drained from the bottom of their pots, return them to their location.

Fertilizing

Don't fertilize when sprouts first emerge from the growing medium. Wait until stem growth begins and a second set of leaves forms. Use the fertilizer at half the recommended strength for seedlings while the vegetable plants are indoors.

Grooming

Continue to *pinch* potted herbs growing indoors to shape them correctly, and to promote dense foliage growth.

Growing Smarter

Rows *vs.* Raised Beds: In the old days when most people lived in rural areas and had plenty of property, vegetable gardens followed the agricultural model–narrow rows of crops with wide paths in between to allow for mechanical tilling and harvesting. These days space is often at a premium in the crowded suburbs, so it makes more sense to have raised beds that are 3 or 4 feet wide with 2- or 3-foot permanent paths between them. While they take more effort to build, especially if you box them, they require less space and less care during the growing season. Once dug, they never need tilling, because they are never stepped on. Carefully nurtured soil within the beds supports intensive planting to produce more food per foot than is possible with traditional rows. Build one and try it.

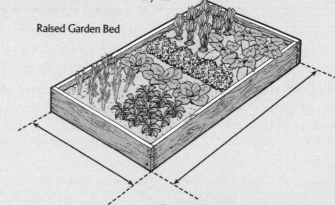

Raised Garden Bed

Typical Dimensions: 3ft. × 8ft.
Rows can be situated in any direction

Problem Solving

Damping off is a fungal disease that kills seedlings—their stems blacken and they flop over, dead. *Water* seedlings sparingly and from below, and use sterile commercial seed-starting medium.

Whiteflies may become a problem, particularly on indoor herb plants.

They fly off leaves like dandruff if you disturb them. Use yellow sticky traps, or *spray* foliage with hot pepper wax, insecticidal soap, or other products listed for whiteflies.

Soluble salts from fertilizer accumulate as deposits of white crust on the pot if plants are constantly watered from the top or if the water is reabsorbed by the growing medium. Repot in fresh medium.

Planning

Experienced food garden-ers have discovered that there can be as many as three growing seasons in the backyard. Certain crops prefer to germinate, grow, and produce in cooler temperatures, so planting them in the spring and then again toward fall adds two more seasons to the main warm-weather one.

After you gain some experience growing warm-weather vegetables during the main season, you may want to experiment with an early-spring cool-weather vegetable garden this year. Buy seedlings for **Broccoli, Cabbage,** and their relatives. Buy seeds for **Peas, Lettuce,** and **Spinach** to plant outdoors late this month.

The temperature of the soil is more critical to plant growth than the air temperature. To speed the warming of the soil for the early cool crops, spread black plastic over the bed to absorb heat from the sun. Cut holes in it, and plant through it so it can continue to warm the soil for the new young plants.

Shopping List: seeds and seedlings for cool-weather vegetables, **Onion** sets, herb seedlings, black plastic for mulch

Planting

As March progresses, it is tempting to go out and garden, but the soil is usually much too wet to cultivate. Attempts to dig it will leave sticky clods that will later harden into stubborn lumps difficult to work with.

If conditions are favorable outdoors, however, you may plant dormant **Asparagus** roots any time after March 15, and set out **Horseradish, Onions,** and **Rhubarb** plants after the 15th as well. To plant **Asparagus** crowns (roots):

1 Soak them in water for several hours before planting.

2 *Dig* a trench about a foot deep.

3 Set crowns in the trench at the spacing recommended.

4 *Cover* them with only a few inches of soil, maintaining the depth until stems appear.

5 Gradually fill in the trench with soil as stems grow taller until the soil is level with the surrounding ground.

Tradition dictates that St. Patrick's Day is the time to plant **Peas** in the garden. Actually, in most areas of Pennsylvania the soil is still too wet and cold for them to germinate. Wait until the end of the month.

Wait several weeks until the soil is in better condition to plant herbs such as **Chives, Cilantro-Coriander, Dill, Fennel, Horseradish, Mint, Oregano, Salad Burnet,** and **Thyme.**

Plant and Garden Care

Dig any **Parsnips, Carrots,** and other root crops that may have overwintered in the garden before the soil warms and they rot.

Begin to *harden-off* seedlings of cool-weather plants scheduled to go into the garden early next month:

- Set them outdoors for a few hours each pleasant day to begin to acclimate them to outside conditions such as wind and sun.

- Increase their exposure gradually over a week or two, bringing them in at night while temperatures are still low.

If you have a cold frame, it is an ideal place to keep seedlings until planting time.

Herbs growing in containers as houseplants will need acclimating to the outdoors, too. If they are not destined to go into the ground, they may need repotting into larger pots with fresh soilless medium. Try planting a large ornamental container with a selection of herbs for the sunny patio later in the season. Be sure the container has drainage holes, and set it on bricks or pieces of wood to facilitate drainage.

Watering

Make certain any overhead water source for indoor seedlings is a very gentle spray. A hard spray will knock them over, increasing the possibility of fungal disease and harm to the tender stems and leaves.

Water young transplants an hour before they go into the soil, just afterward, and again over the next several days to give the roots a good start. Plants lose a lot of moisture through their foliage because of the temporary stress of transplant shock.

Fertilizing

Either mix a granular slow-acting fertilizer into the garden soil when you dig it to prepare it for planting, or add the fertilizer to the soil when you plant each young transplant. If you choose to water in fast-acting (water-soluble) fertilizer every few weeks over the

Growing Smarter

Planting potatoes this year? Plant part of the crop on top of the ground. No digging required.

Simply lay the cut pieces or seed potatoes in a row on top of the soil. Cover them with 8 to 10 inches of organic mulch such as chopped leaves or straw. Make certain it covers the crop at all times through the growing season.

About two weeks after the plants have finished blossoming, lift the mulch on one plant to see how large the potatoes are. If they are too small, drop the mulch and look again in two weeks. Do not allow the potatoes to be exposed to sunlight because they will form green sections under the skin that are harmful if eaten.

When the potatoes are large enough, pull the plant, harvest the potatoes, and enjoy.

season instead, follow the directions on the product label.

If you have access to fresh animal manure to use in the garden, spread it over and dig it into the soil at least thirty days before planting. The earlier the better (fall is best), so that it will have time to age. Fresh manure will burn tender plants; dried or aged manure can be used immediately.

Problem Solving

Unexpected late frost may threaten newly planted seedlings. Throw an airy blanket of white, polyspun gar-

den fleece, called floating row cover, over them for protection during the night. Baskets or shade cloth will also work. *Remove* coverings during the day so the plants can receive sunlight.

Rabbits may eat young plants because there is little else for them to eat. The plants may disappear overnight or suddenly lose their tops. Protect them with garden fleece, low fencing, or netting.

Planning

Gardening season begins as cool-weather crops begin to thrive outdoors in the garden. To maximize production from your garden space, plan to have young warm-weather transplants ready to go into the empty spots when the cool crops are finished. Buy or raise young **Tomato, Pepper,** or **Eggplant** starts, which need hot weather to thrive.

Shopping List: birdbath, seeds, food dryer, Walls-o-Water™, young transplants

Planting

Finally outdoor planting time has arrived. The soil should be workable, and the temperatures are moderating. While the possibility of a frost still exists upstate, cool-weather crops can handle it.

Among the sure planting bets are **Asparagus, Horseradish, Parsnips, Rhubarb, Salsify,** and **Onions.** About mid-April, *plant* or *sow* seeds for **Beets, Cabbage, Lettuce, Mustard,** and **Parsley.** It is not too late to plant **Peas.** *Plant* young homegrown or store-bought cole crop plants such as **Broccoli** and **Cabbage** outside now, too.

Many herbs and veggies (colorful **Lettuces,** dwarf **Basil,** determinant **Tomatoes, Parsley**) grow attractively in windowboxes and hanging baskets. Always plant more seeds than needed because there is seldom 100 percent germination.

Lettuce, Peppers, Radishes, Onions, and most herbs need a container at least 6 inches in diameter and 8 inches deep. Groups of plants need larger, 5- to 15-gallon barrels or containers. Later in the season, **Tomatoes, Squash, Pole Beans,** and **Cucumber** will need containers at least 24 inches deep to handle their larger root mass.

Tomato plants started indoors may be outgrowing their small pots. *Transplant* them into larger, deep pots filled with soilless medium while they grow until May planting time. Bury their stems a bit so they will develop strong root systems.

Plant **Sunflower** seeds as soon as frost is past in your area. Later, plant **Pole Beans,** either **Snap** or **Limas,** so they can climb the sturdy **Sunflower** stems. Enjoy the benefits of raising **Beans,** as well as pretty flowers and birds in the garden.

Plant and Garden Care

Thin plants growing in rows to the spacing specified on the seed packet. *Snip off* or *pull* excess seedlings so the stronger ones will have room to grow.

To discourage weeds and help retain soil moisture, *mulch* plants that are more than 6 inches tall. Plant seedlings through a plastic mulch, which will warm the soil. While black plastic is commonly used, research shows that the new red plastic (SRM-Red Mulch) increases **Tomato, Pepper,** and **Strawberry** yields by 20 percent. The light wavelength reflected by the red color encourages plant stem and foliage growth, and they bear heavier and earlier crops. Punch holes in plastic mulch to allow moisture to get to the soil.

In a hurry to plant warm-weather crops such as **Tomatoes** outdoors way ahead of schedule? This month they will require serious protection. Set up clear plastic tunnels over planted boxed beds, or surround individual plants with Walls-o-Water™, a structure made of heavy plastic sheets sealed together to form chambers to be filled with water. The water-filled structure is then placed teepee-like upright around a seedling for insulation.

Watering

Always *moisten* transplant rootballs before planting them in the ground. *Water* them, and the seeds that you plant afterward, too, to settle them in the soil. Follow up with regular watering if rainfall is undependable. Roots of young plants are shallow and dry out quickly until they develop and penetrate more deeply into the soil. Eventually a layer of organic mulch will reduce watering needs.

Watering is critical for seeds and plants in containers. *Check* moisture levels daily. The soilless medium dries out very quickly, especially if the container is in full sun.
Use a watering can or soft sprayer from the hose.

Fertilizing

Mix a granular, all-purpose (not lawn) slow-acting fertilizer into the soil when you prepare your beds for planting. This will provide uniform, consistent nutrition for crops planted there for up to sixteen weeks, depending on the product.

Delay using fast-acting (water-soluble) fertilizer products until later in the season when heavy producers such as **Tomatoes** need an energy boost.

Remember that soilless media in containers has no nutrition because it has no soil. You must provide the complete diet for plants there. *Mix* a granular, slow-acting fertilizer into

the medium or purchase one that already has it mixed in.

If you prefer to use fast-acting fertilizer, *dilute* it in water, and water it into the container every few weeks as specified on the product label. Do not overdo, or it will burn plant tissues.

Grooming

If you did not cut back woody herbs such as **Sage, Rosemary,** and **Lavender** last fall when you brought them indoors for the winter, do so now. As soon as they can go outdoors they will begin to generate fresh foliage.

Pinch the tops of young **Basil** plants to encourage them to branch and become more compact. Continue pinching after they are planted outdoors next month.

Problem Solving

Cutworms are likely to be in your garden soil where they will chew through the stems of young plants at soil level. *Protect* stems with "collars" made from foam or cardboard coffee cups or similar materials with their bottoms removed. Gently lower the cup over the plant, top

Growing Smarter

Various **Tomato** varieties grow in one of two ways—determinant or indeterminant.

- **Determinant** types grow to a genetically pre-determined height and stop. They typically top out at about 4 or 5 feet and are ideal for use in containers on the patio.
- **Indeterminant Tomato** plants grow indefinitely, putting out numerous vining subsidiary stems that grow rampantly. They may extend 10 or 12 feet during a growing season. They need sturdy trellises and frequent pinching of suckers to discipline their spread.

down, twisting its rim into the soil around the stems of **Tomatoes, Peppers, Eggplants, Cabbage, Broccoli,** and others.

Birds may take an interest in the tender stems and pods of young **Garden Peas.** If the occasional finch, sparrow, or cardinal does too much damage, throw some garden fleece, netting, or shade cloth over the vines. The covering will admit light, air, and water but will thwart the birds. (Put out seed in a bird-feeder for the birds.)

Planning

Now that the weather is warmer and the soil has dried out, there is a lot to do out in the garden.

If you have raised beds established, remove any winter mulch remaining on those that do not already hold cool crops planted earlier this spring. Loosen the soil with a rake, add a little granular, slow-acting fertilizer, and you will be ready to plant.

If you have a traditional row garden, it is time to get out the power tiller or hoe and *cultivate* the entire area. Add organic matter and fertilizer, then lay out paths and rows.

Nesting pairs of various bird species have probably already settled in nearby to start their families. This is a plus for your garden, because the parents will seek insects to feed newborns who are unable to digest seeds for awhile. Your filled bird feeders will spare the adults from having to use up energy while seeking food sources for themselves

Shopping List: more seeds, warm-weather vegetable plants, trellis netting, garden twine, bird seed

Planting

Direct-seeding into the garden is the best planting approach for many crops. Some germinate fairly promptly and grow so rapidly that there is no real advantage to starting them ahead of time indoors, and others simply do not transplant successfully. To plant seeds:

1 *Dig* the area to loosen and aerate the soil. *Remove* stones and debris. Mix in some organic matter such as compost, peat moss, or mushroom soil, and add granular, slow-acting fertilizer. Smooth and level the soil.

2 Trace an indentation or shallow trench in the soil (or poke individual holes for a square-foot pattern), and dribble into it seed from between your thumb and forefinger. Follow seed-packet instructions for depth and spacing.

3 *Cover* the seed lightly with soil, and water lightly to settle it into the ground.

4 Place a label or seed packet nearby to identify what has been planted.

By mid-month it is safe to plant young herb plants such as **Dill, Sweet Marjoram,** and **Basil.** Cut the bottom from a 5-gallon container or use a chimney flue (or any container that won't rot), and sink it into the soil to restrict the roots of **Mint** and other invasive herbs. Allow its top rim to protrude from the soil several inches to prevent roots from climbing over the rim of the container. Fill it with soil and plant. An alternative is to plant **Mint** and others in aboveground containers.

Plant and Garden Care

Begin to *prepare* **Tomato** plants raised indoors to be moved outdoors. They can go into the garden or containers around Memorial Day weekend if danger of frost is past. Set the plants in open shade after the day has warmed, for increasingly longer periods of time each day, to acclimate them to the outdoor conditions. Bring them indoors at night at first, then allow them to stay outdoors if the weather promises to be mild. Don't set them out in heavy winds or heavy rain.

Many types of **Garden Peas** need support. Set up temporary fencing or a trellis of some sort to support those that are developing tall stems. *Mulch* plants over 6 inches tall to keep down weeds.

Watering

Water young plants from the garden center that are waiting to be planted outdoors. They dry out quickly when they grow large in relatively small pots, and even more quickly when they are outdoors.

Water newly planted plants regularly if there is no rain, until they show that they are established by generating new stems and foliage. A 2- or 3-inch layer of organic mulch on the bare soil around (but not touching) plant stems will retard water runoff and drying out.

Until plants grow to maturity there is still time (and space) to install drip irrigation in your garden. Porous hose or soaker hose systems made from recycled automobile tires "leak" moisture along their length. They deliver water directly to plant roots with minimal loss to evaporation. Because foliage stays dry, the chances of mildew diseases are reduced.

Fertilizing

If there is slow-acting fertilizer in the soil or container mix, there is no need to fertilize plants for many weeks. Later, supplement the slow-acting fertilizer with periodic sprays of fish emulsion or a kelp-based product directly on plant foliage for an energy boost, especially beneficial when the plant begins producing fruit.

Carefully dilute fast-acting (water-soluble) fertilizers to be watered in. Too much nitrogen promotes excessive vegetative growth. This attracts pest insects and diverts energy from flowering and fruit formation.

Grooming

Pinch herbs to keep them compact and bushy. This will also delay flowering for awhile so you can enjoy harvesting and using the foliage before it gets bitter.

Keep after branch suckers that form on **Tomato** plants. Pinch or snip them off to channel energy to developing strong central stems to support the plants all season.

Problem Solving

Aphids may cluster at the tips of tender new **Tomato** stems. **Ladybugs** will appear later this month to control them. *Pinch off* infested tips, and put them in a plastic bag for the trash; or wash the aphids off plants with a forceful spray of water from the hose. Use insecticidal soap, as directed, to handle stubborn, well-established infestations.

Slugs, essentially snails without shells, can be a problem on **Lettuce, Beans, Peppers,** and other crops. They lurk in damp mulch during the day and chew ragged holes in leaves after dark. Pick them off plants or trap them in shallow containers of beer or yeast dissolved in water, and throw them in the trash.

Cabbageworms chew holes in cole crops such as **Cabbage** and **Broccoli.** These are the larvae of small white butterflies that flit around the garden. When the little worms are feeding on the foliage, *spray* the foliage thoroughly with a product containing *Bacillus thuringiensis kurstaki*. The bacteria will sicken and kill them in a few days.

Ladybug

Nymph

Planning

Some gardeners grow food for the joy of it, and to have fresh vegetables for the table during the summer. They give the inevitable excess to neighbors or the local food kitchen to feed the hungry. Others also enjoy "putting food by," storing it various ways for use during the winter. For them, maximum production is a goal, and special gardening techniques increase harvests:

- *Plant* intensively to use every inch of soil.

- Use clear plastic tunnels to extend the growing season before and after the main season.

- Succession-plant by immediately replacing harvested plants with new seedlings for the next crop.

- Plant vertically to take advantage of airspace above the beds.

- Plant in containers to take advantage of the sun elsewhere on the property.

- Plant food crops among ornamentals to increase the growing area.

Shopping List: sprayer, seeds for fall crops, tomato cages, a book on pest insects

Planting

June brings good planting weather for warm-weather crops. Soil temperatures are high enough for hardened-off **Tomatoes, Peppers,** and **Eggplants,** and plants that have been displayed outdoors at the garden center are now adjusted to the outdoors. To plant commercially grown or homegrown young vegetable plants:

1 *Prepare* the soil with organic material and fertilizer (as described in May, Planting).

2 Late in the day or on an overcast day, dig holes in the prepared soil, spaced at the distance recommended on their labels. Make the holes the same depth and width as the young transplant's container. (Space plants more closely in raised beds).

3 Gently tip over the plant, and slide the pot off the rootball. Set the plant in the hole, making sure it is at the same depth in the ground that it was in its pot. *Exception:* Plant **Tomatoes** as deeply as possible without covering their foliage.

4 Press the soil firmly around plant stems, and *water* gently to settle the plants in the soil.

5 If it is unavoidably sunny at planting time, rig some garden fleece or shade cloth temporarily to reduce transplant stress.

Sow seeds directly into the garden for **Corn** and later crops of **Beans, Beets, Carrots, Kohlrabi** and **Turnips.** If the **Lettuce, Spinach, Radishes,** and other early crops planted in containers are finished, *pull* them, and plant a **Tomato** or **Pepper** plant there.

Purchase seeds of cool-weather plants for a fall garden now. When it is time to plant **Broccoli, Cabbage,** and **Brussels Sprouts,** plants may not be available at the garden center. Companies offering seedlings over the Web may have them.

Plant and Garden Care

Mulching plants saves weeding time, conserves water, and protects the soil from compaction by rain and harsh sun. It also prevents dirt from splashing up on plant foliage. *Cover* all bare soil over plant roots (but not stems) with a 2- or 3-inch layer of organic material. Cover existing black plastic mulch; make sure the plastic has plenty of holes to allow moisture through if you do not have drip irrigation lines under it. Mulch with your choice of:

- chopped leaves

- dried grass clippings (herbicide-free)

- pine needles

- straw (hay has weed seeds)

- shredded newspaper

- aged sawdust (from untreated wood)

Pull up bolted **Lettuce,** spent **Broccoli** stems, and other cool-weather crops that are finished to make way for new warm-weather plants.

Thin the root crops planted earlier in the season. Use the tops of beets and turnips, and tiny carrots in salads.

Start picking peas as soon as they appear. They are at their best when they are just barely mature.

Train **Tomato** plants onto a fence, stake, trellis, or cage to support them. Fruit held off the ground gets better air circulation and ripens more uniformly, so it is less bothered by pests and diseases.

Watering

Make certain all crops have sufficient water. **Peppers,** especially, need to be well watered. **Tomatoes** like a steady supply rather than a wet-dry cycle. Avoid hot water from a hose that was lying in the sun.

Avoid overhead watering, if possible, because moist foliage promotes fungal disease.

Water all container plants regularly.

Fertilizing

If you incorporated granular, slow-acting fertilizer into the soil at planting time, plants should be fine. *Spray* fish emulsion or a kelp product on their leaves for a snack. Let the liquid drip to the ground. Plants can absorb nutrients directly through their leaves and also through their roots.

Grooming

Continue to *pinch and clip* herb plants to delay flowering and encourage denser growth.

Removing suckers from **Tomato** plants while they are young directs energy and growth to the main stem. Next month, allow a few to develop into real stems with flowers and fruit. **Note:** Take care when removing suckers from determinant **Tomato** plants. They develop flowers and fruit on thin stems that grow at intersections of main stems which are easily mistaken for suckers.

Problem Solving

Whiteflies may flit around **Tomato** plants. They will not affect healthy plants.

Flea beetles are the bane of **Eggplants,** as they make tiny holes all over the leaves. *Spray* foliage with Neem oil or insecticidal soap. Repeat the spray after every overhead watering and when it rains.

Colorado potato beetles are oval yellow-and-black-striped beetles that can be seen on **Potato** foliage and lay soft yellow eggs underneath the foliage. *Pick them off* or *spray* neem oil on both sides of the leaves.

Parsleyworms eat **Parsley, Dill,** and **Celery** foliage. Because they are the larvae of the lovely swallowtail butterfly, you may want to ignore them or transfer them to a nearby **Queen Anne's Lace** plant to eat instead.

Weeds will begin to take over between rows of unmulched crops. They compete with crops for nutrients and moisture and harbor disease-bearing insects. Either *pull* or *hoe* them out of moist soil while they are young.

Planning

Decide whether you want to plant an empty garden spot with a second crop of a vegetable that will tolerate hot weather yet mature before first frost. You might want to leave the soil covered with mulch to prevent weeds, until mid-month when it is about time to plant young cool-weather plants for a fall garden. To time planting properly, *check* seed packets or plant labels to determine how many days to harvest.

Shopping List: seeds, Neem oil or Neem with soap, deer-repellent, insecticidal soap or pepper wax

Planting

Plant cool-weather **Broccoli, Cauliflower,** and late **Cabbage** seedlings by mid-July. *Sow* seeds for **Peas, Beets, Carrots, Chard, Endive, Kale, Kohlrabi,** and **Radishes** directly into the garden or in containers.

Some new varieties of **Lettuce** can handle heat and humidity better than traditional types. *Plant* a summer salad garden under a shade cloth "awning" to reduce the heat.

Plant and Garden Care

Stake **Eggplants** and **Peppers** as they surge in growth. These tropical plants love hot weather.

Mulch all bare garden soil to cool it a bit. The growth of **Tomatoes** and some other crops stalls in soil over 85 degrees F. Mulch also preserves soil moisture, discourages weeds, and keeps foliage clean.

Picking mature fruit promptly stimulates more growth and avoids disease and pest problems from overripe, rotting fruit. Early **Corn** matures about three weeks after tassels form. Early **Tomatoes** will be ready this month. *Dig up* Onions if their tops are dry and flopped over.

Keep pinching stems of herbs to delay flowering and loss of foliage flavor. Use them fresh at twice the amounts recommended for dried ones. Freeze or dry extra herbs.

Watering

Plants use copious amounts of water when it is hot. Sandy soil or soil that lacks adequate organic matter dries out especially quickly. *Water* when the soil under the mulch in garden beds is dry down an inch or two.

- *Avoid* watering in the heat of the day unless you need to cool the soil.

- *Water* in the early morning to give plants a strong start on the day.

- Keep moisture away from plant foliage to avoid sunburn and possible mildew problems.

- Use drip irrigation under the mulch for most economical water use.

- Use a timer with irrigation systems for low-maintenance watering.

Water containers set in the sun twice daily.

Fertilizing

To give plants that are blooming and setting fruit an energy boost, *spray* the foliage with dilute liquid fertilizer featuring fish emulsion or kelp.

Dig more compost or other organic matter into the soil before planting the next round of crops in the garden.

Grooming

Continue to *pinch* suckers from indeterminant **Tomato** vines until their main stems are tall enough to attach securely to their support; then pinch suckers according to how much topgrowth from subsidiary stems you want.

Thin root crops such as **Carrots** and **Beets** to the correct spacing as indicated on the seed packets.

Problem Solving

One or two of a host of potential pest insects may appear in your garden, depending on what crops you grow. Stressed plants will have problems first (see chart in Appendix, p. 336). If your plants are happy, they are less likely to be bothered.

Japanese beetles emerge early to mid-July. Immediately start knocking them off plants into a jar of soapy water to control plant damage, and do this several times a day over the next few weeks. *Spray* heavily infested crops such as **Green Beans** with Neem oil. Do not use bag traps near the garden—they are so effective they will attract beetles from great distances.

Mexican bean beetles may appear on **Green Beans** and the foliage of

other crops this month. *Check* the undersides of the leaves for fuzzy little yellow eggs. Mash them between your fingers, or pick them off the leaves before they turn into beetles.

Squash borers attack both **Squash** plants and **Cucumbers.** A moth lays her eggs at the base of plants, and hatched worms (borers) travel up through the stalk, eating as they go. They also carry a virus disease that infects host plants and causes their stems to rot. To repel the moth, place a piece of aluminum foil around the base of the plant on the ground, or cover young plants temporarily with garden fleece. Many gardeners accept the demise of their **Squash** plants at midseason, having had their fill of zucchini by then.

Squash bugs, Cucumber beetle, slugs, and **Asparagus beetles** are all bad guys. Watch for them, and catch them early before they multiply. *Handpick* the ones you can reach. Following label directions, *spray* major infestations with neem oil or an insecticide product that features pyrethrum.

Fungal diseases show up as gray coatings or soft, dark spots on foliage or fruit. *Pick and discard* affected fruit. A mature, healthy plant is rarely affected by mildew on its foliage.

Critters can sabotage a food garden in short order. Use fencing to deter

Growing Smarter

- Dry soil sometimes delays seed germination. Soak **Corn, Bean, Squash,** and other large seeds in water for several hours before planting. Drain them, then plant.
- Do not waste food. Use thinned beets and carrots in salads. Cook turnip and beet tops from harvested crops for nutritious "greens."
- Pick summer/hybrid squash varieties when they are only 4 to 6 inches long. Large squash slows down the production of more squash. Let them grow a bit larger for stuffing.
- Harvest the main head from each **Broccoli** plant before yellow flowers appear. Later, harvest a second, smaller crop from the subsidiary branches of the main stalk.
- Plant **Dill** seeds every two or three weeks until early August to ensure fresh dill all season.
- Do not mulch with dried grass clippings unless you are sure they are from lawns free of pesticides.

deer, rabbits, and woodchucks. Voles and other rodents are tougher to control—consequently, many gardeners are cat lovers.

Planning

The August pause—when just about everything has been planted and is at some stage of development, and the eating is great—offers an opportunity to reflect on the season so far. It is time to catch up on record-keeping in your garden notebook or journal.

- Check those seed packets and plant labels for plant names.
- Recall planting dates, varieties and yields.
- Note any problems and the solutions you tried.
- Remember dates of last frost, heat arrival, and other weather events.

In a short five months it will be time to plan the garden for next year.

Shopping List: bird seed, freezer storage bags and boxes, more slow-acting fertilizer

Planting

There is still time for a second planting of **Turnips, Spinach, Lettuce, Beets, Radishes, Chard,** and **Winter Onion**s in the garden or in containers. *Check* the maturity dates against your date for expected first frost. Gardeners upstate are short on time. *Plant* seeds a bit deeper and *sow* them more generously, because germination may be unreliable.

Start seeds for growing herbs indoors under lights this fall for holiday gifts. *Plant* in 4-inch pots filled with moist, sterile seed-starting medium and some granular slow-acting fertilizer. Then temporarily sink the pots into the garden. Keep them moist. When young plants are 3 inches high, *spray* some fish emulsion or kelp (seaweed) fertilizer on their foliage. Bring the pots inside before first frost.

In most parts of Pennsylvania, **Rosemary** will not overwinter safely in the garden. *Dig up* your plant and put it in a pot to use and enjoy indoors all winter.

Plant and Garden Care

If it has decomposed in the heat, *renew* the layer of organic mulch under plants such as **Tomatoes, Cucumbers, Bush Beans,** and **Melons.** Mulch blocks the fruit from contact with the ground.

When the stalks and foliage of the **Potato** plants flop over, it is time to harvest potatoes. *Dig them up*, or lift the mulch from the above-ground pile, taking care not to damage them with the fork or shovel in the process. Allow the potatoes to dry, and brush the dirt from them. To avoid rot, do not wash them until you use them.

Dig garlic as soon as the leaves start to turn yellow; their delicate paper covering will rot if they are not dug promptly. Dry them carefully, braid the tops together, and store them hanging in a cool, dry location.

Watering

Watering is critical this month, as plants have just so much energy to expend. If they must spend some of it recovering from wilting, then some other part of the plant will suffer, and this time of year it will probably be the quality and size of the fruit. Give each plant at least 1 inch of water weekly. Regular watering will prevent much cracking on **Tomatoes** and blossom-end rot on **Tomatoes** and **Squash.**

Keep newly planted seeds and seedlings moist. While you may have to water both morning and evening in hot, dry weather, you will not have to water for long periods, as the seeds are close to the soil surface.

Containers dry out in no time, especially the clay (terracotta) ones, because air and moisture can pass through their sides. The hot August sun speeds up this process, and heat from nearby masonry patios, building walls, and paved walkways is much stronger than that generated out in the garden. Water, water, water.

Fertilizing

A monthly liquid fertilizer snack helps all productive plants. Younger plants will do fine on the granular, slow-acting fertilizer you added to the soil at planting time. Remember each crop takes nutrients from the soil, so *replace* the nutrients when planting a succession crop.

If you are growing a second round of **Corn,** give young plants some extra fertilizer. **Corn** is a heavy user of nitrogen.

Grooming

As each crop is completely harvested, take time to *pull up* plants. Chop or cut them up into manageable pieces with pruners or a spade, and put them in the compost bin. *Cover* the bare soil with mulch for protection until the next planting.

Problem Solving

Spider mites curl leaves or make them look sickly or dirty. *Pinch off* infested leaves. *Spray* foliage of heavily affected plants with a forceful water spray to wash off mites every couple of days for a week or two.

Viral diseases attack certain varieties of **Tomatoes** and other vegetables. If plant foliage begins to turn brown and die from the bottom up, promptly *pull up* the plants, and discard them in the trash. Choose disease-resistant varieties next year.

Powdery mildew sometimes develops on plant foliage. *Ignore* it on mature or nearly finished plants. *Spray* all new and emerging foliage on a newly producing plant with a sulfur-based garden fungicide product according to label instructions. It will protect it from further infection.

Bacterial wilt spread by a beetle may infect **Cucumbers,** which will dry up and die just as they start to produce fruit. Watch for and control the beetles early in the season. *Pull up* infected plants, and discard in the trash.

Growing Smarter

To minimize waste from overproduction next year:

- Plant only foods that your family likes to eat.
- Limit the number of different crops to about five until you have learned how to grow and manage them well. Then add two or three new kinds of vegetables and herbs each year.
- Make several successive small plantings of **Beans, Dill, Lettuce,** and others so that you have some to eat all summer rather than having the whole crop all at once.
- Perfect methods of intensive planting and succession planting for more economical use of space, fertilizer, water, and your time and energy.

Weeds will soon go to seed. Pull them up before they scatter seeds for next year.

Raccoons are a major pest of **Sweet Corn.** They can ruin a harvest in no time. An electric fence is your best defense.

Planning

Labor Day weekend signals the end of summer and, in the minds of many, the end of the vegetable garden season. This month is often seen as a time of harvest and winding up gardening activities for the year—which may be true if you are only interested in a summer garden filled with warm-weather crops.

In large areas of Pennsylvania, however, there are weeks of golden, relatively mild days ahead, even if a light frost visits toward the end of the month. There is ample opportunity for extending the gardening season by growing cool-weather crops. The same plants that did well very early last spring also perform in the fall. With some help from plastic mulches, tunnels, or cold frames, crops can be protected from the frost and nurtured to harvest despite days with increasingly less light.

Shopping List: portable cold frame, clear plastic

Planting

Because there are now fewer hours of daylight, seeds sown directly in the garden will take a bit longer to mature. If you have a cold frame or can rig a clear plastic tunnel, **Parsley, Lettuce, Chives, Onions,** and other crops will eventually mature and grow past first frost into November.

To increase your supply of herbs for gifts or for kitchen use, take stem cuttings from outdoor plants before they succumb to frost.

1 *Cut off* 4- to 6-inch-long pieces of tender stem tips.

2 *Remove* all but the top three to five leaves.

3 Place the stems in a glass of water on the window sill,

OR

insert them into a shallow pot or flat filled with moist sand or vermiculite and cover the container with plastic (with some air holes) to maintain humidity around the cuttings.

4 *Check* after two or three weeks for signs that roots have developed.

5 Pot rooted cuttings in soilless potting medium with some granular fertilizer mixed in.

Now is the time to plant **Garlic** for next year. The secret to growing **Garlic** is fall planting and loose soil; add sand to make the soil soft and friable.

Get a jump on spring by planting **Spinach** now. *Sow* seeds, and let the new young plants overwinter in a mulched bed. They will resume growing in the spring.

Plant and Garden Care

Young **Broccoli, Cabbage,** and other cool-weather lovers planted last month may need more mulch.

Plan to leave root crops such as **Parsnips, Turnips,** and **Carrots** in the ground until after frost; the chill will sweeten their flavor.

Pull up dead and dying plants from containers before real cold sets in later this month or next month. Clean out the planting medium, and mix it into the real garden soil. Scrub the empty containers and store them indoors.

Watering

Water the soil in the **Asparagus** bed either now or next month so it will be moist when cold weather comes.

Unless the fall is extremely dry, there is no need to water the remaining vegetables in the garden, especially if they are mulched.

In the absence of rain, *moisten* materials that you put on the compost pile so that microbial activity will continue deep within it even after frost.

Fertilizing

When planted beds are cleared at the end of the season, spread a 3- or 4-inch mulch of some organic material such as chopped leaves to protect the bare soil from compaction during the winter. Living mulches or "green manure" such as a vetch or winter ryegrass are also suitable. These mulches will add nutrients to the soil when they are tilled into it in the spring.

Grooming

Cut off tops of indeterminant **Tomato** plants to prevent more fruit production. This will divert energy to those already formed green tomatoes, which may still have time to ripen.

Pull stems of other plants such as **Corn, Peppers,** and **Eggplants** that have finished producing.

As **Asparagus** fronds turn brown and dry out, cut them back, then *weed* and *mulch* the bare soil in the bed.

Growing Smarter

Double-digging planting areas–either wide rows or raised beds–is a lot of work, but the improved soil offers great benefits for your plants. The soil has more air and nutrients, and holds moisture better. Do the digging in the fall.

Rather than simply pushing a shovel into the ground, lifting clumps of soil, then turning them over as you deposit them back on the ground, follow these steps:

1 Dig a 2-by-2-foot hole and set the soil aside. Partially fill the hole with organic debris such as chopped leaves, leaf mold, straw, non-meat kitchen peelings, or prunings.

2 Dig a similar hole adjacent to the first hole, depositing the soil you remove into the first hole to cover the plant waste at its bottom. Partially fill the second hole with organic debris.

3 Dig a third hole next to the second one. Deposit the soil on the debris in the second hole. Continue this process until you've used up your organic material or you have dug all the planting area you want to.

During the winter the soil over the dug area will sink back to ground level as the organic debris beneath it settles and decomposes. Come spring, a light raking readies it for planting.

Problem Solving

Insect activity virtually halts as temperatures drop. Most have completed their life cycles and have left eggs or larvae to overwinter in the yard.

Diseases are not much of a problem as the season winds down. Their spores may winter over in the soil or on nearby organic debris, so *clean up* the mulch and dead plants where disease problems developed.

Rodents continue to be a problem because they are looking for comfortable nesting places. *Delay* spreading winter mulch until the ground has frozen hard. By that time mice, voles, chipmunks, and other critters will have nested elsewhere.

OCTOBER

Planning

Store unused seeds for use next year. Make sure they are not damp from being outdoors during the summer. Tightly seal them in their packets and put them in an airtight tin or other container in the back of the refrigerator to keep them fresh. Most seeds remain viable for three years if they are stored correctly.

If you do not already have one, this is a good time to **establish a composting operation** on your property. The leaves that fall from trees this month are much too valuable to put in the trash. Collect those that fall in your yard, chop or shred them, and use them to mulch the garden. Use leftovers to start a pile in some out-of-the-way corner where they can sit and decompose over the months to come. Add leaves from the neighbor's yard, kitchen scraps, prunings, dead plants from the garden, straw, dried grass clippings, or any other nonmeat organic material to the pile.

In the spring you can decide whether you want to make compost by one of the following methods:

1 The **simple** (passive) method means you just allow the pile to perpetually sit and decompose within, while you continually add materials on top during the season. It will begin to yield compost at the bottom of the pile in a year.

2 The **managed** (active) method means that you build the pile all at once, turn it periodically to make it heat up, and harvest lots of compost halfway through next season.

Shopping List: electric- or gasoline-powered leaf shredder

Planting

Other than sowing some **Spinach** for next season, there is no more planting to do this season.

Place plants such as **Lettuce** that are still growing in pots in a cold frame to protect them until you have harvested all the leaves. Tender perennial herbs such as **Rosemary** can also winter over in a cold frame if they are in pots. Rooted herb stem cuttings should be ready for potting up any time now.

Last call to bring herbs indoors. *Dig up* viable **Parsley, Chives, Rosemary, Thyme, Basil, Oregano,** and **Sage** plants. Shake soil off the roots and plant them in pots of moist, soilless potting mix. Herbs can grow under lights or in a cool, sunny window. (**Chives** that have been frosted already may not grow until next spring.)

Plant and Garden Care

Harvest all remaining vegetables in anticipation of a serious frost, which will blacken **Tomatoes, Squash, Pumpkins, Peppers,** and **Ornamental Gourds.** Root crops may remain in the soil until after first freeze. *Cover* **Carrots** and **Parsnips** with a heavy mulch, up to a foot thick. This will protect plants from an early freeze but will not protect them from a constant freeze. The alternative is to bury a 5-gallon bucket in the soil, dig the root crops, and place them in moist sand in the bucket. Mulch the lid with a straw bale, and open it only to gather some vegetables for the kitchen. Don't let them freeze.

Thoroughly *clean up and destroy* weeds to control pests and diseases. Remember that pests that annoy vegetable plants are also attracted to many of the weeds growing in and around the garden, and they lay their eggs on them.

Compost remaining plant material. *Cut or shred* the woody plants before dropping them on the compost pile so these tougher materials will break down faster.

Winter Squash and **Pumpkins** can take a frost but not a freeze. When the pumpkins turn solid orange, cut them at their stems with a knife. *Cure* them in a warm, dry location

for a week or two (until they are dried out a bit). *Store* them cool and dry at 55 degrees F, and they will last all winter. **Winter Squash** will be ready to harvest when the pumpkins are.

Green tomatoes may still be on **Tomato** vines, but they require 65 degrees F temperatures to ripen. When the thermometer dips below that, *harvest* the unblemished remaining ones, and wrap them individually in newspaper. Place them in paper bags in a cool, dark area such as the basement to ripen. Periodically check to see if any are turning color. Bring pinkish ones into the kitchen to ripen further in the sun and heat.

Watering

Make certain all perennial herb plants have been watered in anticipation of winter. *Drain* all hose and water lines to the garden to prevent damage from freezing.

Moisture is necessary for decomposition of organic material. *Water* the compost pile only if it is very dry. If the materials were moist when you piled them up, chances are the interior of the pile is still moist. Once the rain or snow moistens the outside of the pile, shelter it from future rain.

Fertilizing

Fertilizing the entire garden can wait until late winter. You might want to sprinkle some slow-acting fertilizer around the **Rhubarb** so it will have nutrition for its very early appearance in the spring.

Sprinkling Slow-Acting Fertilizer

Problem Solving

Squash vine borers winter over in plant debris. Throw suspect debris in the trash.

Growing Smarter

There are lots of ways to chop leaves for use as mulch or to speed up their decomposition in the compost pile. (Whole leaves tend to mat together flatly and prevent moisture and air from reaching the soil).

- Mow them with a mulching lawnmower and collect them in a bag attachment.
- Mow them with a mulching mower so that the side discharge blows them toward the center of the lawn as you make your passes. They will become a pile of chopped leaves ready for use.
- Rake them into a pile and run the lawnmower back and forth over them.
- Use a shredder-vac which collects and shreds the leaves into a bag.
- Rake or blow them into a pile, and put it in a large trash can or other tall container. Then push the string trimmer down among them to shred them.

Planning

Pennsylvania gardeners with extended-season vegetable gardens traditionally have fresh food from their gardens on the Thanksgiving dinner table. What better way to celebrate the harvest!

- Pick B**russels Sprouts, Lettuce, Spinach, Swiss Chard,** and **Chinese Cabbage** from under clear plastic tunnels.

- Pull sweet **Carrots** and **Parsnips** directly from the garden.

- **Pumpkins** and **Winter Squash** are at their best.

Cover or *mulch* all the bare soil in the garden. The microbial life in the soil appreciates some winter protection.

Thanksgiving is an appropriate time to take stock of the past gardening year and make final entries in your notebook or journal. Keep it handy to continue to record weather events and information on the birds and other wildlife that visit your feeder during the winter months.

Shopping List: indoor light garden, black oil sunflower seed, suet cakes, birdbath heater, snow fencing

Planting

Plant Egyptian (walking) **Onions** now. They winter over in bulb form and will begin to grow early next spring. They will be ready to eat two to three weeks earlier than spring-planted **Onion** sets.

Plant and Garden Care

Vent clear plastic tunnels and open cold-frame lids if the weather is mild with strong sun.

If the ground is still workable, this is an excellent time to build a raised bed. Start this first year with just one or two beds; box them with wood planks now so the wood can weather over the winter. (See February Growing Smarter, p. 95.)

Prepare soil for next spring by incorporating organic material into it now. This will allow time for it to decompose and condition the soil.

If enough manure is available now, this is the best time to dig it into or spread it over the entire garden.

Scrape dirt from the surfaces of hand tools. Wire-brush them, and coat the metal with oil. Follow manufacturers' instructions for winterizing power equipment.

Mulch the herb beds after the first hard frost. By this time rodents will have found homes for the winter and they will not nest in the mulch.

Watering

Water any plants growing under clear plastic tunnels, because the rain cannot get at them. Either run drip irrigation, or water by hand with a watering can or hose.

Problem Solving

Poor crop production may be a result of nutrient deficiencies in the soil. Take a soil sample for laboratory analysis (see December). If the soil is too acid for certain plants, this is a good time to spread lime to "sweeten" the soil. It provides calcium too.

Critters may continue to visit the garden in search of leftovers. An 18- or 24-inch fence with the lower portion snugly against the ground or slightly under its surface will deter rabbits. Groundhogs (woodchucks) are a different matter. Sink their fence in a 12-inch-deep trench and extend it at least 2 feet above the ground. You may want to widen the trench to 12 inches so the fence lies flat under the ground for a foot, then bends upward aboveground for 2 or 3 feet. This is a lot of work, but it is the only effective barrier to these destructive creatures.

The best way to keep deer away from the garden is to run a strand of electrified wire around its perimeter at nose height. A lower strand will deter woodchucks and rabbits.

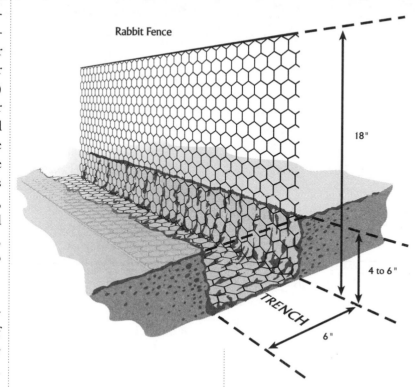

Rabbit Fence

18"

4 to 6"

TRENCH

6"

Planning

Collect new seed catalogs and put them aside for consultation after the hectic holidays are over. There will be lots of enticing new varieties of many of the vegetables and herbs you are already growing. This is where your garden notes will come in handy. They will remind you if you need to try a different variety of a particular plant because the past year's crop was not successful.

Use the off-season to learn more about growing and using herbs. Join a local herb society, and search out herb gardeners who can help you find unusual varieties.

Christmas List: a soil-test kit, a book on vegetable gardening, a rain gauge, a book on herbs, a seed-starting system

Planting

Cover cropping is an agricultural technique used by backyard vegetable gardeners to protect and nourish garden soil. A cover crop is a plant that is temporarily grown on idle soil. It will be dug or tilled into the soil in the spring before planting a vegetable crop in that space.

The best cover crops make rapid growth. Grasses are good for pro-

Growing Smarter

If you have a suspicion that the soil in your garden—or some part of it—is not healthy, test it. Production crops are much heavier feeders than are most ornamental plants, so their soil is more likely to become depleted of certain nutrients or trace elements . . . even when you fertilize with a balanced, slow-acting product and rotate your crops.

Purchase a soil-sample test kit from your county extension service, and mail it to Penn State University. Follow the label instructions exactly. A computer printout will indicate if the soil is overly acid or alkaline; the amounts and proportions of nutrients available to the crops; and any trace elements lacking in your soil. The test will also recommend how to correct deficiencies (see Appendix for extension offices).

ducing maximum organic material in a short time. For fall planting, try **Winter Ryegrass.** Plant it thickly—about 20 or 30 pounds per 1,000 square feet.

Plant and Garden Care

The ground has frozen hard in many parts of Pennsylvania. If you have not already mulched perennial food and herb crops such as **Strawberries, Rhubarb, Oregano, Sage, Chives,** and **Mints,** do so now. Straw, chopped leaves, or pine needles are suitable mulches.

Grooming

Cut back the dead stems of plants in the garden for a final cleanup. To keep the area neat, pick up twigs and branches that drop from trees onto beds.

Problem Solving

Snow is *not* a problem. The cover it provides insulates the soil and protects bulbs, seeds, and microbial life beneath the soil surface. It helps hold in moisture and provides more moisture when it melts.

Houseplants

My first serious houseplant experience was with a small, variegated **Spider Plant.** I consider the experience serious because it was both intentional and successful. Although there had been houseplants in my life before, they were acquired incidentally or accidentally, as holiday gifts or castoffs, and none lasted long enough for me to discover the thrill of success. But the **Spider Plant** was offered to me by a friend, and because I chose it, I valued it, and I consciously set out to care for this plant. Because it happened to be practically the world's easiest houseplant to grow, I was successful at keeping it alive and happy for several years. This gave me confidence to try others.

Houseplant Success

Upon reflection I realize that earlier experiences with other houseplants were doomed to failure because I had no confidence. All it takes to gain confidence is one success. Holiday gift plants do not offer opportunities for success. Often manipulated to perform before their normal time and force-fed to develop a flush of impossibly wonderful flowers and foliage, they are unable to sustain their vigor and performance without expert care. It is the sturdy, unassuming foliage plants—**Philodendron, Peace Lily,** and **Corn Plants**—that help novice indoor gardeners have success. Once they manage to keep a foliage houseplant alive for two or three years and experience the delight of it, novices are motivated to learn the skills necessary to nurture other plants.

My **Spider** was the perfect plant to learn from. Because it was forgiving, it tolerated my inexperience; because it was tough, it was able to survive my fumbling efforts to care for it. Ultimately, my **Spider Plant** taught me many lessons.

Replanting

Lessons Learned

I learned that some plants are more tolerant of indoor conditions than others, but none are truly happy in the house. Most plants are really only happy growing outdoors. Most houseplants are tropical, genetically programmed to thrive in warm, humid environments. Others are typically garden annuals, held over or started from rooted cuttings, grudgingly tolerating house conditions so they can have a chance at outdoor life once again. They are indoors because they have to be—they cannot survive our winters outside. To the degree that we can provide their favorite conditions—appropriate warmth, humidity, and light—we will succeed in keeping them happy. (I also learned that this is the same as keeping them healthy). Putting them outdoors in the summer revitalizes houseplants and enables them to develop the vigor needed to make it through winters indoors.

That said, I learned from my **Spider Plants** that most houseplants do survive life in a home. Most are forgiving of some environmental deficiencies if they have at least two of the four essential requirements

Houseplants

fully provided—optimum light, proper moisture, ideal air temperature, and appropriate ambient humidity. They can compensate, but they may still be stressed. That is why they are constantly vulnerable to pest and disease problems.

I learned about houseplants and water. Many plants like definite wet/dry cycles, others prefer even moisture. It is important to know which is which. One reason **Spider Plants** are so instructive is that they will survive a novice's occasional forgetfulness about watering. They are as happy as the next plant to have adequate moisture on a regular basis, but luckily they can do without for quite awhile. This is helpful for a person who needs to have success growing a houseplant.

I learned what "potbound" means from my **Spider Plant.** After a season or two, I noticed alarming pale protuberances bulging from the surface of the soil in the pot. These, a friend told me, were the plant's roots, and they were running out of space in the pot. Yet the plant seemed happy. Thus I learned that, while most plants prefer plenty of room in the pot for their roots to grow, some do not mind a bit of crowding. Again, it is important to know which plants are which.

Important Caution

Important: Keep certain plants away from children and pets. Some plants that are traditionally grown indoors at least part of the year have parts that are poisonous in some way. They include:

- **Amaryllis**
- **Caladium**
- **English Ivy**
- **Dumb Cane (Dieffenbachia)**
- **Oleander**
- **Peace Lily (Spathiphyllum)**
- **Philodendron**
- **Devil's Ivy (Pothos)**

This is also how I learned about repotting plants.

I learned about propagation. **Spider Plants** produce long, drooping, branching stems from which small shaggy plantlets hang like ornaments. Fortunately, these **Spider Plant** babies develop roots practically on their own. Pinch them off and stick them in a glass of water and the roots promptly develop. In no time they are ready to plant in pots of soilless medium. How easy! Having experienced that kind of success, I eventually dared to try stem cuttings, layering, and other ways to make new plants from my increasing number of houseplants.

Over time I learned to value variegated foliage. My **Spider Plant** had yellow-striped green foliage that brightened the room as the light from the window fell on it. It provided contrast with the other, mostly green plants nearby. I began to seek out houseplants with multicolored foliage.

I learned about displaying houseplants. I regard the gracefully arching foliage of my **Spider Plant** as its greatest asset. It begs to be hung. It never looks better than when the pot is suspended in front of a window, its foliage in full panoply, its limp stems thickly burdened with plantlets hanging beneath.

Mostly I learned from my **Spider Plant** that once you have success caring for certain houseplants, you gain the confidence to adopt others. Soon your house is filled with exotica—**African Violets, Orchids, Citrus,** and **Bromeliads.** Then somewhere along the line you decide to pass along a plant—perhaps a **Spider Plant**—to a friend who is not very experienced with houseplants . . .

Houseplants for Pennsylvania

Common Name (Botanical Name)	Light	Ornamental Features	Easiest Propagation	Comments
African Violet (*Saintpaulia* sp., hybrids)	Bright indirect/medium	Fuzzy, green, rounded leaves; flowers in shades of purple, rose, pink	Leaf cuttings anytime; divide in May	Virtually year-round flowering in right site. Likes some humidity.
Aloe, Medicinal (*Aloe vera* syn. *Aloe barbadensis*)	Medium to low	Stemless succulent green leaves stiffly upright in rosettes; grows to 2 feet	Pull apart offsets in spring	Juice known for healing burns. Yellow flower on stalk.
Aluminum Plant (*Pilea cadierei*)	Medium	Leaves splashed with silver	Stem cuttings late spring	To prevent lankiness, pinch back, repot.
Asparagus Fern (*Asparagus sprengeri*)	Medium	Light-green inch-long, flat needles line arching stems up to 2 feet	Divide late spring	Likes cool site. Tolerates range of light, moisture, and humidity.
Begonia, Rex (*Begonia* × *rex-cultorum*)	Bright indirect/medium	Large, hairy, irregular leaves with red, green, silver patterns	Stem cuttings in April	Strking foliage display. Likes moisture, humidity. Pest-susceptible.
Boston Fern (*Nephrolepis exaltata* 'Bostoniensis')	Medium	Spreading, arching, green fronds droop with age; some types more cutleaf	Divide in spring	Easiest fern to grow. Classic parlor fern. Keep moist. Hanging basket.
Bromeliad (*Bromeliad* sp.)	Bright indirect/medium	Stemless; mottled, stiff leaves grow in rosettes; dramatic flower spike	Pull apart offsets in spring	Easy-care, long-lived. Like warmth, humidity, and water in foliage cups.
Cactus (*Cactus* sp.)	Sun/bright	Green succulent "joints" have areoles where spines/flowers emerge	Pull apart offsets in spring	Needs good drainage. Minimum water in winter.
Cast-Iron Plant (*Aspidistra elatior*)	Medium to low	Tough, glossy, narrow, dark-green leaves on thin stems	Divide large clump in late spring	**"Dungeon plant"** ideal for dark corners. Slow-growing. Pest-free.
Chinese Evergreen (*Aglaonema modestum*)	Medium to low	Medium-green, oblong leaves from central stem	Divide large clump or take stem cuttings	Long-lived; grows to 3 feet. Likes moist air and soil.
Christmas Cactus (*Schlumbergera* sp.)	Bright to medium	Leaves are green, flat-jointed, spineless; tubular flowers in red, orange, white, pink	Stem cuttings in late spring	Flowers in periods of fewer daylight hours. Joints of "Thanksgiving" type are more pointed.

Houseplants for Pennsylvania

Common Name (Botanical Name)	Light	Ornamental Features	Easiest Propagation	Comments
Corn Plant (*Dracaena fragrans*)	Medium to low	Wide blue-green leaves, over 18 inches long, on thick stem; resembles corn	Stem cuttings spring	Easy to grow. Tolerates dungeon sites.
Croton Joseph's Coat (*Codiaeum variegatum* 'Pictum')	Lots of direct sun	Oak-like leaves of varied exotic colors; grows 2 to 4 feet tall	Stem cuttings in summer	Insists on sun, humidity, no drafts.
Dumb Cane (*Dieffenbachia maculata*)	Medium to low	Green oval leaves dotted/splotched with cream	Stem cuttings spring to fall	Sap inflames, numbs mouth if tasted. Reaches 6 feet. Hates overwatering.
English Ivy (*Hedera helix*)	Bright to medium	Three-lobed leaves on trailing stems in hundreds of variations	Stem cuttings early summer	May cause dermatitis. Susceptible to mites in dry, hot air.
Gardenia (*Gardenia jasminoides*)	Bright indirect/ medium	Small, glossy, dark-green leaves; white to cream fragrant flowers	Softwood cuttings early in season	Needs generous water but good drainage, cool nights, regular fertilization, acid soil.
Grape Ivy (*Cissus rhombifolia*)	Bright to medium or low	Dark-green leaves with three leaflets	Stem cuttings anytime	Fast-growing. Trailing, with tendrils to climb. Ideal for hanging.
Hibiscus, Chinese (*Hibiscus rosa-sinensis*)	Bright/direct sun okay	Medium-green oval leaves; large single or double flowers in red, yellow, orange, or pink	Stem cuttings spring or summer	Prune stems in spring to start new wood for flowering. Aphids—a problem indoors.
Jade Plant (*Crassula argentea*)	Bright indirect	Fleshy, thick, oblong, dark-green leaves; pink, star-shaped flowers	Leaf or stem cuttings May	Easy care. Tolerates same pot for years. Blooms for months. Needs special treatment to bloom.
Kaffir Lily (*Clivia miniata*)	Bright	Dark-green strappy leaves; clusters of orange or yellow lily flowers	Division of large clumps, offsets	Likes being a bit potbound.
Mother-in-Law's Tongue (*Sansevieria trifasciata*)	Bright indirect	Stiff, dark, lance-shaped leaves have yellow edges, gray-green bands	Pull apart offshoots in spring	Tolerates low light if it must.
Orchids, Moth (*Phalaenopsis* hybrids)	Bright indirect	Wide, dark-green, straplike leaves; pale flowers line stems	Divide in June	Cool rooms promote flowering for months.

Houseplants for Pennsylvania

Common Name (Botanical Name)	Light	Ornamental Features	Easiest Propagation	Comments
Parlor Palm (*Chamaedorea elegans*)	Bright to medium	Light-green, thin fronds to 6 feet tall; small, low, yellow flower clusters	From seed; difficult	Likes humidity, but tolerates some dryness. Susceptible to mites.
Peace Lily (*Spathiphyllum floribundum*)	Medium to low	Deep-green foliage; in spring or fall, white lily-shaped bract	Divide in February or March, every two years	Tolerates low light, but flowers with more light. Likes moisture.
Peperomia (*Peperomia caperata*)	Medium	'Emerald Ripple': rich green, textured, heart-shaped foliage	Stem cuttings in spring or summer	Avoid overwatering. Compact, 3 to 4 inches tall.
Philodendron (*Philodendron* sp.)	Medium to low	Large, glossy, evergreen leaves; vining or shrub	Stem cuttings	A classic for low light, foliage interest.
Pothos (*Epipremnum aureum*)	Bright indirect	Leathery heart-shaped leaves, bright green with yellow splashes	Stem cuttings spring or summer	Trailing stems good for hanging; relative of Philodendron.
Rubber Plant (*Ficus elastica*)	Bright indirect	Large deep-green, oval leaves, some variegated	Stem cuttings May or June	Easy. Stems to 10 feet tall bleed milky sap.
Schefflera (*Brassaia actinophylla*)	Medium to low	Glossy, green leaflets that spread like umbrella	Air-layer in spring	Elegant tree to 8 feet. Takes some neglect.
Spider Plant (*Chlorophytum comosum*)	Bright indirect/ medium	Grasslike arching foliage, green with white or yellow stripe	Separate and pot plantlets anytime	Easy to grow. Thrives potbound. Tiny plants form on stems.
Wax Plant (*Hoya carnosa*)	Bright	Stiff, waxy, oval pale-green leaves; waxy, off-white flowers	Layering or stem cuttings	Trailing stems, fragrant flowers. Also blooms at night. Needs good drainage; dry soil okay.

JANUARY

Planning

These are literally and figuratively the darkest days for houseplants. Daylight hours are short, heating systems reduce humidity, and opening and closing doors creates cold drafts. These environmental conditions stress plants severely. They cause both the foliage plants that are essentially dormant and the blooming plants that are at peak energy to be vulnerable to pest and disease problems.

This is a time to be proactive in caring for your plants. Take pains to balance your need for greenery and flowers with their need for a healthier environment. Give thoughtful consideration to their location, and move them to areas with lower temperatures, more light, or higher humidity. Examine them closely for signs of insects and disease, and deal with problems promptly.

To cheer you, **Holiday Amaryllis, Poinsettia, Kalanchoe,** and others are still blooming. **Orchids** will bloom next month.

Houseplant Rule of Thumb: Plants need slightly more water when they are blooming than when they just have foliage.

Planting

If you received an **Amaryllis** bulb as a holiday gift, start it anytime.

1 Choose a pot that is just slightly wider than the bulb for a snug fit, and make sure it has drainage holes. (If you are planting several bulbs in one pot, their sides should be touching.)

2 Fill the pot partway with moist potting mix, and set the bulb in it, tapered tip upward, so that its "shoulders," its widest part, are just about an inch below the rim of the pot.

3 Fill in potting mix around the bulb so that it is about 2/3 covered with soil, its shoulders and growing tip exposed. *Water* to settle the potting mix in the pot.

4 Set the potted bulb in a cool room for several weeks with minimal watering so it can develop roots.

5 As soon as a green stem sprouts, bring the plant into a warm room. *Water* it, and enjoy the show.

If you prepared some bulbs for forcing last fall, take them out of their cold storage after they have had eight to ten weeks of chill time. Enjoy watching them grow and bloom.

Care for Your Houseplants

Evaluate the light conditions for your houseplants. While foliage plants do not need as much as light as do those that are flowering, they do suffer from reduced winter daylight hours. To increase the light:

- Move plants to a window where winter sun is more available.

- Wash windows and remove screens.

- Set the plants under fluorescent lights on a kitchen counter or set up a grow light elsewhere.

- Keep curtains open—even sheer ones cut light.

- Limit the size of hanging plants that block light coming through upper windows.

- Wipe dust from plant foliage with a damp cloth.

- Set plants on or near mirrors.

Check for signs of pests as you clean and rearrange plants. Sometimes holiday gift plants become infested seemingly overnight. Throw them away before they infect other plants. Some plants, such as **Ficus** (**Fig**), drop some leaves any time environmental conditions change. *Clean up and discard* fallen leaves promptly. Beware of overwatering.

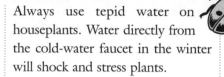

As each of the holiday **Amaryllis** blossoms on a stalk fades, clip it off. When all are finished, *cut off* each stalk down near the top of the bulb, leaving just the leaves. Treat the plant as a foliage houseplant, keeping it moist and giving it sunshine. Plan to put it outdoors when warm weather arrives.

Watering

Overwatering is the single most common cause of houseplant demise. Plants vary in their need for water depending on the season, the temperature, the light, the location, the size and type of pot they are in, and, of course, the plant species. One drink does not suit all.

Customize watering by using a houseplant water meter every time. Insert the probe into the pot's soil down 2 to 3 inches or where most of the plant roots are concentrated, and read the meter. Unless the needle indicates "dry" or nearly dry, delay watering. An alternative is to stick your finger about an inch into the soil. If it is not moist, *water.*

Always use tepid water on houseplants. Water directly from the cold-water faucet in the winter will shock and stress plants.

Fertilizing

The traditional foliage plants are not growing, so they do not need fertilizing. Only plants that are actively growing in anticipation of flowering (**Orchids, Begonias, African Violets,** garden annuals treated as houseplants) or that have been flowering for an extended period (**Cyclamen, Bromeliads**) need nutrition now. Every couple of weeks, add powdered or liquid quick-acting (water-soluble) houseplant fertilizer to their water at about half the dosage recommended on the package label.

Grooming

Since dead and dying plant parts foster disease, promptly *pull off* yellowed or dried leaves from **Ficus, Philodendron, Palms,** and others. *Cut off* faded flowers from **Poinsettias, African Violets,** and other flowering plants. *Snip back* trailing stems of **Ivies** and others if they threaten to overrun their allotted space.

Problem Solving

Mites thrive in hot, dry air. Look for pale, minute stippling on leaves, maybe some fine webbing near their stems. Wash mites off leaf undersides with tepid water from the faucet, and repeat every couple of days for a week. Try to improve the humidity around the plant. Serious infestations may require periodic sprays with insecticidal soap or light horticultural oil.

Scale often affects houseplants stressed by winter indoor conditions. One sign is stickiness on foliage or nearby windowsills. *Check* stems and leaf undersides for pale, waxy bumps. Rub or wash them off, then *spray* the plant foliage thoroughly with light horticultural oil. It will cover and smother those that were missed.

Cats may play with and nibble the arching foliage of **Spider Plants, Ferns,** and others that are accessible. Some scratch in the soil of large potted **Ferns, Ficus,** and **Dracaenas.** Short of getting rid of the cat (unthinkable!), put plants out of reach, or *spray* pots and foliage with a citrus-based pet-repellent product.

Planning

Often our houseplants are informal passalongs from friends who have divided some of their favorites or rooted their stem cuttings, and we may inherit others from friends when they move or develop an allergy. This means it is likely that among our plants are some that we do not particularly like or that are simply not agreeable to conditions in our homes. This is a good month to take dispassionate inventory and discard those plants and make room for new ones. Choose plants you have not tried, such as **Orchids, African Violets, Palms,** or **Ferns,** as replacements. Buy a good book on their care and make an adventure of it.

Houseplant Rule of Thumb: Fertilizers with a higher proportion of nitrogen promote the growth of foliage—those with a lower proportion promote flowering.

Planting

Retrieve from their chill space some of the bulbs you potted for forcing last fall, and watch them grow and bloom. It is not too late to start more **Paper-white Narcissus.**

1 Fill a shallow bowl with gravel or colorful stones.

2 *Set* **Paper-white** bulbs on the gravel, pointed tip upward, nestled close to one another.

3 *Fill* the bowl with water to cover the gravel and the bottoms of the bulbs.

4 *Set* the bowl in a cool, dark room so the bulbs can generate some roots.

5 *Move* the bowl into a warm, bright room when green shoots show at bulb tips.

6 *Expect* flowers to bud and bloom in about six weeks.

If you plant an **Amaryllis** bulb (see January) by Ash Wednesday, it will bloom for Easter.

Root stem cuttings of some of your favorite plants to create more plants.

1 *Cut* 4- to 6-inch lengths of the newest, tenderest stem tips. Remove the bottom leaves.

2 *Dip* the cut ends of the stems in powdered rooting hormone (available in garden centers).

3 *Insert* them into a pot or shallow container filled with moistened vermiculite or perlite, alone or combined with peat moss.

4 *Water* them, then cover them with clear plastic to maintain humidity.

5 Set them in bright, indirect light.

6 In three or four weeks, resistance to a tug on the cuttings will indicate that roots have developed roots.

7 *Pot them up* in soilless potting medium.

Some plants such as **Piggyback Plant** develop tiny plantlets at the ends of stems. Root them by "layering." While they are still attached to the mother plant, lay them on a bed of moistened potting medium, and fasten them so their undersides are in contact with the soil. In a few weeks when they become attached to the soil by their own new roots, cut the stem that connects them to the mother plant.

Care for Your Houseplants

• *Monitor* humidity around your plants. If the air is dry, only the **Cactus** will be happy!

• *Wipe or rinse* dust from foliage regularly and check for problems. The foliage always tells the tale.

Remove dust from foliage

- *Look* for spots, wilting, color change, or drooping that indicate problems.

- *Reevaluate* all plants' environments periodically as the sun changes position, thermostats get moved up and down, and plants grow larger.

A brownish or whitish crust on the surface of the soil or around the inside edge of the pot is accumulated salts from water-soluble fertilizer. *Leach* them from the potting medium by letting running water from the faucet wash through it, or repot the plant in fresh potting medium. Go easy on the fertilizer in the future.

Watering

Do not have a set watering schedule for houseplants. *Customize* watering to their needs and situation.

Orchids potted in wood chips dry out quickly. *Water* them under a running faucet, allowing them to drain so there is no accumulated water. An alternative is to set ice cubes on the wood chips (not touching any plant part) and let them melt slowly at room temperature. They dampen the wood chips gradually and thoroughly without messy dripping.

Fertilizing

Continue to *water* dilute fertilizer into plants that are blooming or about to bloom. Those that shake off dormancy by month's end will appreciate either the slow-acting granular fertilizer added to their potting mix when you potted them last, or a dilute water-soluble product in their water every couple of weeks.

Grooming

This month **African Violet** blooms may be fading and will need cutting off. Remove, also, the colorful bracts and tiny center flowers of **Poinsettia** plants if you intend to keep them over the summer. *Cut back* a **Poinsettia's** stems to about 6 or 8 inches, and let it enjoy the light indoors until it is safe for it to go outdoors.

Stretching for limited light causes some plants to develop leggy stems, with few, widely spaced leaves. To promote more compact plants, *cut back* these stems and improve their light.

Problem Solving

Aphids, scale, mites, or whiteflies may be back. It is not uncommon for these pests to have several generations, and some eggs may escape earlier spray treatments. Sometimes plants are reinfected by new or neighboring plants. *Wash* them with water, and *spray* foliage and stems with insecticidal soap or light horticultural oil again. Be sure to spray every nook and cranny—stems, leaf undersides, and buds.

Ants are embarrassing and annoying indoors, but their presence is helpful in alerting us to insect problems on plants. They like the sweet honeydew that aphids and others pests create when they feed on plant tissues. Investigate. *Wash and spray* infested plants as described above.

Wilted leaves do not always mean dry soil—they may mean the soil is too wet and the rotting of plant crowns and stems may be under way. *Throw away* the plant.

Planning

Finally, the daylight hours are beginning to lengthen noticeably. Houseplants respond to the arrival of spring with their greatest growth spurt, in root runners, new trailing stems, and new foliage. Assume that many will outgrow their pots and will need dividing or larger pots. Plan to have a selection of larger pots, soilless potting medium, and granular slow-acting fertilizer on hand. You may want to purchase potting mixes specially formulated with wood chips and other ingredients for **Cactus, Orchids, Bromeliads,** and **African Violets.**

The inability of older, overgrown houseplants to generate lots of fresh new growth signals decision time. Either *renovate* them by cutting back and removing woody stems, or *cut off* offshoots or tender stems to root and create new plants. Throw away the old plants.

Houseplant Rule of Thumb: The more leaves a plant has, the more moisture it needs.

Planting

This is a good time to transplant houseplants into fresh, clean containers.

Remove the plants and scrub the pots if fertilizer salts encrust them. Vinegar helps dissolve the stains. Repot in the same cleaned pot if the plant has not outgrown it, or use a larger pot.

Remove plant from container.

Remove a potbound plant from its container to expose the tangled mass of roots. Gently tease the roots loose with your fingers or a small screwdriver or ice pick, so that the soil falls away and the roots hang free. *Trim* overlong or tightly circling roots, and *repot* in a larger container. Follow these steps to pot up houseplants:

1 *Choose* a pot that has drainage holes and is large enough to comfortably accommodate the plant's existing rootball with at least an inch leeway on the sides. The deeper the pot, the better the drainage.

2 *Cover* the drainage holes with pieces of broken clay pot, landscape fabric, or other porous material that will keep potting mix from falling through.

3 *Fill* the pot roughly half-full of potting medium. *Mix in* some granular, slow-acting fertilizer, then set the plant on it to measure the height. **The plant should rest at exactly the same depth in its new soil as it did in its former soil.** Add or remove soil as necessary.

4 *Center* the plant on the bed of planting mix, and spread its roots outward. Add soil to cover the roots, and fill the pot to within a half-inch of its rim. Firm it gently by hand around the stems.

5 *Water* the plant well, and set it in a shaded area while the plant adjusts. Then return it to its accustomed spot in the house.

Care for Your Houseplants

Plants that are growing rapidly need more nutrition, water, light, and space, yet it is too early to put them outdoors. Adjust their inside locations to accommodate their needs until the weather is more dependably mild. Notice how the sunlight is shifting and affects available light for those plants that are blooming.

Houseplants appreciate a foliage cleaning every so often. *Wash* leaves of foliage plants under a faucet or the shower. Contrary to popular myth, **African Violets** do not mind wet foliage, as long as the water is at least room temperature.

Stake plants that have lengthening stems, such as **Begonia** and **Poinsettia,** before the stems get crooked.

Watering

Water newly potted plants generously until the water pours readily from the drainage holes at the bottom of the pot. This will settle the soil so you can confirm that the plant is at the correct depth in the pot. It also assures that the planting medium is thoroughly moistened for excellent root contact. Thereafter, *do not* routinely water plants without checking soil dryness to avoid soggy medium.

Fertilizing

Soilless potting mixes have no nutrients because they have no soil, so houseplants depend on fertilizer. Resume regular fertilization of houseplants when they have emerged from dormancy.

Repotting presents an excellent opportunity to add granular, slow-acting fertilizer to the medium to eliminate the need for frequent feedings over the season. Both synthetic and natural granular slow-acting products release nutrients slowly over many weeks—even months, depending on the product—and plants will receive consistent, uniform nutrition. Some potting mixes are now formulated with slow-acting fertilizer included, so *check* the label when you buy.

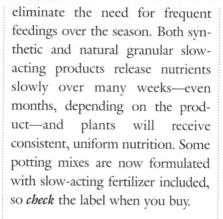

Grooming

Keep houseplants compact and bushy the same way you do outdoor plants. *Cut back* woody stems, or *pinch back* growing tips. Because plants are in an active growth mode now, they will regenerate quickly.

Plants such as **Corn Plant** (**Dracaena**) and **Dumb Cane** (**Dieffenbachia**) develop expanses of bare lower stems as they mature and grow tall. Cutting them back will help them fill out with foliage.

Problem Solving

Tender new growth is a target for plant pest insects, so examine plants regularly for signs of pest infestation.

Aphids are tiny, soft-bodied, pear-shaped yellow, white, or pinkish insects that suck juices from plant tissues. They create a sweet, sticky honeydew that makes the top surface of infested leaves shiny. Sometimes the honeydew promotes a sooty mold on the leaves; sometimes it attracts ants, which love the sweetness. *Snip off* heavily infested stem tips, and put them in a plastic bag for the trash. Wash aphids off small plants under the kitchen faucet. *Spray* larger plants outdoors on a mild day with the hose. Spray heavily infested plants with insecticidal soap, thoroughly covering all leaf and stem surfaces. Repeat treatments every few days for a few weeks.

Mites are always a potential threat to houseplants. *Check* for pale stippling on leaves, maybe some fine webbing near their stems. Give affected plants a shower with tepid water to wash mites off upper and lower leaf surfaces.

Growing Smarter

Some indoor and outdoor gardeners are so enthusiastic about certain favorite plants that they join together to organize plant societies such as the American Ivy Society, the Orchid Society, or the African Violet Society. If you are deeply interested in learning more about your favorite houseplants and meeting other people who share your passion, check the list of plant societies on pg. 343.

Planning

Rather than continually increasing the size of the pot to accommodate an ever-larger plant, sometimes it makes more sense to divide an overlarge plant into several smaller plants and pot them up individually. Thus the result of a spring houseplant repotting project is often lots of extra plants. What to do with the extras?

1 Give them away as hostess gifts when you visit friends.

2 Wait until mild weather to repot so you can put them outdoors on the porch or patio.

3 Take them to plant-swap events at the local garden club, arboretum, or plant society.

4 Donate them to local offices, the library, post office, doctor's office.

5 Plant them outdoors in the garden when the weather permits.

6 Locate them in bedrooms, bathrooms, and hallways where space is more available.

7 Offer them to institutions that have horticultural programs—retirement homes, prisons, school clubs, rehabilitation hospitals, scouts.

8 Sell them at yard sales.

Houseplant Rule of Thumb: The softer or more succulent the stem, the more readily it will root in a glass of water on the windowsill.

Planting

If you haven't already cut back the stems of the holiday **Poinsettia** you are keeping through summer, do so now. Soon you can put it outdoors, where it will regenerate into a bushy landscape shrub and grow all summer.

Some people enjoy propagating new houseplants in addition to caring for the ones they have. Propagating plants by various means is one way to acquire more of your particular favorites for free. Some, such as **African Violets,** are easily divided into many smaller rooted plants. **Spider Plants, Strawberry Begonia,** some **Bromeliads,** and many others develop tiny plantlets, or miniature plants that readily root in a glass of water.

Propagating many other houseplants, such as **Begonias** and **Ivies,** is almost as easy—it is simply a matter of rooting pieces of cut stem:

1 Measure roughly 4 to 6 inches back from the growing tip of a healthy young stem. Cut it off at the spot where some leaves are emerging from it.

2 *Remove* the leaves from the lower 2 or 3 inches of the cut stem, but leave the others. Remove any flowers or buds from its tip.

3 EITHER stick the cut ends into a glass of tepid water, and set them on the windowsill for a few weeks until roots become visible . . .

4 OR dip the cut ends of the stems into a powdered rooting hormone available at the garden center, and insert them into a pot filled with damp vermiculite or perlite. *Cover* them loosely with plastic to maintain the humidity. Make sure they do not dry out.

5 After a few weeks, when substantial roots have formed, plant each rooted cutting in a pot of soilless potting medium (see March).

Care for Your Houseplants

Resist the temptation to transfer houseplants outdoors to the porch or patio too soon. It is important to wait until the overnight air temperature is reliably at least 55 degrees F and there is no danger of light frost.

While you are waiting to move plants outdoors, guide their growth. Use small sticks to support supple stems or train vining stems.

Clean up fallen leaves, flower petals, and other debris from floors and windowsills promptly to prevent disease problems.

Watering

Plants that are actively growing need more water than they did when they were dormant. Most like a wet/dry cycle rather than being evenly moist all of the time, so water well but infrequently. *Test* the soil down an inch or more into each pot with the end of your finger or a houseplant water meter. If the planting medium feels dry, *water* until water appears in the drainage dish beneath the pot. Use room-temperature water that is unsoftened (to avoid sodium accumulation). Distilled water from a basement dehumidifier is ideal.

Fertilizing

If there is no fresh, granular, slow-acting fertilizer in or on a plant's potting medium, add fast-acting (water-soluble) fertilizer to its water rations every couple of weeks as directed on the package label. Do not exceed the recommended amount. Continue this regimen all summer.

Grooming

Snip off brown parts of leaves.

Cut off flower stems from **Orchids** as soon as their blossoms begin to fade and fall. Snip off dead or brown parts of leaves. Routinely cut off faded flowers from all flowering houseplants. Cutting back or pinching stems and deadheading flowers helps houseplants in many ways:

- It creates and maintains a pleasing shape, especially in the case of topiary or espalier.

- It removes breeding grounds for pest insects.

- It makes plants more compact and bushy for a healthier look.

- It stimulates new foliage growth with better color.

- It removes damaged or diseased leaves and stems.

- It provides stems and leaves to root for additional plants.

Problem Solving

Pest and disease problems are most easily solved when they are discovered and treated at an early stage. Continue to *check* your plants for problems each time you water them. Regular showers will take care of dust and pollen on leaf surfaces.

Growing Smarter

Some plants have stems that root easily in water or moist vermiculite:

- **Aluminum Plant**
- **Begonia**
- **Coleus**
- **English Ivy**
- **Impatiens** (and other garden annuals)
- **Grape Ivy**
- **Philodendron**
- **Swedish Ivy**
- **Wandering Jew**

Planning

The danger of an errant late frost is diminishing as daytime temperatures steadily moderate. Any time now it will be safe to begin to acclimate your houseplants to the outdoors. Set them outside during the day for short periods of time and then return them indoors overnight, gradually increasing their exposure over a week or two. Bring them in evenings until you are sure that nighttime temperatures will stay above 55 or 60 degrees F. Do not set them directly in the sun. Even those that crave bright light will suffer sunburned foliage if they are not able to adjust to the brightness gradually.

Taking houseplants outdoors is good for them and for you. It exposes them to good light and air circulation, and they benefit from watering with rainwater. Best of all, any pest insects will now be vulnerable to the natural populations of beneficial insects that are protecting your landscape plants—they will deal with aphids, scale, and whiteflies on the houseplants, too. Meanwhile, you can reclaim and enjoy the areas of your home that have been taken over by a growing collection of houseplants!

Houseplant Rule of Thumb: Bromeliads need regular moisture; **Cacti** need very little.

Planting

Some houseplants do very well out in the garden or in shrub beds for the summer. Either dig a hole and sink them—pots and all—into the ground, or remove their pots and plant them directly into the soil. **Poinsettias** will grow into attractive shrubs. **Coleus, Hibiscus, Spider Plant,** and many **Ferns, Ivies,** and **Bromeliads** will feel quite at home in the yard as long as their light and moisture requirements are met.

If the **Orchids** are finished blooming, *repot* them. Some are growing bigger and will soon produce longer roots that will require a roomier pot. Others may simply need fresh potting medium in the same pot.

1   *Remove* each plant from its pot and loosen its roots, allowing the old potting medium to fall away.

2   *Cut off* any damaged or dead parts of roots, and clip excessively long ones so they are in rough proportion to the others.

3   *Select* a clean pot large enough to accommodate the roots of the **Orchid,** and fill the bottom of it with potting medium formulated for **Orchids.** Set the plant on this medium at the same depth in this new pot as it was in its former one. Then add more potting medium.

4   Because the growing medium is typically coarse and chunky to promote the excellent drainage that **Orchids** need, it may need coaxing to fill in over and around the roots and support the plant crown. Gently *shake* the pot or rap its base on a table to distribute the material evenly as you fill up the pot to within an inch of its rim.

5   *Place* the newly potted **Orchid** under the kitchen faucet spray or hose, and thoroughly wet the potting medium to help it settle. Add more if necessary. If the plant sits too low in the pot, tug it upward gently to raise it, allowing more of the potting medium to fall under and among its roots.

Care for Your Houseplants

Take pains to assure that houseplants both indoors and out receive the type of light they prefer. "Dungeon plants," such as **Cast-iron Plant** and **Philodendron,** that are used to very low light will do best in shaded outdoor sites.

Once they are accustomed to sunlight, set or hang sun-loving plants, such as citrus and other tropicals, out in the open where they can get maximum light.

Plants such as **Ivies, Tuberous Begonias, Gardenia, Orchids, Bromeliads,** and **Clivias** prefer indirect bright light outdoors just as they do indoors.

Some plants, such as **Ficus,** are quite adaptable—tolerating either sun, bright light, or light shade with equanimity.

Set pots on bricks or decorative "feet" so they are off the ground. This will prevent slugs and bugs from climbing into the pots via drainage holes.

Do not crowd pots of plants when arranging them outdoors. Plant foliage needs good air circulation to prevent mildew problems.

Watering

Watering plants outdoors has two potential problems.

1 Plants may be overwatered by rainfall. Be sure that pot drainage is good and that pots are not sitting in saucers that collect water and prevent drainage.

2 Plants may be underwatered. Many will be in pots that are clay, or hanging in the sun, which increases their potential

for rapidly drying out. Locate these near the house so it is convenient to check them frequently when days become hot. Large, treelike **Palms, Ficus, Citrus,** or **Dracaenas** located under trees or roof overhangs may miss out on rainfall. Because they are in pots, they will dry out sooner than surrounding plantings.

Fertilizing

Plants with granular, slow-acting fertilizer incorporated into their potting medium can manage just fine without extra feeding. *Feed* others with water laced with soluble fertilizer on a schedule recommended by the manufacturer. Either water it into the potting medium, or *spray* the dilute fertilizer directly on plant foliage for a rapid energy boost to sustain blooming.

Grooming

Continue to *clip off* damaged stems and yellowed leaves and flowers from houseplants. Periodically pinching back actively growing stems will keep them compact and bushy.

Problem Solving

Deer may be a problem to houseplants that are temporarily outdoors. *Protect* vulnerable plants by hanging them or keeping them on a screened-in porch.

Squirrels sometimes dig in the soil of potted houseplants on decks and patios. They break stems and expose the roots to drying out, and they may knock over the pots as they scamper about. *Spray* plants with a commercial repellent if it is impossible to move them to a less vulnerable spot.

Temporary **leaf drop** when plants are in transition is not unusual, especially with **Ficus.** Caused by stress, it stops when the plant adjusts to its new situation.

Planning

Summer's onset affects houseplants indoors, too. As household routines change to accommodate seasonal activities, vacations, guests, plus heat and humidity, plants may be neglected. They are also affected by the turning on of air conditioning. It is especially easy to fall into the "out of sight, out of mind" mode when most houseplants are outdoors.

Arrange your houseplants outdoors to enhance your outdoor living spaces, just as they enhance your indoor spaces the rest of the year. Hang plants from arbors, pergolas, porches, and roof overhangs to soften their lines. Set potted flowering houseplants in empty spaces in the garden where hardy bulbs or other spring-blooming plants have died back. Use taller palms and small trees to soften corners on the deck or near stairways.

Houseplant Rule of Thumb: Houseplants are more likely to die from overwatering than from underwatering.

Planting

Plan to complete repotting projects before the season advances much farther. This is a good time to repot **African Violets.** Vigorous ones often develop secondary crowns that also generate foliage and flower clusters. Each of these should be separated from the main plant and given a pot of its own.

1   *Remove* the **Violet** from its pot.

2   Gently *loosen* the roots so they hang down and excess potting mix falls away. Then *tease apart* the distinct crowns at the soil surface, taking pains to be sure their respective roots are not damaged.

3   *Fill* a clean pot with **African Violet** potting mix or regular soilless potting medium, and set the second plant into it at roughly the same depth it was in its former pot.

4   *Press* the potting mix around the plant crown, and *water* well.

5   *Return* the original **Violet** plant to its former pot, after washing the pot and filling it with fresh potting medium. Plant at the same depth as before, firm the soil around it, and water.

Care for Your Houseplants

Evaluate the locations of those houseplants, such as **African Violets,** that remain indoors to be sure they are getting the light they need. Remember that window air-conditioner units reduce available light.

Thoroughly clean areas where houseplants were located all winter. Windowsills, glass windowpanes, plant stands, and countertops may be sticky with honeydew from insect infestations. There may be litter composed of dead insects, the webs of spiders that attacked them, or fallen leaves in the area. Wash macramé rope pot hangers, nearby curtains, and tablecloths or placemats that have been underneath houseplants.

Outdoors, insert small stakes into pots of any houseplants that show signs of toppling stems. Readjust the ties of those already attached to stakes or small trellises as the plants grow and produce more and longer stems.

Make sure the potted **Amaryllis** bulb is located in a sunny spot so its leaves can soak up energy from the sun for this winter's bloom.

Watering

Group smaller plants to facilitate watering and grooming. Locate all houseplants that are vacationing outdoors near the house for convenient watering and feeding.

Those in pots will need more attention than those planted in the soil. Attach a wand to the hose to make watering hanging plants easier. *Mulch* the surface of the potting medium with sphagnum moss, nut hulls, or other attractive organic material to help it retain moisture.

Fertilizing

If you accidentally use too much water-soluble fertilizer, *flood* the potting medium with water several times and let it drain freely from the bottom of the pot. This dilutes the fertilizer and washes most of it through and out of the potting medium.

If you forget whether you recently put fast-acting (water-soluble) fertilizer on your plants, delay a dose. It is better to err on the side of too little rather than too much fertilizer.

Grooming

Although their major spring growth spurt has passed, houseplants will respond to the outdoors with steady, but slower, growth. Keep pinching back stems of ivy-type plants that threaten to grow too leggy and get out of bounds. *Pinch* **Poinsettia** stems to maintain compact bushiness.

Remove dead and dying foliage and flowers from all plants regularly.

Problem Solving

Warm weather brings insects in droves, so extra vigilance is important.

Aphids will threaten as long as there is tender new growth at plant stem tips. **Scale** is partial to **Ferns, Spider Plants,** and **Orchids** that are experiencing stress from too much sun or lack of water. Keep the hose handy for washing minor infestations off plants. Use insecticidal soap or horticultural oil as directed on their labels to treat more significant infestations. Remember to repeat treatments, since most pest insects have several generations over the season.

Weeds may be a problem with houseplants that are outdoors, as seeds blow onto the surface of the potting mix and germinate. Pull them out promptly while their roots are tiny so they will not disturb the houseplant's roots.

Growing Smarter

Even though they are outdoors and perhaps even have their pots sunk into a garden bed, houseplants require more care than other plants growing outdoors. That is because they are not planted in soil that contains the microbial life that creates fertility and provides nutrients. Houseplants are planted in various kinds of "soilless" mixes that lack plant nutrients, providing only air and some degree of moisture retention. Whether they are primarily wood chips, sand, peat moss, vermiculite, or a combination of these materials, professional–or soilless–potting mixes are designed to provide a sterile medium to support the plant root system in its pot. They have the advantage of being lightweight and disease-free, but the bottom line is that you must provide all the nutrition for your potted plants in the form of fertilizer.

Birds may pester certain houseplants. Purple finches have been known to nest in hanging plants. Others occasionally drop seeds on their way to and from the feeder. These may become weeds in the potting medium.

Planning

Some of the tropicals that have served off-season as indoor houseplants will repay you for your care now that they are outdoors. Be on the lookout for hummingbird and butterfly visitors to potted **Mandevilla, Hibiscus,** and **Bougainvillea** plants that are now out on the deck. **Clivias** and **Tuberous** and **Rex Begonias** will get some attention, too.

This is yard-sale season, and there is no better place to find wonderful pots, hangers, plant stands, and stools for houseplants. Stop by and browse for bargains and great ideas for creative ways to pot and display plants. Look for decorative bowls, jars, and crocks that would make good cache pots: lacking drainage holes, they provide attractive outer containers for plants in ho-hum conventional pots.

You may see an advertisement for a houseplant tent sale at the parking lot of a nearby mall. This is one way that Southern growers clear out their inventory of foliage plants in time for their next growing season. While the plants can be had at bargain prices, they will require more careful, gradual acclimating to the indoors at the end of the summer.

Houseplant Rule of Thumb: The larger and thinner the leaves, the more moisture the plant will need.

Planting

Plant low-growing foliage plants such as **Asparagus Fern, Swedish Ivy, Crotons,** or something similar at the base of tall plants such as **Corn Plant** or **Ficus.** As they share the pot, they mask and soften the expanse of bare stem.

If you have been rooting stem cuttings harvested when pinching back leggy stems of **Begonia, Wandering Jew, Ivy, Coleus,** and others, pot them up in soilless mix as soon as their roots are developed. Also pot up rooted **Spider Plant, Bromeliad, Piggyback Plant** babies, segments of **Christmas Cactus,** and others. Cuttings rooted in water alone may take longer to adjust to their new situation than those rooted in moist vermiculite. Keep them away from harsh light until they have adjusted to life in a pot.

Pot up stem cuttings.

Care for Your Houseplants

Properly sited outdoor houseplants need little special care.

- *Hose down* plants to wash off dust if rainfall is not available to do the job. Allow time for the foliage to dry before dark.

- *Shelter* outdoor houseplants from wind and heavy rains if thunderstorms are predicted. Drain water accumulated from rain or the hose from cache pots and saucers under pots.

- *Secure* tall plants in low or small pots so they will not topple over in breezes.

- *Protect* plants from injury from kids, games, pets, and family activities around the pool.

- *Move* unhappy plants to improve their light or air circulation.

Watering

Houseplants that remain indoors in moderately cool air-conditioned areas do not require watering as often as those that spend the summer outdoors. Wherever they are located, plants in plastic pots will not need watering as often as those in clay (terracotta) pots.

Individual hanging plants are likely to need watering more often than those grouped on a counter or on the floor. *Check* each plant individually to determine moisture needs before routinely watering it.

Outdoor houseplants do best if they begin summer days with plenty of moisture; they tolerate heat better than plants that are watered after they have wilted from dry soil. If it does not rain every day or two during very hot spells, routinely *check* outdoor houseplants in the morning, and *water* the thirsty ones.

Fertilizing

When houseplants have finished their spring growth and flowering, they will not need as much nutrition. Granular, slow-acting fertilizer mixed into or put on top of their potting medium will provide sufficient general nutrition to maintain their health and vigor over the season. Tropicals that flower steadily all summer will benefit from additional periodic foliar sprays or waterings with dilute fast-acting fertilizer. As usual, beware of overdoing.

Never fertilize a plant that is wilted from dryness, heat stress, or disease attack. Wait until it has recovered.

Grooming

Certain foliage houseplants that are enjoying the outdoors will grow vigorously. **Philodendrons; English, Grape,** and **Swedish Ivy; Wandering Jew;** and similar plants may rapidly outgrow their space. You have two choices:

1 Continue to *clip back* or *pinch off* the ends of the stems. While this temporarily controls the size of the plant, it also stimulates it to grow even more to replace the lost foliage. The plant will eventually grow larger overall, which is fine if there is room for it indoors.

2 Radically *cut back* all stems to only a few inches long, in effect renovating the entire plant. This too will stimulate new growth, but the plant will return to its former size by the time it is due to go indoors and into winter dormancy.

Problem Solving

Usually it is their foliage that tells the tale when indoor and outdoor houseplants have their occasional summer problems.

Leaves are pale but veins are a dark green: The plant lacks iron, probably because the root environment is not acid enough. **Gardenias** may have this problem. *Sprinkle* powdered sulfur or used coffee grounds on the surface of the planting mix, and water-in.

Leaves coated with gray powder: This is a mildew infection, due to crowding, lack of air circulation, and damp foliage. Move the plant into better ventilation. Clean up fallen, infected leaves. If necessary, *spray* new foliage with a houseplant fungicide product to protect it from infection.

Leaves show pale stippling, webbing on stems: Mites love the hot, dry conditions that stress plants in summer. *Isolate* the plant to prevent the mites' spread. Wash them off under the hose or faucet every day or two for a couple of weeks to disrupt their life cycle.

Growing Smarter

Try planting a bowl garden with those rooted cuttings from various houseplants. It is easy to make a miniature garden in a large bowl or other shallow container by planting several types of young/small plants together as a mini-garden. It saves space, and showcases contrasting foliage color and texture to create strong interest.

Planning

This traditional vacation month is hard on houseplants because of the heat, humidity, and reduced rainfall. If you plan to be away more than five to seven days, it is vitally important to arrange for your plants to be watered somehow. Leave instructions for anyone who will be coming to water for you.

1   For convenience, *collect* all indoor houseplants that will need moisture (succulents and **Cacti** will be fine without) in one or two central locations—the kitchen sink, bathtub, shower stall, or someplace similar near a faucet. Although the plants may suffer reduced light, they will lose less moisture. If you have no one who will visit and water, water the plants well yourself, perhaps leaving a half-inch or so of water in the bottom of the sink, tub, or tray. *Cover* them lightly with plastic to help retain the humidity.

2   *Group* all houseplants that are summering outdoors in the shade in an area that is handy to the hose faucet. Plants in very large pots or that have water-saving crystals mixed into their planting medium can probably stay in place if it is at least partially shady. (This is a good time to *discard* any plants that are already struggling with major vigor or bug problems.)

If you are traveling to Florida or Hawaii, don't be surprised to see giant versions of your houseplants growing in people's front yards!

Houseplant Rule of Thumb: Houseplants with succulent stems or foliage require less moisture than other plants.

Planting

Take some time off from potting duties. Unless there are some rooted cuttings badly in need of potting, or some situations where pots have broken or plants have become horribly overgrown, let houseplants enjoy the rest of the summer.

Care for Your Houseplants

Continue to provide support for climbing or tall plants. Tropicals will be in their glory and growing vigorously.

Think about which plants you will eventually bring back indoors and which will be discarded.

- If you plan to bring in some garden annuals such as **Impatiens, Geranium,** or **Coleus** to overwinter as houseplants, *cut back* their leggy stems fairly severely to about 4 to 6 inches late in the month. Dig them up from the garden, keeping some of the garden soil around the roots to protect them. Set the rootball in a pot slightly larger than the rootball and partly filled with potting medium. Fill potting medium around the rootball, firm it, and water well. Let the newly potted plant stay outdoors in a protected area while it adjusts to its pot. As evenings grow cooler, it will come inside with the other houseplants.

- If you plan to overwinter garden annuals as cuttings to be rooted and potted for houseplants in a few months, take stem cuttings by month's end and get them started in a glass of water or a tray of damp vermiculite (see April).

Watering

Watering continues to be of critical importance to houseplants, especially those outdoors. Many are accustomed to a wet/dry cycle, which is easier to provide indoors when the watering is entirely up to you. Out on the deck or by the pool or patio, houseplants get supplemental water when it rains. Sometimes it is difficult to tell whether a nighttime rainfall was sufficient to truly moisten their medium, especially those in large pots. Use the trusty houseplant moisture meter or lift the pot and judge by its weight whether it needs more water.

Houseplants summering in indoor air-conditioned comfort—especially those in clay pots—will need regular watering attention because the humidity will be fairly low and potting medium will dry out faster.

Fertilizing

There is no need to fertilize houseplants long established in their pots at this point in the season. Their growth will slow as the daylight hours shorten and they anticipate the onset of dormancy.

When potting up rooted cuttings, add some granular slow-acting fertilizer to the potting medium.

Grooming

By month's end, cutting back and pinching will no longer be necessary because growth will have slowed.

Growing Smarter

Many kinds of plants grown as houseplants in Pennsylvania have similarly named hardy relatives which are capable of growing outdoors year-round here because they can survive the cold. Others have common names that are similar to those of some outdoor plants, even though they are not related, which further confuses the issue. *Hibiscus syriacus* (**Rose of Sharon**), for instance, is cold hardy and grows in many Pennsylvania gardens, but *Hibiscus rosa-sinensis* (**Chinese Hibiscus**) is tender here, so it is a houseplant. Other examples of similarly named plants with both tender and hardy versions:

- *Ficus benjamina/ Ficus carica* (**Fig**)
- **Florist Azalea/Hardy Azalea**
- **Florist Chrysanthemum /Hardy Chrysanthemum** (**Mum**)
- *Citrus sinensis* (edible **Orange**)/**Osage Orange**

Using the complete botanical name of a plant will help avoid confusion when shopping for any plant.

Continue to *deadhead*, and *clip off* discolored foliage and broken or damaged stems.

Problem Solving

Pest insects are responding to the natural signals of a season winding down. They are still nuisances on plants that have had chronic stress and lack of vigor all season, but their numbers are declining. This is the time to identify those plants to throw away, rather than take the trouble to spray them again with insecticidal soap or horticultural oil. Others will need careful cleaning and debugging before they are allowed back indoors for the winter.

Rots are sometimes a problem on houseplants that have been constantly exposed to rain during damp summers in their outdoor sites. Their stems darken and collapse, or their foliage and stems turn to mush. There is no way to save them. To prevent problems in the future: 1) empty or eliminate saucers under pots, 2) use a lighter potting medium for better drainage, 3) make sure the pot has several drainage holes in case one becomes clogged, 4) shelter plants from the rain and take over all watering chores yourself.

Planning

Even though the weather does not change dramatically in only three days, Labor Day weekend marks a seasonal transition for most gardeners. This is particularly true for houseplant care, because routines shift from summer maintenance to fall preparation of plants to resume indoor life. Which plants will be invited back indoors, and which will be discarded to make room for healthier or newer plants?

Allow enough time for plants to make the trip gradually, spending increasingly more of their days inside over several weeks. Bring them in for overnights before first frost is expected in your area. This reverse acclimatizing will minimize the stress they experience in adjusting to indoor conditions. They need to adjust gradually to lower humidity before the heat comes on.

Many houseplants are bigger now, some are in different types of pots, and you may have acquired some new hangers or plant stands. Give some thought to where you will display each plant in the house.

- Has the light situation changed at the window where the **Palm** or the **Orchid** was last winter?

- Perhaps a tree that once shaded a window has been cut down.

- Perhaps you have new, heavier curtains or replacement windows with slightly smaller glazed areas.

These things affect houseplants' access to light.

Houseplant Rule of Thumb: Natural sunlight is about twice as effective at maintaining houseplants as artificial light.

Planting

It's repotting time again. Several of your houseplants, particularly those that summered outdoors, may have outgrown their pots. Lift them from their pots to see if they are potbound. Roots peeking through the drainage holes, showing at the surface of the planting medium, or wrapped in a circle around the outside of the rootball are the signs. Either *divide* them into several smaller plants for smaller pots, or *repot* the large one into an even roomier pot (see March).

Dig up planted **Poinsettia** shrubs, or lift those that are in pots sunk in the ground. Repot them if you intend to keep them for the holidays. Otherwise, treat them like annuals—leave them in place and let them succumb to the frost.

Continue to *pot up* any rooted stem cuttings that have been sitting on the kitchen windowsill and have developed nice root systems.

Care for Your Houseplants

Set up a routine for preparing all houseplants for their indoor season. Avoid bringing pest insects inside with them.

1 *Clip off* dried foliage and flowers.

Clip off dried foliage.

2 *Remove* any decorative mulch on the potting medium.

3 *Pull* out any tiny weeds growing in the pot.

4 *Wash* plants under the hose to remove dust and insects. Wash the outside of the pot, too.

5 Then *spray* all plant surfaces thoroughly with light horticultural oil or hot pepper wax to kill any eggs or larvae that might survive the washing.

Start acclimatizing recently purchased bargain foliage plants to indoor conditions early this month while outdoor temperatures are still moderate. Any that were raised in the South have never been indoors and will face a major adjustment.

Let **Amaryllis** bulbs that you intend to force for December holiday bloom go dry; the leaves will wither and drop off. Keep potted bulbs in a cool, dark cellar or garage for eight to ten weeks without watering.

Watering

Keep a special eye on repotted plants that are indoors after a summer outdoors and are in a different kind of pot. Those in clay (terracotta) pots after being in plastic ones will dry out faster than you may be prepared for. Conversely, those in plastic pots will not need watering as often as before. Use the houseplant water meter probe to test moisture before watering (see April).

Fertilizing

Unless a plant is about to flower (some, such as "Christmas" and "Thanksgiving" **Cactus** respond to fewer daylight hours

Growing Smarter

People who prefer to get used to the water gradually before diving into the ocean or a swimming pool will understand the desirability of gradually acclimating plants to new environments. It is easier on their systems to bring outdoor houseplants indoors in a series of steps. It is a bit of a shock to them if they suddenly experience lower light levels, less humidity, and cooler temperatures.

1 Move plants destined for low-light areas indoors into deeper shade outdoors first.

2 Then move them onto a sheltered porch or balcony for awhile.

3 Then move them indoors to enjoy maximum light from a window.

4 Then move them to their designated site.

with blossoms), do not give it fertilizer. The lower light availability is signaling time for dormancy, so nutrition needs are minimal.

Grooming

Plants that are newly placed indoors after a summer outdoors will glow with good health. Those that are small trees, such as **Citrus, Ficus,** and **Palms,** may have grown so much they will need pruning to allow them to fit into their designated spot.

Do not pinch back **Poinsettia** stems anymore if you plan to encourage it to bloom in December.

Problem Solving

Leaf drop is common with certain plants, especially when they must adjust to new circumstances. **Ficus** and **Asparagus Fern** commonly lose foliage under stress, but the dropping will eventually stop as the stress subsides.

Pest insects will inevitably find their way into the house and plague houseplants. Be vigilant while the weather is still mild enough during the day to take an infested plant outdoors to wash and spray it.

Planning

If you plan to encourage last year's holiday **Amaryllis** *and* **Poinsettia** *to bloom again in December, start the process this month.*

Now that it has dried out, the **Amaryllis** bulb needs many weeks of dormancy, so leave it in a cool, dry place from now until late November.

The **Poinsettia** shrub needs fourteen hours of *complete* darkness each night to prompt it to develop flowers and its trademark red bracts in time for the year-end holidays. Because this is ahead of its normal schedule, *you* must extend the long darkness at night. Designate a nighttime location—a closet, unused room, or paper bag cover—to simulate December nights. During the day it needs sunlight. Continue this routine until early December, when expanding bracts will show a tinge of color.

Houseplant Rule of Thumb: The thicker and fleshier a plant's stems and leaves are, the drier they can become between waterings.

Planting

Many hardy bulbs are easily forced to bloom indoors as colorful house-plants in midwinter. **Paper-white Narcissus** are the easiest of all to force. Purchase some at the garden center as soon as possible (see February). This is also a good time to plant a new **Amaryllis** bulb if you want to have it bloom for late-December holidays.

Engage children in a planting activity to enjoy over the winter months. Start houseplants from food served in the kitchen.

1 Grow a pineapple plant from the top of a fresh pineapple from the grocery store. *Slice* off the top, and *scrape away* any flesh remaining under the tough skin and tuft of foliage. Let it dry for about a week. Then fill a pot with moist potting medium and gently press the pineapple into its surface, where it will develop roots.

2 Support an avocado pit with toothpicks inserted in its sides and resting on the edges of a glass of water. *Suspend* it so its narrow tip is immersed in the water. *Maintain* the water level until roots grow from the tip. Then plant in a pot with soilless potting medium.

3 *Suspend* a sweet potato upright in a glass of water so that it is immersed halfway. Watch for roots and leaves, then *pot up* the potato.

4 Grow a Citrus plant from seeds from a grocery store grapefruit, orange, or lemon. Save some seeds and let them dry out for a week or two. Then *plant* them about 1/2 inch deep in a pot of moist potting medium, and watch them sprout and grow on a sunny windowsill. Choose the strongest to maintain as a plant; clip off the others.

Care for Your Houseplants

Start putting the **Poinsettia** in a closet or other cool, totally dark space where it will not receive even a trace of light every night from 5:00 p.m. until 7:00 a.m. During the day, set it in a well-lighted area, and *water* when it needs it.

A cool plant "rest" room really comes in handy. If possible, keep an unused bedroom cooler than the rest of the house and in it put potted annuals that are not flowering, pans of forced bulbs that are rooting, and plants such as **Clivia** which need a cool environment for six to eight weeks to produce flowers.

OCTOBER

Watering

When the heating system starts running with the advent of cold weather, it takes awhile to get a feel for how often each houseplant needs watering. *Check* plants frequently at first.

Most hot-air systems simultaneously overheat the room and lower the humidity—a double problem. These conditions dry out potting medium rapidly; at the same time, they are forcing plants to transpire moisture from their leaves even faster to try to keep cool. Plants continue to draw on moisture in the soil through their roots to replace what they lose through transpiration, even though the potting medium is drying up. Wilting foliage signals this distress. The wilt becomes permanent when moisture is not replaced in the soil, even if the transpiration rate has slowed. Then the plant dies.

Fertilizing

There is no need to fertilize any plants, unless they are preparing to bloom.

Grooming

Minor clipping and grooming tasks continue all winter to assure that houseplants look their best. Cutting back stems now will not stimulate rapid growth, because plants are preparing for dormancy.

Remove damaged or discolored leaves and stems. Use this opportunity to closely examine plants for problems.

Do *not* clip stems of plants such as **Thanksgiving** or **Christmas Cactus.** They are forming buds at this time.

Problem Solving

Leaf drop may continue for some weeks while houseplants brought in from a summer outdoors struggle to adapt to the indoor environment. *Check* the undersides of leaves that are discolored, but have not yet dropped, for insect problems.

Scale shows up fairly quickly on certain houseplants that are stressed by their new indoor environment. By the time scale is visible as small, whitish, waxy bumps on plant leaves and stems, it is well established. *Isolate* the plant, and try to scrape off minor infestations with a fingernail. *Spray* all plant surfaces

Growing Smarter

Thanksgiving **Cactus** and **Christmas Cactus** do not resemble **Cactus** at all. Different varieties of *Schlumbergera,* both have distinctive green, spineless, flat, jointed stems which proffer iridescent tubular flowers in shades of pink, rose, and white at their tips. You can tell the difference between the two types by closely examining their stem segments. Those of **Christmas Cactus** are wider, with scalloped edges. Those of **Thanksgiving Cactus** are smaller and have two to four pointy teeth on their edges. Each blooms at a different time, in late fall and winter.

with light horticultural oil to smother major infestations. Follow product label instructions.

Whiteflies love **Poinsettias** and **Hibiscus.** Hang yellow sticky traps near these plants to alert you to an infestation. Hang more to trap them. Whiteflies are difficult to spray because they instantly fly away. Wash plant foliage to destroy eggs and larvae.

Planning

There are lots of opportunities ahead for giving gift plants. Slip those small plants that you potted up last month from rooted cuttings into unusual decorative wrappings or containers—flea market finds, coffee mugs, candy bowls, wine goblets—and bring one along for your host or hostess. Include a label with its name and how to care for it. There is always room for one more plant in any house, especially if it is a small plant.

The way florists prompt plants to bloom for holidays (and late-winter flower shows such as the one in Philadelphia in early March) is by manipulating the amount of light they receive. More light is provided to simulate spring, less light to simulate winter. A similar technique is necessary to encourage last year's **Poinsettias** to bloom on the holiday schedule this year.

As the number of daylight hours shrinks, houseplants typically enter their dormant period. They rest during the dark winter days and await the return of longer days of daylight when they will produce flowers. **Poinsettias** do the reverse, responding to increasingly less light by preparing to bloom. If they have been enjoying fourteen-hour periods of complete darkness daily since October, their bracts will start to turn red and flower buds will form

in their centers by late this month. The need for extra-long nights in a separate dark room will be over. They will be ready to bring out and set on display for the next few weeks.

Houseplant Rule of Thumb: The cooler the room, the less moisture a plant needs.

Planting

Plant and start to water an **Amaryllis** bulb at the beginning of this month if you want to enjoy it for the year-end holidays. Start watering those you have kept over from last year. You may not have to repot them because they do not mind being potbound.

While this is not an optimum time to propagate plants, you can root stem cuttings in water any time.

Care for Your Houseplants

Periodically *check* houseplants to be sure their natural shapes are not becoming distorted on one side because they are reaching for the light. *Rotate* their pots every few days to make sure they receive even light.

Keeping the humidity up will help reduce houseplant stress and potential pest problems. While misting with a small sprayer has traditionally been a recommended way to provide humidity, recent research has shown that it is almost useless because the effects last only minutes. These are some more effective ways to increase ambient humidity around plants:

- Set high-humidity lovers in the bathroom or kitchen where the air is more likely to be moist.

- Lower the thermostat. Hot air heat dries out the air.

- Put dishes of water on the floor near heat ducts in rooms where there are houseplants. Refill them regularly.

- Install a humidifier on your furnace.

- Purchase a room humidifier for the hallway to humidify adjacent rooms where plants are located.

- Set up a small sickroom-type humidifier near plants that need more humidity.

- Group plants so they will benefit from mutual transpiration.

- Set plants on shallow trays of small gravel kept barely covered with water.

Watering

If humidity levels are improved, plants will not need watering quite so often, even though the heating system is on. *Check* each plant to determine if the soil has dried down at least an inch before automatically watering it.

If the planting medium dries out nearly completely, it will shrink and pull away from the edges of the pot. *Water* it a little bit at a time to fully saturate the medium. Otherwise, the water may bypass the roots and just pour out the bottom of the pot into the saucer. You might try setting the pot in a saucer of water and letting it absorb it from below for a half-hour or so. Then *empty* the saucer of any remaining water.

Fertilizing

There is no need to fertilize any plants unless they are preparing to bloom.

Grooming

Continue to *clip off* withered leaves and stems. If insects or diseases distort and discolor plant parts, *remove* the parts immediately.

Clip off dead **Palm** fronds. **Caution:** Never pinch back the tips of **Palm** stalks. Their life support systems are located there.

Problem Solving

Mealybugs are a problem for many plants, especially **Gardenias.** They are flattened, off-white ovals about $1/4$ inch long, and their bodies are covered with a thin, textured, waxy coating. They nestle in the crevices where leaves join stems or at the base of buds, and their feeding mars the foliage and stunts the growth of houseplants. Deal with these pests promptly: 1) *Move* affected plants away from healthy ones. 2) *Remove* mealybugs with your fingers or a forceful spray of water. 3) *Spray* major infestations with insecticidal soap or horticultural oil as directed on the product label.

Evergreen plants such as **Norfolk Island Pine, Holly, Ficus,** and others are constantly replacing leaves, so there are likely to be a few fallen leaves to remove from the floor or the surface of the potting medium now and then.

Many plants adjust to lower light levels by dropping their smaller, thicker "sun leaves" and growing new more efficient, larger "shade leaves."

Growing Smarter

Some houseplants that need high humidity:

* **African Violets**
* **Anthuriums**
* **Begonia, Riegers**
* **Bromeliads**
* **Croton**
* **Ferns**
* **Gardenia**
* **Gloxinia**
* **Hydrangea**
* **Ixora**
* **Orchids**
* **Poinsettia**
* **Primrose**
* **Saxafraga**
* **Schefflera**
* **Streptocarpus**

DECEMBER

Planning

Houseplants often take a backseat to seasonal decor this month, including boughs and berries from outdoors and newly arrived seasonal hothouse flowering plants. Often the houseplants are moved to less visible sites, subject to drafts, underwatered, and ignored. Include them in the decorations instead.

- Hang small bird or ball ornaments on treelike large **Citrus, Ficus, Palms,** and **Norfolk Island Pines.**

- Attach bows to stems of **Ivies, Philodendrons,** and **Spider Plants.**

- Decorate pots with ribbons or colored foil.

Houseplant Rule of Thumb: Pinching or clipping off faded flowers stimulates more blooms on flowering plants.

Planting

Pot up any rooted cuttings.

Plant **Paper-white Narcissus** bulbs if you have not already done so (see February). Store them in a cool place to develop roots over the next couple of months.

Care for Your Houseplants

Temporarily move houseplants that may interfere with holiday decorations and activities.

If you purchase new plants, *protect* them from weather shock on the way home from the store. If it is colder than 50 degrees F outdoors, have the store wrap them, and warm up the car ahead of time as well.

Remove or *puncture* the bottoms of foil wrappers of potted gift plants to assure that water will drain freely from their pots into saucers. *Quarantine* newcomers for a few days to make sure they are free of pest and disease problems.

Watering

Watch **Poinsettias** carefully. They may seem fine one minute and horribly wilted from dry soil the next. *Soak* their soil, and let it drain well.

Assure that your houseplants will not suffer if you are away over the holidays. If possible, leave them in their locations so they can continue to enjoy what meager light is available in late December. Entreat a neighbor to check on them. If they must go it alone while you are away:

- *Group* the smaller ones in the kitchen sink or bathtub, water them well, and cover them lightly with clear plastic to maintain humidity and some access to light.

- *Open* curtains and shades to maximize light, and turn down the thermostat.

Grooming

Clip off broken or damaged stems, yellowing leaves, and faded flowers from houseplants to improve their appearance and prevent disease problems.

Problem Solving

Aphids, whiteflies, scale, and mites never quit. Some are from eggs or larvae responding to the indoor heat. Others arrive on holiday gift plants. Treat problems promptly. Wash insects off infested foliage and stems. *Cut off* heavily infested stem tips (they will regenerate). Thoroughly *spray* repeat infestation on plant stems and leaf surfaces with insecticidal soap or a product containing pyrethrum, as directed on its label.

Lawns

Lawns have always been a luxury. Historically, having one's own plot of grass rather than sharing a common "green" with the neighbors symbolized high economic and social status in the community. To maintain the lawn required the services of servants, which came with the elevated status. Today lawns continue to be an emblem of prosperity. They enhance the curb appeal of a home and thus its value. But the servants are gone now. It is now up to homeowners to maintain their lawns, either themselves or by hiring a service.

Lawn care has become America's real national pastime. Through good times and bad over the last half of the 20th Century, homeowners have faithfully mowed, sowed, sprayed, weeded, and fertilized their lawns. Enormous amounts of time, energy, money, and, regrettably, chemicals have been consumed in the process. A drive through any community, however, suggests that after all the work and worry, the prize of a thick, healthy turf continues to elude most homeowners.

Good Soil Makes Good Grass

The key to healthy, vigorous plants, including grass plants, is good soil. Good soil has a light, airy texture because it contains lots of spongy organic matter that helps it hold moisture and drain well. It is alive with millions of microscopic organisms that process nutrients from organic sources in the soil and from fertilizer. Good soil also teems with earthworms, which process organic matter and aerate the soil as they travel.

It is safe to say that most lawns are growing in horrible soil. Builders routinely remove the fertile top layer of soil at a site before they begin construction of new homes. More often than not, they skimp on returning the topsoil, then seed the new lawn on thin, dead soil that has been compacted by heavy construction equipment.

The soil around established homes is also likely to be poor. It has been compacted by years of foot traffic and mowing, and the organic matter in it has long been used up. Grass roots must somehow penetrate this hard, lifeless soil, and they must depend on fertilizer for nutrients.

To reverse the situation, follow these ten steps:

1 **Aerate the soil that your grass grows in.** If soil is to be alive, it must have oxygen for the organisms that live in it. To aerate the soil under living turf, make holes in it so oxygen can get below the soil surface. The best equipment for this is either a core aerating hand tool, which is useful for smaller yards and tight spaces, or a rented core aerating machine for larger yards. Both punch hollow tubes down into the turf and pull up cores of soil, which they deposit on top of the lawn to gradually dissolve in the rain. This one step alone will make an enormous difference in your lawn within a few weeks.

2 **Add organic material to improve the soil's texture.** Sometimes called "humus," it hosts the living organisms in soil. It is the activity of these living organisms that makes soil fertile. The organisms also use up the organic material, so it will need to be replaced periodically. One way is to topdress the lawn by raking a one-inch layer of peat moss, topsoil,

spent mushroom soil, compost, or something similar into the grass. Another way is to leave a layer of chopped leaves on the turf after the last fall mowing with a mulching mower. Always add organic matter when there is an opportunity to work the soil (such as patching or installing a new lawn).

3 Leave the clippings. A mulching mower chops mown grass into very short clippings that fall down easily between the grass plants. These clippings are almost entirely nitrogen, and this natural nitrogen can provide slow, steady nutrition for the grass all season. Collectively, over the entire season, they can supply one-quarter of a lawn's nitrogen requirements.

4 Fertilize at least once a year with a granular, slow-acting product. Grass plants are heavy feeders, requiring lots of nutrients over the growing season. Even the healthiest soil has a hard time keeping up with the demands of a thick turf, so it is important to add supplemental nutrients by spreading a granular (dry) fertilizer every year, either in the spring or fall. Whatever the brand of fertilizer, the nitrogen in it should be mostly "slow-acting," which means it dissolves gradually in

the soil. This is better for the grass and the soil.

5 Spread lime in fall to adjust soil pH. The chemical environment of soil has a lot to do with how well plants can access the nutrients it contains. In Pennsylvania the soil tends to be fairly acidic, and lawn grasses prefer soil that is more alkaline. To alter the chemistry of the soil so it can take better care of the grass (to raise its pH, or "sweeten" it), spread lime over the turf every year or so. Lime also contributes some valuable calcium and magnesium to the soil.

Good Care Makes Good Grass

Fall is the best time to do a lot of the soil-improvement steps outlined above. Meanwhile, a few simple changes in routine lawn maintenance practices during the growing season will have a major impact on grass health and beauty.

1 Cut the grass tall. Keep it at least 2 inches tall—$2^1/2$ inches is even better. Cutting the foliage of grass plants reduces the area of their leaf surface that collects the sunshine necessary to metabolize energy. The more leaf it loses, the more urgent its struggle to quickly replace the

essential foliage, leaving little energy to develop the all-important root systems. Less-stressed, taller grass builds deeper roots that reach water and nutrients more efficiently.

2 Cut the grass properly. Use a sharp mower blade. To minimize stress, never cut more than one-third of the grass blade at one time. This means that to maintain grass at 2 inches tall, you need to mow when it reaches about 3 inches tall. If it is longer than 3 inches, set the mower so that it cuts about one-third of the longer length, then mow a few days later down to 2 inches. Mow when the grass is dry to minimize the possibility of spreading fungal disease.

3 Patch bare spots with seed immediately. Weed seeds are always lurking in soil, and they will germinate before grass can spread to fill in a bare spot. Have some **Perennial Ryegrass** on hand to sprinkle over bare spots any time during the season. Unlike other Northern grasses, it will germinate quickly and withstand heat.

4 Overseed with top-quality seed periodically. Even nice lawns decline, because grass plants eventually age, tire, and

Lawns

thin out. To maintain a lush turf that is dense enough to crowd out weeds, overseed the existing grass with new seed every three or four years in the fall. Introducing new seed into your lawn will upgrade its disease-, drought-, and insect-resistance. Expect to pay a little more for the highest-quality seed—it has been produced with the most modern technology and has the fewest weed seeds.

5 **Choose appropriate grass seed.** Grass seed is usually packaged and sold as a mixture of several varieties of grasses (see Planting Chart). Your local garden center, home center, or hardware store stocks seed appropriate for your part of Pennsylvania. Choose seed labeled for sun if your lawn receives six hours or more of direct sun each day. Choose seed labeled for shade for lawn areas that receive only four to six hours of bright light and/or sun each day. (Their labels notwithstanding, shade grasses still need a fair amount of light, so use ground cover plants instead in truly shady areas under trees.) If your yard doubles as an athletic field, choose a mixture designed for heavy use.

Turfgrasses for Pennsylvania Lawns

Name	Characteristics	Start As	Uses	Problems
Fine Fescues (Chewings, Fine, Hard, Creeping, Red, Sheep)	Very thin blades for fine texture. Tolerates shade best. Tolerates poor soils.	Seed—fall.	Use in mixtures with other turfgrasses. Good for shade and/or dry areas.	Does not recover quickly from damage. Tends to lie flat and cause uneven mowing.
Kentucky Bluegrass	Fine, uniform texture. Excellent color. Repairs itself well under normal use. Full sun best, also light shade.	Seed—fall. Sod—spring or fall.	Areas on display.	Heavy feeder, needs lots of water. Vulnerable to powdery mildew, fungal diseases; chinch bugs, cutworms, grubs, sod webworms.
Perennial Ryegrass	Nice texture and color. Germinates quickly.	Seed—spring, early summer, or fall. Sod—spring, early summer, fall.	Use as "nurse" grass in mixtures. Patch bare spots in summer.	Suffers in extreme heat—may get pythium. Vulnerable to brown patch, red thread, rust, snow mold, dollar spot.
Tall Fescue	Durable, withstands foot traffic. Relatively drought-tolerant. Needs less fertilizer.	Seed—fall. Sod—spring, early summer, or fall	Ideal alone or in mixture for lawns with heavy use, athletic fields, public areas.	Older versions tend to clump. Vulnerable to pythium, brown patch diseases; cutworms, sod webworms, billbugs.
Zoysia	Spreads rapidly and vigorously. Drought-tolerant, resists weeds when established. Is dormant (brown) 8 months of the year.	Plugs or sod in spring.	A warm-climate grass not intended for Pennsylvania climate. Once established, looks good over entire yard during summers.	Chronic heavy thatch buildup. Spreads to the point of being invasive.

Planning

It seems that it's finally okay to take time off from thinking about the lawn. However, January is actually a great time to think about it, about its size and manageability. It is also a good time to maintain and upgrade the equipment you use to care for it. Seeing to this now will reduce the time and effort required to do it during the busy official lawn-care season.

- **Check equipment.** Have your mower blade sharpened during this slow period. Be sure the gasoline is drained from gas-powered engines, the oil is changed, and the sparkplugs are replaced if necessary.

- **Purchase new equipment.** If your mower is an older model, upgrade to a modern mulching model. Consider a battery-rechargeable electric one.

- **Evaluate your property.** If lawn-care chores are growing burdensome, consider reducing the lawn size. Think about the kinds of ground cover plants that would look nice around trees and on slopes where grass now grows. When the weather improves, you might put in a patio or a new growing bed where there is now turf.

Planting

If you did not have a chance to seed some bare patches in the turf last fall, do it now when there is no snow. Seed of cool-weather grasses such as **Kentucky Bluegrass, Perennial Ryegrass,** and **Tall Fescue** don't mind the chill. They will happily wait around until milder late-winter temperatures and moisture stimulate their germination.

Care for Your Lawn

Protective snow cover is not reliable in the eastern and southeastern part of the state, so turfgrasses are vulnerable to some damage from drying winter sun and winds, even though they are dormant. As long as the crown of the grass plant survives, the grass will return in the spring.

Do not walk on frosted or snow-covered lawns. Even though the grass is dormant, ice crystals in crushed plant tissues will damage the plants.

Watering

Since turfgrasses are dormant at this time of year, they can manage on minimal moisture. If rain or snowfall is sparse for over three or four weeks, however, it is a good idea to water the lawn to make sure grass plant crowns—especially those in the direct sun—do not dry out and die.

Fertilizing

If you spread a granular fertilizer product around Thanksgiving, it will be good until June. If you did not, you can spread some now—even on top of snow (in flat areas)—and it will soak in with spring thaw or rains. A granular, slow-acting product will last for many weeks over the spring and into early summer.

Problem Solving

Compaction of the soil under lawns is a problem any time of year. The soil under lawns that are semi-soggy with melting snow for weeks on end is even more vulnerable. Foot traffic compresses the soil particles, expelling the air that is essential to fertile soil. When it dries out, the soil is so hard that grass roots can barely penetrate. Discourage everyone, including the mail carrier, from cutting across the lawn.

Planning

Reminder: Take the lawn mower and other lawn-care equipment to the dealer for servicing while it is the slow period. In a few short weeks the dealer will not have time for you.

One of the advantages of cool weather–loving grasses such as **Kentucky Bluegrass** is that they often hold their green color a bit during their dormant period in the wintertime. In areas that do not have reliable snow cover all winter, the green redeems an otherwise bleak landscape. If you notice patches or expanses of beige, dried-looking grass in your lawn, that is probably a warm weather–lover, **Zoysia** grass from a neighbor's lawn. **Zoysia** is an invasive grass and will take over other turfgrasses unless its progress is checked. Decide whether you want to eradicate it in the spring before it spreads farther.

Planting

If the ground is not frozen, you can *lay sod* on prepared bare spots in the lawn. Keep it moist. As soon as temperatures moderate, the sod grass roots will begin to grow in soil moistened by winter thaw.

Care for Your Lawn

Do not walk on lawn that is frosted or snow-covered. Not only does it compact the soil, but ice crystals in grass foliage tear its membranes when they are crushed, and snow packed around crowns of plants promotes disease.

Make sure that de-icing salt does not run onto turf areas. While it may be unavoidable along the curb if that is what the municipal plows use on the streets, use non-salt alternatives on sidewalks, drives, and patios on your property.

Watering

Even though the grass is dormant, it still needs some moisture. If there has been no rain or snow for more than four weeks during the winter and the ground is not frozen, *water* the grass—particularly grass newly sown last fall.

Fertilizing

Lawn grass is still dormant. Because it is not actively growing, it has no need for supplemental nutrition over and above what is already in the soil.

Problem Solving

Snow mold is a term for two fungal diseases that occur in turfgrass that suffers prolonged cold, wet conditions or compacted snow cover in winter. After spring thaw, patches up to 2 feet in diameter may be covered with a white or gray fungus or matted, dead grass that is pink in color. More easily prevented than cured, the best defense against this disease is a good offense. In the fall, remove any thatch that is more than $1/4$ inch thick. Avoid overdosing the grass on nitrogen late in the season, and cut the lawn no taller than 2 inches. With the onset of winter, initiate a "no walking on the lawn" policy, and do not pile shoveled snow into large mountains on the lawn. The disease will subside when warm weather arrives.

Planning

Although the lawn is probably still dormant, this will not be true for much longer. It's time, then, to service the gasoline-powered lawn mower. By now the dealer may be overloaded with work, so you can do it yourself:

1. *Remove and discard* the sparkplug.

2. Uncover the engine, and *clean off* any accumulated gunk and grass clippings from the fan and engine parts.

3. If the gas tank was not emptied for winter storage, *drain* it now. Leave it empty while you tip over the mower to access the blade.

4. *Remove* the blade for sharpening. Re-install it, or install a new one.

5. *Replace* the fuel filter, and clean or replace the air filter.

6. *Drain* the oil from the crankcase (in 4-cycle engines), and refill it with fresh oil.

7. *Fill* the gas tank with fresh gasoline (and oil if a 2-cycle engine).

8. *Install* a new sparkplug.

Planting

If temperatures are mild and the soil is not too wet, patch bare spots in the lawn with either pieces of sod cut to fit, or seed. Take the time to *prepare* the soil by pulling any weeds, and trimming the grass at the edges of the spot if necessary. Loosen the bare soil, and *scratch in* some granular, slow-acting fertilizer. Smooth the soil, then sow seed or lay sod, pressing either into the seedbed a bit to establish contact with the soil. *Water* these areas daily if spring rains are insufficient to keep them constantly moist.

Care for Your Lawn

If your lawn has chronic annual weed problems such as crabgrass and chickweed, consider using a pre-emergent herbicide this year. Pre-emergents kill seeds before they germinate. An environmentally safe type made from corn gluten also contributes some fertilizer in the process. Because many pre-emergent products do not distinguish between "good" seeds and "bad" seeds, do not plan to reseed areas of the lawn on which you have spread this herbicide for several weeks. Have the herbicide down before the **Forsythia** is in full bloom in your area. Follow the directions on the package label carefully. Do not spike or aerate the turf afterward.

If your soil is acidic and you forgot to lime the lawn last fall, look for a liquid lime product. Faster-acting than the traditional granular or powered products, it will modify soil pH relatively quickly—in time to get the lawn off to a good start this spring.

Watering

Spring can usually be depended on to bring adequate rainfall to support turfgrasses that are emerging from dormancy. If this spring is dry, *water* the grass so it can get growing. Established grass needs deep watering because its roots are deep, but young grass plants newly planted last fall do not need quite so much water. Keep newly sown seed or new sod in patched bare spots moist.

Fertilizing

If you did not spread fertilizer last fall or winter, *spread* a granular, slow-acting product this month, toward the end of the month. Depending on the number of weeks listed on the label, it might last until midsummer. If you did spread slow-acting fertilizer last fall or winter, it will begin to kick in this month and will last until early summer. A synthetic, slow-acting fertilizer may also have a small proportion of water-soluble nitrogen, which will jumpstart grass growth—then the slow-acting type of nitrogen will take over for the longer haul.

Drop-type (Gravity) Spreader

Growing Smarter

The best way to discourage weeds in the lawn is to encourage thick, dense turf to crowd and shade them out. Your lawn-care practices can do the job.

1 Build fertile, loose soil by topdressing the lawn with organic matter. Core aerate periodically so grass roots can grow deep and support tall, healthy grass plants.

2 To keep lawn grass vigorous, overseed existing turf with new seed every couple of years.

3 Mow tall so grass foliage will shade the soil and deny weed seeds the light they need to germinate.

4 Deal with young weeds promptly, before they spread by runners, or flower and set seed.

5 After weeds die, patch bare spots with sod or seed to prevent new weeds.

Mowing

In all but the warmest areas in Pennsylvania, turfgrasses are still dormant and will not need mowing for a few more weeks. Before the grass grows to 3 inches or more, however, a light mowing early in the season will remove frayed foliage tips and stimulate growth. Remember, if you fertilize with a fast-acting (water-soluble) fertilizer this season, you will have to mow quite frequently in early spring as the grass responds to the sudden, rich nitrogen diet.

Problem Solving

Annual weeds that have been allowed to go to seed in the lawn in the fall leave lots of seeds behind when they die, and they will germinate later in the spring. Either deal with them now by using a pre-emergent herbicide, or wait until they sprout. Once weed seedlings are green and growing, either *pull* them up, or *spot-treat* them with a spritz of herbicide spray just as you would the perennial weeds such as oxalis or plantain. Try to avoid routine broad applications of general herbicides over the entire lawn.

Dandelions seem to appear earlier every year. Be prepared with a strategy. Either treat them as an edible crop and harvest the leaves for salads and wine, or resolve to *pull* or *spray* them before they develop their trademark fuzzy seedheads and proliferate.

Planning

Don't let the new lawn-care season sneak up on you. Check the mower, string trimmer, rakes, and other equipment. Have slow-acting fertilizer and other supplies on hand so you can take advantage of the arrival of real spring weather. Cool-weather grasses glory in the early spring weather, just as we do. They seem to green up suddenly—over a weekend, almost.

Take time to look over some of the gardening and lawn-care catalogs that turn up in the mail. This is a good way to become familiar with new developments in products and equipment. If you are having trouble finding an organic lawn fertilizer, a certain pesticide, or a hand aerating tool, many mail-order firms offer such products.

Planting

Sow grass seed as early as possible so it will have maximum time to develop roots before the heat arrives in June. The best grass for spring sowing is **Perennial Ryegrass** because it germinates in only four or five days, giving seedlings a head start on maturity. Other cool-climate grasses take two weeks or more to germinate; they are still so young by June that they often shrivel up in the first heat wave.

If the lawn looks sparse:

1   To hold you over the summer, ***overseed*** temporarily with **Perennial Rye,** then plan to do a thorough lawn renovation in the fall.

OR

2   ***Lay sod.*** This is a much more elaborate undertaking, but it will give you a marvelous instant lawn. Spring rains will help with the watering chores for awhile, but it will be up to you to provide most of the critical moisture while the sod establishes during the summer. (See September Planting for steps.)

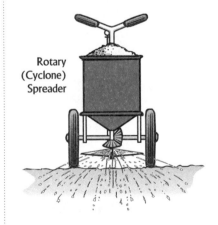

Rotary (Cyclone) Spreader

Care for Your Lawn

It is never too early to begin weed control. ***Handpick*** young weeds when the soil is moist, pulling them carefully so the entire root system is dislodged. If the ground is not compacted, even stubborn perennial weeds will come out when they are young.

Until the soil has dried out, ***limit*** lawn work to picking up sticks and raking dead leaves and other debris. Constant foot traffic on soggy soil compacts it and deprives grass roots of oxygen.

Watering

If rainfall is scarce, keep newly sown seed continually moist with frequent light sprinklings. ***Water*** new seedlings enough that the moisture penetrates the soil a few inches to encourage deep root growth.

Water newly laid sod very generously. The moisture must be sufficient to penetrate beyond the mat of grass and roots and into the soilbed where the roots must take hold. Watch the edges of the sod—they dry out quickly.

Fertilizing

If you already spread a slow-acting granular fertilizer in late fall or winter, there is no need to do so again until May or June.

If you are planning a program of repeat fertilizations with fast-acting fertilizer, the first application will be sometime this month, depending on where you live. *Check* the product label for exact timing and amounts. *Do not overdo.* Grass plants soak up water-soluble fertilizer as they take up moisture through their roots, and foliage greens up rapidly as the grass absorbs the readily available nitrogen, prompting rapid growth.

To minimize stress on lawns from periodic rich doses of nitrogen followed by a dropoff of its availability, strive to *maintain* the fertilizing schedule suggested by the product manufacturer. This may mean three or more applications over the season. The more consistent the nutrition, the less stress on grass. The less stress it experiences, the more resistant it will be to pests and diseases.

Mowing

The lawn-mowing season typically begins sometime this month. Set your mower blade at about 2 inches for the first cut, then raise it to cut at 2 1/2 or 3 inches as the weather warms. The longer grass will shade and cool the soil and prevent the sun from getting to weed seeds. Here are some mowing tips to assure healthy grass:

1 Mow dry. This will assure a more uniform cut. Dry clippings fall into turf rather than mat in clumps, and there will be less chance of promoting and spreading fungal disease.

2 Mow sharp. Dull blades bruise grass foliage and fray their tips, permitting loss of moisture, entry for disease, stress, and a brownish appearance.

3 Mow often. Do not allow the grass to get so tall that you cut more than 1/3 of its foliage at any one time—having to replace more than 1/3 of the foliage stresses grass plants. In the spring grass grows quickly, so expect to mow more often. Later in the season growth will slow.

Problem Solving

Thatch typically develops in all lawns over time. Some grass varieties seem to develop it more quickly than others. A thin layer is not a problem, but as the layer thickens it will threaten the health of the grass plants. Thatch is composed of the roots and crowns of grass plants near the surface of the soil that have died—often because compacted soil has prevented their access to air and nutrition. They trap other lawn debris and gradually build up a thick mat on the soil around the live grass plants. This mat blocks moisture from the soil and harbors pests and disease spores. It also blocks the air that is necessary for the accumulated organic debris to decompose and become part of the soil. Sometimes grass clippings are visible on top of the thatch, but they are *not* the cause of the problem. To deal with severe thatch problems:

- *Remove* thatch mechanically with a power rake or dethatching tool.

- *Remove* thatch biologically with an enzyme product.

- *Core aerate* the lawn every couple of years to break up the soil and the thatch layer.

- *Topdress* the lawn with a thin layer of organic material to improve the microbial activity in the soil so it can break down debris.

- Lightly *spread* lime or even beer (1 pint per 500 square feet diluted with a thorough watering) over the lawn.

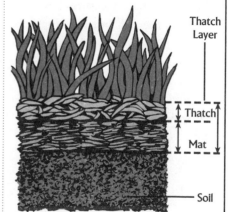

Thatch Layer

Thatch

Mat

Soil

Planning

Your lawn-care goal in the spring is to help grass plants develop deep roots so they can withstand the coming heat and possible droughty periods. If they are able to access moisture deep in the soil, they can handle longer periods without rain. So, again, the key to healthy, vigorous lawns is healthy soil. If it is loose it will have air in it. If it has air in it, it will allow roots to penetrate deeply and will also support lots of microbial life, which will turn raw materials into nutrients for those roots. This season, plan to:

- *Aerate* the soil.

- *Topdress* with organic material to improve microbial activity.

- *Mow tall* so energy is available to grow roots instead of to constantly replace foliage.

- *Water* deeply and infrequently.

- *Use* slow-acting fertilizer.

Most of these measures are best taken in the fall, but mowing happens almost every week. Your grass will become healthier because of the improved soil, and the lawn will require less maintenance, as the soil will do some of the work you used to do.

By this time all the neighbors' lawns are looking green and healthy except, perhaps, for one or two that are still a golden beige. These lawns are not dead; they are still dormant. They are planted with a warm weather–loving turfgrass called **Zoysia** grass. A very dense, fine-textured grass, it was developed for use in the South where warm weather persists over many months. Here in the North it loves the summer but goes dormant at the first hint of chill, and is brown nearly nine months out of the year.

Planting

Where grass seed is needed to fill in bare spots in the turf, *plant* **Perennial Ryegrass** early this month at the latest. It is the only cool-weather grass that has a chance of surviving the impending onset of summer heat in many areas of Pennsylvania. If planted immediately, it will germinate quickly enough to develop sufficient roots before heat comes in late June in the southeastern part of the state and soon after statewide.

Care for Your Lawn

Although the season is rapidly advancing toward summer, it is still okay to aerate the lawn if soil has dried somewhat. Do it soon, or wait until fall if you are planning a major lawn renovation then. A good way to start improving the soil is to *topdress* the lawn with a thin layer of compost or mushroom soil, then core aerate. Rent a power aerator or use a simple mechanical one, (and do a small area every few days) until you cover the turf that needs work. Make many holes—the lawn should look thoroughly chewed up. Leave the soil cores on the ground to break down in the next rain. You will see improvement in the lawn in a month or less.

If there are areas in the lawn that get unusual wear, do what the golf course managers do and *spike* the turf and soil in those spots. Do this every couple of weeks to prevent soil compaction and the formation of bare spots and paths. Use a compost or spading fork to punch deep holes in moist soil to let in air for grass roots (the spikes on golf shoes are not long enough for this task).

Watering

If you have seeded or sodded certain areas, *do not* let the soil there dry out. As it gets warmer, these areas may require two sprinklings a day if it does not rain. Established turfgrass can go ten days without rain or watering if its soil is decent.

MAY

Fertilizing

If you have not spread fertilizer since last September, choose a product that has some fast-acting (water-soluble) nitrogen for rapid greenup to get grass going, as well as a large proportion of slow-acting nitrogen to maintain uniform, consistent nutrition over many weeks. Spread it as directed on the product label.

Mowing

After the first mowing or two, *raise* the blade on the mower to 2½ or 3 inches. **Cut tall** so the grass will have maximum foliage to produce energy for its spring growth spurt during the last of the cool weather it loves. When it gets warmer, grass this tall will shade the soil to discourage weed seed germination and keep soil cool. It looks greener, too.

Growing Smarter

One of the best ways to keep grass green and healthy is to make sure your mower blade is sharp. Sharp blades cut grass foliage cleanly rather than bludgeon its tips. A dull mower blade will fray the tips of the grass, and the tips will turn brown and unsightly. The ragged tips also promote moisture loss and offer a way for disease to enter the foliage. With clean cuts, the tips heal more quickly.

Problem Solving

Ants may be obvious now because it is their time to swarm. They are basically beneficial for lawns because they feed on pest insect eggs and help control lawn pest populations. Ants normally nest at the edges of the lawn in a stone wall or near pavement. From there they venture into the lawn on pest patrol. When ants become a problem— their little hills are turning up all through the lawn—that is a signal that the soil is poor and needs restoring. If your lawn has not experienced extensive pest problems in the past, **do not** spray or spread broad-spectrum pesticides. They will kill the resident beneficial ants and ground spiders who are allies in pest control.

Weeds have a growth spurt in spring too, sometimes overtaking grass and crowding it out. Try to **pull** them when you see them, a few at a time, and stay on top of the situation. Catch them before they go to seed. Even if you used pre-emergent herbicide in the early spring, expect that some weeds will always appear. Many blow into the yard or are brought by birds and other wildlife; if they find bare soil, they will sprout.

Broadleaf Weed: Dandelion

Planning

In the warmest areas of Pennsylvania, the great lawn days will soon be over. They will not return until fall. Cool-weather turfgrasses such as **Kentucky Bluegrass, Tall Fescue,** and **Perennial Ryegrass** look their very best when temperatures are cool—daytimes in the 70s and nighttimes in the 50s and 60s. In the spring and in the fall when these temperatures prevail, these grasses do their serious growing. They send roots deep into moist soil and launch stems outward to spread for denser turf. Aided and abetted by late fall/winter fertilizer or an early spring application, these grasses have been growing lots of foliage to enable them to produce the energy necessary to support their rapid growth. This has meant frequent mowing.

The spring growth spurt will stall now, as soon as heat and humidity arrive. Grass will need less-frequent mowing and will depend on the vigor it has developed so far to help it withstand the harsh summer conditions. If you have improved the soil, the grass will need less maintenance during the summer months—improved soil will provide nutrients and hold moisture.

Planting

Patching bare spots in the lawn caused by wear or by weeds that have since been removed is about the only grass planting that will succeed during the summer. Fill any bare area that is larger than a saucer (roughly 8 inches in diameter) with grass, or weeds will rapidly move in and take over. *Prepare* the soil, then sow seed or cut a measured piece of sod that fits the space.

Care for Your Lawn

Fight the development of thin spots that become bare paths in the turf. Periodically *spike* areas that get extra wear as a result of foot traffic or water from downspouts or construction or maintenance equipment. To prevent compaction, poke holes down 3 or 4 inches into the soil to let in air.

Watering

In recent summer-drought years, reduced rainfall actually began in early spring, but it was not immediately obvious that a real drought had begun until late June, when homeowners began to realize their lawns were suffering. Even under normal conditions, cool-weather grasses need lots of moisture to stay green in the summer. Their natural inclination is to deal with heat by going dormant. To help them manage during the summer, encourage them to grow deep roots so they can still get moisture way down in the soil when rainfall is scarce. Make sure that thatch is not preventing moisture from penetrating the soil.

Water established lawns in decent soil only when it has not rained for over a week or ten days. Then water deeply. Lawns in poor soil will dry out much sooner.

Water new sod or young seedlings daily until they are established. Keep an eye on these areas if rainfall is sparse or temperatures heat up ahead of schedule.

Fertilizing

If you used a fast-acting, water-soluble fertilizer product on the lawn in the spring, it will probably be time to repeat the application before June is over. It is important that nitrogen continues to be available to the grass. Slow-acting fertilizer spread on the lawn in the spring is still on the job and should last anywhere from ten to sixteen weeks, depending on the product. *Check* the package label.

Never fertilize lawns that are already stressed by drought or heat. Either *skip* the fast-acting dose, or wait until the weather breaks and use it at partial strength. Follow the directions on the package label carefully.

Mowing

Unless there is generous rainfall, you will be mowing less often now that warmer weather is slowing grass growth. Make sure your mower blade is set at 2$\frac{1}{2}$ or 3 inches so the grass will not brown out in the summer sun.

Alter your mowing pattern to minimize wear on the turf. Mow in horizontal rows one week, in vertical rows the next, and in diagonal rows the third week.

Problem Solving

White grubs, larvae of Japanese and other beetles, have migrated closer to the surface from deep in the soil where they had burrowed to escape frost. This month they are feeding on grass roots as they prepare to develop into their beetle stage and emerge from the soil into

Growing Smarter

There are several good reasons to mow your lawn tall:

- Tall grass grows more slowly because it does not need to replace so much foliage, which is essential to metabolism.
- Tall grass needs less water because it shades the soil, minimizing evaporation of moisture.
- Tall grass needs less fertilizer because it has more leaf surface to capture sunlight and produce its own food.
- Tall grass reduces weed problems because it prevents sunlight from reaching weed seeds in the soil.
- Tall grass has fewer pest and disease problems because it is less stressed.
- Tall grass shelters beneficial spiders and ants that feed on pest insect eggs and larvae.
- Tall grass discourages Japanese beetles from laying their eggs in the lawn, so it helps control white grubs.

the air. Patches of grass will become browned and die, and the grass will pull up out of the soil easily because the roots are gone. Healthy lawns can handle a fair number of grubs and will not be harmed, because grass roots are thick and deep. Thin lawns show serious damage from even minor grub activity. Be suspicious if you see flocks of starlings on your lawn: they feed on white grubs.

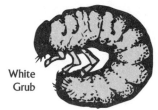

White Grub

Early this month is a good time to spread a grub-control product. Try using a biological one featuring predatory nematodes or milky spore (*Bacillus popilliae*), a bacterium that kills soil-dwelling beetle larvae. Both give fairly long-term control. Follow the directions on the product label carefully.

Planning

Plan to have someone mow your lawn if you are going to be away on vacation for more than two weeks. Although grass grows more slowly in hot weather, after ten to fourteen days it will begin to look neglected and reveal that no one is at home.

As pest or disease problems appear in the lawn over the summer, give some thought to developing a long-term strategy for preventing these problems. Rather than simply treating them each year, year after year, why not deal with the underlying causes and try to prevent them? The first step is to make some notes about problems that develop—the time of year, the location, the symptoms—to determine if they are chronic. If so, it may be time to change the grass variety to one more resistant to the disease, or to topdress more often to improve grass root systems. Consider keeping a lawn notebook or journal to help you track your lawn-care activities.

Reminder: This is a good time to sharpen your mower blade again.

Planting

Heat is the enemy of new plantings of any kind. Seed of cool-weather grass varieties does not have a chance to really thrive, even if it germinates and starts to grow. If you need to fill a bare spot to prevent the inevitable opportunistic weeds from taking over, use sod. *Water* well and often until the roots establish down in the soil.

Care for Your Lawn

There is not much to do once summer heat arrives except mow the lawn. Be sure to leave the clippings when you mow (unless you have waited way too long and the clippings are so long that they clump). They will decompose rapidly because they are mostly water. To minimize soil compaction, *avoid walking* on the lawn. Grass is likely to be stressed now, so do not aerate, fertilize, or treat for pest and disease problems while it struggles with heat, humidity, and possible drought.

Watering

Now that summer is in full swing everywhere in the state, cool-weather turfgrasses suffer unavoidable stress if they lack regular moisture. (**Zoysia,** however, a Southern grass and warm-weather fan, finally comes into its own after sulking as a beige carpet since last September.)

Water lawns of cool-weather grasses every ten days or so if it does not rain regularly. To encourage grass to develop deep roots and therefore some drought resistance, *water* deeply—soak down at least 6 or 8 inches—then do not water again for another ten days to two weeks. Compacted or clay soil may require a pause between watering sessions to allow the water to soak into the soil and avoid wasteful runoff.

Resist the temptation to "sprinkle" the grass daily. This encourages grass roots to stay near the surface, promoting thatch buildup. Having foliage wet all the time may cause fungal disease problems.

Fertilizing

Even though you may not be actually spreading a fertilizer product, you are providing nutrition to the lawn when you leave the clippings every time you mow. Over the season, their accumulated nitrogen represents fully $1/4$ of the annual nitrogen needs of your grass, and the clippings break down into organic matter that improves the soil.

If you used a lawn-fertilizer product with fast-acting water-soluble nitrogen in the spring, it is time to repeat the fertilization to maintain reasonably consistent nitrogen levels and avoid stressing the cool-climate grasses. Wait until severe heat subsides, *dilute* it to half-strength, and *water it in* deeply.

Mowing

Continue to mow often enough to remove only ⅓ of the length of the grass blade each time. Keep the mower blade at 3 inches to help grass plants withstand heat and possible drought. If you have **Zoysia,** it can be mowed at 2 or 2½ inches tall.

Problem Solving

Japanese beetles emerge from the soil around the Fourth of July weekend in the warm region around Philadelphia. They are likely to appear elsewhere within two weeks or so. (Most insects are amazingly punctual, appearing in a given place at almost the same time every year.) While they do not eat and destroy grass foliage the way they do the foliage of other plants, it is important to control the adult beetles.

Growing Smarter

Three ways to tell if your grass is thirsty:

1 The grass wilts and acquires a bluish tinge, and the edges of the blades start to curl or fold.

2 The soil is hard and resists insertion of a screwdriver.

3 Footprints where grass is crushed from walking on it remain for several hours instead of regaining their upright posture within a short time.

Remember—brown tips do not indicate drought stress. They are a result of a dull mower blade, which frays the tips. Sharpen your blade.

Prevent them from laying eggs in the lawn; the eggs will produce white grubs, which do harm grass. Watch for the early arrivals and *pick them off* plants they are known to frequent, such as **Roses, Raspberries,** and tender annuals. Brush them into a jar of soapy water or a plastic bag to seal and put in the trash. Keep grass tall to discourage their laying eggs. Do not use bag traps with scented lures; they are so effective they actually entice more beetles into your yard from the surrounding neighborhood, and not all of them end up in the bag.

Weeds will need spot treatment. *Spray* individual, tough perennial weeds such as thistle, plantain, and dandelion. Use a product such as Roundup® that travels to the roots and kills them. Unless you destroy their roots, weeds will regrow. *Spot-treat* annual weeds with a herbicide that desiccates foliage. Those made from fatty acids of soap work quickly and safely. Try to deal with weeds before they go to seed.

Sod webworm activity in the grass is often signaled by the presence of small moths flitting above the turf. They are laying eggs that will hatch into larvae (caterpillars) later in the season. Watch for them on trees and shrubs in the fall.

Sod Webworm

Planning

In the typical lawn, disease problems begin to show up this month. That is partly because the typical lawn is growing in poor soil, and partly because the weather is so harsh that the grass is now stressed to its limits. Old grass plants die from exhaustion. New ones shrivel in the heat. Many grasses develop fungal infections from the extremes of weather. Uncontrolled weeds rapidly move in to exploit their opportunity to fill bare ground.

If your lawn has all these problems, a major lawn overhaul will be necessary to prevent its total collapse. If only one or two problems exist, then some remedial measures such as overseeding or aerating may turn things around. In any case, nothing can be done until around Labor Day weekend, except to plan.

Inspect your lawn carefully to identify its problems. Plan your fall lawn rehabilitation program now, and buy supplies so they will be on hand. The earlier you start, the more time the lawn will have to establish before hard frost arrives. Many regions of Pennsylvania enjoy prolonged, mild autumn weather, which cool-weather grasses prefer. They can use this time to great advantage to grow deep roots and develop strong constitutions.

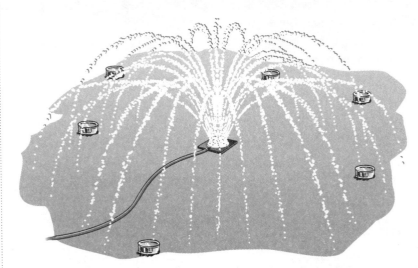

Measuring 1 Inch of Water

Planting

In most of Pennsylvania it is too hot and probably too dry to do any major lawn work. It is best to wait until after Labor Day. In the cooler, zone 5 regions upstate, however, mid-August marks the beginning of prime time for overseeding existing lawns or installing new lawns with seed or sod of cool-climate grasses (**Kentucky Bluegrass, Perennial Rye,** and **Tall Fescue**). Decide if this is a project you will do yourself, or if you will hire someone to do it for you. The size of your lawn has a lot to do with that decision. Sodding is more difficult to perform than seeding (see steps in September).

Care for Your Lawn

If the summer has featured prolonged drought, the best thing for cool-weather grasses is to allow them to go dormant. Not only will this save valuable water, but it is healthier for the grass. It is natural for grasses to deal with heat and water deprivation by turning brown, and they will actually survive better than if you try to keep them watered. Sprinklers and hoses water inadequately and intermittently, causing more stress for grass plants that they prevent. When normal rainfall resumes, they will green up in a matter of days. (Warm-weather **Zoysia** will probably need some water, but it is naturally able to handle the heat better.)

Watering

Water grass deeply if there is no significant rainfall for two weeks or if it indicates by a bluish tinge and curled blades that it is suffering. The quality of the soil in which grass plants are growing will determine how long they can go between waterings. In good soil, grass will have long roots that can find moisture deep in the soil. In poor soil, grass roots will be near the surface and dry out quickly.

Fertilizing

Delay any fertilizing until next month when summer temperatures moderate. It is okay to wait until even later in the fall.

Mowing

Continue to *mow tall*. Taller grass shades the soil to minimize evaporation of moisture, and it is likely to have deeper roots. Leave clippings as usual.

Problem Solving

White grubs can be treated now as a followup to Japanese beetle–control methods used in July. Spiking the soil kills grubs newly hatched from the beetle eggs while they are still near the soil surface. An effective long-term alternative is to *spray* predatory nematodes (**Steinernema carpocapsae**) on the turf. Active in soil above 75 degrees F, these microscopic worms enter the soil on droplets of moisture and parasitize the grubs over successive generations. Use as directed on the product label.

Fungal diseases can strike any time, but they are the most troublesome problem of lawns at this time of year. While most thrive in moist conditions, certain ones prefer dry conditions, so some infection is almost inevitable. Sometimes infected areas appear as a gray powdery coating on a patch of grass foliage. At other times, patches of lawn, especially those areas in full sun, seem to melt away—if there is no sign of pest insect infestation, it is a fungal infection. *Protect* nearby healthy grass from infection by spraying its foliage with a fungicide product such as wettable sulfur labeled for use on lawns. *Avoid* walking on the lawn, if possible, to minimize spreading the infection. A change in the weather will eventually eliminate the fungus. Some grass varieties are more prone to certain fungal diseases than others. *Overseed* with a mixture of several types of grass, so that each contributes resistance to the various turfgrass fungal diseases.

Crabgrass plants that have escaped your scrutiny all summer will form seeds this month. Mow with a bag attachment to catch the seeds with the grass clippings, and *dispose* of them in the trash to minimize problems next season. The plants will die when frost comes, because crabgrass is an annual plant. If seeds have proliferated, plan to spread pre-emergent herbicide next spring.

Growing Smarter

Leaving clippings is one of the best things you can do for your lawn. Modern mulching mowers are designed with roomy bells that suspend clippings in the air while the blade cuts them several times. They are small enough to fall down among the grass blades and avoid clumping. Because clippings are mostly water, they decompose very quickly, releasing nitrogen as they do, and they also provide a bit of organic material. While they do not create thatch, an existing thatch problem in your lawn will retard the breakdown of the clippings and make them more visible.

SEPTEMBER

Planning

Traditionally, Labor Day weekend opens the window of opportunity for major lawn-repair work. If sown or sodded at this time, the cool-climate grasses that are appropriate for Pennsylvania will still have warm weather for germination, then several increasingly cool weeks to develop strong root systems before the ground freezes.

The key to a healthy lawn is healthy soil, and this month is also ideal for upgrading your soil various ways. Plan to do the bulk of the work in the next week or two.

Planting

Overseed an existing lawn to thicken and invigorate it:

1 *Spot-treat* patches of weeds in the lawn with Roundup® about ten days ahead.

2 *Mow* the grass as short as possible without scraping crowns of existing grass plants.

3 *Collect* grass blades and litter to expose the soil between grass plants.

4 *Sow* a premium seed mixture with a hand or mechanical spreader onto the bare soil.

5 [*Optional*] Cover the seedbed with garden fleece or straw mulch, or roll it with a roller.

6 *Water* to keep the seed moist for maximum germination.

7 *Mow* when the new grass seedlings and the existing grass exceed 3 inches in height.

Seed a completely new lawn that is thin, tired, and weed-infested:

1 Either *remove* the sod or kill all existing grass with Roundup®, and wait about ten days.

2 *Add* organic material such as compost, peat moss, or high-quality topsoil to the soil and rake, rototill, or aerate to mix in.

3 *Smooth* the soil to make a seedbed, then water it to germinate weed seeds that surfaced when the soil was disturbed.

4 *Kill* the weeds with Roundup®, and wait a week to ten days.

5 *Sow* a premium seed mixture according to package directions. *Water* to keep seeds constantly moist.

6 [*Optional*] Mulch the seedbed with straw or fabric, or roll it with a roller.

7 *Mow* when the grass seedlings exceed 3 inches in height.

Lay sod for an instant new lawn to replace a thin, weedy turf.

1 *Remove* the existing lawn sod to expose the bare soil beneath.

2 *Prepare* the soilbed as described above. Mix in organic material to improve soil quality, and add granular, slow-acting fertilizer.

3 Smooth and level the soilbed. *Moisten* it the evening before you lay the sod.

4 *Select* sod grown from a premium mixture of cool-weather grasses. Have it delivered the morning it is to be laid.

5 *Lay* strips of sod, beginning along the edges of paved walks or driveways and snugging the edges of the sod pieces close together. *Stagger* the seams as illustrated below.

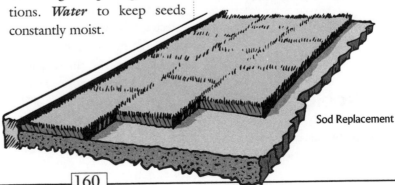

Sod Replacement

6 *Roll* the completed tapestry of sod strips with a roller filled to $1/3$ with water to assure good contact with the soilbed.

7 *Water* well and often to soak the soilbed below grass roots. Pay particular attention to the seams, which will dry out first.

8 *Avoid* walking on newly sodded areas for three or four weeks.

Growing Smarter

There are some advantages to using sod when installing a brand-new lawn:

- *instant* green, weed-free lawn
- can be done almost anytime during the growing season
- no erosion problems on slopes
- smothers weed seeds on bare soil
- no need for followup seeding next year

There are some advantages to using seed when installing a brand-new lawn:

- less expensive
- easier to do yourself
- wider choice of grass varieties
- covers a larger area faster

Care for Your Lawn

Seed care: Mulching newly seeded areas helps improve the germination rate of newly sown seed. A layer of straw or a cover of white, polyspun garden fabric will discourage birds and help prevent erosion from heavy rain. These mulches hold in heat and moisture to speed growth and reduce watering frequency.

Soil care: *Every fall*, topdress the lawn with organic material such as peat moss, or leaves mulched into the turf with a mulching mower. *Every year or two*, thoroughly core aerate your lawn to reduce soil compaction and thatch problems and stimulate soil microbial life. Leave the cores of soil on the lawn to dissolve in the rain.

Watering

Water newly seeded areas so the seeds stay moist continuously. As sprouts grow into seedlings, water deeply to encourage their roots to stretch downward.

Water newly sodded lawns deeply so the water soaks into the soilbed below. If it is hot and there is no rain, you may have to water twice a day.

Fertilizing

For a newly seeded or over-seeded lawn, you might use a seed-starter lawn fertilizer product at sowing time as directed on the package label. Oherwise, wait a few weeks and spread a granular, slow-acting fertilizer when the young grass plants are about 3 or 4 inches tall.

Mowing

Continue to *mow* grass at 3 inches until the weather cools. Put clippings in the compost pile (if they are not contaminated with weed seeds or don't contain pesticide residues).

Problem Solving

If **mildew** has been a problem over several seasons, *overseed* the affected parts of the lawn with grass varieties that are labeled as mildew-resistant. They will thrive and eventually supercede the susceptible grass.

Planning

This is prime time for all lawns. Existing ones respond to the cooling temperatures with renewed enthusiasm. As their foliage prepares for dormancy, they are able to divert their energy to growing and repairing roots. New and renovated lawns become greener and healthier daily as the cool-weather grasses revel in the increasingly cooler weather. A long, languid fall is just the thing for seedlings of **Kentucky Bluegrass, Tall Fescue,** and **Perennial Ryegrass** newly planted last month. The goal is to have them well rooted before a heavy frost freezes the soil.

There is no time like the fall to begin to record in a journal or notebook your ongoing lawn-care adventures, if you have not already done so.

- *Record* when you lime, aerate, topdress, or install a new lawn.

- Each time you purchase and sow a turfgrass seed mixture, keep the label for future reference.

- Note when you purchased and serviced your mower and when you sharpened the blade.

Planting

In many parts of the state it is getting past time to plant new grass by mid-month. There is not enough time before serious frost and cold weather for grass seedlings to establish enough to survive the winter. Lawns in areas without snow cover are exposed to harsh wind and sun, too.

Care for Your Lawn

One of the problems with brand-new seedlings at this time is that falling leaves from deciduous trees can crush and smother the new, young plants. It is trickier to remove the leaves without damaging the seedlings' tender stems than it is to remove them from an established lawn.

Rake or blow fallen leaves from newly sodded or established lawns—do this frequently so that leaves will not mat and smother the grass. To avoid promoting fungal disease, do not allow leaves to accumulate for any length of time, especially if they are wet.

Turfgrasses prefer soil that is less acid and more toward neutral than most other cultivated plants like. In most regions of Pennsylvania the soil is naturally on the more acidic side, so spread lime on the lawn in the fall to temporarily reduce acidity and "sweeten" the soil for turfgrasses. Granular and powdered lime products take many months to dissolve and change soil chemistry, so do the job this month or next month to benefit next spring.

Warning: Do not spread lime at the same time you fertilize. Wait a month or more between these projects, or delay fertilization until late winter or early spring.

One way to provide some organic material to improve the soil under your turf is to mow the last of the leaf fall with the mulching mower. The finely cut leaf fragments will filter down between the grass blades to decompose and enrich the soil over the winter. In effect, you are mulching the grass plants, just as you do the other plants in the yard.

Watering

If it does not rain regularly, *water* newly planted lawn areas so that shallow-rooted young seedlings will not dry out and shrivel up.

Fertilizing

If you did not use a starter fertilizer when overseeding or patching the lawn with seed, *spread* a slow-acting, granular product formulated for fall any time now. If you decide to spread lime this month, delay fertilization.

Many forms of powdered or granulated lime also provide magnesium and calcium, and most lawn fertilizers do not have these nutrients. This alone is good reason to lime the lawn every year or two.

Mowing

In the warmer regions of Pennsylvania, lawn mowing seems to go on forever . . . but the last mowing will probably take place this month.

1 *Rake* the heavy leaf fall from the turf before mowing each time to assure an even cut. Toward the end of the leaf fall, when the layer of leaves is thin, mow the lawn and leaves with a mulching mower whether the grass actually needs it or not. This will chop the leaves into organic confetti that will fall between the blades of grass and mulch the grass plants for the winter.

Growing Smarter

Fungal diseases are a nuisance in lawns. They occur most commonly in the form of rusts and mildews. Fungal spores are always present, but certain environmental conditions–lots of rain, no rain, excessive heat or humidity, poor air flow–trigger periodic flareups in even the best of lawns. In most cases the best response is to wait it out. As soon as the environmental conditions change, the fungal infection will subside.

- Spray a fungicide such as wettable sulfur to protect neighboring healthy grass.
- Keep grass as stress-free as possible.
- Control excessive buildup of the thatch layer.

2 For the last grass mowing, *lower* the mower blade to cut grass at about 2 inches tall.

3 *Trim* the weeds and grass around lawn edges. If it is a bit on the short side, grass is less likely to mat under snow cover and develop mold diseases.

Problem Solving

White grubs may damage lawns in the early fall. Watch for dead patches of turf. Evidence of skunk visits and/or flocks of starlings on the lawn suggests grubs are present in the soil (both love to eat white grubs)—but if the soil has cooled below 75 degrees F, it is too late to treat the problem now. The grubs migrate deep in the soil below the frost line for the winter. Spread predatory nematodes or inoculate the lawn with milky spore disease (*Bacillus popilliae*) next June when they return to near the soil surface. Resolve to control Japanese beetles next summer to reduce the grub population in the fall. Keep soil and grass healthy so the lawn can tolerate a degree of grub damage.

Broadleaf weeds may still be green and growing. If air temperatures are still mild, it is possible to *spot-treat* dandelion, plantain, clover, and others with herbicide. This will give you a head start on next season. *Check* product labels for optimum air temperatures for their use.

Planning

As the mowing and lawn-care season finally winds down, there is time to reflect on the past year's activities. If you have worked on improving the quality of the soil under the lawn so the grass can depend on it rather than you for its sustenance, you will begin to reap the rewards next season. Simply by changing your mowing habits a bit, taking measures to add organic material to the soil, and adding some new grass to replace old, tired grass, you will have made a huge difference.

This is also a good time to evaluate the size of your lawn. Traditionally, Americans tend to overdo, creating vast swaths of green turf that dominate the landscape. Consider ways to make better use of your yard and reduce lawn-care chores as well. You might be able to start work on a yard project if the weather is nice.

Identify areas where grass has chronically failed or been sub-par. This is often the case under shade trees. Think about giving up on trying to have turf there, and grow ground cover plants instead. Evergreen plants such as **Pachysandra, Vinca,** and **Liriope** make great lawn substitutes. They provide interesting green foliage all winter and require less moisture and little fertilizer. Other ways to reduce lawn area:

- Widen shrub borders or garden beds.

- Build a deck or patio.

- Create a dog run.

- Set up an area for a child's swingset or playhouse.

- Put in a swimming pool.

- Widen the driveway or front walk.

- Extend the ring of mulch under a tree as far as the branches reach.

- Establish a water garden.

Planning

Delay any planting of seed or sod until next spring. The ground will freeze soon, and grass plant roots will not be able to penetrate the soil.

Care for Your Lawn

There is little to do for the lawn now. Care for it over the winter by protecting it from damage from shovels, snow blowers, de-icing compounds, and compaction.

Watering

Continue to *water* newly planted lawns if rainfall is scarce. It is important for them to go into the winter in moist soil. If you are lucky enough to be able to count on snow cover during the really cold months, you will not have to think about watering until spring.

Fertilizing

If you have not fertilized this fall with a granular, slow-acting lawn fertilizer formulated for fall, you can delay until late winter. Wait until early next spring, and use one that is higher in nitrogen to promote the new growth then. The grass is dormant and can get along fine over the winter. If you want to, you can still fertilize with a granular, slow-acting product now and get the job out of the way. The fertilizer will begin to activate when the soil warms up again in spring, and that will be one less thing you will have to do then.

Mowing

Some years you may find yourself doing the final mowing this month. It is better to cut the lawn again to about 2 inches than to have it go into the winter too long. When covered with snow, overlong grass mats and develops fungal diseases. Leave the clippings as usual unless they are very long.

Problem Solving

Dog urine is a real problem in lawns where owners allow dogs to run in the yard. The nitrogen in their urine burns the grass foliage and often kills plant crowns, leaving a dead, brown patch in the turf. This happens more often with female dogs because they "puddle" on the lawn, leaving a large concentration of urine in one spot. Male dogs "piddle" at many sites as they mark them, and the nitrogen in any one spot is minimal. To prevent burning of the grass, pour a pail of water on the spot where urine is puddled to dilute it and wash it off the grass and down through the soil.

Weeds that are still obvious will have to remain until spring unless the soil is still soft enough that you can dig them out. Most herbicides do not work when the air or soil is below a certain temperature.

Growing Smarter

If you are planning to move to a newly built home, talk to the builder about the lawn. Let him know you want more than the perfunctory "builder's special." This will save you time and energy next season.

- Insist that he replace ***all*** the topsoil he removed before construction began. He has probably sold it or used it elsewhere, so request an equal volume of high-quality topsoil instead.
- Ask if there is a seed allowance. If so, ask him if you can add to it so he will buy and sow a premium seed rather than the bargain special which is full of weed seeds. An alternative is to ask for the money, then choose the seed yourself.
- Ask him to have his crew sow the seed thicker than they normally do. Offer to pay for an extra supply of seed so this will happen.
- Request a mixture of several kinds of seed, rather than a single type. If the builder sows **Kentucky Bluegrass** varieties mixed with some **Tall Fescues** and **Perennial Rye** varieties, your lawn will be more disease-resistant.

Erosion of the lawn soil is a problem in newly built homes where the grass has not yet become established. Often builders rush to complete new construction by the onset of winter and manage to throw some seed on the sea of mud around the house at the last minute. Spread some straw over the soil as a mulch to break the force of rain and subsequent runoff.

Crabgrass

DECEMBER

Planning

If you have succeeded over the past year in caring for the lawn, it should look pretty good even in December. If there is no snow yet, cool-climate grasses may even be somewhat green, even though they are essentially dormant. If any **Zoysia** grass has invaded, this warm weather–lover will be clearly visible as dried brown patches. Plan to eradicate it next spring. (If you prefer **Zoysia,** this is an opportunity to determine how much of the cool-weather turf remains to eliminate next spring.)

Planting

If the soil is not frozen, it is still possible to *lay sod* in limited areas of the lawn that were damaged by construction projects or affected by other traumatic events (see steps in September). It is better to lay sod over bare soil than to leave the soil exposed to compaction by winter rain, harsh sun and wind, or foot traffic. Sod will prevent erosion of the soil, too. Be sure to keep new sod well watered. Winter sun and dry, cold air will cause it to dry out quickly, especially along the edges of the pieces and where the sod meets paving. Whether it will actually put down roots and establish before spring depends on the weather over the next couple of months.

Growing Smarter

Salt is a big problem for turfgrasses. Runoff from sodium de-icing products or spray from municipal plows as they scrape salted streets often ends up on the lawn. It dissolves in the melted snow and ice water and is taken up by plant roots, causing plant tissues to die.

- Pour fresh water on turf areas you know have been soaked with salty water. This will leach out the sodium and wash it down into the soil beyond plant roots.
- Use non-salt de-icing products—sand, kitty litter, or something similar—on your own driveways and sidewalks.

Care for Your Lawn

Dormant turfgrass does not need special care. Whether covered with snow or not, the most important thing you can do is avoid walking on it. Alert your family and the mail carrier, and keep walks clear so people are not tempted to take a shortcut.

Watering

If it has been a dry fall, monitor the soil moisture under your turf. If you are not sure whether the soil is dry, use a houseplant water meter. Insert its probe into the soil under the grass down about 6 inches. If the meter reads "dry," it is time to water. Do not wait more than a couple of days to water young grass that was sown earlier in the fall.

It has not had time to develop deep roots and will be in danger of desiccation long before established grass is thirsty. *Water* turf near trees, because competition from tree roots for water will have dried the soil under grass even more.

Fertilizing

If you intend to fertilize and have not done so, spread a granular, slow-acting lawn fertilizer intended for winter use now so it will be available to the grass first thing in the spring.

Problem Solving

Annual weeds seem to have disappeared, but they have left behind seeds for next year. Perennial weeds are dormant.

Perennials

Whether you are a novice gardener or an experienced one, selecting perennials for the garden can be a daunting experience. It may not be difficult to choose an occasional perennial flowering plant to fill a particular space in the garden, but it can be a challenge to buy many plants for a brand-new garden or a renovated bed or border: you will have to assess the virtues of many different plants and factor color, bloom time, size, and shape into your decisions.

Perennial plants are considerably more expensive than annuals, which means that choosing perennials is a financial as well as an aesthetic decision. Because they can be expected to be around for a long time, making good choices from the beginning makes good sense . . . and cents.

The heart often overrules the head when choosing perennials, so it is important to take the time to think about what qualities you want your plants to have before you make the shopping trip. It is tempting to choose the newest or most glamorous plants that are being promoted for the current season. But new, relatively untested perennials may not be reliable, easy-care choices for your particular garden. Once the honeymoon is over, a new plant may develop problems and require special attention that you may not be able to give.

A Better Plant

All gardeners are looking for what horticulturists call a "better plant," one that is gardenworthy. Professional plant hybridizers and growers interpret this to mean a perennial that has attractive foliage, sturdy stems, and handsome, long-lasting flowers. They are constantly trying to find and develop plants that are adaptable to a wide range of soils and various light and moisture conditions. They are always on the lookout for new versions of an existing perennial, versions that display superior qualities. In fact, the running joke is that the perfect perennial blooms all summer like an annual, stands tall without staking, does not need deadheading, has no pests, never needs dividing, and likes both sun and shade, drought and wet. This "perfect" perennial has not yet been found, but "better" ones are constantly being developed.

A new plant will be evaluated against existing plants to try to determine if it is truly better. Various organizations and plant societies conduct trials in different parts of the country and put promising plants through their paces. Perennials that demonstrate true superiority often win recognition by the Perennial Plant Association or a similar organization. Look for special tags or labels that indicate the perennial you are considering has won an award.

Perennials

Another way to judge whether a certain perennial is reliable and easy to care for is to notice how popular it is with other gardeners. Groups that track sales of various perennials throughout the country year after year report that a consensus exists among gardeners and homeowners about the best garden perennials. While some may shift position over time, the following plants appear on the list time after time:

- **Hosta**
- **Daylily**
- **Coreopsis**
- **Geranium**
- **Veronica**
- **Ferns**
- **Salvia (Sage)**
- **Ornamental Grass**
- **Astilbe**
- **Purple Coneflower**

Your Better Plants

The best way to determine which perennials will be "better plants" in your own garden is to establish your own personal criteria. Growers and evaluators apply good standards to determine a plant's superiority, but they cannot take into account the special circumstances that exist on your particular property. They may assume that easy care, beauty, and reliability are near the top of your personal list of desirable traits in a plant, but they cannot know *all* the qualities you deem important.

A perennial selected by you must be hardy in the horticultural zone where you garden. Zone numbers traditionally reflect cold hardiness, but plants also have varying heat hardiness. A plant that can handle the winter cold in the State College area may not be also able to handle the summer heat and humidity near Philadelphia, and plant labels are now listing heat-hardiness as well as cold-hardiness information.

Pay attention to the different varieties of a perennial that are available. A certain variety of **Hosta** or **Phlox** may be a fantastic success in one region, but another variety may do better in your region. Every yard has its microclimates—pockets where it is warmer, colder, moister, or drier than conditions that prevail in the yard as a whole. Plant choices must be suited to these sites if they are to flourish. If you garden, you have already been conducting unofficial trials to determine the better plants for your yard.

Favorite Plant Checklist

Take a moment to think about the plants that have done exceptionally well for you, those that come through year after year regardless of the rainfall or heat. Chances are these are your favorites. List the reasons you love them. Chances are this list reflects the qualities you most value in a plant.

Do not be surprised if your favorite perennials are the same ones you see in neighbors' gardens and elsewhere. This is no coincidence. The **'Stella d'Oro' Daylily** or the **'Sum and Substance' Hosta** are truly better plants: they perform reliably under a variety of conditions with a minimum of care.

Complete your checklist by *checking* (on the next page) the qualities you consider virtues in perennials. Then *prioritize* them to fit the circumstances in your life and in your garden. Take the list with you when you go shopping at the garden center. It will help you narrow your choices in your search for a better plant for your garden.

Checklist

What Makes a Better Perennial in My Garden?

Priority	Quality	
____	____	Low water demand
____	____	Tolerates a variety of soils
____	____	Needs little fertilizing
____	____	Likes acid soil
____	____	Deer-resistant
____	____	Dries easily for floral crafts
____	____	Low-growing
____	____	Evergreen foliage
____	____	Variegated/textured foliage
____	____	Native to Pennsylvania
____	____	Good for cutting
____	____	Fragrant (flower or foliage)
____	____	Pest- and disease-resistant
____	____	Does not need staking
____	____	Clumps rather than spreads
____	____	Persistent bloom (more than 2 weeks)
____	____	Easily propagated
____	____	New or unusual
____	____	Takes shade
____	____	Attracts beneficial insects
____	____	Attracts butterflies and hummingbirds
____	____	Multi-season interest
____	____	Great flower color
____	____	Other _____
____	____	Other _____

Perennials for Pennsylvania

Common Name (Botanical Name)	Bloom Time Height (Spread)	PA Cold Hardiness Zones	Cultural Requirements	Comments
Aster (native) New York Aster New England Aster (*Aster* species)	August through October 2 to 6 feet	Most 4 to 8	Most need sun; some tolerate part shade. Well-drained to moist soil.	Daisylike flowers perk up the garden in late summer. Needs good air circulation to control mildew.
Baby's Breath (*Gypsophila paniculata*)	June to August 3 to 4 feet	3 to 8	Full sun. Moist, well-drained, neutral to alkaline soil.	Tiny white, pink florets on airy stems. Filler for flower beds. Easily cut and dried, too.
Beebalm (*Monarda* sp. and hybrids)	Late June through July 2 to 4 feet (spreading)	4 to 8	Sun to part shade. Moist soil.	Attracts butterflies and bees. Aromatic foliage. Red, pink mophead flowers. Spreads aggressively. Plant mildew-resistant cultivars.
Bellflower (*Campanula* sp. and hybrids)	Late May, early June 4 to 36 inches	3 to 8	Sun, part shade. Moist to well-drained soil.	A large clan featuring bell-shaped flowers in blues, white, pink. May rebloom if deadheaded.
Black-eyed Susan (*Rudbeckia fulgida* 'Goldsturm')	July through September 2 to 3 feet (2 feet)	Most 3 to 9	Sun. Moist, well-drained soil. Established plants tolerate drought.	Classic yellow daisy flower. Spreads quickly; self-seeds readily. Attracts butterflies and goldfinches. Disease-resistant. Seedheads provide winter interest as well as bird food.
Blazing Star Spike Gayfeather (*Liatris spicata*)	July and August 2 to 3 feet (2 feet)	Most 4 to 9	Sun. Moist, well-drained soil. Tolerates drought.	Fuzzy purple or white flower spikes, grassy foliage. Long-lived, reintroduced native. No pests or significant diesease.
Bleeding Heart (*Dicentra eximia*)	April and May 2 to 3 feet	Most 3 to 8	Sun, part shade, shade. Moist, acidic soil.	Heart-shaped pink or white flowers dangle from thin stems that arch above feathery foliage.
Candytuft (*Iberis sempervirens*)	Late May 8 to 10 inches	3 to 9	Sun, well-drained soil.	Neat, low-growing, evergreen foliage; white flowers. May rebloom if sheared after early flowering. For edging, filler.

Perennials for Pennsylvania

Common Name (Botanical Name)	Bloom Time Height (Spread)	PA Cold Hardiness Zones	Cultural Requirements	Comments
Chrysanthemum Hardy Mum (*Chrysanthemum × morifolium*)	August to November 1 to 3 feet (1 to 3 feet)	3 to 7	Sun. Good garden soil.	Available in lots of bright fall colors, flower shapes. Pinch back throughout summer for branching and later blooming.
Columbine (*Aquilegia* sp. and hybrids)	May 1 to 3 feet (1 foot)	3 to 8	Sun, part shade. Moist, well-drained soil.	Elegant, airy, delicate plants. Flowers are spurred cups in blues, white, yellow. Leafminer problems. Cut back midsummer for new foliage.
Coral Bells (*Heuchera* sp. and hybrids)	May and June 2 feet (2 feet)	Most 3 to 8	Sun, part shade. Moist soil.	Semi-evergreen and many fascinating leaf patterns. Sprays of tiny bell flowers on long stems.
Coreopsis, Tickseed (*Coreopsis* sp. and hybrids)	June through September 6 to 24 inches	Most 3 to 8	Sun. Moist, well-drained soil; can handle drought.	Jaunty yellow flowers rebloom if deadheaded. Some have threadleaf, others lanceleaf foliage. Easy care.
Cranesbill Hardy Geranium (*Geranium* sp. and hybrids)	May to July 6 inches to 4 feet tall (1 to 2 feet); clumping or spreading types	Most 4 to 8	Sun, part shade, shade. Moist, well-drained soil.	White, pink, blue, magenta flowers have main bloom period, occasional rebloom. Finely cut foliage. Long-lived.
Daylily (*Hemerocallis* hybrid)	June throught September 1 to 4 feet (2 to 4 feet)	Most 4 to 9	Sun for best bloom.	Trumpet flowers in shades of yellow, red, orange, lilac, and cream grow on stems among strappy green foliage. Deer favorites.
False Spirea (*Astilbe* sp. and hybrids)	June to late summer, depending on species 1 to 4 feet	Most 4 to 8	Part shade. Moist, slightly acidic soil.	Spires of white, pink, lavender florets; ferny foliage. Make beautiful cut flowers.
Goldenrod (*Solidago* sp. and hybrids)	Midsummer to fall 2 to 6 feet (2 to 4 feet)	4 to 9	Sun, part shade. Moist, well-drained soil. Drought-resistant when established.	Sprays of tiny yellow florets on feathery spikes. Attracts butterflies and beneficial insects. Good as cut flowers, fresh or dried.

Perennials for Pennsylvania

Common Name (Botanical Name)	Bloom Time Height (Spread)	PA Cold Hardiness Zones	Cultural Requirements	Comments
Hardy Begonia (*Begonia grandis*)	Late summer and fall 1 to 3 feet	5 to 10	Part to full shade. Moist soil.	Late-season pink flowers on arched stems. Distinctive purple-backed, veined foliage. Easy care for color and texture.
Hellebore Lenten Rose (*Helleborus orientalis*)	March to April 15 to 20 inches (15 to 20 inches)	6 to 8	Part shade, shade. Moist, well-drained soil.	Cream, maroon, speckled open-cupped flowers on stems among glossy, leathery, deeply divided leaves. Winter interest plus early flowering.
Hosta Plantain Lily (*Hosta* sp. and hybrids)	July or August 6 to 24 inches (1 to 3 feet)	3 to 8	Part shade, shade. Moist, slightly acidic soil.	Variegated, ruffled, or rippled, foliage in greens, blue-green, yellow, chartreuse. Deer and slug favorites.
Lady's Mantle (*Alchemilla mollis*)	Spring and early summer 1 foot	3 to 7	Sun, part shade, shade. Moist soil.	Attractive fan-shaped foliage with clusters of yellow flowers on flexible stems. Charming; easy care.
Lobelia (*Lobelia* sp. and hybrids)	Summer and fall 2 to 4 feet	Most 4 to 8	Part shade. Moist soil.	Tall flower spikes bring reds, blues, white, and pastels to late-season shade garden.
Peony, Garden (*Paeonia* sp. and hybrids)	Late May to June 2 to 3 feet (3 feet)	4 to 8	Sun, part shade. Well-drained soil.	Fragrant; tissue-petaled flowers in reds, pinks, white, and yellow. Long-lived and carefree.
Phlox, Garden (*Phlox paniculata*)	July and August 2 to 40 inches	4 to 8	Full sun.	Domed flower clusters in reds, pinks, white on straight stems. Look for mildew-resistant cultivars.
Pinks Cottage Pink (*Dianthus plumarius*)	June 10 to 12 inches	4 to 8	Sun. Well-drained alkaline soil.	Evergreen narrow, grayish foliage. Fragrant white, red, pink, bicolored flowers. Drought-resistant.

Perennials for Pennsylvania

Common Name (Botanical Name)	Bloom Time Height (Spread)	PA Cold Hardiness Zones	Cultural Requirements	Comments
Primrose (*Primula × polyantha*)	April to May 6 to 12 inches (8 to 10 inches)	3 to 8	Part shade. Moist, clay or garden soil.	Open-faced flowers in pastels and crayon colors with yellow centers. Textured leaves.
Purple Coneflower (*Echinacea purpurea*)	July to August 2 to 4 feet; **'Kim's Knee High'** is short version	3 to 9	Sun. Ordinary soil. Drought-tolerant.	Purple-petaled daisy with dark center. Attracts butterflies, gold finches. No pest or disease problems.
Shasta Daisy (*Chrysanthemum × superbum*)	June and July 1 to 3 feet (2 feet); there are dwarf varieties	4 to 8	Sun, part shade. Moist, well-drained soil.	Classic white daisy. Attracts butterflies and beneficial insects. Easy care in flower border and Cutting garden.
Showy Stonecrop (*Sedum spectable* sp. and hybrids syn. *Telephium*)	August to October	3 to 8	Sun, part shade. Well-drained soil. Drought-tolerant.	**'Autumn Joy'** and **'Brilliant'** are favorites. Large, flat clusters of tiny flowers that turn russet in fall. Winter interest; attract butterflies, beneficial insects. Three-season interest.
Veronica Speedwell (*Veronica* sp. and hybrids)	June and July 1½ to 3 feet (1½ to 2 feet)	4 to 8	Sun. Moist, well-drained soil.	Spires of blue, pink, or white florets. Easy care; long bloom time. Deadhead for rebloom. Attracts butterflies. Most types pest- and insect-free.
Wormwood (*Artemisia* sp. and hybrids)	August to October 12 inches (36 inches)	4 to 8	Sun. Tolerates dry soil.	Silvery, fine-textured foliage more important than flowers. No pests. Deer-resistant.
Yarrow Milfoil (*Achillea* sp. and hybrids)	June to August 1 to 4 feet (up to 3 feet)	3 to 10	Full sun. Well-drained soil.	Flat clusters of florets in shades of red/pink, yellow, gold. Deer-resistant. Basically pest-free. Cut flowers for drying.

Planning

As the new year begins on the calendar, it is time to think about the new year in the garden. Winter weather may just now be truly closing in, with ground-freezing temperatures and some snowfall—nevertheless, the new gardening season has begun! The amount of daylight is gradually increasing, and it's time to follow up on the New Year's resolution and begin a garden notebook or journal. If you already keep one, get it out this month and read the entries from last January.

If you have a sketch or chart of where your perennials are planted on the property, *review* that to determine where new ones might be planted this spring. If you do not have a sketch, begin one, and fill it in as emerging plants appear this spring to remind you where they are.

Get out the catalogs that have been accumulating since early last month. Take some time to get acquainted with the featured perennials for this coming season. The wonderful color photographs and information about their cultural requirements will help you identify some that you may want to plant in the garden this spring.

Garden Plan

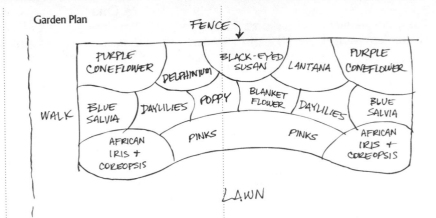

Planting

While it is too early to plant any perennials outdoors, it is not too early to select a few varieties from catalogs to start from seed next month.

- *Choose* perennials that will sprout fairly easily and quickly. Unlike most annuals, many perennials are fussy about their conditions for germination—unless you want a new hobby, let the professionals do the complicated propagation.

- *Choose* varieties that will come true from seed. Some perennials are hybrids, and their offspring will resemble one of their grandparents rather than their hybrid parent.

Care for Your Perennials

At this time of year the soil needs protection from winter weather, for the soil protects the perennials lying under it. If you have not already done so, *spread* a 3- to 4-inch layer of organic material as a mulch over any bare soil in the garden. The cheapest and easiest mulch is chopped leaves (whole ones tend to form a mat that blocks air and moisture).

Some perennials, like **Chrysanthemums, Veronica, Loosestrife,** and others, retain green foliage at soil level during the winter. Make sure this foliage is lightly mulched, too. Lay some boughs of needled evergreens (**Pine, Spruce,** or **Fir**) over them if you do not have chopped leaves or pine needles or something similar.

174

JANUARY

Watering

If it has been an extremely dry late fall, check soil moisture around new or divided perennials planted within the past couple of months. *Water* them if the soil is not frozen and seems dry.

Grooming

If you have not already done so, *cut back* the dead, dried stems from fall-flowering perennials such as **Asters, Mums,** and **Goldenrod.**

Leave ornamental grasses uncut to provide some color and movement in the garden for another month or two.

Growing Smarter

Some perennials for a winter garden include:

- **Hellebores**—glossy, evergreen foliage and late-winter flowers
- **Basket of Gold**—gray leaves and stems, trailing
- **Snow in Summer**—mat of gray-white leaves
- **Threadleaf Coreopsis**—dried, fine-textured, needlelike foliage on straight stems
- **Coralbells**—variegated, evergreen foliage
- **Lavender**—grayish, thin leaves on straight stems
- **Black-eyed Susans**—black, rounded seedheads
- **Purple Coneflower**—large, rounded, bristly seedheads
- **Tall Sedums**—large, flat, dried flowerheads on dark stalks
- **Yucca**—stiff, toothed, swordlike foliage in green, gray-green, or gold-and-green

Problem Solving

Deer and rabbits may visit your yard to investigate. Since most perennials are dormant and have died back to the soil, these critters will focus more on the woody shrubs and young trees, and **Hellebores** have such leathery foliage, they are usually ignored.

Planning

Technically, a perennial plant is any plant whose life support system is designed to ensure its survival over many seasons; it is genetically programmed to grow roots and foliage that collect and store energy from the sun in the form of starches that carry it through a dormant season. Woody plants such as trees and shrubs are perennial, of course, but when gardeners talk about perennials, they are usually referring to herbaceous ornamental plants—those whose tops die back with frost but whose roots survive to send up new shoots next year.

Even though they are designed to return each spring, not all perennials are equally capable of surviving cold winter temperatures. Some are constitutionally more cold hardy than others. To be sure that you select plants this spring that will survive in your garden for years, *check* the zone number on the plant description in the catalog or the plant label at the garden center. To be successful in most parts of Pennsylvania, perennials should be rated for at least zone 5 or 6. Look at the state Hardiness Zone Map in the Appendix to double-check the zone in which you live. While most garden centers routinely carry only those plants that are suited to the local climate, mail-order companies serve the entire country, so make sure any plants you order are cold hardy for your part of Pennsylvania.

Planting

If you would like to try starting some perennials from seed indoors under lights, consult the discussion of seed-starting procedures for annuals (see February Annuals). Be sure to read and follow the specific directions on the seed packets as well. Remember that if you are not successful starting from seed, there will be plenty of time to purchase professionally grown young plants in a month or two. Seed-starting things to remember:

- *Use* soilless potting soil or seed-starting mix.

- *Cover* planted pots or flats to maintain humidity around sown seeds.

- *Label* the pots or flat with the name of the plant.

- *Provide* the correct temperature—warmth from beneath is best unless cool temperatures are specified.

As the indoor seedlings grow:

- *Maintain* fluorescent lights within an inch or two of the sprouts as they grow.

- *Provide* sixteen hours of bright light per day.

- *Do not* let the seedlings dry out.

Care for Your Perennials

Take a tour of the yard to check on current conditions:

1 Where frost has heaved the soil, make sure the crowns and roots of perennials have not been exposed to the drying, cold air. *Replant* any that have been disturbed. If the ground is too hard to work the soil, pile mulch or compost over the plants. *Replace* mulch that may have blown away from beds exposed to wind.

2 To prevent early perennials from appearing prematurely during a sunny, relatively warm period, *maintain* their layer of mulch. It will hold some chill in the soil and delay their growth until there is less risk of damage from late freezes and snow.

Watering

Mulched beds will not dry out if the soil was moist before the mulch was spread. Often a late

January thaw melts any snow cover a bit and the water soaks into the soil. Dormant perennials do not use much moisture, and the moisture in the soil outdoors should be just fine.

After you have removed their plastic cover, new seedlings will need watering. When the soil is dry, either water from beneath or *sprinkle* lightly to avoid damaging the tender sprouts. Do not overdo watering and risk damping-off disease.

Growing Smarter

Even though you live and garden in a particular cold-hardiness zone, climatic conditions are never uniform everywhere on your property. There are several microclimates in every yard–pockets where it is a bit warmer, colder, drier, or more humid than everywhere else. Over the years you will become aware of these places and choose plants that can handle the special conditions that prevail in each. Watch the patterns of snow melt this month, which will indicate warmer, more sheltered spots. A few other things to be aware of as you learn the microclimates in your yard:

- Masonry walls absorb heat and reflect light to create a warmer, brighter spot that encourages plants to bloom a bit ahead of schedule.
- Fences and shrub hedges create niches sheltered from harsh winds.
- Dips and low-lying areas tend to trap frost and humidity and remain winterish even when most areas are feeling springish.

Fertilizing

As soon as seedlings begin to develop real leaves (not just the initial small ones), they will need some nutrition. Because soilless planting medium contains no real soil, it has no nutrients. Every other watering, add some fast-acting (water-soluble) fertilizer to the water. Use it at about half the strength recommended on the package.

If you do not already have a supply of granular slow-acting fertilizer for flowering plants, buy some this month when you buy lawn fertilizer and other supplies for the spring gardening season.

Grooming

It is tempting to do something out in the garden toward the end of the month. This is a good time to *pick up* twigs and debris that have fallen onto garden beds, and to *check* for the first bulbs. To prevent soil compaction if the soil is very wet, avoid walking on the beds or lawn.

Problem Solving

Weeds will not be a problem yet, if you kept after them last fall. Most perennial weed plants are dormant, just like their ornamental cousins.

Damping off is a fungal disease that plagues seedlings. To avoid it, plant seeds in sterile potting medium or soilless mix, water sparingly and from beneath, and maintain good air circulation around developing seedlings.

Planning

Early this month there are hints of the season to come. Out in the woods **Skunk Cabbage** is beginning to emerge from the soil, and **Mayapples** will be along before you know it. In the garden, the flowers on the **Lenten Rose** are on display, and tiny, delicate stems of **Barrenwort** are about to emerge. Most flowering perennials lag behind the small, cold-loving, early-flowering bulbs, but they are stirring. Get organized for the imminent new season.

- Locate trowels, shovels, and rakes.

- Sharpen pruners and garden scissors.

- Inventory the supply of stakes, wire cages, and other supports for tall perennials.

- Buy new stakes, garden twine, and plant labels at the garden centers now, to beat the rush.

- Have on hand sufficient supplies of slow-acting fertilizer, soilless potting mix, insecticidal soap, and horticultural oil.

- Start doing mild stretching exercises to get in shape.

While you wait for the soil to dry out and warm up this month, decide what new garden projects will need doing this spring. Thinking about expanding an exist-ing flower bed or border? How about a new island bed? Pencil it in on the sketch of your garden in your notebook or journal. Estimate how many new plants the additional garden space will accept.

Planting

Traditionally, March is mud month. Melting snow and early spring rains conspire to turn even great garden soil into sticky slop. The temptation is to get outdoors and dig in the garden the minute the air temperature is milder; the danger is that you will ruin the soil. Do not begin to dig a new bed or extend an existing one until you can grasp a handful of soil, squeeze it, and see it crumble in your hand when you release it. If water drips from it as you squeeze, or if it is a sodden ball when you open your hand, wait a week or two before digging.

To break new ground for a perennial garden:

- Shove the flat blade of a garden spade under turfgrass sod or ground cover plants to *break* their roots.

- *Peel* the grass sod or mat of plants off the soil, leaving as much valuable topsoil as possible behind.

- *Dig* down into the bare soil at least 18 inches. Lift and dump shovelsful of soil back onto the bed to loosen and aerate it.

- *Add* several inches of organic material such as peat moss, chopped leaves, or compost to the piles of newly overturned soil to help clay or sandy soil hold air and moisture and drain well.

- *Sprinkle* granular, slow-acting fertilizer over the newly dug soil as recommended on the package label.

- *Mix* the organic material and the fertilizer into the loose soil. Break up the large clods, and remove small stones, roots, and other debris.

- *Rake* the soil smooth and level, and cover it with a mulch of chopped leaves or pine needles to await planting as soon as all danger of frost is past.

Seedlings raised indoors under lights are ready for larger pots if their roots are peeking out through the drainage holes in their current containers:

- *Mix* some granular, slow-acting fertilizer (as recommended on the label for young plants) into moistened soilless potting medium.

- *Fill* plastic or peat pots half-full of the medium.

- Gently *remove* each young plant from its container and set it on the medium.

- *Fill* in around it with more medium. Be sure the plant is at the same depth in the new pot that it was in its former one.

- *Water*, and return the seedlings to their lights.

Care for Your Perennials

Perennials that are already established in the garden can cope with some chill and the occasional setback provided by a late frost. The growth and eventual emergence of their new shoots from the soil is governed by their internal clocks, soil temperature, and the increasing amount of daylight. Plants that you will plant this spring are young and inexperienced in the ways of the world, let alone your yard. Those that arrive mail-order are typically bare-root and dormant. If they arrive this month, delay planting (unless otherwise instructed on the plant label) until at least late April or May. Keep them in a cool dark place so they stay dormant until planting time. Make sure their roots stay moist.

Watering

Perennials that are about to make their season debut in the garden probably have sufficient soil moisture if they have been mulched all winter and there has been normal snow cover or rainfall.

Water newly transplanted seedlings to prevent them from drying out. When the outside of peat pots become dry, they turn a pale brown—it is a signal that it is time to water.

Fertilizing

Granular, slow-acting fertilizer mixed into soilless planting medium for seedlings or into garden soil will provide consistent, uniform nutrition for as many weeks as are indicated on the package label.

Grooming

This is garden cleanup month. *Cut back* colorful and interesting dried stems of grasses and other plants that you enjoyed over the winter. This will neaten up the yard and make way for the new shoots these plants will be sending up soon.

Do not remove mulch until danger of frost is past. If the sun warms the soil prematurely, shoots of new plants may emerge ahead of schedule and get frosted.

Problem Solving

Slugs always appear sooner than we expect. Unless there is still snow on the ground, it is not too early to put out some traps. They catch the earliest arrivals so that populations do not become established before their natural enemies are on duty. Slugs typically lurk in damp, shady places where soil is acid; they hide under boards, rocks, and other debris. Set out a shallow pie plate or a commercial slug trap baited with beer or baking yeast dissolved in water. If there are slugs in the area, they will come to investigate, fall in the trap, and drown. *Check traps daily* to determine when they first appear. Make a note in your journal.

Weeds will begin to appear when other plants do. *Pull them up* while they are young.

Planning

Wonderful shade trees are a hallmark of Pennsylvania landscapes. They are a legacy of the hardwood forests that once carpeted the entire East Coast. In residential yards they create shade that cools homes and makes it possible to have woodland gardens, and it is here that so many lovely perennial flowers make an early-season appearance. Keep your eyes out for signs that **Bleeding Heart, Virginia Bluebells, Wild Phlox, Ferns,** and **Barrenwort** are emerging. If you have trees and do not already have a shade garden, think about adding one.

Other activities for this month:

- Repair nearby walls or walks.

- Evaluate your plants.

- Discard those that have never performed up to expectation.

- Divide overgrown clumps of plants.

- Introduce new plants.

- Improve the soil.

- Change the planting design.

Planting

Although the perennial plants in beds and borders can be depended on to return every spring, that does not mean a perennial garden can be taken for granted. After a few years the soil will need attention. Because there is not a lot of planting and replanting activity in long-established beds of perennial plants, their soil is not regularly aerated and conditioned; it becomes compacted and no longer holds moisture or drains as well. Long-time resident perennials will have depleted the soil of certain nutrients, and they begin to show signs of age and lose vigor.

After five or six years, perennial beds and borders need a thorough renovation. Establish a rotation by scheduling renovation of a different bed every year or two. It is a great way to continually update and upgrade the garden. When all danger of frost is past and the soil has dried out enough to be workable, it is time to **renovate a garden bed:**

1   *Remove* existing plants. Dig the rootballs as large as possible to avoid harming their roots.

2   *Set* each plant in the shade on a piece of burlap or tarp or in a roomy pot. *Cover* its rootball to keep it moist and hold the soil in contact with the roots.

3   *Dig* down into the soil at least 18 inches, if possible, then lift and dump the shovelsful of soil back onto the bed.

4   *Incorporate* a 2- to 3-inch layer of organic material and granular, slow-acting fertilizer into the soil.

5   *Break up* clods; remove stones, roots, and other debris. Rake the soil smooth and level.

6   *Replant* those plants that you wish to retain; leave space for new ones.

It is probably time to *repot* young perennials that you started from seed indoors under lights. They will not be going outdoors into the garden for another month at least.

Care for Your Perennials

Mulch the newly replanted perennials in the renovated bed to prevent drying out, and to discourage weeds from seeds that surfaced during the digging and aeration of the soil.

Take care of indoor seedlings:

- *Maintain* the fluorescent lights at about 2 or 3 inches above their foliage and provide good air circulation around each plant.

- *Brush* your open hand gently across their foliage daily to promote sturdy stems.

- *Inspect* regularly for signs of pest or disease problems.

Watering

April showers should be sufficient to keep emerging perennials happy. If it has been a dry spring, *check* the soil under the mulch to see if it is moist. Water if it is not. Continue to water young perennials you are raising indoors under lights.

Fertilizing

If the soil in established beds is not very fertile, *sprinkle* a little granular, slow-acting fertilizer around newly emerging perennials to get them off to a good start for the growing season.

If you have not mixed slow-acting fertilizer into the potting medium when you repotted young perennials growing indoors under lights, add some liquid fertilizer to their water every two weeks. Use it at about half the dilution strength recommended on the package label.

Grooming

Cut back any remaining dried stems from last season on grasses, vines, and other perennials. When the garden begins to fill in with emerging plants in a few weeks, it

---

Growing Smarter

Chrysanthemums are familiar favorites in fall perennial gardens or containers. If you planted some last year, they are already developing fresh foliage and new stems. Since they do not bloom until late summer, gardeners handle them several ways.

- Leave them in place and pinch stems often until late July.
- Some pull up last year's plants and throw them away. They buy new, full-grown ones in late summer to plant in beds and containers.
- Some take cuttings from the young shoots of last year's plants that are still in the garden and discard the plants. They root the cuttings, pot or plant them in a nursery bed, and raise them for planting in the garden late in the summer when they are ready to bloom.
- Some treat **Mums** as annuals. They buy full-grown, budded plants in the fall, plant them in the garden while they bloom, then pull and discard them when they finish blooming.

---

will be more difficult to move around in it and reach plants at the back of the border.

If the young perennials raised from seed indoors are developing thin, leggy stems, *pinch them back* to a place above the second set of leaves. This will stimulate them to develop multiple stems for a more compact plant.

Problem Solving

Slugs are the biggest potential problem in shade gardens when the delicate, ephemeral spring flowers appear. Put out slug traps (see

---

March) a short distance from potential target plants.

Deer and rabbits love the tender new shoots of many perennials, but if you have lots of **Crocus** and **Tulips** on the property, they are likely to focus on them (see Bulbs, March).

Squirrels dig in the soil to try to find the nuts they buried last fall or to find bulbs. They make holes in lawns and garden beds, occasionally disturbing early perennials. They do not harm established perennials, but they may expose the roots of newly planted ones to drying out. Just push the roots back into the soil, and fill in any holes with soil.

Planning

This is planting month throughout most of Pennsylvania. Local garden centers have lots of fresh new perennials available in different sizes. Small young plants in 4- or 6-inch pots are least expensive. Larger plants in individual quart, one-gallon, two-gallon, and larger pots cost more, but these plants have more of an immediate presence in the garden. Unlike annuals, perennials are slow to establish. It is not until their second year in your garden that they really show their stuff. It is vitally important to choose healthy perennials at the garden center. Their stems and foliage will indicate if they have problems:

- Wilted foliage—improperly watered

- Yellow, limp foliage—insufficient light or fertilizer

- Holes in foliage—insects

- Dark blotches or gray coating on foliage—possible fungal disease

- Blotches on the stems—injury or disease

- Tiny pale spots or dark specks on leaf undersides—insects

- Thin, lanky stem—insufficient light

- Lots of flowers on undersized plant—overfertilized or aged plant

- Roots emerging from pot drainage holes—plant cramped

- Weeds in the container—poor care

Planting

No matter how healthy a new perennial is, unless it is happy where it is planted, it will not thrive. *Check* plant labels for the correct cold-hardiness zone number and the plant's cultural requirements. Choose a planting site where its needs will be met.

Keep newly purchased perennials moist until planting time. Then dig a hole as deep as the plant's container and slightly wider. Slip the plant from its pot and set it in its hole. Make sure it is at the same depth it was in its pot. Fill in loose soil around the rootball, and firm it around the stem. Water well.

Dig a hole for the perennial.

You can plant perennials in large decorative outdoor containers as you would plant annuals, perhaps combining them so the annuals can provide colorful flowers during the time the perennials display foliage only. Use soilless planting medium with a granular, slow-acting fertilizer mixed in.

Rx Care for Your Perennials

Established perennials send out stem or root runners to form new plants nearby, or they develop larger clumps as their crowns enlarge and send up more stems. Either way, they will reach a point when they are too large for their space in your garden bed. They are crowding neighboring plants, and may begin to die out in the center of the clump. To renew the plants, *divide* them. The commonly recommended time to divide perennials is in either spring or fall after they bloom. However, for many plants you can get away with doing it when you have time (other than midsummer).

1 For easier handling, try to time the division so emerging shoots are only 2 or 3 inches tall.

2 Dig under the roots and their soil, and *lift* the plant from the soil.

3 Use a sharp knife, flat spade, garden fork, or something similar to cut through the clump of roots to make rooted chunks of plant.

4 *Discard* woody, thin, or dead centers of old plants.

5 *Replant* one of the viable rooted chunks in the former planting spot, and plant the others elsewhere or in pots for gifts.

Mulch all newly planted perennials with a 2- to 3-inch layer of organic material such as shredded leaves, pine needles, or compost.

Some perennials will need support as they mature. Individual, unobtrusive green bamboo stakes are suitable for single-stemmed plants such as **Delphiniums** and **Foxgloves.** Use several with a matrix of twine to support large clumps of stems of plants such as **Beebalm, Asters,** and **Black-eyed Susans.** The stakes should be just slightly shorter than the plant's maximum height when they are inserted into the soil 10 to 12 inches.

By month's end it should be safe to acclimate the young perennials that were raised indoors to the outdoors. Set them in a shaded place for a few hours daily, gradually increasing the light and outdoor time. After a few overnight stays, they will be ready

to be planted in the garden or in a container.

Watering

Water newly planted perennials well at planting time. If rainfall is unreliable, *check* them every four or five days—more often if you have not mulched.

Fertilizing

Perennials planted in beds where granular, slow-acting fertilizer has been dug into the soil do not need fertilizing this spring. *Check* the product label for the number of weeks the fertilizer will last.

Grooming

Some spring-blooming perennials will have finished blooming by now. Removing their faded flowers neatens their appearance and sometimes stimulates a few more blooms later in the summer. Use hedge shears to clip off the small flowers from low-growing mats of **Candytuft, Pinks,** and **Phlox** quickly and evenly. Use handpruners for larger, faded blossoms.

The flower spikes of **Lamb's Ears** and some kinds of **Coral Bells** and the flowers on **Coleus** and **Artemisia** are regarded by many as dispensable. *Cut them off* as they develop over the season.

Problem Solving

Skunks leave small conical holes in the lawn or garden soil and paths where they dig for grubs. The occasional plant they might disturb is a small price to pay for the service of grub control.

Ants may crawl all over the swollen buds on **Peonies.** They are not harming them—they are seeking the sweet juices that healthy buds secrete.

Aphids will probably show up clustered at the tender growing tips of certain perennials. Until their natural predators arrive in your yard, control them by pinching off the infested stem tips and discarding them in the trash.

Plants may disappear after blooming. This is normal for **Bleeding Heart, Virginia Bluebells, Oriental Poppies,** and certain other early-season bloomers. They go dormant for the summer and they will return next year.

JUNE

Planning

It is important to record in a garden notebook, calendar, or journal when your perennials begin to bloom and how long they bloom. Because most perennials bloom for a relatively short time, each typically shows mostly foliage for much of the season. Without planning and careful choice of plants, the garden is likely to be mainly green foliage for the bulk of the season. If your records indicate that you have mostly spring-blooming perennials, plan to acquire some later-season bloomers now while there is still a good selection at the garden center. To assure some color in the garden all summer:

- Choose perennials that bloom in midsummer, late summer, and early fall.

- Choose plants with variegated foliage.

- Plant annuals among the perennials.

- Choose perennials that have long bloom periods.

- *Cut off* faded flowers and stems to promote repeat bloom later in the season.

- *Record* those companion plants that look good.

Planting

Plant perennial plants as soon as possible after you purchase them. If they sit around in pots, they are likely to dry out and/or become pot-bound, stressing them unnecessarily. Any perennials that you grew indoors from seed should be planted early this month.

Plant any divisions of plants that you have made or been given as soon as possible. They dry out very easily, and they need as much growing season as possible to get well-established in the soil.

Care for Your Perennials

Make sure the mulch layer around perennials is no thicker than 3 inches. That is sufficient to discourage weeds and maintain soil moisture, but it will not interfere with the roots' access to air.

Do not delay setting up supporting stakes for plants that will develop tall stems or clumps. Once the stems fall to the ground or begin to develop crookedly, it is difficult to train them to grow straight.

Watering

Established perennials need about 1 inch of water a week from the rain or from watering. Those in sandy soil need more because the soil drains so quickly. Mix in some organic matter at planting time to help the soil hold more moisture. Perennials that are mulched need less-frequent watering because soil moisture is not lost to evaporation and runoff.

Check soil moisture around newly planted perennials every week or so if it does not rain; their soil dries out a bit faster than that of established plants.

Staking perennials

Fertilizing

The granular, slow-acting fertilizer you added to the soil when preparing the garden bed or at planting time will continue to offer nutrition to perennials for several weeks, as indicated on the package label.

If there is no granular fertilizer mixed into the potting medium of perennials in decorative containers, remember to *water-in* some diluted fertilizer for them every two weeks all season long, or as recommended on the package label.

Grooming

Pinch back the lengthening stems of **Chrysanthemums** by half to encourage denser branching and more flowers in the fall. Because this practice also delays the development of buds, do so every few weeks until the end of next month if you want the **Mums** to bloom in October. Otherwise, they will bloom earlier, in September.

To guide and control the growth of other summer- and fall-blooming perennials that tend to become overtall and lanky—**Beebalm, Artemisias, Asters, Goldenrod,** and others—cut back newly developing stems by about half after they grow to about 10 or 12 inches long. This will delay flowering somewhat, but it will result in shorter, fuller plants that may not need staking.

Cut off stems of **Daylilies** whose flowers have all faded. In reblooming varieties, this will encourage the continuous development of new stems and buds. It improves the appearance of any **Daylily.**

Growing Smarter

There are all kinds of perennial gardens. The classic one is the perennial border. Typically a potentially stunning, high-maintenance effort, it features as many perennials as can possibly be crammed into a long, relatively narrow bed along a fence, hedge, walkway, or building. More common is the mixed border, which features perennial flowering and foliage plants, small shrubs, and maybe even a small tree. There are other types of gardens where perennials are at home:

- an island bed that is viewed from all sides
- a naturalistic woodland/shade garden
- a rock garden
- a meadow
- a cutting garden for producing flowers, foliage, and dried pods for bouquets

Problem Solving

Leafminer activity usually becomes obvious on plant foliage (especially **Columbine**) after flowering. Their tunneling in leaf tissues makes visible white serpentine trails. *Cut back* the infested foliage to the ground, and put it in the trash. Cutting back will stimulate new foliage growth.

Slugs may be making inroads on shade-loving perennials. Look for chewed leaves and shiny mucous trails. Turn over boards and other debris to find them hiding during the day, and put them in a plastic bag for the trash. Set out traps (see March) to catch others.

Weeds steal nutrients and moisture in the soil intended for your cultivated plants. They may harbor insects and disease pathogens. *Pull them* as soon as you notice them. Use mulch to cover bare soil and prevent their seeds from germinating.

Runaway plants spread so rampantly that they crowd out their neighbors and monopolize soil moisture and nutrients. Known offenders are **Running Bamboo, Mint, Japanese Loosestrife, Glory Bower,** and **Creeping Lilyturf.** Plant them where their growth is restricted, perhaps in containers or between paved areas and walls.

Planning

After the Fourth, there is usually a flowering pause in the garden. Spring bloomers have had their day in the sun, and the summer bloomers are not quite ready to perform. In years where a hot spell comes early, the pause is not so noticeable. Other years it is more obvious. Include in your seasonal notes details about the weather and the onset of summer blooms. You might want to choose some plants to fill in the gap. Adding some annuals will do this nicely.

Some plants are in season all season long. These are the perennials that sport interesting and colorful foliage rather than fancy, striking flowers; they provide nonstop color to bridge the peak flowering times of other perennials. Plants with silver-and-white or bright-yellow foliage add to the color mix even if their flowers are absent or insignificant.

Many familiar perennials are also available with variegated foliage in green-and-white or green-and-yellow (or -cream) stripes, speckles, or blotches, doubling their color contribution to a garden. Certain **Hosta, Jacob's Ladder, Phlox,** and ornamental grass varieties are good examples.

Planting

Once summer heat arrives, it is not advisable to plant or transplant perennials if it can possibly be avoided. Either they are about to bloom, or have just bloomed and their vigor is already being drained. Adding the stress of being uprooted and then planted in a new environment while trying to cope with heat and humidity may compromise their health for the rest of the season. Although many perennial plants survive summer transplanting, they are at risk for insect attack or disease.

To avoid as much transplant stress as possible:

- ***Plant*** on a cloudy day or in the evening.

- ***Shade*** new transplants for a day or two if they are in a sunny site.

- ***Delay planting*** until the heat breaks and temperatures are cooler.

- ***Cut back*** foliage by $^1/_3$ to $^1/_2$ to minimize moisture loss through transpiration.

- ***Water and mulch*** new transplants to assure sufficient soil moisture.

Care for Your Perennials

With the onset of summer heat, the organic material in the mulch around perennials and other plants begins to decompose, and the layer will grow thinner. ***Spread*** fresh material to maintain 2 to 3 inches in depth. Pull any weeds that may have taken hold when the mulch was thin.

Stake plants before they grow so wide or tall that their stems flop. It takes only a few minutes for a summer rainstorm to flatten stately stalks of **Phlox, Beebalm, Meadow Rue,** and similar plants. A child's runaway soccer ball or a heedless dog will accomplish the same thing. Plants that are growing upright have cleaner, healthier flowers and foliage, and a better appearance.

Stake perennials.

Watering

If it is to be a dry summer, it is usually apparent by mid-July. Well-mulched, established perennials growing in decent soil can manage a week or ten days between rainfalls or waterings. *Check* the soil moisture of recently planted perennials more frequently. Feel an inch or two down in the soil under the mulch layer, or insert the probe of a houseplant water meter into the soil a few inches to determine if the soil is dry. Pay particular attention to shallow-rooted plants and moisture lovers such as **Astilbe.** They may need watering more often.

Fertilizing

As organic mulch gradually decomposes in the hot weather, it adds valuable humus to the soil around perennials. Earthworms and weather help incorporate the humus into the soil to increase its moisture absorption. The humus also stimulates the activity of the soil's resident microbial life, which maintains the fertility of the soil. This infusion of humus often boosts nutrition at midseason for perennials that already have granular, slow-acting fertilizer in their soil.

If more than ten weeks have passed since a slow-acting product was added to their soil, late-summer bloomers will benefit from a light dose of granular fertilizer scratched into the soil now.

Grooming

Cut off any broken or diseased stems promptly.

Clip off dead flowers to prevent disease and stimulate new bloom. With plants like **Coreopsis,** where the flowers are at the ends of bare stems, cut the stems off as well, back to where some leaves appear. This will keep the flowers at the ends of bare stems, and keep them looking nice.

If plants that have already bloomed are looking really ragged, exhausted, and unsightly, *cut them back* to the ground and they will develop fresh, new foliage for the remainder of the season. Sometimes they even manage to bloom again before frost.

Continue to *pinch back* stems of **Chrysanthemums** to delay their blooming until mid-fall.

Problem Solving

Japanese beetles appear early this month in many areas of Pennsylvania. Make a note of when you first spot them in the garden, as they return every year at almost the same time. Look for chewed leaves and flowerbuds, and you will find the metallic-colored beetles nearby. Start control with the first arrivals; knock them from plant foliage into a jar of soapy water. *Check* the plants they seem to favor several times a day, if possible. The more you destroy, the fewer will have an opportunity to lay eggs in the soil to become next year's pests.

Mites may infest plants such as **Chrysanthemums** that are stressed by heat and drought. Look for light stippling on the leaves and fine webbing around stems. *Wash them off* foliage with a forceful water spray from the hose. Repeat several times a week for two weeks. *Check* after a week or two to be sure they have not returned.

Powdery mildew may develop on the foliage of certain perennials like **Phlox, Beebalm,** and **Veronica.** The fungus forms a gray coating on the foliage in humid weather. It is unsightly, but rarely life-threatening. If the plants have bloomed, *cut back* stems to the ground to promote uninfected new growth. Try plant varieties that are labeled disease-resistant.

AUGUST

Planning

One of the many things to consider when planning and managing gardens that feature perennials is that many plants self-sow their seeds. Plants such as **Black-eyed Susan, Columbine, Coreopsis, Fringed Bleeding Heart, Purple Coneflower, Hardy Begonia, Goldenrod, Hellebore, Shasta Daisy,** and others do this to varying degrees. Some gardeners welcome this—new young plants that appear in the garden next season are easily pulled up and discarded, dug up and moved to a desirable location, or potted for friends. To encourage perennials to seed themselves, leave faded flowers on the plants so seeds will dry and scatter.

Another good reason to leave seedheads on late-season perennials is to provide seed for visiting wildlife. Finches of all kinds love the seeds of **Purple Coneflower** and **Black-eyed Susan.**

This is **Goldenrod** month, and open fields and meadows are aglow. There are several really nice garden varieties of **Goldenrod** that will become a hallmark of your late-summer landscape. Contrary to popular myth, they do not cause allergies.

Planting

While the weather is typically too hot and oppressive for planting in the garden this month, you might want to **propagate** some favorite perennials from soft-stem cuttings. This can be done almost anytime during the growing season.

1 **Cut** each stem about 6 inches back from its tip just above a node, the point where leaves emerge from it. Choose stems tipped with foliage only, or **pinch off** any incipient buds or flowers.

2 **Remove** the lowest leaves so that an inch or so of stem is bare. Dip the cut end into rooting hormone powder (available at most garden centers).

3 **Insert** a pencil into a pot filled with moist vermiculite, perlite, and peat moss to make a hole for the stem cutting. Then stick the powdered end of the cutting into the moist rooting medium.

4 **Water** well, and **cover** the pot with clear plastic wrap or a plastic bag to maintain a moist environment around the cutting.

5 **Set** pots of cuttings in light, but not direct sun. Make sure they do not dry out. When small leaves begin to emerge, that is a signal that roots have established.

6 **Remove** the plastic, and increase the sunlight (if the plants are sun lovers). Water-in a very dilute fertilizer when you water, as the rooting medium has no nutrients in it.

The softer, more succulent its stem, the more likely a perennial will root in a glass of water on the windowsill.

Care for Your Perennials

Toward the end of the growing season the number of daylight hours decreases daily, and new young plants made from rooted stem cuttings will not have the luxury of a full growing season in the garden to build their vigor. Rather than plant them directly into a garden bed, provide a temporary winter location where they are more protected. Designate a sheltered area as a nursery bed, and either set their pots in the soil or remove them from the pots and plant them in the soil.

Check the supports of large late-summer perennials to be sure they can handle the full weight of the plant in bloom.

AUGUST

Watering

Established perennials can survive without water for ten days to two weeks—*if* they are first mulched and watered well.

Perennials in decorative containers, either alone or with annuals, will dry out in a day or two if it is hot. At this point in the season their root systems are crowding the pot and the planting medium dries out even more quickly than it would in June or July.

Ways to conserve water:

- *Group* plants by water preference. Locate low-water-demand plants farther from the house. Locate those that need more regular moisture near the house and hose for convenient watering.

- *Mulch* garden beds well to reduce evaporation of moisture from the soil and prevent runoff from rain or watering.

- *Use* drip irrigation systems, which leak water slowly directly into the soil to minimize waste.

- *Plant* perennials that do not require lots of moisture— **Yarrow, Artemisia, Coreopsis, Baby's Breath,** and **Daylilies.**

Fertilizing

Do not fertilize perennials after mid-month. Except for those that bloom in the fall, most perennials are now preparing to enter dormancy. Unless plants have six weeks or more before frost arrives in your area, the new growth stimulated by the fertilizer will likely be killed by frost.

Grooming

As the summer wanes, the perennial garden may begin to look a bit shabby. Some primping and clipping will soon restore a groomed look.

- To neaten their appearance, *cut back* leggy stems of plants such as **Artemisia, Goldenrod,** and **Black-eyed Susan** after they bloom.

- To improve the appearance of plants such as **Lady's Mantle,** *pluck* aged, discolored foliage, allowing younger, fresher foliage to show.

- Clip off the spent flowerheads on **Phlox** to stimulate a second, sparser flowering.

- *Cut off* flower stems from **Hostas** as soon as the flowers fade.

Problem Solving

Mites love the dry, hot conditions that stress plants. *Check* perennials for pale, stippled leaves and fine webbing on stems. Wash mites off infected plants with a forceful spray of water from the hose. *Repeat* in a week or two.

Fungal diseases, usually in the form of mildews, thrive in heat and humidity. They appear on plant foliage as a gray or white coating and cause leaves to droop, shrivel, and eventually dry out and drop off stems. At this point in the season it is easiest to *cut off* plant stems to the ground. Pick up fallen leaves and debris, and discard in the trash.

Viral and bacterial diseases sometimes attack perennials. When they do, symptoms such as wilting foliage seem to appear suddenly. These diseases typically infect the roots or crown of the plant, causing it to rot. Since there are no cures for these diseases, prevention is the key. Immediately dig up the plant, including as many roots as possible and the soil surrounding them. Put it in a plastic bag and discard in the trash. *Disinfect* any tools you use by dipping them in a solution of hot water and household bleach.

Planning

Traditionally, Labor Day weekend marks the end of summer. That may be true for schoolchildren, but it's not true for gardeners. Often this is one of the best times in the perennial garden, as the cooler temperatures bring out colors and crisp up foliage. The golden light created by the changing angle of the sun casts a warm glow on your yard. Many earlier-blooming perennials may sport pods or seedheads that punctuate beds abounding with **Boltonia, Asters, Black-eyed Susans, Datura, Turtlehead, Tall Sedums, Mums,** and other late-season bloomers. Since many annuals will still be going strong, a mixed border can be as exciting now as at any other time during the season.

Continue to *record* in your garden notebook or journal what is blooming this month as the season winds down. If you notice glaring gaps in the bloom sequence over the season—times when nothing is in flower and foliage carries the ball for quite a while—think about acquiring plants to add bloom during these times. You may have plenty of sun-lovers, but the shade garden may need an infusion of late-summer bloom. Or vice versa.

Try to find time to visit nearby public gardens and arboreta, and see how they do the fall season. *Write down* the names of the plants you like, and note the conditions they seem to like. You can find out more about them from books or the catalogs that will start arriving soon.

Planting

Fall is a great time to plant perennials. Those in pots at the garden center may not look great this time of year, because they are starting to die back for the winter just like the ones in your garden. Some may have spent the season in their pots and are rootbound. However, they may also be on sale.

Planting or transplanting perennials now affords them several weeks to get comfortable before the ground freezes. This time of year they do not have to produce foliage and flowers, so they can concentrate on expanding their root systems.

Take special care if plants have roots that are matted and wrapped around themselves from long confinement in their pots. Tease apart the roots, or pry them loose so that they hang free before you set the plant in its hole.

Perennials with single, long taproots like **Balloon Flower, Globe Thistle, Columbine** and **Butterfly Weed** are particularly tricky to transplant. It is essential to dig deeply to be sure you get the entire brittle, tapering root. It tends to break off, leaving critical root fibers in the soil and reducing the chances for the plant to succeed in its new site.

This is also a good time to *divide* clumps of perennials that have grown too large over the summer. Wait to divide spring bloomers until after they bloom next spring (see division steps in May).

Care for Your Perennials

Stake tall plants that are blooming or are about to bloom. If they have already started to flop and their stems are bent, prop them up the best you can so their flowers are visible.

If plants in certain areas of the yard have not performed well this season despite your attention, there may be a problem with the soil. The problem is often signaled by off-color foliage and lack of vigor. Take a soil test to determine if it is deficient in one or more essential nutrients. Call your county extension office to order a mailer for sending a soil sample for laboratory analysis. You will receive a computer printout of the results.

SEPTEMBER

Watering

Water potted **Chrysanthemums** and other perennials. They will dry out very quickly if the weather is mild and they are in the sun.

Water newly planted divisions and transplants well if there is not enough rain to provide about an inch of water a week. If they are mulched well, they will need moisture less frequently.

If it has been a dry late summer, garden areas that are usually damp, or even boggy, may dry up. Remember to *check* moisture levels so that **Turtlehead, Lobelia, Astilbe, Joe-pye Weed, Swamp Milkweed**, and **Red (Swamp) Hibiscus,** all plants that love to have their feet in damp soil, do not suffer.

Grooming

If the birds have pretty much eaten all the seeds from **Purple Cone-flowers** and **Black-eyed Susans,** cut back the plants' stems to the ground.

To maintain the appearance of the garden, continue to *deadhead* faded flowers from plants that are still blooming. Next month will be major cleanup time.

Problem Solving

Weeds become very obvious now that garden perennials and other plants are dying back. Many of the perennial weeds such as nutsedge, wild grape, plantain, and Pennsylvania smartweed are still green. As long as the weather is mild and they are growing, they will be susceptible to herbicide. *Spray* them now with Roundup® or a similar product that kills their roots.

Pest insects normally represent only about 10 percent of all the insects in your yard. The others are either beneficial or benign. Chronic pest insect infestations on perennials suggests that populations of beneficial insects in your yard are low. This may be caused by a number of garden problems:

1 Plants have been unusually stressed, and are more vulnerable. Think about the possible causes of the stress—poor site or soil—and *correct* it for next season.

2 Frequently used general insecticides have killed off many resident beneficials. Use methods that target specific pests (see Appendix).

3 There is not a large enough diversity of plants in the yard to support a healthy population of beneficial insects. Next spring, *plant* an insectary garden filled with lots of different plants.

Growing Smarter

The Perennial Plant Association (PPA) is an organization of producers, growers, and sellers of perennial plants. They promote the use of perennial plants in civic spaces and public and private gardens. In an effort to educate gardeners about perennials, each year the membership selects a Plant of the Year, a perennial which is exceptionally hardy, beautiful, and easy to grow.

1990 *Phlox stolonifera*
1991 *Heuchera* '**Palace Purple**'
1992 *Coreopsis* '**Moonbeam**'
1993 *Veronica* '**Sunny Border**'
1994 *Astilbe* '**Sprite**'
1995 *Perovskia atriplicifolia*
1996 *Penstemon* '**Husker Red**'
1997 *Salvia nemerosa*
1998 *Echinacea* '**Magnus**'
1999 *Rudbeckia* '**Goldsturm**'
2000 *Scabiosa* '**Butterfly Blue**'

Planning

The one thing gardeners in most of Pennsylvania can count on this month is a fresh supply of leaves. What a gift! The trees that grow so well here have been providing humus from their decomposed foliage in the forest for ages. Harvest this resource to build and renew your soil so it will resemble the soft, rich soil in the woods. Ways to use fallen leaves in the landscape:

- *Chop or shred* them to spread as a mulch on all bare soil on the property.

- Chop or shred them, and *mix* them into soil cultivated to create or renovate planting beds.

- *Pile* them to partially decompose into leaf mold for mulch or soil conditioning.

- *Pile* them with other organic materials such as weeds, prunings, kitchen peelings, or straw to completely decompose into compost.

- *Mow* them with a mulching mower as they lie on the lawn, and bag them with grass clippings for use as mulch or, eventually, compost.

Cool weather inspires outdoor projects now that plant-care chores are about over for the year. This is a great time to build or repair a walk, fence, or patio. *Dig* new beds or renovate existing ones so that you will be ready to plant in the spring.

Look around the house, garage, and tool shed for plant labels, equipment warranties, and product packaging that has instructions for use and storage of garden supplies. Collect them to store in an envelope in your garden notebook or journal. Don't forget to include photographs you have taken over the season to document the location and performance of your plants.

Planting

Theoretically, you can plant perennials that are in containers practically any time the ground is not frozen. It is better to plant them than leave them in their cramped containers all winter.

If one of your fall landscape projects is building a stone wall or laying a stone terrace or patio, try planting some plants among the stones:

- Choose sturdy, low-growing perennials such as **Moneywort** or **Moss Pinks** that love the excellent drainage of coarse, gravelly, or sandy soil.

- Tuck plants in the crevices created when you lay a course of rock in a dry wall, or plant them as you build the wall in spaces you purposely leave between the stones.

Care for Your Perennials

Herbaceous perennials disappear with the arrival of frost, although their roots still grow underground. Clean up flopped leaves and dried stems, then *mulch* the soil over their roots for the winter. Do this after the ground freezes hard. If you live in the warmer area of the state near Philadelphia, sometimes that does not happen until January—in that case, spread winter mulch around Thanksgiving to have the job done.

Some plants in your garden will continue to show green foliage over the winter. These are not true perennials. Called **biennials** because their life cycle spans two seasons, they will survive just one winter. They are genetically programmed to grow vegetation the first season, and then send up flower spikes or stems for blooming the second. If this is their first fall, mulch biennials well. If it is their second fall, they will die with frost, and you can pull them out. Next spring, check the area for seedlings from the seeds they leave behind.

Watering

Water any plants you have moved or added to the garden if there is not sufficient rainfall during the time before the ground freezes hard. Make sure wintering-over biennials get sufficient moisture, too.

When the perennials have died back to the ground, *install* drip irrigation. Snake lengths of porous hose through beds among the plants, and attach them to a feeder line that links them to an outdoor faucet. Then spread fresh winter mulch, which will cover the irrigation lines. Water leaking slowly from the entire length of the hose and soaking slowly into the soil near plant roots reduces fungal disease due to wet leaves.

Grooming

Frosty mornings blacken annuals dramatically, but perennials preparing for dormancy may have already begun to turn brown and die back. First frost is a signal to gardeners that it is time for major cleanup.

- *Cut back* remaining soggy or dried stems, and *clean up* fallen leaves that may harbor fungal spores. Pull or cut back weeds.

Growing Smarter

Hellebores and their hybrids provide interesting evergreen foliage and flowers when most garden perennials are dormant.

- **Christmas Rose** (*Helleborus niger*) forms clumps of dark-green leaves with toothed leaflets that spring directly from the soil. In late December, purple stems arise among them, bearing saucerlike white or pink-tinged flowers with greenish centers.
- **Lenten Rose** (*Helleborus hybridus*) forms open mounds of glossy, leathery, deeply divided leaves year 'round. Slightly nodding flowers in wonderful variations of cream, pink, and maroon—with and without speckles—appear mid-winter.
- **Bearsfoot Hellebore** (*Helleborus foetidus*) features a burst of narrow, rich-green, toothed leaves at the top of sturdy 3- to 5-inch stems. About midwinter it produces stalks of yellow-green, bell-shaped flowers that sometimes have purple edges.

- *Leave* ornamental grasses in full-blown glory. Their bleached stems and fluffy seedheads will provide something interesting to see in the garden over the winter.

- *Pick up* boards, twigs, old pots, and other debris.

- *Pull out* stakes and other supports, and *store them*.

- *Bring in* any decorative pots, statuary, and birdbaths that may crack in cold weather.

Problem Solving

Rodents like to nest in deep, soft mulch. If you have vole, mice, or chipmunk problems, *delay* spreading winter mulch until the ground freezes. By then the rodents will have found alternative nesting sites.

Fallen leaves lying on garden beds may mat together and prevent moisture from soaking into the soil. Rake or vacuum up leaves and *shred* them. Then cover the beds with them.

Planning

It is possible to have a winter perennial garden. It does not feature flowers, but it offers a welcome alternative to the typical bleak, empty winter garden bed. With judicious selection of plants and careful planning, you can create a garden that is interesting during the winter months when there is sparse snowfall. Choose a site that is visible from the windows of the house so you can enjoy it when you are shut in by the weather. A winter garden might include:

- Colorful evergreen foliage of **Hellebores, Hardy Ferns, European Ginger, Ivy,** and **Pachysandra**

- The semi-evergreen foliage on **Barrenwort** and some other perennials—it turns purplish or yellow and persists for many weeks

- Bright berries from plants such as **Arum** and **Jack-in-the-pulpit**

- Interesting dried stems of ornamental grasses, **Blazing Star,** and **Dwarf Astilbe**

- Silver foliage that persists on some **Artemisias**

- Architectural lines provided by dried stems topped with seedpods and seedheads of **Yarrow, Tall Sedums,** and others

Take inventory of supplies—pots, potting medium, fertilizer, insecticidal soap, twine—used up during the season, and start a list in your garden notebook of what you will need to purchase early next season.

Planting

Outdoor planting time is past in parts of the state where hard frost has shut down the season. Because the roots of any perennials still in pots are vulnerable to freezing if they are aboveground, do not leave them outdoors over the winter without protection. Either sink the pots into the compost or mulch pile, or bring them into a cool, dry place such as a cold frame, garage, or cellar where the temperature does not go below freezing.

If you feel the urge to plant, try planting some seeds. Certain perennial seeds require a period of moist cold in order to germinate. After frost arrives, conditions are good for planting seeds in pots filled with moist potting medium.

1   *Cover* the pots with plastic to keep their moisture from drying out.

2   *Set* them outdoors in a protected location where they can experience winter weather but will not be damaged by winds and snow. A porch or cold frame where the temperature dependably stays below 40 degrees F is ideal. Leave them there for four to eight weeks.

3   *Check* pots for sprouts as the winter wanes and temperatures warm 10 or 15 degrees. Different perennials respond to slightly different conditions.

4   When sprouts emerge, remove the plastic, *move* the sprouts into bright, indirect light, and begin to water them. Make sure they continue to experience roughly the same air temperatures that perennials outdoors are experiencing.

5   As seedlings develop in late winter or spring, *provide* dilute doses of fertilizer every few waterings, as well as larger pots. Plan to plant them in late spring—or early fall if they have not grown large enough to go into the garden safely.

 ## Care for Your Perennials

Spread winter mulch up to 6 inches deep on the soil over the root zones of perennials. Use pine needles, shredded leaves, wood chips, or straw. Spreading the mulch after the soil is cold or frozen will:

- protect soil from compaction by heavy rain, or snow.

- insulate soil by buffering temperature extremes of freeze-thaw cycles that heave soil and disturb plant roots.

- help soil absorb and retain moisture.

- keep soil cold in early spring to avoid premature emergence of perennials.

- discourage early growth of weeds.

To forestall the recurrence of disease problems next season, before snow flies, pick up all fallen leaves from the area where infected perennials grew. Remove the remaining summer-season mulch, which might harbor spores, and spread fresh mulch.

Watering

Every so often Pennsylvania autumns are mild and dry, and a prolonged Indian Summer occurs. When this happens, *water* perennial gardens and other planted areas well before the ground freezes hard. Pay particular attention to newly planted and transplanted perennials.

Grooming

Garden cleanup should finally be finished by Thanksgiving. Except for those plants that will provide some winter interest, cut back the dried, ratty stems of all perennials. There is no need to cut them off at ground level—in fact, it is a good idea to leave short lengths of stem on plants to mark where they are located. This is especially helpful for late arrivals such as **Balloon Flower**. Otherwise, there is a danger of forgetting that they are there and digging or planting on top of them in spring.

Problem Solving

Wind may be a problem in certain beds located in exposed areas. If there is no snow cover, wind may blow mulch off soil, leaving it bare and drying it out. There are several possible solutions to the blowing mulch problem: 1) Use pine needles as mulch—they are less likely to blow around. 2) Leave 4- to 6-inch lengths of stem on perennials when cutting them back for garden cleanup; they will trap and hold chopped leaf mulch so that it is less likely to blow. 3) Erect a low wind screen made from burlap or landscape fabric; fasten it to stakes at the front of the affected beds to block the wind.

Growing Smarter

Compost is a wonderful garden resource for improving the soil. The fact that it is easily made at home from yard and some kitchen waste, and is therefore free, makes it even more valuable. Essentially the tough, fibrous parts that remain after organic materials decompose, compost is soft and spongy. Whether your soil tends toward clay or sand, the humus that compost provides creates a better environment for most plants. When mixed into soil, it improves the soil's ability to hold air and water, and simultaneously helps it drain better. The microbial life that lives in soil transforms its nutrients into a form that plant roots can easily take up, and these microbes thrive when soil provides oxygen and some (not too much) moisture. When the microbes are on the job, soil is fertile and plants thrive.

DECEMBER

Planning

A review of your notes from the season just past will remind you of some of the changes you want to make next year. The health of certain perennials which are not quite in the ideal spot can be improved by moving them. They may need more sun, moister soil, or more room than you anticipated. Perhaps you will want to add more plants to fine-tune bloom sequences or color coordination. Sometimes a garden bed needs more variety in plant height or foliage color or texture to look its best. Make a list now of changes you are considering before end-of-year holidays divert your attention.

Some ideas for a holiday gift list:

- certificate for a purchase at a favorite garden center

- membership at the local botanic garden or arboretum

- comprehensive reference book on perennials

- book on designing a garden

- new garden journal for the coming year

One way to learn more about gardening is to enroll in the Master Gardener program. Call your local county extension office to inquire about classes (see Appendix for county extension offices).

Planting

As you planted and transplanted perennials last season, no doubt you became aware that soil type varies somewhat at different locations on your property. There are probably places where the soil is less than ideal, possibly areas near the house that feature builder's fill, silty subsoil laced with pieces of mortar, bricks or stone, and the occasional nail or piece of glass. Other areas may be sandy, soggy, or rock-hard clay.

Take this into account when choosing and locating perennials next year. Some plants actually prefer soggy, boggy soil. Others love gritty, fast-draining soil. On the theory that it is easier to adapt the plant to the soil, rather than vice versa, aim to plant the right plant in the right place.

Care for Your Perennials

- Have you groomed and mulched all perennial beds?

- Have you planted outdoors or protected all potted perennials?

- Have you collected and stored all stakes and other plant supports?

- Have you brought indoors all ornaments and pots that are vulnerable to winter weather?

- Have you set up and filled bird feeders and birdbaths?

Watering

Until and unless there is a major freeze in the forecast, keep the outdoor water turned on in case you need to use the hose or drip irrigation. If the soil in perennial beds was moist before it was mulched, plants should be fine if there is a week or two of dry weather. *Check* unmulched areas, especially if temperatures are mild for an extended period.

Grooming

If the pods, seedheads, and berries that remained on perennials have already been depleted by the birds and other wildlife, *cut back* the stems to neaten the yard.

Roses

I confess to feeling extremely ambivalent about roses. I love to receive them on birthdays and Valentine's Day, I enjoy the fragrance of those varieties that still have fragrance, and I love the idea of cutting them in the garden and bringing them indoors to display on the dining room table. It is growing them that causes me to have mixed emotions, for I did not have much success in the past. They are basically a flowering shrub, and how difficult can it be to grow a shrub and have it bloom? In my early experience, very difficult.

The Reign of the Hybrid Teas

I know now that was because in my youth (and until relatively recently), the rose reality for home gardeners was the **Hybrid Tea** rose and bush roses such as **Grandifloras** and **Floribundas.** Devoted rosarians knew about other kinds of roses, and so did horticulturists and world-class gardeners, but it was the **Hybrid Tea** type that was promoted to the unwitting public as the quintessential rose, the Platonic ideal, the "classic" rose. Some **Teas,** such as **'Peace'** or **'Mr. Lincoln',** were inextricably linked to our historical memory. Ultimately the **Rose,** typically pictured as a **Hybrid Tea,** became our national flower.

The result of intense breeding efforts over many years, most **Hybrid Tea** rose varieties manifested some of the classic signs of overbreeding. They were temperamental, fragile, disease-prone, and demanding. Stars of the garden, they behaved, much like some human celebrities, as prima donnas. They required a lot of tender, loving care, giving new meaning to the term "high-maintenance plant."

Conventional garden wisdom decreed that **Hybrid Tea** roses should be grown "in their own garden." As a matter of practical fact, this was a good idea. They took so much tending that it was much more efficient to have them all together in one place, and their typical stiff, upright posture did not suit them to cozy placement among other shrubs or flowering plants. As befitted their exalted status, the **Hybrid Teas** usually claimed the best sun in the garden, and there they required soil with superb drainage. They needed plenty of space, too—generous space between them assured the gardener could avoid being pricked while proceeding to prune, mulch, spray, deadhead, spray, cut, spray, and spray over the season.

Landscape Roses

My, how things have changed. Somewhere along the line, rose fanciers and breeders were inspired to broaden the definition of roses for the home garden and to embrace different kinds of these remarkable plants. They recalled and revived old-timers that unselfconsciously tumbled over walls and arbors in even the humblest gardens in England. They took an appreciative look at the roses that grew unceremoniously and sturdily at our summer homes at the seashore.

Breeders applied their skills to these other kinds of roses and came up with modern versions that retained the sturdy qualities of their parents yet featured great color and fine blossoms. They offered a whole new assortment of rose varieties dubbed **Landscape,** or **Shrub, Roses.** No prima donnas here! These new roses are tough, adaptable, disease- and pest-resistant, long-blooming, drought-tolerant—and many are fragrant. Less formal in habit than **Hybrid Tea** roses, the

Roses

new **Shrub** roses are comfortably at home in many places throughout a residential landscape. As ground covers, they hold the soil on slopes and replace high-maintenance turfgrass. When grown vertically, they create spaces, screen views, and soften hardscape. All this and beauty, too.

And what about the **Hybrid Teas?** They have benefited from the renewed interest and enthusiasm for roses that followed the introduction of the **Landscape** types. Breeders have redoubled their efforts to create **Hybrid Tea**–type roses that emulate the best qualities of their more self-reliant **Landscape** sisters. Experts are breeding for greater disease resistance, greater adaptability to a range of light and soil conditions, and general hardiness. Best of all, more varieties have fragrance.

All-America Rose Selections

In the constant search for even more wonderful roses, the rose industry is supported by organizations of professionals and amateur rose enthusiasts. All-America Rose Selections (AARS) is a nonprofit association dedicated to the introduction and promotion of exceptional roses. Since 1938 this organization has aided and abetted the constant improvement in garden roses by running a trial program that rigorously evaluates rose performance. The association challenges the rose industry to improve the vitality, strength, and beauty of roses, and confers the AARS imprimatur on the tags of the superior performers chosen each year.

The AARS accredits certain public gardens all over the country as showcases for their award winners. In Pennsylvania, there are display gardens at the following locations.

- Allentown: Malcolm W. Gross Memorial Rose Garden

- Hershey: Hershey Gardens

- McKeesport: Garden Club of McKeesport Arboretum at Renziehausen Park

- Philadelphia: The Morris Arboretum of the University of Pennsylvania

- West Grove: Robert Pyle Memorial Rose Garden

American Rose Society

The American Rose Society (ARS) also evaluates new rose varieties annually, grading them according to fragrance, shape, and disease-resistance. Evaluators are ARS members who are rose gardeners at all levels, from beginner to expert. The ARS rose ratings, also known as Proof of the Pudding, are averages of over five years of testing. They set the perfect rose at 10. Generally, it's best to select roses that rate from 7 to 10. The American Rose Society website, which includes Consulting Rosarians OnLine (a schedule of rose shows and more), can be found at **http://www.ars.org.** The ARS American Rose Center near Shreveport, Louisiana, contains more than 20,000 rosebushes of nearly 400 varieties of old and modern roses. Events are listed on the ARS website.

Cutting Roses

Roses for Pennsylvania

Name	Type	Uses	Bloom	Comments
'Autumn Sunblaze'™ 'Cherry Sunblaze'™	Miniature	Edging, specimen, container.	Orange-red. Cherry red. Continuous through the season.	Bushy. Can handle hot, dry conditions.
'Betty Prior'	Floribunda	Specimen or accent.	Single pink flower.	Tall, bushy. Generous blooms. Slightly fragrant.
'Bonica'	Landscape	Mass, hedge, screen, specimen.	Pastel-pink, double flowers all season.	AARS. Orange-red hips in fall.
'Carefree Delight'	Landscape	Mass, hedge, screen, foundation.	Single, deep-pink flowers.	Consistent color. Generous blooms.
'Carefree Sunshine'	Landscape	Border, foundation, hedge, massing.	Single, bright-yellow flowers.	New for 2001.
'Chevy Chase'	Rambler	Soften corners of buildings; cover landscape eyesores.	Small red flowers on 12- to 15-foot canes in early summer.	Mildew-resistant. Prune away old canes yearly.
'Cinderella'	Miniature	Edging, rock garden, container; good cut flower.	Pink-tinged white flowers. Continuous through the season.	Micro at 12 inches high. Nearly thornless. Disease-resistent.
'Eden Climber'	Climber	Woody sprawler reaches 10 to 15 feet tall; good for large space.	Fragrant, creamy-pink, double flowers in spring. Some rebloom later.	Fasten arching cane to support structure. Special pruning considerations.
Flower Carpet™	Landscape	Ground cover, slopes, screen.	Magenta, white, appleblossom, yellow. Continual.	Low, arching stems. Tough, pest-resistant.
'Fragrant Cloud'	Hybrid Tea	Group for flower border.	Double, orange-red, intensely fragrant flowers.	Susceptible to insect and disease problems.
'Guy de Maupassant'	Floribunda	Four-foot plants for specimens, accents.	Old-fashioned pink flowers.	Fragrance suggests apples.
'Knock Out'	Landscape	Medium height. Border, foundation, mass planting.	Single, cherry-red flowers.	AARS. Incredible disease resistance.
'New Dawn'	Climber	Enthusiastic, vigorous grower. Train on fences and walls.	Medium-sized, double, shell-pink flowers.	Spring, then rebloomer. Great disease resistance.
'Peter Mayle'™	Hybrid Tea	Large upright specimen. Great for cutting.	Double, deep-fuchsia flowers, 4 inches or more	Wonderful long-lasting rose fragrance. Tolerates heat and humidity.
'Queen Elizabeth'	Grandiflora	Large upright specimen. Great for cutting.	Large, flat, pink flowers.	AARS. Some fragrance. An all-time favorite.
'Red Cascade'	Miniature	Arching, spreading canes for ground cover, border, or container.	Small red flowers in clusters.	Versatile addition to the landscape.
'Regatta'	Hybrid Tea	Specimen, cutting.	Medium, double, soft peach-pink flowers.	Fruity fragrance.
Rosa rugosa hybrids	Landscape	Border, screen, windbreak hedge.	White, or various shades of red, pink. Textured foliage.	Handle drought and sandy or compacted soil. Disease resistant.
'Sun Sprinkles'	Miniature	Upright and mounded for edging, containers.	Bright-yellow 2-inch flowers.	AARS. Blooms all summer.
'The Fairy'	Polyantha / Landscape	Mass for ground cover, low hedge. Specimen for container planting.	Continual production of small, pink, double flowers in large sprays.	Compact 2-foot shrub. Versatile. Blooms until frost.
'Traviata'	Hybrid Tea	Good for cutting.	Clear-red 4-inch flowers.	Disease-tolerant foliage. Turns burgundy in fall.

Planning

It takes some imagination to visualize lovely roses out in the yard where now there are only some humps of mulch and soil around stubby canes. Exercise your imagination by browsing the new garden catalogs that have started to arrive in the mail. If you have some roses, you may want to try more. If you do not yet have any roses in your yard, why not plan to try some? This New Year's resolution will be easy to keep.

Roses are actually many different kinds of shrubs of different colors, sizes, and habits. They do not have to be planted in a bed of their own—or even in a garden. There is bound to be one that will fit comfortably into your landscape, whether it is formal or informal, small or large. The key to selection is identifying the reasons you want to grow roses. Some reasons might be:

- cutting for indoor display
- drying for floral crafts
- fragrance in the garden
- season-long color in the yard
- solving a landscape problem
- an enjoyable hobby

As you review the catalogs, look for improved varieties that are low-maintenance, hardy, and disease-resistant. Think about where there is lots of sun in your yard or garden and whether there is sufficient room there for a full-sized shrub. Otherwise, you may want to consider growing a rosebush in a container on a deck or patio. **Miniature Roses** are ideal for balconies and window-boxes. Think vertically, and consider **Climbers** or **Ramblers** on trellises or arbors where space is limited.

It is time to start a new garden journal or notebook for the new year. If you have lots of roses on your property, you may want to devote your journal exclusively to your experiences over the coming year with roses. Otherwise, *keep records* for all your plants to help you remember names, weather events, planting times, and pruning and blooming times. It is important to record problems that your roses encounter and how you solved them.

Care for Your Roses

If you are growing **Miniature Roses** indoors as houseplants, keep a close eye on them. This is a tough time for them. Their environment is very stressful because of cold drafts from opening doors, low humidity from central heating, and low light. Stress makes them vulnerable to pest and disease problems.

If possible, set potted **Miniature Roses** under fluorescent lights to increase the amount and duration of their daily light. *Group* them (but don't crowd them) to promote ambient humidity, and *check* their soil moisture often.

Outdoors, check to be sure rose shrubs are still nestled deeply in mulch, soil, or other protective materials such as pine boughs or water-permeable shrub jackets. *Replace* protection that has blown away and exposed the rose crowns to harsh wind and sun. In most parts of Pennsylvania, the coldest weather is yet to come.

Watering

Monitor indoor **Miniature Roses** closely for sufficient soil moisture—especially if they are in clay (terracotta) pots. In heated homes where humidity is low, the soil medium can dry out quickly, and the plants may need watering twice a week or more. Beware of overwatering, which will induce root rot and kill the plant.

A houseplant water meter or the pencil test will determine whether the soil is dry and watering is needed. Insert a sharpened pencil point about 2 inches into the soil, then remove it. If wet soil sticks fast to the pencil, check again in a few days. If there's some soil on the pencil, check again in a day. If the point comes up without any soil, it's time to water.

Ways to increase humidity:

- use a room humidifier

- cluster plants

- keep plants in the kitchen or bathroom

- set plants on shallow trays of damp gravel

Fertilizing

If **Miniature Roses** are actively blooming indoors, they will need nutrition. If you mixed some granular, slow-acting fertilizer into their potting medium when you potted them last fall, it will suffice. Otherwise, *water-in* some liquid fertilizer as directed on the product label. It is a good idea to dilute it more than suggested if plants are only producing new foliage.

Pruning

During the period that **Miniature Roses** bloom indoors, *pinch off* the faded blooms. This will improve their appearance and encourage more buds to form.

Pick off any yellowed leaves, and remove fallen leaves from the soil surface promptly to prevent disease problems.

Sometimes high winds outdoors will cause breakage on dormant roses, especially of long canes of **Climbing Roses** that come loose from their supports. *Prune off* any broken or injured canes on outdoor rose shrubs as soon as you notice them.

Problem Solving

Spider mites are problems for all indoor plants, especially **Miniature Roses.** Too tiny to detect without a hand lens, these spiderlike pests cause pale stippling on foliage. Sometimes their fine webbing is visible among the stems. The simplest solution for these small plants is to wash them thoroughly in tepid water from the kitchen faucet every couple of days for two weeks. Persistent infestations may need a spray of insecticidal soap.

Aphids may also attack **Miniature Roses** growing indoors. They cluster on tender new growth at tips of stems and on buds. *Pinch off* stem tips, and discard them in the trash. Wash insects off the plant with tepid water from the faucet. *Spray* stubborn infestations with insecticidal soap as directed.

Powdery mildew appears on foliage of **Miniature Roses** as a gray or whitish coating. There is no cure for already infected leaves, but you can *spray* uninfected foliage and new foliage with horticultural oil or a garden fungicide listed for this use. Follow the label directions. Promote better air circulation around your roses with a small fan.

Planning

This month roses are in the minds of many who hope to be in the hearts of others on Valentine's Day. While bouquets of long-stemmed beauties are a classic gift of love, the gift of a rose shrub is a more enduring expression of affection. A gift certificate for a garden center or mail-order rose supplier tucked in the Valentine card may be just the thing to touch his or her heart all year.

If roses are in your future this season, it is time to plan where to locate them in your yard and garden. A simple sketch of existing plantings on your property in your notebook or journal will help you identify available space. *Review* last month's thoughts about why you want roses. If you want them for flower production for cutting, crafts, competition, or a hobby, you may want to establish a separate rose garden on your property. This requires significant space and sunshine.

Roses are also easy to integrate into the yard like any flowering shrub. As they beautify a home landscape, the many kinds and sizes of rose shrubs also solve problems. Roses can:

- make a hedge to enclose an area.

- screen a view.

- mask an eyesore.

- anchor a mixed flower border.

- cover and soften an arbor or pergola.

- control erosion on a slope.

- replace lawn as a ground cover.

- cool a wall.

- accent a doorway.

- soften architectural lines.

- serve as barrier plants along the property line.

Planting

Although it is too early to plant rose shrubs outdoors, it is time to order roses by mail. Suppliers will send the plants to you about the time it is safe to plant in your area. They will come bare-root—lightweight, and therefore easiest to handle and ship. A bare-root plant is dormant. It is just three or four bare, stubby brown stems joined at the plant crown. Its exposed roots are temporarily covered with moist sawdust, sphagnum moss, or shredded paper, all covered by a plastic bag with a few air holes.

Store bare-root roses in a cool (above freezing), dark place so they will remain dormant. Make sure the material around their roots stays moist. *Soak* their roots in water for about twenty-four hours prior to planting (plant as soon as possible after they arrive in March or April).

Care for Your Roses

If the winter weather is severe, *check* to make sure there is still plenty of insulating mulch piled generously around the crowns and stems of rose shrubs out in the yard and garden. **Hybrid Tea** roses are at special risk for winter damage because they are typically grafted—they are actually two different shrubs that have been encouraged to grow together. The top one produces the special flowers, the bottom one provides sturdy roots. The bud union, or graft, where they meld is a small knob low on the stem near or under the soil. If it is not well protected against winterkill, the top part of the rose shrub will die and the new growth will come from the root stock. It will be a real surprise, because it will not resemble the hybrid rose at all. **Shrub Roses** that are typically on their own roots may suffer winter damage, but as long as their roots and crown survive, they will regrow true to variety.

This is also a good time to *spray* horticultural oil on the bare, stubby stems of rose shrubs that have a history of insect pest problems. It will smother any overwintering eggs before they can cause problems this coming season. Follow the directions on the product label. Spray heavy, or dormant oil, only before leaves appear. Spray light, or superior, oil at any time during the year.

Watering

Continue to *watch* soil moisture in potted **Miniature Roses** indoors. Do not let them dry out so that they wilt; this seriously undermines their health.

Dormant plants do not require much moisture. Unless there has been an unusual drought period, there is no need to water rose shrubs outdoors.

Fertilizing

Miniatures that have been coping with less-than-ideal indoor conditions would appreciate a boost from some kelp (seaweed)–based plant tonic. *Mix* it in water as directed, and water it in. The trace minerals will boost plant resistance to insects and diseases. There is no need to fertilize plants to boost blooming until the return of bright sun and warmer temperatures signals them to begin a new bloom period.

If you are suffering from cabin fever and feel you must get outdoors and do something for the

roses, *spread* a thin layer of some organic matter such as rotted manure, mushroom soil, or compost on soil over the root zone of the rose shrubs. It doesn't matter if the ground is still frozen—spring rains will soak it in at just the right speed as it thaws.

Pruning

Indoors, carefully *check* **Miniatures** for insects and diseases. *Remove and discard* any dropped, discolored leaves that could harbor black spot fungal spores or insect eggs. *Prune away* bare stems and excess twigginess from plant centers to encourage good air circulation.

Problem Solving

Rabbits and deer are notorious for nibbling woody plants in the winter.

When food is scarce, they may nibble the bases or tops of rose canes. To protect shrubs, either surround them with wire cages tall enough so that deer cannot reach down inside, and/or *spray* stem surfaces with a critter-repellent. Remember, if there is deep snow, critters will be able to reach higher than usual.

Mice and voles may be nesting in the mulch piled up around dormant rose shrubs. They will chew on the bark and damage canes. To prevent this in the future, delay mulching until after the ground freezes hard so the rodents will seek another place to nest. For now, *spray* stem surfaces with a repellent product as directed, repeating the spray after rains or snowfall. If you can identify the nest site, *pull* the mulch away and destroy it. Then *replace* the pile of mulch, and surround the plant with a wire cage.

Planning

This is a good time to examine your pruning tools. They will be in use before you know it. Sharpen or buy replacement blades for handpruners. Shop for loppers, handpruners, and pruning saw. You might also pick up some supplies such as:

- granular, slow-acting fertilizer formulated for roses

- shredded bark mulch

- tough gloves for handling thorny rose canes

- bags of compost or peat moss if you do not have another source of organic material for improving the soil

- film for your camera to record events for your notebook or journal

Planting

Planting roses begins this month wherever the soil has thawed and is not too wet to be worked. It is important to plant rose shrubs ordered by mail while they are still dormant. To plant a bare-root rose shrub:

1 *Set* the plant in a pail of water so its roots are immersed for up to eight hours prior to planting.

2 *Dig* a saucer-shaped hole about as deep as the roots are long, and 2 feet wide.

3 *Mix* some slow-acting, granular fertilizer for shrubs or roses into the soil you remove from the hole. Add organic material such as peat moss or compost to make clay soil hold moisture and drain better. Reserve this to fill the hole later.

4 From the regular soil at the bottom of the hole, form a mound to support the crown of the rosebush so the bare roots splay down along its sides. The bud union (graft) on the main stem should be about 2 inches below ground level when the plant is in position. (Adjust nongrafted **Landscape, Old Garden,** and **Species** varieties so that shrub crowns are just level with the ground.)

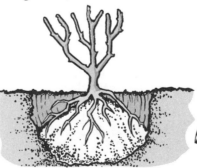

Plant a bare-root rose over a mound.

5 *Fill* the hole with the fill soil, firming it gently around and over the roots. *Water* well.

6 *Hill* more soil or some mulch up over the crown and base of the stubby canes until temperatures moderate and leaf buds start to swell.

Care for Your Roses

When leaf buds start to swell, begin gently removing the piled protective soil or mulch from around the canes of both established and newly planted rose shrubs. Use gloved hands or a soft water flow from a hose. Wait until temperatures are consistently above freezing at night and at least 45 degrees F during the day.

Check the canes, especially at crown level, for insect and rodent damage. Spread the mulch in a 2-inch layer over the shrub root zone out as far as its potential branching area (it should never touch the shrub's crown or canes while they are growing).

Watering

If less than an inch of rain falls weekly, water newly planted roses deeply. *Water* the soil, not the leaves, to minimize the potential for fungal disease. Properly mulched shrubs will manage longer between rains than unmulched ones.

Fertilizing

If you haven't yet done so, *spread* organic matter such as rotted manure and compost around the bushes for an early spring tonic. Spring rains will soak nutrients in. If you do not have these materials, simply *mulch* the soil.

Established rose shrubs will need their dose of granular, slow-acting fertilizer. Following package directions, sprinkle the granules over the entire root area, and *scratch* them into the mulch. The rain or your watering will soak them in.

Pruning

When all winter protection has been removed, prune rose shrubs. *Cut out* all dead and damaged canes on all types of roses. If some canes show winterkill at their ends, cut them back to live wood; cut as low as you must.

Use sharp pruners, loppers, and pruning saw blades for a clean cut. *Disinfect* pruner blades between plants and cuts by spraying the blades with rubbing alcohol or household disinfectant.

Further pruning can be done now or early next month for the health and beauty of the roses. How much

Growing Smarter

When working with roses (and sphagnum moss), a gardener should be aware of the potential for contracting the fungal disease *sporotrichosis.* Rose thorns can carry this fungus, which enters the skin through small cuts and punctures. The first symptom of infection is usually a small painless bump (red, pink, or purple) resembling an insect bite on the finger, hand, or arm. Sporotrichosis is serious, so contact your doctor. For more information, see the Center for Disease Control and Prevention's website at http://www.cdc.gov/ncidod/dbmd/diseaseinfo/sporotrichosis.

and what you do depends on the type of rose shrub. Always *pick up and discard* fallen debris. New roses arrive from the nursery pruned properly.

- **Hybrid Teas, Floribundas, and Grandifloras require hard pruning.** To keep the center of the shrub open to light and air, select three to six healthy young canes spaced openly to form a vase shape. Cut them back to 8 to 12 inches tall. Cut off all other canes at the base. Make the cuts about 1/4 inch above an outward-facing leaf bud, angled so that rain water will drip away from it.

- **Landscape roses need renovating.** Prune away about 1/3 of their older canes and weak branches. Reduce the length of remaining canes by 1/3 their length.

- **Polyanthas and Miniatures need grooming.** Prune back

stems to 3 to 5 inches. Clip off twiggy growth, especially from the center.

- **Ground Cover and Hedge Roses need shearing.** Cut all canes to about 6 inches.

Problem Solving

The early season is a time for prevention measures. Proper pruning assures removal of dead and diseased tissues and possible overwintering insect eggs. It also establishes good air access to prevent fungal disease on foliage.

Fungal diseases plague certain types of roses. *Spray* new foliage with the anti-desiccant spray used on evergreens to limit moisture loss. The coating will discourage fungal spores from attaching to leaf surfaces. Choose disease-resistant rose varieties from now on.

Planning

As the season unfolds, consult your garden notebook or journal to refresh your memory about your roses. Were there trouble spots in the bed of **Hybrid Teas,** or with the rose shrubs elsewhere in the yard? Did you identify any new opportunities for using roses in the landscape?

More and more roses are being sold in containers at the nursery or garden center. If you delay shopping until next month, their flower buds will begin to show color for earlier selection.

Hybrid Teas, Miniatures, and others adapt well to planters on the sunny deck or patio. When pruned as Standards, each on a single stem like a small tree, **Hybrid Teas** provide a formal touch. **Miniatures** can go in windowboxes and hanging baskets. Their colors blend well with tropical plants such as **Canna** and **Hibiscus,** possible neighbors on the deck. Plant fragrant roses where you sit to relax and entertain so the fragrance can be fully appreciated.

Planting

Plant container roses any time when the ground is not frozen.

1 *Keep* the soil in the container moist until planting time. Temporarily tie overlong canes up out of your way with twine to prevent damage to you and the shrub.

2 *Dig* a saucer-shaped planting hole as deep as the rootball is high and about twice as wide. The sloping sides will encourage roots to spread into the natural soil around them.

3 *Slide* the rootball out of its container, taking care not to break up the soil or damage the roots. Prune or untangle any roots that are matted or circling due to confinement in the pot.

4 *Set* the rootball in the hole. *Check* that the top of the rootball is level with the surrounding ground. In cold upstate areas the bud union on grafted rose shrubs should be underground. If it is showing while the plant is in the container, plant the rose deeper so the knob will be covered with an inch or two of soil when the fill is returned to the hole.

5 *Fill* the hole with the soil you dug out of it. *Mix* in some granular, slow-acting fertilizer formulated for woody plants, or for roses specifically. If your soil is impossibly clayey, add some organic matter such as chopped leaves or compost to improve its drainage. Firm it over and around the rootball.

6 *Water* the entire area thoroughly. To help reduce transplant shock and safely stimulate root and leaf growth, add some kelp-based fertilizer to the water if you have it.

7 *Spread* a 2- or 3-inch layer of some organic material over the root zone. If more cold weather is a possibility, pile some soil or mulch over the crown and lower stems temporarily.

Care for Your Roses

By month's end it is probably safe to *remove* winter protection from rose shrubs. If an overnight frost threatens, throw some garden fleece or a light blanket over vulnerable shrubs for a few hours.

As the leaves begin to show on rose shrubs, softening their profile in the wake of severe early-season pruning, spruce up their beds by spreading fresh mulch under them. Add just enough to provide 2 to 3 inches, and do not allow it to touch shrub crowns or stems. The mulch will discourage weeds and help control leaf diseases by reducing splashing of fungal spores from the soil onto the leaves. It also reduces water loss from runoff and evaporation, and insulates roots from extreme summer heat and winter cold.

Begin to train climbing roses as their canes grow. They produce the most blossoms on canes that grow horizontally, within a 45-degree angle of the ground.

Watering

Remember to *water* newly planted roses deeply every week or so if less than an inch of rain falls. Check unmulched soil with a houseplant water meter probe to determine its dryness after about five days without rain. When watering, avoid wetting the rose foliage.

Fertilizing

If you have not already sprinkled a granular, slow-acting rose or nursery fertilizer into the fill soil of newly planted roses or onto the soil of established shrubs, do so now. The package label will indicate how long it is effective. Later, when warm weather arrives and plants have been flowering for a time, an energy boost from fast-acting (water-soluble) fertilizer is optional.

Pruning

One pruning rule of thumb is: *Prune when the* **Daffodils** *bloom.* If you have not done the job yet, do it this month. It is best done just as the leaf buds are beginning to enlarge, but it is better to do it later than not at all.

Prune climbing and rambling types of roses this month. Because **Climbers** take two years to establish themselves and bloom, wait three seasons after planting to do the maintenance pruning described below. It's okay to prune dead and damaged canes anytime.

- **Ramblers** flower on one-year canes, so prune all canes that are two years old or older— prune them away at the crown.

- Flowers on **Climbers** develop on short, 6- to 12-inch laterals on two- to three-year-old canes. Keep all tall canes except the oldest (dark brown). *Prune off* dead ends to just above a healthy, outward-facing bud. If the long canes have come loose from their support structure (trellis, fence, etc.), reattach them.

- Just before spring budbreak, prune the short laterals to 3 to 6 inches or three to four buds.

Problem Solving

Aphids may cluster on tender new growth at the foliage tips or flowerbuds of rose shrubs. Masses of these pear-shaped, soft-bodied insects are visible to the eye. *Pinch off* infested shoots, and discard tips in the trash. Squish the occasional cluster between your fingers. If it seems necessary, *spray* more serious aphid infestations with insecticidal soap or Neem. Spray the aphids directly.

Aphid

Blackspot is a major fungal disease that attacks the foliage of many rose varieties, especially **Hybrid Teas.** Watch for sunken black rings and then yellowing in lower leaves. Limit its spread by spraying healthy foliage with garden or rose fungicide products featuring wettable sulfur or horticultural oil.

Planning

May is a feast for rose gardeners. By mid-month, garden centers are stocked with the latest varieties such as **David Austin English** roses as well as familiar old favorites. Take the trouble to seek out disease-resistant varieties of the types of roses you are considering. The AARS label attached to the stem of a rose shrub indicates that it is a good choice.

While you are at the garden center, take a look at rose accessories. You might need a sturdy trellis or handsome arbor for your **Climbing Rose.** Any of the new lightweight planters that resemble terracotta or concrete would make a wonderful Mother's Day gift for a special lady. So would a good book devoted to the history, selection, and cultivation of roses.

Planting

Cool nights and comfortably warm days make this an excellent planting time for roses as well as gardeners. Follow the March and April planting directions for bare-root and container-grown rose shrubs. You may see some at the garden center that are neither bare-root nor planted in containers—the roots of these shrubs are packaged in cardboard containers intended for planting directly into the planting hole. Follow the instructions on the package label.

Roses thrive in rich soil and open space with good air circulation. Place bushes 3 to 5 feet away from surrounding plants in a garden bed with other flowering plants in it. If they are in a bed of their own, be sure to allow enough space to move among them to prune and harvest flowers without getting pricked by the thorns. Those planted as hedges should be far enough apart so their fully-grown branches just barely touch. **Climbers** should be at least 1 foot from a wall or trellis to allow room for air circulation and pruning.

As the season progresses, do not forget to take some photographs, and record the date of the last frost in your journal.

As spring becomes warmer, consider taking stem cuttings from your favorite **Miniature Rose.** They root easily and make delightful gifts throughout the summer.

Care for Your Roses

Spread fresh mulch or augment existing mulch on the soil around all roses in the yard. Do not make it deeper than 3 inches. Shredded leaves, leaf mold (partially decomposed leaves), or dried grass clippings are perfectly fine. For specimen plants or entire beds devoted to roses, you may prefer something a bit more elegant such as:

- shredded bark
- licorice root
- pecan hulls
- wood chips
- bark nuggets

The coarser the material, the longer it takes to break down during the hot summer. Be sure to keep mulch from touching the rose canes or crown, lest it provide a moist, warm place for insects and fungi.

The long canes of **Climbing Roses** will need fastening to their supporting trellis or arbor as they grow. They are not able to cling or twine on their own. Use brown or green jute twine ties or commercial plant ties. Loop them around the cane, then around the trellis, and fasten. Do not tie them tautly; leave a bit of flex in the ties.

Warm weather brings indoor **Miniature Roses** outdoors. *Acclimate* them gradually by setting them outside for just a few hours daily, extending the time every couple of days until they are comfortable staying out all night, too. Do not put them in the sun immediately; it will burn their foliage.

Watering

Be sure to *water* new transplants generously until new green sprouts show they're getting established. Because they are in the sun a large portion of the day, rose shrubs need lots of water, especially when the weather warms. Well-mulched established roses will manage fine with the usual spring rains, but they, too, will need supplemental watering in the summer sun and heat.

If there's no rain, *water* all young plants and continuously blooming roses thoroughly once a week. Using a water wand rather than a hose sprayer will help direct water to the soil and root area, not the leaves. Wet leaves can lead to fungal diseases. If you must use an overhead sprinkler, try to water early in the day so that any damp leaves will dry before nightfall.

Fertilizing

If you haven't yet sprinkled a granular, slow-acting rose or nursery fertilizer on the mulch and soil around rose shrubs, do so now.

They will need the consistent, uniform nutrition because warm weather promotes vigorous growth. Follow label instructions. Because **Hybrid Tea** roses are heavy feeders, they also benefit from some supplemental foliar sprays of a fast-acting fertilizer every few weeks over the summer.

Pruning

Once rose foliage fully emerges, basic maintenance pruning should be finished. If stems are beginning to grow from below the graft, clip them off promptly. Their foliage will look different from that of the main plant. *Remove* all fallen leaves and plant debris, and discard them in the trash, as they might harbor insect eggs and fungi. *Trim* the edges of rose beds to create an attractive border and to halt encroaching weeds and grasses.

Problem Solving

Newly planted roses may be slow to establish for several reasons. They may not have received sufficient water, or their roots may have dried out prior to planting. Sometimes being planted when it is extremely warm, as with later spring planting, retards devel-

opment temporarily. Be sure plants have sufficient moisture. When planting in sun and heat, erect an awning to shade rose shrubs for a few days.

Leggy stem growth along with few or no flowerbuds usually signals that a rose shrub is not getting enough sunlight. *Trim* overhanging tree branches that may be shading its site. *Move* the shrub to a sunnier place.

Raspberry cane borer causes unopened buds to droop. Look carefully for a tiny, discolored entrance hole just below the affected bud. *Prune* the rose cane well below the hole, near a full-sized leaf.

Canker causes canes to turn brown in the spring or fall as if winter-burned. It is caused by a fungal infection abetted by poor air circulation and improper pruning cuts. *Remove* cankered canes by cutting them off well below the infection. Improve air circulation, and *sterilize* pruners by dipping them in a solution of hot water and rubbing alcohol after each cut.

Planning

Many rose varieties—the older one-time bloomers, the **Hybrid Teas,** *the continual bloomers, the rebloomers—begin to flower in early to mid-June in most of Pennsylvania.* This is the peak time for roses. The first flushes of blooms are the freshest and most abundant. It is a perfect time to plan leisurely visits to public (and private) gardens where roses abound. Keep notes on the roses that appeal to you most. Are you attracted to their color, fragrance, flower form? Will they suit your garden?

Later this month there are usually a few steamy days, advance warning of the summer heat and humidity to come. While the bush roses that are integrated into your landscape as ground covers, hedges, or screens will manage pretty well on their own, expect to devote considerable time to **Hybrid Tea** specimens. Careful tending will yield the best, healthiest flowers over the weeks ahead. When several rosebushes are planted in relatively close proximity, the incidence of pest and disease problems is greater. Having resistant varieties helps a great deal.

Planting

It is best to have planting and transplanting of roses completed well before their major bloom time this month. This is especially important for bare-root shrubs. If they are planted when dormant early in the spring, new acquisitions can concentrate on growing roots and foliage all spring. Then they will be ready to produce buds and flowers on schedule now in June.

Many rose shrubs are available in containers at the nursery or garden center this month. By this time they have already produced foliage and flower buds. They will transplant fairly well over the next few weeks as long as it is not too hot. If you want to plant, do so on an overcast day to reduce transplant stress.

Care for Your Roses

Since this is display time for your roses, take some time to enhance their surroundings. Make sure the mulch is fresh and the edges of beds of rose shrubs are trimmed. *Pull* any weeds, and *mow* adjacent lawn areas.

Check **Climbers** and **Ramblers** to make sure they are securely fastened to their supports. Rapid early-season growth sometimes loosens the ties. Newly planted **Climbers** may need some guidance as their canes grow long enough to reach the bottom of the trellis or arbor they are intended to climb.

Watering

If less than an inch of rain per week falls, *water newly planted* roses deeply every week. Properly mulched, *established* roses can go longer between waterings—as long as two or three weeks. Roses are sensitive to heat, and their foliage will wilt dramatically if it gets unusually hot. *Check* their soil moisture. Sometimes it helps to water them even if their soil is still moist, because adding water helps cool the soil. *Avoid* making the soil soggy, though. Apply water to the soil and root area, not the leaves; wet leaves promote the spread of fungal diseases.

Fertilizing

Sprinkle a granular, slow-acting rose or nursery fertilizer product on the soil around any roses newly planted this month. *Scratch* it into the soil surface. The rain or your watering will soak it in.

All roses that will continue blooming over the summer need a followup dose if they received slow-acting fertilizer as early as March or April. Most slow-acting products last eight to ten weeks.

Repeat-blooming **Hybrid Teas** also appreciate a monthly snack of a very dilute fast-acting fertilizer product sprayed on their foliage for an energy boost. Follow the label directions.

Pruning

Cut and enjoy your **Hybrid Tea** roses indoors in bouquets. *Clip off* all spent blossoms that remain on the rosebush. Cut stems back to just above a point where a second five-leaflet leaf faces outward on the stem. This practice stimulates repeat bloom and controls the shape of the shrub.

Continuous bloomers such as **Meidiland®, Carefree,** and **Polyantha** varieties do not require deadheading of spent blossoms to maintain flowerbud production—however, it does improve their appearance and helps keep the shrubs compact.

Problem Solving

Mites infest roses stressed by heat and drought. *Disrupt* light infestations with a vigorous water spray from the hose on leaf undersides every day or two for a week.

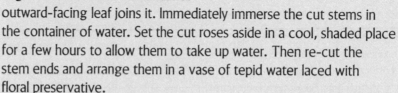

Growing Smarter

To prolong the life of cut roses, cut them in early morning or at dusk when the air is cool. Cut flowers that are in the late bud stage, open just enough so you can see their colored petals. Carry a bucket of tepid water into the garden with you. Use sharp pruners for a clean cut, and cut each selected stem at a 45-degree angle back to where a five-leaflet outward-facing leaf joins it. Immediately immerse the cut stems in the container of water. Set the cut roses aside in a cool, shaded place for a few hours to allow them to take up water. Then re-cut the stem ends and arrange them in a vase of tepid water laced with floral preservative.

Cutting Roses

Established, stubborn mite infestations, as evidenced by fine webbing on twigs and leaf stems, may require further treatment with insecticidal soap or Neem spray as directed on the product label.

Thrips may become a problem when heat and drought arrive. These tiny insects target rose flowerbuds—especially light-colored ones. They burrow into the unfurled petals, which become deformed and fail to open properly. Hang a yellow sticky trap near plants where they are suspected. If thrips appear on the trap, *spray* buds with a pyrethrum-based insecticide as directed on the label.

Caterpillars such as the rose budworm or fall webworm or rose slugs sometimes chew leaves and buds of roses. Tentlike webs among the foliage may be the first clue that they are present. Destroy the web nests, pick off visible caterpillars, and clip off ruined buds and leaves. *Spray* the foliage of heavily infested rosebushes with a product containing *Bacillus thurengiensis* (**Bt**); do so while the caterpillars are feeding on the foliage, following label directions. The caterpillars will soon sicken and die. Neem works on all caterpillars, including the rose slug.

Planning

Now that your continuous-flowering roses are in full show and early bloomers are on the wane, take time to enjoy and evaluate. While the garden's display is fresh in your mind, make a few notes on the highlights and disappointments. If the foliage of certain rose shrubs is off-color, take a soil test to ascertain that the soil pH is in the correct range and nutrients are in balance. There is still time to alter and adjust them for a healthy season.

If certain rose shrubs have died or their health has been seriously compromised by winter conditions or chronic disease and pest problems, dig them up and *throw them away.* This will make space for one of the newer interesting varieties.

Planting

If you must, you can still plant container roses in the ground (see steps for planting container roses in April, Planting). Now that summer has arrived, sufficient soil moisture is even more important. Put extra effort into followup watering. If rainfall is scarce, keep up the extra watering until you see the plants are growing new foliage; water-in some liquid kelp as a tonic to help them withstand transplant stress. *Avoid* feeding with a fast-acting fertilizer—it will overstimulate growth, which a newly planted shrub does not yet have the root system to support.

Alternatively keep a rosebush in its pot until the fall, when it will be safer to plant it. You may have to repot it in a larger container as the shrub develops. **Miniature Roses** are as at home in a pot (indoors or outdoors) as they are in the ground. **Rose Standards,** the tree forms with single stems, always grow in pots here in Pennsylvania.

Care for Your Roses

Roses in full summer sun can suffer in extreme heat. When temperatures reach 90 degrees F, their leaves may wilt dramatically because they are losing moisture through them faster than their roots can pull it out of the soil. Never fertilize a plant that is under stress, whatever the cause of the stress. Deep watering and occasional foliar sprays of liquid kelp (in the morning when the sun is low) will help them through the summer.

A layer of organic mulch on the soil beneath rosebushes will cool the soil and also keep weeds to a minimum. When weeds do appear, they will pull out easily from the mulch.

Landscape, or **Shrub, Roses** are typically much tougher than the classic traditional bush types such as **Hybrid Teas.** Freer in habit, more rambunctious, they can handle a wider range of soil types and conditions. As long as they get sufficient water, they can pretty much manage on their own.

Watering

Check moisture of containerized roses with a houseplant meter probe, and water when the needle on the meter registers toward "dry"—do not wait until it is already there. Be sure containers have good drainage holes.

If less than an inch of rain falls, continue to water newly planted roses deeply every week or so. Give established roses a good soaking every two or three weeks during summer drought.

Fertilizing

Don't fertilize roses in extremely hot weather. Their slow-acting fertilizer from earlier in the season will sustain them nicely through these hot weeks.

Pruning

Routinely *check* rosebushes for damaged canes, dead twigs, and faded flowers. *Remove* them promptly to improve their appearance and forestall disease. Remove dead leaves and other debris on the ground to prevent splashing soilborne fungal spores onto the lower leaves of rose shrubs.

Prune varieties such as spring-flowering, **Perpetual Hybrid,** early-blooming **Climbers,** and some **Rambling Roses** shortly after the flowers drop. This will give the bushes time to set buds on new wood for next year.

Problem Solving

Japanese beetles love roses. In July they emerge from the soil, where they have lurked in their larval (white grub) stage since last year, to feed on rose leaves, flowers, and buds. Be on the lookout for the early arrivals, and start picking them off plants and dropping them into a jar of soapy water. Patrol your rose garden several times a day, if possible. If their numbers overwhelm, *spray* them with an insecticide product containing pyrethrum, making sure it contacts them directly. Do

Growing Smarter

Fight Japanese beetles year 'round. Go after them where they live—the lawn. After they devour your roses they will lay their eggs in the lawn. These eggs hatch and become white grubs, which feed on grass roots until it gets cold and then migrate deeper into the soil to overwinter. Next spring they will come back near the soil surface and eat more grass roots until it is time to emerge as adult beetles. Some things to try:

1 This fall, treat your lawn with predatory nematodes or milky spore disease to destroy the white grubs. It will take a season or two for these agents to establish and make inroads on the white grub population, but they are very effective.

2 Meanwhile, cut your grass tall—at 3 inches—to discourage the beetles from laying eggs there.

3 Aerate your lawn. Some white grubs will fall victim to this machine.

4 Put out birdfeed to encourage birds to hang around your yard. When you see flocks of starlings on the lawn, they are eating white grubs.

not hang bag traps near roses or anywhere else on your property, because their lures will attract even more beetles to your property.

White Grub

Rose midge larvae cause deformed buds and dead stem tips. They can quickly infest and devastate an entire rose garden. *Prune off and destroy* infested buds and stem tips.

Spray with Neem every five days, as directed on the package.

Leafcutter bees cut precise ovals and circles from leaf surfaces, sometimes causing stems to die back. Just *prune off* the dead and dying stems, and *remove* dead debris. As pollinators, leafcutter bees are beneficial to the garden environment, so don't treat them with a pesticide.

213

Planning

It takes a sturdy plant to flower with gusto during this month of serious heat and, perhaps, drought. There are roses which can take all this in stride. In fact, they are just getting their second wind about this time. Take note of those roses blooming in yards this month as you travel in the neighborhood and on your way to work. Typically, it is the informal landscape types rather than the formal display type of rose shrubs that are most visible. They are producing abundant colorful flowers as they serve as hedges, ground covers, and screens around the yard. Plan to integrate some of these roses into your landscape if you like what you see this month.

When you go on vacation, watering your roses will be a concern if rainfall has been scarce all summer. While established **Landscape Roses** can manage for several weeks, others may not be able to. Try to arrange for a neighbor to water, especially those roses planted in containers. Think about installing a drip irrigation system on the property this fall to handle the roses and other plants as well.

If you vacation at the seashore, you may be familiar with **Rugosa Roses.** These sturdy plants are adapted to coastal conditions and can handle drought well. By late this month they will be showing gorgeous bright-orange hips that are as decorative as their flowers. You might want to plant some at your house down the shore.

Planting

By late August and through September as summer heat subsides, you can plant **Landscape Shrub Roses.** If they have been sitting in a garden center in a container all summer, it is best to get them into the ground as soon as possible. They are tough enough to manage in any residual heat and drought.

- *Follow* the instructions on planting container rose shrubs in April, Planting.

- *Untangle* and clip off matted or circling roots caused by confinement in the pot for an extended period.

- *Prune off* flower buds that are close to opening. The shrub can then concentrate its energy on growing new roots to withstand the winter.

- *Do not* add fertilizer at planting time.

Care for Your Roses

Maintain a 2- or 3-inch layer of mulch over the soil in beds where roses are planted. Chopped leaves tend to decompose quickly in the heat, so you may have to *spread* a fresh layer to keep down weeds and help the soil retain moisture. The decomposed material is excellent for conditioning the soil over shrub roots.

Many varieties of roses will develop rose hips where flowers fade on the stems—this is their way of setting seed. By late this month, *stop deadheading* faded flowers, and allow the hips to form. This, combined with the increasingly fewer hours of daylight daily, will signal the shrub to slow its growth and prepare for winter. Later in the season, the hips will provide a nutritious meal for birds and other wildlife.

Check **Climbers** to be sure their new growth is securely fastened to their trellis or arbor. The high winds that accompany late-summer storms will loosen the long canes and thrash them about, causing major damage.

Watering

Continue to water if rainfall is sparse.

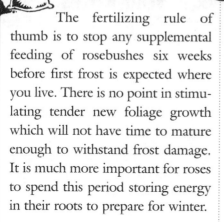

Fertilizing

The fertilizing rule of thumb is to stop any supplemental feeding of rosebushes six weeks before first frost is expected where you live. There is no point in stimulating tender new foliage growth which will not have time to mature enough to withstand frost damage. It is much more important for roses to spend this period storing energy in their roots to prepare for winter.

Pruning

Routinely *remove* dead, diseased, and dying branches from rosebushes that are in full view in the garden. Dispose of the debris in the trash. Carefully inspect the remaining leaves, canes, and flowers for signs of insects or disease. Large groupings of rose shrubs around the property—such as plantings of ground covers or hedges—will not need such meticulous grooming.

Prune off any suckers that may have sprung up from below the bulging bud union on the bush stem. Suckers have a different look from the flowering plant—coarser or different-colored foliage—because they are from another plant, the rootstock, that the desirable flowering variety is grafted to.

Problem Solving

For answers to specific disease or insect problems or other questions, *check* with your local rose society, state agricultural college or university, county agricultural agent, or horticultural society. You can learn about local trends and conditions and receive the latest information on solutions and research. (See Appendix.)

Mites, aphids, and Japanese beetles may still turn up on rose foliage. They will focus on those shrubs that are stressed or weak for some reason. Consider their appearance an alert, and try to discover why the plant is struggling. It may just be in the wrong place. If so, you can move it in the fall. *Check* leaves and flowers periodically. Prevention, early detection, and prompt treatment are your best defenses. Neem is effective for all these problems.

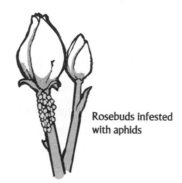

Rosebuds infested with aphids

Viral diseases such as rose mosaic virus occasionally appear in rosebushes, which may have become infected at the nursery. Infections

Growing Smarter

Floribundas are a relatively recent development in the world of roses. They originated in the early 1900s as a cross between the **Polyantha** rose and **Hybrid Teas,** which yielded the hybrid **Polyanthas** now known as **Poulsen** roses. Instead of single flowers, they feature proportioned flower heads, or clusters, of several blooms at the tips of their stems. They are free-flowering and hardy, with a long bloom season. If you want a low-maintenance **Garden** and **Landscape Rose,** consider the **Floribunda 'Europeana',** an All-America Rose Selection (AARS) in 1968, rated 8.8 on a scale of 10 by the American Rose Society (ARS). **'Charisma', 'Cherish',** and **'First Edition'** are other AARS selections also rated 8 or higher by the ARS.

are systemic, established throughout the plants. The plants' growth will be stunted and they will develop increasingly more splotchy colored, puckered leaves and malformed buds. Infected plants decline over time. There is no cure for plant viruses. *Dig up* the shrub immediately, and put it in a plastic bag for the trash. *Wash* your shovel and other tools with hot water and disinfectant.

Planning

While we think of fall starting after Labor Day, summer actually continues for several weeks on the calendar, and good weather continues in many parts of Pennsylvania. Expect to enjoy your roses during this time. They will respond to a break in the heat with a fresh flush of blooms.

A season's experience with roses yields a lot of helpful information on how to grow these wonderful shrubs even more successfully next year. The key to their health and, thus, their beauty, is proper siting. Plan now, so when the weather cools and plants begin to go dormant, you can move those that did not perform well because they were in the wrong place in your yard or garden. The various **Landscape** or **Shrub** types generally tolerate a range of soils and moisture conditions. They can do with less sunlight. However, high-performance **Hybrid Tea** roses have stricter requirements. Do yours have:

- at least six hours of sun (more in the morning so some shade cools them in summer afternoons)?

- excellent soil drainage?

- a soil pH of about 6.5?

- good air circulation?

- at least 2 feet of distance from walls and solid fences?

Coming up—lots of yard sales and flea markets. Garden centers hold fall sales to clear their merchandise, and bargains are to be found. Here are opportunities to acquire garden accessories inexpensively. You might find a lovely arbor or trellis to support some more roses next year. Now is the time to add that Victorian-style gazing ball or unusual planter to your garden.

Planting

Plant container roses from the garden center now through the fall until the ground is frozen. Sooner is better, because their roots will have more time to adjust to the new soil and site and begin to grow. Follow the planting steps in April, Planting. Do not fertilize until next spring.

Some of the roses growing in planters and decorative pots may be outgrowing them. Either *repot* them into larger planters, or put them in the ground in an appropriate place in the yard. In the case of **Miniatures,** either plant outdoors, repot for outdoors, or repot and bring them indoors for the winter.

Care for Your Roses

Topdressing the soil around roses with compost or composted manure is not essential, but it is a good thing to do if you have a source of these organic materials. They condition the soil and gradually provide some nutrients to give the plants a good start come spring. Combine this task with season-end cleanup. *Remove* the thinning, old mulch that may be contaminated with fungal spores and pest insect eggs. Spread the organic material, then spread a layer of fresh mulch over it.

Shortly you will be piling more mulch up over the crowns and lower stems of the roses for winter protection. Delay doing so until plants are dormant and freezing is imminent.

Prepare any **Miniature Roses** destined to overwinter indoors:

1 *Wash* their leaves and stems with water, then spray their foliage with horticultural oil to eliminate any residual insect life, including mite eggs. A repeat spray a week or so later will nail the next generation for good measure.

2 *Reverse-acclimate* them to help them with their adjustment to indoor conditions—particularly the reduced light. Bring them in gradually, before the heat goes on in the house. Have them spend just a few hours at a time indoors—more every few days—for a week or more. Eventually they will stay overnight and settle in at your sunniest (usually south-facing) window.

Watering

When rainfall is limited, continue to water container and garden roses while the weather is mild and they are still blooming. It is important that they go into the winter in as healthy condition as possible.

Fertilizing

Do not fertilize outdoor roses. Newly planted ones will do fine, and all rose shrubs on your property will get their fertilizer next March.

Growing Smarter

One way to enjoy your roses long after the season is past is to dry some of their petals for use in potpourris. Pick opened blossoms of fragrant varieties after morning dew has evaporated, but early enough in the day so their essential oils are still strong.

- For a moist potpourri, pull the petals from the blossoms. Then spread them on a drying rack away from the light for a few days until they are limp. The petals will retain their color well.
- For a dried potpourri, pull the petals as above. Set them on a cookie sheet in a warm oven. Keep the oven door ajar to allow the moisture to escape. Stir the petals occasionally so they dry evenly and completely. They will lose some color intensity with this technique. Drying the petals in the microwave oven is faster, and the color holds better. Experiment with timing, because each appliance is somewhat different.

Pruning

Continue to *pick up and discard* any dropped foliage or other debris. Prune only damaged twigs or canes now; delay other pruning a few weeks until the rose shrubs have dropped their leaves and are dormant.

Problem Solving

Weeds may be a problem now. If the mulch over beds of rose shrubs has decomposed and thinned, perennial weeds can enjoy more light, and annual weed seeds may germinate in the rich residue. *Handpull* them when they are young. Wait until the soil is moist. It is difficult and risky to spray herbicide near the rose foliage, so avoid doing so if at all possible.

Powdery mildew is a potential problem as long as there are leaves on the rosebushes. At this point in the season it is not practical to treat it. Soon the leaves will drop. Clean them up promptly.

Planning

It has been customary in this country and abroad to plant **Hybrid Tea** *roses in beds of their own.* These roses are the stars, the specimen plants that exist to be on display. Their stunning blossoms are their reason for being. In their own bed they are easy to prune, spray, and, of course, pick. Their typical stiff, upright posture makes them difficult to blend in with other shrubs or flowering plants, so a separate bed makes sense.

This is a good time of year to make a rose garden—a separate bed or area of beds—or to renovate an existing bed to be dedicated to **Hybrid Tea** and other specimen roses. Establishing it from scratch provides a great opportunity to create optimum conditions—strong light, good air circulation, and great soil.

1 *Choose* a site that receives at least six hours of direct sunlight daily in the summer. (Remember, the sun's angle shifts in fall and winter, so it lights a slightly different portion of the yard now.)

2 Designate a measured area with string or other marker. *Remove* the turf or other existing plants to expose the soil.

3 *Dig down* at least 2 feet, and turn over the shovelsful of soil in place. If the soil is hard and clayey, improve its drainage. Dig a deep trench and lay drainage pipes or tiles and gravel beneath the bed. An alternative is to build up the bed a foot or two above ground level to facilitate drainage.

4 *Add* an inch or two of some organic material such as compost, peat moss, or mushroom soil over the soil, and dig it in to improve the soil's ability to drain well yet retain moisture. Rake the soil smooth and level.

5 *Move* rosebushes from elsewhere in the yard, or plant new ones now, or wait until spring to plant.

6 *Cover* the bed(s) with a 3- or 4-inch layer of winter mulch in the form of pine needles, chopped leaves, wood chips, or shredded bark.

Planting

Although it is pushing things a bit, until a major frost hits it is still okay to transplant rosebushes. It is also important to *dig up and discard* any that are so ill or stressed they are unlikely to make it through the winter. This will make room for new plants next spring. Transplant roses when the soil is moist:

1 *Prune out* dead wood, and *cut back* overlong canes to 2 or 3 feet.

2 *Tie* the canes together with twine for better access to the plant crown and root zone.

3 *Estimate* a distance of a foot out from the shrub crown on all sides. Shove a sharp spade or shovel into the soil around this perimeter so that it cuts through roots. This will create a soilball with the roots embedded.

4 *Lift* the rootball out of the ground with a shovel or spading fork. Try to keep the soil around the roots, and set it on a tarp or piece of burlap. (If the soil falls off the roots, proceed to plant as you would a bareroot rose, described in March, Planting.)

5 *Dig* a saucer-shaped hole the depth of the rootball. Use the tarp or burlap to lower the rootball into the hole, and position it as you wish. Then lift the plant slightly to remove the fabric.

6 *Check* to be sure the rosebush is at the same depth in its new hole that it was in its former one.

7 *Fill in* the hole with soil, water, and mulch, as you do when planting any shrub. *Remove* the twine. Do not fertilize until next spring.

Care for Your Roses

Rose trees, also known as **Rose Standards,** aren't hardy in most of Pennsylvania. They involve two grafts, so they have two bud unions, and are therefore doubly vulnerable to weather extremes. For winter protection, place the entire plant, pot and all, horizontally in a trough, and *cover* it with mulch. An alternative is to put it in a cold frame or cool shelter where the temperature never drops much below freezing.

Light frost is usually not a problem with roses. If you have warning, throw a light cover over the tops of the shrubs where frost is likely to alight. White polyspun garden fleece, a bedsheet, or newspaper will do the trick. If the frost is a surprise, damage will be limited to a few browned petals and leaf tips.

Watering

Water newly planted roses well to assure good root-to-soil contact. If it does not rain, *check* them every week or ten days to see if they need water. Mulched roses can go longer between waterings now than they can in the summer.

If keeping up with summer watering of roses has been a problem, consider installing an irrigation system where roses are planted in beds. This is a good time of year to do the job, because it is cool and the plants are dormant.

Snake porous hoses (made from recycled automobile tires) over the bed between the rosebushes, where they will sweat moisture along their entire length. Because it delivers water slowly and directly into the soil, a porous hose system conserves water. It also avoids wetting rose foliage. Once the length of hose is installed, cover it with mulch. Next season, attach a timer to the faucet.

Fertilizing

Do not fertilize any outdoor roses. *Delay* fertilizing newly planted ones until next spring.

If you have brought **Miniature Roses** indoors and they are producing new foliage, *water-in* a very dilute fast-acting fertilizer every couple of weeks.

Pruning

Clean up leaves that are falling from trees promptly. If allowed to lie on the ground and mat together, they will block rain from access to the soil around rose shrubs in the landscape. When leaf fall is finished, *mulch* any bare soil around roses everywhere on the property.

Problem Solving

Deer may nibble on rose canes and any foliage that remains on shrubs prior to hard freeze. Given alternatives, they typically avoid plants with thorns, but if there is not much else available, they will go for the roses. *Spray* roses with repellent, or cage them.

Rodents and rabbits may be inclined to nest in the mulch near rosebushes. Wait until a hard frost to *spread* winter mulch—by that time they will have found an alternative nesting site.

Planning

Before the extended end-of-year holiday period begins with Thanksgiving, take some time to review your experiences with your roses this past year. Have you:

- updated your notebook or garden journal?

- built or renovated a bed for **Hybrid Teas** and other specimen rosebushes?

- removed any dead or dying rosebushes?

- transplanted roses to better sites?

- installed drip irrigation in rosebeds?

- winterized the roses?

Planting

If you have decided to pot up a rose shrub that has been growing in the ground, it is best to do it this month after a hard frost. Otherwise, wait until spring. Dig only when the shrub is fully dormant.

1 *Water* the soil around the shrub the night before to soften it and hydrate the roots.

2 *Tie* the canes of the rose shrub to prevent damage while you dig and move it.

3 *Dig* a rootball as described for transplanting roses (see October, Planting). Pots should have a drainage hole and be roughly 6×8 inches for **Miniature Roses**, 14×18 inches for standard-size roses.

4 *Set* the rosebush in the pot so the top of the rootball is an inch or two below the edge. Fill in the edges with soil if necessary, but do not pile it higher over the roots.

5 *Water* well. **Remove** the twine.

Care for Your Roses

Rose shrubs in containers are more vulnerable to winter cold than those in the ground, as their roots are aboveground, subject to drying and cold. There are several ways to overwinter them safely:

- Set them in a cold frame.

- Sink the container into the ground out in the garden.

- Leave it in place, and pile up mulch around the container and over the soil around the shrub crown.

- Bring it indoors. Treat **Miniature Roses** as houseplants.

The conclusion of leaf fall from shade trees and the arrival of hard frost signals time to winterize roses. They are now fully dormant.

- **Landscape** type roses around the property are pretty tough and need minimal care. *Water* them well if rain has been sparse, and *mulch* them with chopped leaves or something similar.

- **Hybrid Teas** and other grafted roses need more care. **Cut back** any overlong canes that might whip around in the winter wind. No canes should be shorter than 24 inches or so. Pile up soil or other organic material such as pine needles, wood chips, shredded bark, or chopped leaves over the crown and lower parts of the canes. Be sure to cover the knobby graft with mulch.

- **Climbing Roses** need protection if winter temperatures dip below zero with any regularity. Unfasten the canes from their support, and gather them in a horizontal bundle on the ground. *Cover* them and the plant crown with soil, straw, leaf mold, or other organic material. If it is too difficult to remove the canes, tie them very securely to their support, and *mound* soil or mulch as high as possible on the plant.

Check any nametags wired on new and existing rose shrubs. Make sure their wires are not strangling the canes as they mature and grow thicker.

Miniature Roses kept indoors as winter houseplants need lots of light to avoid the loss of vigor that invites pest and disease problems. As the sun drops lower in the sky and the number of daylight hours shrinks, they cannot get the requisite minimum of four hours of direct sunshine on the windowsill. Set them under fluorescent lights to compensate. Rig the lights so they are about 2 or 3 inches above the tips of the branches. Use a timer to assure that the lights are on sixteen hours a day.

Growing Smarter

Flowers are not the only ornamental assets of roses. Many kinds of roses develop large, colorful hips after their flowers fade. Their rich orange color enhances the autumn landscape well into early winter if the local wildlife does not eat them first.

Rose hips are a source of seeds if you want to try to propagate roses yourself. Remember that seedlings of hybrid varieties of roses will not resemble their hybrid parent.

Rose hips are also a rich source of vitamin C. In fact, the vitamin C in commercially produced natural vitamin supplements is made from them. Another way to benefit from their vitamin C is to make rose hip jelly. Do not use hips from roses that have been sprayed with chemical pesticides. Horticultural oil or insecticidal soap are not harmful.

Watering

If it has been a dry fall, *water* all shrubs in the yard and garden before the ground freezes hard.

Check soil moisture for **Miniature Roses** growing indoors. They tend to dry out quickly when the indoor heating runs regularly. Do not let them dry out.

Fertilizing

If budded or blooming indoor **Miniature Roses** do not have slow-acting fertilizer in their potting mix, *fertilize* with a water-soluble fertilizer when you water.

Pruning

From now until spring, limit any pruning to removing injured canes from dormant rose shrubs. Resist the urge to neaten them up ahead of schedule by cutting canes way back. There will be a certain amount of winterkill at the tips of canes, so they should remain at 18 to 24 inches. That will assure there is live, healthy wood lower on them when official pruning time arrives in the spring.

Problem Solving

Spider mites are always a potential problem on indoor **Miniature Roses.** They love hot, dry conditions, and these are often the norm inside homes when cold weather arrives. To catch infestations early, regulary *check* for pale, fine stippling on leaves. Wash plants under the kitchen faucet every week or so to prevent mites from getting established at all.

Planning

An appropriate year-end activity is to revise the sketch of your yard and garden. Before the possibility of a cover of snow, tour the property and identify changes that have occurred during the past season. Alter the drawing of your landscape to reflect:

- new planting beds

- roses and other shrubs that have been moved

- any trees that were removed (affects available sunshine)

- changes in walkways, and grades (might affect rainfall drainage)

- drip irrigation installed

- arbors or pergolas established

- new pools, decks, or patios

If you have been taking photographs of your roses over the past season, label them and put them in your journal for future reference.

Planting

If the ground is not yet frozen, it is still possible to plant or transplant rosebushes outdoors. It is not recommended, however.

Care for Your Roses

For winter protections, *hill up* mulch—chopped leaves, shredded bark, pine needles, wood chips—over the crown graft and bottoms of the canes of **Hybrid Tea** and other grafted rosebushes. (The graft, or bud union, should be below the soil level in most parts of Pennsylvania.) A 3- or 4-inch layer over the ground around and between bushes in a bed will insulate the soil so it does not alternately freeze and thaw and disturb the roots over the winter.

Watering

Water **Miniature Roses** wintering indoors. *Check* their soil every few days with a houseplant water meter, or stick your finger down into the soil about 2 inches to feel for moisture.

Fertilizing

If there is no granular, slow-acting fertilizer in the soil of indoor **Miniature Roses**, *sprinkle* some on top of the soil instead.

Problem Solving

Wind is the enemy of roses in the winter. *Check* to be sure **Climbers** are securely tied to their arbors and trellises. If the canes of other rose shrubs are becoming too battered, tie some twine around them all to steady them.

Lack of sufficient light will stress **Miniature Roses** growing indoors. Make sure there are only 2 or 3 inches between stem tips and the fluorescent lightbulb. Set a timer to run the lights for sixteen hours daily.

Insufficient humidity is a problem for all indoor plants. Put them in a cool room, or set them in a tray of moist gravel. If they are located in the bathroom or kitchen, they will get more humidity.

Growing Smarter

Gloves that best protect against thorns are usually made from heavy canvas or leather and/or are coated with nitrile. The best have generous cuffs that reach up the arm toward the elbow to protect against scratches. Maybe new gloves for rose care should be on your holiday gift list.

Shrubs

It is something of a mystery to me why caring for residential lawns is virtually a national pastime in this country, yet caring for shrubs seems to have such a low priority on the homeowner's to-do list. These incredibly important landscape plants are typically taken for granted. The fact that most shrubs survive many years of benign neglect is a tribute to their sturdy constitutions. When someone does pay attention to them, it is usually to prune them within an inch of their lives. A utilitarian rather than an artistic effort, the pruning usually distorts their natural habit and destroys their health.

Yet shrubs are so essential to our sense of a residential landscape that builders always put a few around newly built homes that need buyers, even before they seed-in lawns. These perfunctory shrub plantings are serviceable evergreens familiar to one and all. They do the job and grow reliably over the years, until one day they completely obscure the house from the view of the street. Unless and until there are new owners or the house desperately needs painting or repair, the faithful shrubs continue to grow wildly, unnoticed and neglected.

What's wrong with this scenario? It reflects an unfortunate failure to appreciate shrubs both as handsome plants of enormous variety and as important ornamental assets to every property. When carefully selected and strategically planted around the yard to showcase their beautiful foliage, flowers, bark, berries, and shapes, a variety of shrubs contributes significant monetary value to a property. Shrubs also feed and shelter wildlife, they screen wind, and they soften architectural lines of buildings.

Shrubs are **woody plants.** This means they have stems that do not die back every fall, but instead develop thick tissues that survive year after year, growing harder as they age. Shrubs are usually distinguished from trees, which are also woody plants, by their smaller size and multiple stems. Like trees, shrubs may bear deciduous foliage that drops every fall, or either needled or broadleaf evergreen foliage that remains throughout the winter. Many shrubs are valued for their blooms in spring, summer, or fall. Others offer unusual growth habits or foliage shapes and textures. Still others withstand shearing and make great formal hedges.

Shrubs provide an infrastructure for the landscape. They unify its disparate elements—low ground covers, lawn, plants, buildings, and tall trees. They do lots of things, sometimes all at the same time. They:

- soften hardscape features.
- define spaces.
- punctuate doorways.
- screen utilities.
- delineate property lines.
- buffer noise.
- anchor flower beds and borders.
- provide winter interest.
- bear flowers and fruit.

Assessing Your Shrubs

The first step in appreciating how shrubs can enhance your landscape is to *identify* the ones you have. Enlist the aid of a knowledgeable friend or a landscape design professional to help you answer the following questions about a shrub you are thinking of purchasing:

1 What is the common name of this shrub?

Shrubs

2 What is the formal scientific (botanical) name of this shrub?

3 What are its ornamental qualities?

4 Is this a high- or low-maintenance shrub?

5 What is the mature height and spread of this shrub?

The next step is to evaluate the condition of each existing shrub on your property:

1 How old is this shrub?

2 Is the foliage healthy?

3 Is there any sign of girdling roots?

4 Do the stems have dead bark, insect holes, or fungal disease?

5 Has either overpruning or neglect compromised this shrub's health?

6 Is this shrub worth keeping, or should it be replaced?

Evaluate the shrub's location on your property:

1 Is this shrub in the best site for the light it needs?

2 Is it too close to another shrub? to a building or wall?

3 What function does this shrub perform here?

4 Would the ornamental features of this shrub show better elsewhere in the yard?

5 Will this location still be suitable when the shrub grows to mature height?

6 Is this shrub able to tolerate the soil conditions at this site?

Upgrading Your Shrubs

The answers to all the foregoing questions will help you make some decisions about the shrubs on your property.

Removal. It may be clear that certain shrubs should be removed and discarded. They are either old, sick, or so overgrown that efforts to reestablish their shape will unavoidably ruin their health. In some cases there are modern hybrids or new varieties of a shrub that are so superior, there is no point in keeping the older one.

Renovation. Shrubs that are healthy, not too old, and appropriately sited are worth the trouble it takes to restore. Since most often the problem is tangled, woody overgrowth, the solution is to revitalize the shrub by pruning. This is not pruning to control its size, this is pruning to remove its old, overgrown stems and stimulate new stem growth. The pruning can be pretty radical, involving either cutting all the stems back to the ground all at once, or cutting back one-third of the oldest, thickest stems each year for three years.

Transplanting. Some shrubs may be perfectly fine but they are not in the best location. Many can be transplanted fairly easily to another site in the yard. The best site for a shrub may not be available on your property, so it may make sense to sell the shrub. There is a brisk market in healthy, mature shrubs to provide instant landscapes for upscale homes. Inquire at a local nursery or garden center for the name of a plant broker who might handle the transaction.

Once the existing shrubs on a property have been inventoried and attended to, there remains the wonderful task of purchasing new ones. If this seems like a daunting task, seek the advice of a professional landscape designer, which may be especially helpful if your plan is to add many shrubs over a newly developed area. It is certainly not difficult to choose a few shrubs on your own. Just be sure that when you set out for the nursery you have in mind the specifications for the site—the mature size, the ornamental features, and the purpose the shrub must serve.

Shrubs for Pennsylvania

Deciduous Landscape Shrubs

Common Name (Botanical Name)	Zones	Ornamental Qualities	Uses	Comments
Azalea, Deciduous (*Azalea* sp. and hybrids)	4 to 8 (Native)	Bright-colored pink, orange, gold flowers in May/June prior to leaves.	Container, woodland foundation.	More open than evergreen types. Needs some shade. Some are fragrant.
Barberry, Japanese (*Berberis thungergii* 'Atropurpurea')	4 to 8	Tiny yellow spring flowers; red berries late summer. Foliage turns red in fall.	Hedges, bed edging, ground cover.	Tough, takes shearing. Good barrier plants near foundations to discourage intruders. Good dwarf forms available.
Beautyberry, Purple (*Callicarpa dichotoma*)	5 to 8	August flowers become showy berry clusters in intense pinks, shades of purple, white.	Shrub border, hedgerows.	Plant in front of evergreens. Drought-resistant.
Blueberry (*Vaccinium corymbosum*)	3 to 7 (Native)	Lovely white May flowers, then edible blue berries. Reddish fall foliage color.	Hedge, food garden, specimen, border.	Virtually problem-free. Attracts birds, likes very acid soil, tolerates drought.
Butterfly Bush (*Buddleia davidii*)	5 to 9	Blooms June to frost in lilac, pink, white, purple. Green-gray foliage.	Specimen, garden bed, hedgerow. Butterfly garden.	Vigorous grower, low maintenance. Attracts lots of butterflies.
Daphne 'Carol Mackie' (*Daphne × burkwoodii* 'Carol Mackie')	4 to 8	Fragrant May flowers; semi-evergreen variegated foliage.	Specimen.	Low-growing densely twiggy. Deer do not eat. Wet feet equals certain death.
Deutzia (*Deutzia gracilis* 'Nikko')	5 to 8	Small white flowers in May. Fine-textured blue-green leaves turn red in fall.	Ground cover, flower bed or border.	Compact, low-growing mound. Spreads slowly by rooted stems.
Forsythia (*Forsythia × intermedia*)	5 to 8	Yellow flowers in April, then medium-green leaves.	Specimen, foundation, hedge border.	Tough, tolerates poor soil. Takes pruning well. No disease and insect problems. Long-lived.

Shrubs for Pennsylvania

Common Name (Botanical Name)	Zones	Ornamental Qualities	Uses	Comments
Fothergilla (*Fothergilla gardenii*)	5 to 9 (Native)	Scented white bottlebrush-type flowers in spring. Fall foliage color.	Group as accent; specimen; anchor flower bed.	Sturdy, decorative.
Glossy Abelia (*Abelia × grandiflora*)	6 to 9	Fragrant white or pink flowers July to frost. Fine-textured semi-evergreen foliage, tinged maroon in fall.	Group as accent; specimen; anchor flower bed, hedge.	Multi-season interest. Prune hard in spring before new growth.
Lilac (*Syringa vulgaris* hybrids)	4 to 7	Cone-shaped clusters of fragrant tubular florets late April into May.	Shrub border.	Old-fashioned favorite. Long-lived. Foliage tends to get mildew.
Oakleaf Hydrangea (*Hydrangea quercifolia*)	5 to 9 (Native)	Upright cones of cream-petaled florets in late spring. Deep-red fall foliage, peeling bark.	Woodland, specimen, hedge, foundation.	Stunning year 'round. Likes woodsy, acidic soil. Flowers dry beautifully; great for floral crafts.
Mockorange (*Philadelphus coronarious* hybrids)	4 to 8	White single or double flowers with citrus fragrance in May.	Specimen, shrub border.	Old-fashioned favorite. Will take shade. Virtually pest- and disease-free. Prune to neaten.
Rose of Sharon (*Hibiscus syriacus*)	5 to 8	White, dark-pink, blue, or lilac flowers July through September.	Specimen, hedge, or butterfly garden; fence line.	Upright summer blooms. Tough. Adapts to any soil, air pollution, road salt. 'Diana' for evening garden. Older nonsterile types are self-sowers, weedy.
Shadblow Serviceberry (*Amelanchier* sp.)	3 to 8 (Native)	White flowers early spring. Red or blue edible fruits. Pale-red fall foliage.	Woodland, streamside.	A harbinger of spring in Pennsylvania woods. Supports wildlife. Edible berries.
Smokebush (*Cotinus coggygria*)	5 to 8	Airy "flower" clusters in June become puffy plumes on pink or gray stalks. Foliage bluish green or deep purple.	Specimen, flower bed, shrub border, hedge.	Needs hard pruning to maintain residential yard scale.

Shrubs for Pennsylvania

Common Name (Botanical Name)	Zones	Ornamental Qualities	Uses	Comments
Spirea, Vanhoutte (*Spirea × vanhouttei*)	3 to 8	White floret clusters in May on arching branches.	Specimen, foundation, fence line.	Fast-growing, easy to care for; drought-tolerant.
Summersweet Sweetpepper Bush (*Clethra alnifolia*)	4 to 9 (Native)	Fragrant white or pink floret spikes July into August. Fragrant.	Specimen, foundation, accent.	Wet soil–tolerant; spreads slowly by underground roots for erosion control. Attracts honeybees.
Viburnum, Doublefile (*Viburnum plicatum tomentosum*)	5 to 8	Parallel rows of flat white May flowers; red, then black fruit in fall. Purplish-red fall foliage.	Specimen, shrub border, fence line.	**Japanese Snowball** version has sterile flowers in white balls. Plant beneath porch or slope to view from above.
Virginia Sweetspire (*Itea virginica*)	5 to 9 (Native)	Dripping strands of white florets in May; purple fall foliage color.	Specimen, foundation, woodland.	Spreads by rooted suckers. Likes wet soil.
Weigela (*Weigela florida*)	5 to 8	Tubular white, pink, or rose flowers late May and June. Some have variegated or purple-tinged foliage.	Shrub border; anchor flower bed.	Old-fashioned favorite. attracts hummingbirds. Newer cultivars more compact, colorful.
Winged Euonymus Burning Bush (*Euonymus alata*)	4 to 8	Fiery red fall foliage; ridged, corky edges on stems visible in winter.	Specimen, hedge, screen.	Adaptable, self-relant, low-maintenance. Deer may eat. May seed around.
Winterberry Holly (*Ilex verticillata*)	3 to 9 (Native)	Tiny white flowers in June. On females, red or orange berries along bare stems in winter.	Accent, focal point, shrub border, property line.	Likes moist soil. Spreads slowly by suckering roots. Attracts winter birds. Needs a male pollinator to guarantee fruiting.
Witchhazel (*Hamamelis* sp. and hybrids)	5 to 9	Fragrant yellow flowers in late winter; fall foliage color.	Streetside, specimen.	Force branches indoors for winter bloom.

Shrubs for Pennsylvania

Needled Evergreen Shrubs

Common Name (Botanical Name)	Zones	Ornamental Qualities	Uses	Comments
Chinese Juniper (*Juniperus chinensis* 'Torulosa')	3 to 9	Dark-green foliage. This is female, so it has berries.	Screen, hedge, foundation.	Tolerates heat, drought, all soils except boggy.
Dwarf Mugo Pine (*Pinus mugo* var. *pumilo*)	3 to 7	Dense, fine-textured; mounded compact form.	Specimen, anchor bed, container, rock garden.	Good contrast to vertical plants; easy maintenance. Not a deer favorite in most areas.
Yew (*Taxus* × *media*)	5 to 7	Deep-green, flat, round-tipped needles in neat rows along stems. Red berries on females.	Foundation, hedge, screen, container, topiary.	Accepts radical pruning to renew. Lots of cultivars with different habits. A deer favorite.

Broadleaf Evergreen Shrubs

Common Name (Botanical Name)	Zones	Ornamental Qualities	Uses	Comments
Aucuba (*Aucuba japonica* 'Variegata')	6 to 10	Small red spring flowers, berries on females in fall. Foliage speckled green or green-gold.	Specimen, hedge, screen, dark corner.	Variegation in foliage best in partial shade. Protect from winter sun. Tolerates dry soil, pollution, full shade.
Azalea, Evergreen (*Rhododendron* sp. and hybrids)	Most 4 to 7	Flowers early May in pink, white, red. Bronze or maroon fall foliage color.	Foundation, hedge, border, woodland.	Funnel-shaped flowers attract butterflies. Likes acid soil. Deer may eat.
Boxwood (*Buxus* sp.)	6 to 8	Fine, oval, glossy dark-green foliage; dense.	Hedge, edge of garden, topiary, mazes.	Elegant, formal. Takes shearing. Distinctive musky foliage scent in some. Long-lived.
Cherrylaurel (*Prunus laurocerasus* 'Otto Luyken')	6 to 9	Off-white upright flower clusters late spring; glossy deep-green foliage.	Foundation, hedge, shrub border.	Tolerates shade; compact and virtually pest-free. Deer do not eat.

Shrubs for Pennsylvania

Common Name (Botanical Name)	Zones	Ornamental Qualities	Uses	Comments
Cotoneaster, Willowleaf (*Cotoneaster salicifolius*)	6 to 8	Flat clusters of white florets in May and June become bright-red berries. Narrow, leathery foliage is maroon in in fall and winter.	Screen, hedge, specimen, espalier.	Leaves purple-tinged in cold. Open, rangy habit and berries provide winter interest. Tolerates poor soil, some drought.
Firethorn (*Pyracantha coccinea*)	6 to 8	White flower clusters in May; orange or reddish-orange berries in fall.	Barrier plant, espalier, hedgerow.	Has thorns. Tough and drought-tolerant. Resists deer.
Japanese Pieris (*Pieris japonica*)	5 to 8	Sprays of scented, cream, urn-shaped flowers in April. Semi-glossy, narrow foliage.	Foundation, accent, woodland.	Shade, acid soil. Newer varieties have red- or pink-tinged new foliage.
Mountain Laurel (*Kalmia latifolia*)	4 to 9 (Native)	Clusters of starlike white or pink cupped flowers late May into June.	Woodland, specimen, foundation.	PA state flower. Few problems. Lots of colorful flowered hybrids available.
Nandina Heavenly Bamboo (*Nandina domestica*)	6 to 9	Loose clusters of white flowers in late June or early July, then red berries. Foliage glows reddish when new and in winter.	Specimen, foundation, hedge. Dwarfs for ground cover.	May lose some foliage in coolest regions. Virtually problem-free.
Oregon Grapeholly (*Mahonia aquifolium*)	5 to 8 (Native)	Fragrant tiny yellow urn-shaped florets in April, then blue berries. Glossy, hollylike foliage; purplish in fall and winter.	Specimen, shrub border.	Likes some shade. Provides strong profile in the winter landscape. Deer tend to avoid. Attracts honeybees.
Rhododendron (*Rhododendron* sp. and hybrids)	4 to 8	Clusters of tubular flowers April through June. Many colors. Can get as tall as 15 feet.	Specimen, woodland, foundation, screen, hedge, container.	Available dwarf. Both large- and small-leaf types. Flowers attract humming-birds and butterflies. Deer have a taste for Rhodys.
Yucca (*Yucca* sp. and hybrids)	5 to 9 (Native)	Spikes tipped with creamy-white bell flowers in July.	Accent, flower bed or border, barrier.	Tough, dramatic, and easy-care. Loves sun and poor, dry soil.

JANUARY

Planning

If you did not have a chance to do so last month, this is a good time to study your yard and appreciate the role played in it by shrubs. What do you see from the various windows in the house? Are shrubs in view, or are they all up near the house to be viewed and appreciated only by passersby on the street? Here are some other questions to answer:

- Do your shrubs have ornamental features—berries, cones, interesting bark, dark or golden evergreen foliage—that relieve the winter bleakness?

- Do your shrubs have a variety of sizes and shapes?

- Are there some evergreens? They are particularly nice this time of year, softening the scene and providing color, plus shelter and food for wildlife.

- Are there places on the property where shrubs would help define its border, screen an unattractive view, or block the wind?

Make a New Year's resolution to plant at least one new shrub this year.

Shopping List: an illustrated book on shrubs; admission to the local arboretum

Planting

This is not a good time to plant, even if the soil is not frozen. The possible exception might be a living Christmas tree if you chose one for the holiday just past. It is better to get it into the ground to keep the roots moist and safe from frost than to let it sit around until spring with its rootball under a tarp. Timely planting is important enough that if you live in areas where the soil is usually frozen by late December, it is advisable to *dig* the hole in the fall and store or cover the fill soil so it will not freeze. Then you can *plant* the tree as soon as possible after the holidays. Such a tree will have a better chance of survival, which is the point of having a living tree in the first place (see Trees, January).

- If the soil is not frozen, *dig* a saucer-shaped hole twice as wide as the tree's rootball and exactly as deep.

- Set the Christmas tree in the hole, *remove* as much of the burlap or wire wrapping around the rootball as possible, then fill up the hole with soil.

- Firm it over and around the rootball, and *water* it. *Do not fertilize* until next fall.

- Spray a needled evergreen's foliage with an anti-desiccant spray to help retard loss of moisture if you did not do so while it was indoors for the holidays.

- Keep it mulched and well watered through the winter if snow or rainfall is scarce.

Care for Your Shrubs

Renew the anti-desiccant spray on any evergreen shrubs in sites exposed to harsh winter sun and wind. Choose a (relatively) mild day, and follow the directions on the product label. This coating on their leaves will reduce moisture loss through transpiration and protect the shrubs from drying out.

Check the winter mulch under shrubs for signs of rodent nests. Stamp snow down around the base of shrub stems to collapse any vole burrows. If some of the lower branches are buried in deep snow or bent over with ice, leave them as is to prevent injury to brittle stems. The snow will protect them, and gradual melting will release them gently.

Shrubs that are located just at the edge of a roof overhang are vulnerable to damage by avalanche. Snow that accumulates on the roof will gradually slide off as temperatures moderate. It falls in a clump on the unfortunate shrub, splitting and breaking branches. To take the brunt of the snow, erect an A frame–type shelter that resembles an opened stepladder placed over the shrub. *Avoid planting* shrubs in these positions in the future.

Watering

If it has been a mild, dry winter and the soil has not frozen, check under the mulch around shrubs to see if the soil is still moist. If it is not, *water* the shrubs. Foundation shrubs near the house, garage, or other buildings often dry out because they are partially under a roof overhang, which may block rain or snowfall. *Check* them often.

Pruning

Limit pruning to cutting off injured and broken branches. Make clean cuts back where the branch joins a larger branch or a main stem. Take care not to cut into tissue on the main branch or trunk. Leave the wound as is to heal in the air.

Growing Smarter

Winter damage to shrubs and other landscape plants does not come from bitter cold, frozen ground, or lots of snow. If they are correctly chosen for the cold-hardiness zone, shrubs can handle all these winter conditions. Damage is more likely to come from bright, glaring sun that reflects off snow or glossy evergreen leaf surfaces and dries foliage and tender bark. Strong winds whip branches around so that they break, or cause broadleaf evergreen foliage to puncture itself and lose excess moisture. Frozen soil prevents shrub roots from drawing replacement moisture from the soil. Fluctuating temperatures in areas with mild winters alternately freeze and thaw the soil around shrub roots—as it expands and contracts, it shifts, damaging roots or even heaving recently planted shrub rootballs out of the soil altogether. Snow cover or winter mulch insulates soil against these freeze-thaw cycles.

Problem Solving

Deer and rabbit damage peaks these next few weeks as natural food supplies are depleted or covered with snow. Deer will be bolder about venturing into your yard, even if they have not previously been much of a problem. Make sure protective wire cages around shrubs are high enough to deter deer standing on deep snow. If you are depending on spray repellents to protect evergreen foliage, *renew* the sprays. Alternate taste and odor repellents every couple of weeks to maintain their effect. Power up the electric fence.

Planning

As the late-winter planting time approaches, it is a good idea to look closely at the shrubs already on your property. If there are some that are obviously in the wrong place (bumping into the sides of the house, so tall that they have covered up windows), think about moving them. If they are otherwise healthy and lovely, give them a new site where they have room to grow, and spare yourself constant pruning. *Move* them yourself, or hire a landscape contractor to do it for you. If you decide you do not want them at all, instead of just cutting them down, consider selling them. Many mature, healthy shrubs are worth hundreds of dollars. Contact a local nursery or garden center for more information and potential buyers. Other questions to think about before the season commences:

- Is this the year to deal with the growing deer problem?

- Will a border of shrubs make the property line prettier or more private?

- What shrubs will encourage more birds to visit the yard?

- Would shrubs with colorful golden, bluish, or purple foliage improve the yard?

- Are all the shrubs spring bloomers, or do you have some that bloom in summer?

- Would a hedge help to define a garden area?

Shopping List: a good pair of work gloves, floral preservative, more birdseed and suet, a platform feeder for birds

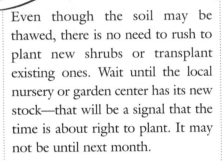

Planting

Even though the soil may be thawed, there is no need to rush to plant new shrubs or transplant existing ones. Wait until the local nursery or garden center has its new stock—that will be a signal that the time is about right to plant. It may not be until next month.

1. First *dig up and discard* very old, dead, or diseased shrubs.

2. Then *transplant* existing shrubs that are too big for their site to new locations in the yard to make way for new plantings in their former locations.

3. Finally, *plant* newly acquired shrubs in their designated spots.

Bare-root shrubs that come in the mail can be planted any time now, but it is easier when the weather is a bit milder (see March for planting steps). Store the bare-root shrubs in a cool place, and keep their roots moist until planting time.

Many summer-blooming shrubs are not available for planting until later spring. In the warmer regions of Pennsylvania, **Crape Myrtles, Camellias,** and **Rose of Sharon** arrive in garden centers in May.

Care for Your Shrubs

Remove snow from heavily laden conifer boughs with a broom, to avoid compounding the weight problem. Using upward strokes from beneath, start knocking the snow from the lower branches first. If you do this, snow knocked from above will not overburden, and possibly break, the lower branches. Work toward the upper branches, bumping them upward from underneath to dislodge and scatter the snow. To finish up, redo the lower ones to clear snow fallen from above. If shrub stems or branches are iced over, do not disturb them—they may be so brittle they will break. When the ice melts, they will resume their former posture.

Watering

Water shrubs whose soil is not frozen if there has been no appreciable rain or snow for a month or more. Well-mulched,

FEBRUARY

established shrubs usually can go that long in winter. If shrubs are not mulched, are newly planted, or are under a roof overhang or other structure that may deflect rainfall from their soil, *check* under their mulch to see if the soil is still moist.

Pruning

To get that spring feeling, *clip off* some budded branches from spring-flowering shrubs to bring indoors to force bloom ahead of schedule. Try **Quince, Forsythia, Dogwood, Winterhazel, Shadblow (Serviceberry), Crabapple, Pussy Willow,** or **Azalea.** The closer to their natural bloom time you cut them, the sooner they will bloom indoors.

Limit any other pruning to removing damaged stems or branches.

Problem Solving

Deer continue to be a potential problem, especially if there is snow on the ground. They will nibble on tender branch tips and twigs of young shrubs. Those under extreme pressure from starvation will eat almost anything in desperation, even **Holly** and other plants with prickly foliage. The only truly dependable deterrent is a fence. Electric fences or ten-foot-tall black polynetting around the perimeter of the property are effective. Some electric fences can be easily reconfig-ured around limited areas of the yard to protect groves of certain vulnerable shrubs such as **Yews** or **Rhododendrons.** If relying on repellent sprays, change the type every two weeks. Many products require repeat sprays after it rains.

Growing Smarter

To force branches of spring-flowering shrubs for indoor bloom:

1 On a relatively mild day, cut branches that have flowerbuds on them. The more swollen the buds, the sooner they will open in the warmth of the house.

2 To maintain its pleasing natural shape, choose branches that the shrub will never miss. The longer the selected branches, the more flowers there will be. Long stems are also more versatile for indoor arrangements.

3 Once indoors, **cut off** the ends of the branches for a fresh cut, and immediately immerse them in a container of tepid water laced with commercial floral preservative or some citrus-based (non-diet) soda to keep it from fouling.

optional To increase water uptake, crush or slit the last inch or two of each woody stem before immersing them in water.

4 Set the branches in their temporary container in a cool room away from direct sunlight. When the flower buds swell so much that you can see their color, put them in fresh water with more preservative in a nice vase. Move them into a warmer room, and enjoy the unfolding display.

MARCH

Planning

It is time to get serious about choosing new shrubs for the yard. Start with a particular site in mind, and choose a shrub whose mature size will not overwhelm the space available. If the site receives lots of sun, mostly shade, or some of each, choose shrubs accordingly. If the soil is chronically soggy, very acid, or very sandy, choose a shrub that can handle those special conditions.

These days the trend is away from planting shrubs up near the house to obscure the view of the concrete foundation. Think about putting a shrub out in the lawn as a focal point, or in a flower bed or shrub border.

Shopping List: a new shrub, bark mulch, granular, slow-acting fertilizer for nursery stock, birdbath, sharp replacement blades for handpruners

Planting

Like trees, shrubs are sold retail either in containers or with their roots in a ball of soil wrapped in burlap and sometimes a wire cage. If ordered by mail, they will likely arrive bare-root—stubby, leafless stems with a tangle of naked roots wrapped in damp paper, moss, or sawdust. Keep the plant cool and the wrapping moist until you can get it outside and into the ground when it thaws. **To plant a bare-root shrub:**

1 *Dig* a hole with sloping sides, slightly more than wide enough to accommodate the root system. Make it about as deep as the roots measure from their tips to the crown of the shrub (the knob where its roots join its stems).

2 Take some loose soil, and build a cone of packed soil in the center of the bottom of the otherwise empty hole.

3 Set the shrub in the hole so its crown rests on top of the mounded soil and the roots splay down along its sides. *Check* that the shrub crown is level with, or slightly above, the surface of the surrounding ground.

4 Fill the hole with plain soil, intermittently firming it lightly around the roots. (Stamping on it may break off fragile root fibers). Then *water* well to eliminate air pockets in the fill soil. *Check* the shrub depth again to make sure it has not sunk below ground level.

5 *Spread* a 2- or 3-inch layer of organic mulch over the planting area. Do not pile it against the stems of the shrub.

Care for Your Shrubs

It's time to deal with neglected shrubs that are tired, overgrown, tangled, and showing lots of dead wood or twigginess. Basically healthy shrubs will respond to renovation. One way to renew them is to gradually *prune out* dead wood over several seasons (see Pruning, this month). In cases where the entire shrub is a mess, the best way to renew it is to cut all the stems back severely. This radical measure stimulates vigorous growth of new shoots, giving the shrub a whole new lease on life.

1 *Renovate* before spring growth begins, either before leaf or flower buds break or new soft needles form on evergreens.

2 Using sharp loppers or pruners, systematically *cut off* every stem at 6 to 12 inches from the ground.

3 When young replacement shoots begin to appear, signaling renewed growth, *clip or pinch off* some of the weaker ones to encourage the development of fewer, but stronger,

remaining ones. They will constitute the basic architecture of the shrub.

4 If the shrub is a naturally well-balanced and full plant, every time stems grow 5 to 8 inches, *pinch out* the terminal bud to promote branching. New branches will emerge just below the cuts.

Remove winter protection from shrubs by mid-month. An exception to this rule is a tender shrub such as a **Garden Fig,** which is extremely vulnerable to frost and chill.

Watering

Water newly planted shrubs well. Follow up every week or so if rainfall is limited. To avoid overwatering, always *check* soil moisture under the mulch layer first.

Fertilizing

When signs of new growth appear, *fertilize* shrubs (don't forget those that are planted as hedges) if you did not do so last fall. Newly renovated shrubs will especially appreciate the nutrition as they strive to regenerate stems. *Sprinkle* a granular, slow-acting fertilizer

formulated for nursery stock on the soil over the shrub root zone. Use the amount suggested on the package label, or less—never more. The rain will soak it in. Evergreens and some other shrubs such as **Holly, Rhododendron,** and **Azalea** like acid soil, so you might use a product formulated for acid-loving trees and shrubs.

Pruning

This is a good time for cosmetic pruning of spring-blooming shrubs. *Remove* those twigs that you determine are dead, as well as any injured ones. Do not assume evergreen foliage that has pale or dark blotchy foliage is dead and remove a branch without testing it to see if it is brittle and dry—it might just be wind or sunburn damage. Wait until after shrubs bloom to prune for size or shape if it seems necessary.

With rejuvenation, you *renew* neglected shrubs a step at a time. This gradual process allows you to enjoy the shrub while it is undergoing renewal. **Spireas, Forsythias,** and **Lilacs** (which produce many stems at soil level) tolerate the technique well.

- This spring, identify and *cut back* the oldest, thickest, woodiest stems to 4 to 6 inches above

the soil level (do only about 1/3 of the total number of stems).

- *Cut back* another third next year.

- *Cut back* the final third the year after that.

Rejuvenation

Problem Solving

Rots may develop in roots planted in overly wet soil during the cool early spring. *Plant* shrubs a bit above ground level if soil is terrible clay.

Brown needles dropping from **Pines** and other evergreens are not necessarily cause for alarm. This is aged foliage that has been around for two or three years, giving way to new replacement leaves.

Weeds will begin to turn up this month. Pull them promptly. *Mulch* bare soil to discourage them.

Planning

Let the show begin. Over the next few months, take some photographs of the shrubs in your yard and other places where particularly attractive shrubs are on display. If taken every couple of weeks, photographs make a terrific record of the succession of bloom and foliage over the growing season. Sometimes a picture helps us be more objective about the problems in the landscape.

In Pennsylvania, our lovely native shrub **Shadblow** is about the first shrub to bloom, deep in the woods. Its white flowers are visible from the highway about the time the shad start running in the Delaware River. Hence, the name. It is also called **Serviceberry.** A bit later our state shrub, **Mountain Laurel,** will be in bloom in the same woods.

Watch the flowers on the conifers develop—**Pines** and **Spruces** first. On a windy day you can see the pollen float toward the female flowers. Later in the season the flowers will become cones.

Shopping List: rain gauge, garden sulfur, insecticidal soap, film for the camera

Planting

To plant or transplant balled-and-burlapped shrubs:

1 Loosely *tie* the shrub stems together so the rootball is visible and easier to lift and move. Keep the rootball moist prior to planting so the soil stays in contact with the roots.

2 *Dig* a saucer-shaped hole with sloping sides about twice as wide as the rootball and only as deep as the rootball is high.

3 *Set* the shrub in the empty hole, oriented as you wish. Make very sure that it does not sit lower than the surrounding ground level. (Set it slightly above level if the soil is clay.) *Cut away* as much of the burlap wrapping as you can reach. If there is a wire cage, *remove* as many rows of wire as you can. Brush off the soil at the top of the rootball until the root flare at the base of the stems is exposed and level with the ground.

4 *Fill* the hole with plain soil, and firm it snugly around and over the rootball. Then fashion a rim of soil beyond its edge to create a water-holding reservoir.

5 *Spread* a 2- or 3-inch layer of organic material such as chopped leaves, pine needles, compost, or commercial bark product over and slightly beyond the planting area.

6 *Water* the planting area well so that the soil is moist down at least 10 inches. If soil is clay, *water* for a while; then stop for a half-hour; then resume for a while longer. *Do not fertilize* for at least a year.

Care for Your Shrubs

Mulching shrubs is the best way to care for them. *Spread* a 2- or 3-inch layer of organic material over the bare soil under and around shrubs. Do not let it touch the stems, though. If there are no chopped leaves left from last fall, use pine needles or wood chips, or buy a commercial bark mulch. The mulch layer discourages weeds, holds in soil moisture, and enriches the soil with nutrients and microbial organisms as it gradually decomposes in warm weather.

Watering

Most shrubs are fairly shallow-rooted, so they tend to get dry quickly. They need, on average, about 1 inch of water a week from you or the rain—more in the hot summer months, less when it is cool. Mulched shrubs may go two or three weeks before their soil begins to dry out. April showers should take care of watering the newly planted shrubs, too.

Fertilizing

If you did not fertilize established shrubs last fall, do so now. Recently planted shrubs need at least a season to begin to grow roots outward into the soil before they are fertilized. Use a granular, slow-acting "nursery" product labeled for the shrubs you have, in the amount suggested on the label.

Because they also produce a berry crop, **Blueberry** bushes need fertilizer every year in spring or fall. Use a product for acid-loving plants to assure rich foliage color (and good fruiting).

Pruning

Prune shrubs soon after they flower if you feel you need to either shape them or gradually renew

Growing Smarter

The key to healthy shrubs is keeping them free of stress. If they are in the right location—one that provides their favorite soil, enough moisture, correct light, and room to grow—then they will be at the peak of their form. They can defend themselves against most insect and disease attacks. When injury or environmental conditions such as drought, pollution, compacted soil, or excessive heat stresses them, they become vulnerable to pest insects and diseases. When there is a problem, treat the pest or disease, then address the cause of the underlying stress. Otherwise, the problem may return.

them. Now that they have leaves, lightly prune hedges that were cut back severely for rejuvenation last month. This will encourage uniform growth and narrower tops. Subsequent prunings should never cut off all this season's new growth.

If you did not do so last fall, *prune* the stems of **Butterfly Bushes** back to within 4 to 6 inches of soil level.

Problem Solving

Aphids and other pest insects that have wintered over as eggs will begin to appear now. They will cluster on the tender new growth at the tips of shrub branches and suck their juices. You may see ants running along stems because they like the sweet honeydew aphids create.

Unfortunately, the beneficial insects that prey on aphids are not yet on the scene. Until they appear, you can: 1) *wash* aphids off stems with a strong water spray from the hose; 2) *clip* or *pinch off* infested stem tips, and toss them in the trash; 3) *spray* the aphids with insecticidal soap as directed on the label.

Weeds respond to spring. Pull them promptly. *Spot-spray* stubborn, perennial ones such as dandelion, poison ivy, and thistle with Roundup®, which will kill their roots, too.

MAY

Planning

May is the month when spring really happens in most of Pennsylvania. The air softens, and the warm days gradually begin to outnumber the cool ones. Shrubs respond to this weather by growing vigorously. Spring bloomers follow up their gorgeous show by pushing foliage and extending their stems. Later bloomers are developing ever larger buds. The paler, soft needles at the tips of needled evergreen boughs signal that they are growing, too.

Because there are lots of species and cultivars of shrubs such as **Viburnum** and **Hydrangea** that bloom at slightly different times, these wonderful spring bloomers decorate landscapes over many weeks. Watch as first the **Oakleaf Hydrangeas** bloom, followed by the **Seashore Hydrangeas,** then as the **Panicle Hydrangeas** flower in succession at your local arboretum or public garden. When you think about buying a new shrub, consider the various bloom periods of its hybrids and cultivars.

Shopping List: a new hose, a hat for sun protection

Planting

Many shrubs are grown and sold in containers these days. They are easier to handle and can be planted almost any time of the year except during severe heat and drought or when the ground is frozen. Planting them is slightly different from planting bare-root (see March) or balled-and-burlapped shrubs (see April). **To plant container-grown shrubs:**

1. *Dig* a hole with sloping sides somewhat wider and just as deep as the container that the shrub came in from the nursery.

2. *Remove* the shrub from its container, and gently knock or brush off excess potting medium from around the roots and the top of the rootball onto a tarp.

3. *Set* the rootball in the hole, positioned as you prefer, and level with or slightly above the surrounding soil. Make sure the root flare at the base of the stems is visible at the top of the rootball.

4. *Mix* the excess potting medium from the container with some of the dirt dug from the hole, and fill in around the rootball. This soil mixture provides a transition for the roots to the harsh reality of the soil in your yard. Shrub roots need encouragement to venture beyond the medium they are used to.

5. *Firm* the soil over the rootball, using the excess to make a ridge beyond the filled hole to create a water-holding reservoir. *Spread* a 2-inch layer of mulch over the planting area up to the root flare, and water well.

Care for Your Shrubs

Is it dead? Browned or dried-looking foliage on some or all branches of a shrub does not necessarily mean that the shrub is dead. Bend the stem or branch. If it is flexible rather than dried and brittle, it may still be alive. Scrape a bit of bark off the stem with a fingernail. If there is green or pale moist tissue beneath, it is still alive. *Cut back* the stem about halfway, and see if it generates new growth.

 # MAY

Add some fresh wood chips, chopped leaves, or pine needles if the mulch layer under shrubs has thinned to less than 2 inches.

Many shrubs grow well in decorative containers or planters outdoors year 'round. To prevent loss of water from the potting medium, *mulch* the top of the planting medium with chopped leaves, sphagnum moss, decorative pecan shells, or cocoa hulls.

If a shrub has a poor appearance and suddenly dies, several consecutive summers of drought may be the reason. *Pull it up* right away, and plant a new shrub.

 ## Watering

Water shrubs when rainfall is unreliable. If they are well mulched, they should be able to go two to three weeks without water.

Newly planted shrubs and those in containers will need more-frequent watering, especially if it is hot.

 ## Fertilizing

Any fertilizing of shrubs in the ground should have been done by now.

If you did not mix a complete granular, slow-acting product into the potting medium of shrubs that are in decorative containers and planters, sprinkle it on top of the medium now. Rains and waterings will activate it over time. Otherwise, add a dilute water-soluble (fast-acting) fertilizer intended for shrubs to the watering can every couple of weeks when you water these shrubs. Measure it according to package directions. Do not overdo.

 ## Pruning

After they have bloomed, prune **Forsythia, Quince, Azalea, Daphne,** and other spring bloomers.

Deadhead faded blossoms from **Rhododendrons** as they finish blooming. This is an opportunity to make **Rhodys** denser by clipping off individual branches to encourage branching. Do not shear these plants. In a few weeks many of these shrubs will set buds for next year, so don't delay—later pruning will cut off the buds and reduce flowering next year.

Problem Solving

De-icing-salt problems may show up now as scorched lower leaves or twig dieback on shrubs that are near the street or sidewalk. The sodium chloride gets into the soil and absorbs the moisture, dehydrating shrub roots. If you suspect this problem, *drench* the soil with lots of water to leach out remaining salts.

Pine sawfly larvae are brownish-black caterpillars that resemble the bark on branches of **Mugo Pine** and some other needled evergreens. They chew on the needles, denuding branches. Look closely to detect their movement, and knock them off into a plastic bag, or squish them between thumb and forefinger. *Spray* a product containing **Bt** (*Bacillus thuringiensis*) on the infested foliage you cannot reach while the sawfly larvae are eating it. They will sicken, stop eating, then die in a matter of days.

Dog urine may be the culprit if foliage yellows on lower branches of shrubs at corners or along edges of the yard. *Mulch* well, put up a little wire fence, or *plant* prickly ground cover plants around the shrub to deter the dogs.

JUNE

Planning

This month is a transition time. Late spring gives way to true summer and things are, literally, heating up. This is when shrubs demonstrate their versatility and dependability, providing dense, colorful foliage to cool the yard. They have many other jobs in the landscape as well. They define borders, enclose spaces, screen views and noise, and form a pleasing backdrop to showcase the herbaceous annual and perennial flowers that are going strong now. During this pause before summer-flowering shrubs begin to bloom, take note of how your shrubs look.

It is not too late to add some summer-flowering shrubs to the yard if you have none. If all you have are spring bloomers, many that bloom later in the summer or through to fall are available in containers at garden centers:

- **Annabelle Hydrangea** (*Hydrangea arborescens* 'Annabelle')

- **Butterfly Bush** (*Buddleia* **sp.**)

- **Chaste Tree** (*Vitex* **sp.**, only for warmer parts of PA)

- **Crape Myrtle** (*Lagerstroemia indica*)

- **Fringe Tree** (*Chionanthus* **sp.**)

- **Peegee Hydrangea** (*Hydrangea paniculata* 'Grandiflora')

- **Rose of Sharon** (*Hibiscus syriacus*)

- **St. Johnswort** (*Hypericum* **sp.**)

The flowers on the following summer bloomers are small, but their fall berries are wonderful:

- **Beautyberry** (*Callicarpa* **sp.**)

- **Chokeberry** (*Aronia* **sp.**)

- **Winterberry** (*Ilex verticillata*)

Shopping List: hose storage reel, new watering can, houseplant water meter

Planting

Last call for safely planting or moving shrubs. Theoretically, you can plant container-grown plants all summer, but it is a lot more stressful for both the shrub and you after heat arrives.

If the shrubs in a border or hedge are too close together now that they have matured a bit, *thin* them by digging up and transplanting every other one. Take care to disturb the roots of those that remain in place as little as possible. They will welcome the improved air circulation and room to grow.

Shrubs whose branches droop, such as **Forsythia** and **Deutzia**, sometimes root where their tips touch the soil. If you notice this, *clip off* the main branch above the rooted tip to separate it from the main plant, then *dig up* the small rooted piece and pot it for a gift, or replant it elsewhere.

Care for Your Shrubs

Gradually move potted tender shrubs—**Gardenia, Norfolk Island Pine, Fig, Citrus,** and others—outdoors to the porch. Allow them a few days to acclimate to outdoor conditions by returning them indoors at night if it is cool. Do not set them immediately in sunlight, or their foliage will burn. When they are acclimated to the outdoors, place them in spots around the property that have their desired light conditions. Tender tropicals are really useful for filling in spaces in planted beds vacated by spring-blooming bulbs and other plants that disappear when heat arrives. *Mulch* the soil in their containers to help it retain moisture.

New, fast-growing stems of **Butterfly Bushes** may need supporting stakes to minimize flopping.

Watering

If it has been a moist spring, shrubs' moisture levels will probably be fine. *Check* the soil under the mulch of recently planted ones, and water if it is dry. Do not forget those in large planters and containers that are out in the garden.

Do not automatically water if a shrub's foliage is wilted. It may not mean that it is thirsty—wilt is also a reaction to transplanting stress, excessive heat and humidity, or a root rot problem. Later in the day, *check* to see if foliage is still wilted. If not, it was the heat.

Fertilizing

The main growth period for most shrubs has passed, so there is no point in fertilizing now. It will only stimulate excessive stem and foliage growth, which stresses the shrub (especially if drought develops) and attracts aphids and other pests.

Pruning

Continue to *prune* any late-spring bloomers, such as certain **Rhododendrons,** after their flowers fade. Other evergreens to prune are **Pieris, Daphne, Fir, Heath,** **Mountain Laurel,** and **Pine.** Otherwise, limit pruning to cutting off broken or diseased stems and branches from now until fall.

Remember, once you give your hedge its major cutback in the spring, subsequent clippings should be light trims only. Do not keep cutting or shearing back to the major cut and eliminating all new growth.

If you are maintaining a shrub hedge, topiary, or espalier, it will need only minor clipping for training now that its major growth phase is past.

Problem Solving

Chlorosis causes foliage of **Rhododendrons, Mountain Laurel,** and other acid-loving shrubs to become pale or yellowish between dark-green veins. This is usually due to iron deficiency. Although there may be iron in the soil, the soil environment may not be acid enough to convert it into a form these shrubs can use, so they become iron-deprived. Acidify the soil by sprinkling powdered garden sulfur on the area over their root zones and watering it in. If the leaves do not grow darker green in a few weeks, add iron to the soil with a product from the garden center. A soil test will confirm if soil problems are serious.

Pest insect activity in the yard is to be expected now. As soon as you notice aphids, whiteflies, or mites, *pinch off* or squish those you can reach. *Wash off* others with a strong water spray from the hose. Do not assume that any insect is a pest—most insects are either benign or beneficial. If your yard has diverse plantings and some bird feeders, beneficial insects and birds will keep most problems under control.

Scale may turn up on evergreen **Euonymus** and other shrubs. Either powdery white spots or waxy hard bumps will dot leaf and stem surfaces. *Spray* affected shrub foliage thoroughly—top and bottom—with light (superior) horticultural oil as directed on the product label.

Growing Smarter

It's too late now, but evergreen shrubs to be pruned in late winter include:

- **American Holly**
- **Aucuba**
- **Boxwood**
- **Cherrylaurel**
- **Falsecypress**
- **Hemlock**
- **Japanese Holly**
- **Junipers**
- **Nandina**
- **Oregon Grape**
- **Privet**
- **Wintercreeper**
- **Yew**
- Most needled evergreens

JULY

Planning

One of the ways shrubs can be used to enhance a landscape is by forming hedges. Hedges along property boundaries are gentle fences. They provide the same privacy, enclosure, and barrier to foot traffic as walls or fences, but are not as isolating or intimidating to the people on the other side. Hedges along planted beds, as edging for herb gardens for instance, add color and definition to gardens. They enhance them as a frame does a picture.

While low hedges that edge formal beds typically require frequent close clipping, hedges in general are not necessarily high-maintenance. If the shrubs are properly chosen and sited, their natural growth habit will create a soft continuous row of dense branches and foliage of the desired height when they are mature. Periodic intense clipping is necessary only in situations where large shrubs must be forced to stay short or where a strictly classical, formal sheared hedge is the goal.

Think about planting shrubs this fall to form a hedge on the property. Observe hedges this summer to get some ideas. Many kinds of shrubs make good hedges—they do not have to be privet or boxwood. Consider evergreens such as:

- **Azalea**
- **Blue Holly**
- **Cherrylaurel**

Some deciduous shrubs also make attractive hedges:

- **Deutzia**
- **'The Fairy' Rose**
- **Forsythia**
- **Virginia Sweetspire**
- Most **Viburnum**

Prickly shrubs that have thorns also act as barriers, discouraging kids, salespeople, mail carriers, and errant dogs from cutting across the yard:

- **Barberry**
- **Hardy Orange**
- **Holly**
- **Pyracantha**
- **Quince**

Shopping List: polynetting to deter birds and squirrels from edible fruit crops, drip irrigation system, mechanical timer

Planting

It is probably too hot to plant shrubs now. If you must, arrange for temporary shade at the site to reduce transplant stress.

Care for Your Shrubs

Blueberry shrubs serve double duty. They are wonderful landscape assets when they bloom in the spring and then, again, when their leaves turn a rich red color in the fall. In between, they yield wonderful berries. As blueberries ripen, *pick* them promptly. Discourage birds from stealing the harvest by draping netting over the shrubs.

Check the organic mulch layer under shrubs. As heat accelerates its decomposition, the layer of leaves, wood chips, or pine needles gets thinner and gradually disappears. To discourage weeds and cool the soil, mulch should be 2 or 3 inches thick. If it is thicker, it may deprive root fibers of essential air; **never pile mulch against shrub stems.**

Be careful with the weed-trimmer. Nicks in the soft bark of young shrubs will allow pests and disease pathogens access to tender tissues under their bark.

Watering

If there is to be a drought, it is probably already apparent by mid-month. Because drought conditions have pretty much become the norm these last few summers, it makes sense to invest in a simple irrigation system for shrubs. In the long run it will save money, water, and time.

Choose the porous-hose type of drip irrigation made from recycled automobile tires; it sweats water along its length for hedges and shrub borders. Another type that has individual emitters every 12 to 18 inches or more is good for shrubs that are planted farther apart. Nestled under the mulch, these systems use scarce water efficiently because they deliver it directly to shrub roots, and there is no loss from runoff or evaporation.

Pruning

Limit any pruning to removing dead or injured branches.

Problem Solving

Japanese beetles arrive early this month. Watch for the first ones, and start knocking them off shrub foliage into a jar of soapy water

Growing Smarter

Some woody plants are both trees and shrubs. How can that be? Well, it is mostly an arbitrary matter. If they have several stems instead of a single leader, or trunk, and if they are smaller than about 20 feet (give or take a foot or two), then most horticultural authorities call them shrubs. There are also some plants, such as **Juniper,** that exist as both trees and as shrubs, with lots of species and varieties that have different forms. Even more confusion results because certain shrubs are grown as single-stem, or trunk, plants. Some have a few stems, but they are limbed up so their branching canopy resembles a tree. Some examples of shrubs that are often made into trees are:

- **Crape Myrtle**
- **Fringe Tree**
- **Witchhazel**
- **Serviceberry/Shadblow**
- **Smokebush**
- **Juniper**

immediately. *Avoid* pheromone traps that lure beetles from other yards into yours. Not all the beetles will fall into the bag that is a part of a pheromone trap. *Spray* major infestations with a product containing pyrethrum, according to label directions.

Lacebugs may appear on the foliage of **Rhododendron, Azalea, Pieris,** and other shrubs that are stressed by exposure to too much sun. Leaf surfaces are dull, pale, and speckled, and the undersides are littered with dark specks of insect excrement. Install some temporary shade for now, and plan to move the plant to a shadier site in the fall. *Spray* infested foliage periodically with insecticidal soap or horticultural oil to catch the inevitable next generation of lacebugs.

Bagworms and other worm/ caterpillar pests may feed on foliage of needled evergreen shrubs. Pick as many dangling, twiggy "bag" nests as possible from shrub branches. *Spray* heavily infested foliage with *Bt* (*Bacillus thuringiensis*) as directed—the caterpillars in the remaining, out-of-reach bags will eat it as they feed on the foliage. They will sicken and die within days.

Aphids should not be much of a problem now, as their beneficial insect enemies are out in full force. Check tender new growth tips that have developed on recently pruned shrubs to make sure. If you find some, *wash them off* with a stiff spray from the hose.

Planning

Of all the plants in your yard, shrubs are among the most self-reliant. If you are planning to be away on vacation for several weeks, even during this hot and possibly dry month, your established shrubs will do fine. As long as they have been watered well and properly mulched, they can go for quite a while without rain.

This is a good time to think about buying a chipper or shredder-chipper to turn the leaves and branches pruned from shrubs into valuable mulch. Shredders also help with composting, as organic yard waste decomposes more quickly if it is shredded. If you have lots of trees and shrubs on the property, it makes environmental and economic sense to have this equipment. It makes sense to recycle the wonderful organic material back onto your property. Think about owning this equipment cooperatively and splitting the cost with one or two neighbors.

Shopping List: a shredder-chipper, composting fork, safety glasses, ear protection

Planting

This is not a good time to plant shrubs, as high soil temperatures shut down root growth in many plants. If planted now, shrubs will just sit and be miserable. Container-grown ones may be available for sale at the local nursery or garden center, left over from spring inventory. If you find one you like, bring it home and *water* it, but leave it in the container until next month.

After Labor Day, nurseries will be getting some fresh new shrubs in stock. Even then, there will still be several weeks for newly planted ones to develop extended roots and become established before the ground freezes hard. Deciduous shrubs will not have to worry about generating energy to make leaves until next spring—by then, they will be in good shape.

Care for Your Shrubs

There's not much to do for shrubs this month. Just harvest the blueberries and *check* the mulch on all shrubs.

Shrubs planted last fall should be strong enough to cope with heat and drought if necessary. Those planted this past spring or early summer may be struggling a bit. If they are in very sunny sites, you might erect some temporary shade for them during the really hot weeks. Fashion a kind of "awning" with commercial shade cloth or white polyspun garden fleece stapled to tall stakes to block the afternoon sun. Do not let the awning interfere with air circulation around the shrub.

Watering

Watch newly planted shrubs to be sure they have enough water. Proper mulching will retard evaporation of soil moisture and help cool the soil.

Understory shrubs such as **Azaleas, Mountain Laurel,** and **Pieris** that nestle partly under large shade trees often lose their share of the soil moisture to thirsty nearby tree roots, and unless a rain is very hard, it may not fall through the leaf canopy to saturate the soil under a large tree. When it is hot, *check* the soil moisture around these shrubs often.

Shrubs in planters around the pool or patio are very stressed by August sun. Test frequently with a houseplant moisture-meter probe to make sure their planting medium is still moist. Shrubs in clay (terracotta) pots tend to dry out more quickly than those in plastic or wooden planters. *Mulch* the planting medium, or add some low cascading plants to the container to cover the soil. Experiment with fancy mulches such as cocoa or pecan hulls, sphagnum moss, or special decorative wood chips. Do not use stones or gravel; they absorb and hold heat.

Fertilizing

Delay fertilizing for another few weeks until shrubs go dormant. Fertilizing now will only stimulate tender new growth that will get caught by the first frost. Never fertilize a shrub that is stressed by heat or pest problems. Wait until the stress is reduced.

Pruning

Continue to limit any pruning to removing dead or injured branches from shrubs.

Problem Solving

Mildew month has arrived. If this grayish-white coating on the foliage of **Common Lilacs, Exbury Azaleas,** and other victims has not yet appeared, it will now. While it mars the appearance of mature shrubs, it does not harm them. In a few weeks the leaves will drop any-

Growing Smarter

Shrubs may be used as ground covers! The typical image of a ground cover plant is something low-growing, green, and crawly. However, lots of different kinds of plants—grasses, annual flowers, wildflowers, perennial flowers or foliage plants, flowering bulbs—do a good job of covering bare soil and protecting it from compaction and erosion, and lots of shrubs make great ground cover plantings, too. The carpet types of **Junipers** that grow horizontally in colorful, textured mats over the soil are standouts. Here are some others:

- **Cotoneaster (***Cotoneaster salicifolius* 'Repens')
- **Red Twig Dogwood (***Cornus sericea***)**
- **Shore Juniper (***Juniperus conferta***)**
- **Slender Deutzia (***Deutzia gracilis* 'Nikko')
- **St. Johnswort (***Hypericum calycinum***)**
- **Wintercreeper (***Euonymus fortunei***)**

way. If it threatens to overwhelm young, new shrubs, thoroughly *spray* all uninfected foliage with an anti-desiccant product or wettable garden sulfur to prevent the spread of the fungus. Make sure shrubs are not too close together. Good air circulation helps control fungal diseases such as mildew.

Mites on **Junipers** and other conifers are more likely if you routinely *spray* your property with the chemical pesticides that also kill the resident beneficial insects that prey on mites. Mites thrive on plants stressed by heat and dryness. Look for sickly or dried foliage and thin webbing among twigs or foliage. Use a strong water spray from the hose to wash them off. Repeat this every other day or so for a couple of

weeks to aggravate the mites so much they will give up and move on. Horticultural oil sprays are effective, too. Use as directed on the product label.

Weeds do not seem to mind heat and drought. Keep after them to prevent their developing seeds and self-sowing. The tough ones (dandelion, thistle) will probably need a herbicide such as Roundup® to kill the deep taproot that is almost impossible to dig out completely. Any remnant in the soil generates a new weed next year.

SEPTEMBER

Planning

In some areas of Pennsylvania it still feels a lot like summer, but the number of minutes of daylight each day is shrinking rapidly with every passing week. As shrubs and other plants respond to this and prepare for their upcoming period of dormancy, it is time to do the jobs that have been delayed until cooler weather prevails. This is a good time to start a compost pile, if you have not already done so:

1 *Designate* an area out of plain sight—behind the garage or tool shed will do—for depositing yard waste.

2 *Collect* prunings, weeds, dead plants, and fallen leaves, and throw them into a heap.

3 *Cut or shred* the organic debris into small pieces to speed the action of the microbes, whose eating and reproducing activities will promote decomposition.

4 To improve the appearance of the compost pile, *enclose* it with chicken wire, wooden pallets, or a commercial bin.

5 Next spring, *harvest* the material at the bottom of the pile that has been transformed into compost.

Shopping List: potting mix, a book on composting, a compost fork, granular slow-acting fall fertilizer for shrubs

Planting

Coming up soon—last opportunity to move or add shrubs to the landscape for this year. Nurseries and garden centers are well stocked with supplies and plants with signs to remind that "Fall is for Planting"— and most shrubs do prefer fall planting to spring planting. It gives them time to develop strong root systems before they have to muster the energy to make new branches and foliage.

Since there are no buds or flowers to guide your choice, read the plant labels carefully to ascertain the flower color and variety name of flowering shrubs. **Mountain Laurel,** for instance, is available in several colors. Note the shrub's light and soil requirements. While conifers and flowering deciduous shrubs usually love sunshine, many broadleaf evergreens are used to woodland settings and need some shade. Be sure to note each shrub's mature height and width.

Review the steps for planting container and balled-and-burlapped shrubs (see April and May). Bare-root shrubs will not be available now, as they are usually planted in the spring.

Care for Your Shrubs

Tender shrubs—**Gardenia, Citrus, Fig,** and others that have summered outdoors—must come indoors before frost. *Check* to see if they need repotting after a season's growth. Increase the size of the pot an inch or two, no more, and make sure it has a drainage hole. Fill it with fresh soilless potting medium mixed with a complete granular slow-acting fertilizer. (Since there is no soil in potting medium, there is no nutrition, either.) Set the shrub at the same level in the new pot that it was in its previous one, add extra medium to fill in the space, and *water* well.

Before bringing tender shrubs indoors, *check* each one carefully for signs of insects or disease. Wash their foliage well with water. Assume there are likely to be pest insect eggs somewhere, and thoroughly *spray* the stems and foliage with light horticultural oil. This will forestall most pest problems.

Gradually *acclimatize* them to reduced-light indoor conditions by setting them in the shade for a few

SEPTEMBER

days, then moving them indoors to a location with bright light.

If you have acquired a **Bonsai** specimen, bear in mind that it must stay outdoors for the winter if it is a hardy shrub. It needs the same conditions to thrive that its normal-sized counterparts need.

However, if a plant is in a container you must protect the roots from freezing temperatures. Put the container in a cold frame or sink it down in the ground.

Watering

When rainfall is scarce, *water* shrubs if the soil under the mulch is dry. Do not forget that shrubs in containers in the sun (**Bonsai** specimens, especially) will dry out more quickly than those in the ground.

Fertilizing

Fertilizing is okay only if frost arrives in your yard this month and shrubs begin their dormant period. It's better to wait a few weeks more to be sure. *Delay* feeding newly planted shrubs until next year.

Pruning

Hurricane season sometimes brings high winds to the eastern part of the state, which take their toll on trees and shrubs. *Cut off* cleanly any branches that are snapped off in a storm. Make the cut back at a joint where the branch joins a larger one or a main stem. This avoids unsightly stub ends of branches. *Delay* other pruning until late winter or early spring.

Problem Solving

Keep after the **weeds.** Pull easy ones as you notice them. Perennial weeds will be alive until frost. Roundup® or a similar herbicide product works best when weeds are actively growing, so *spray* them as soon as possible—hopefully before they release seed for next year. Be especially careful around poison ivy, which will be developing berries and lovely purplish-red or yellow foliage. All parts of it are poisonous to those who are sensitive.

Deer will reappear if they are in the neighborhood. Set up the electric fence or make other preparations. Put wire cages around newly planted young shrubs. Young stems and twigs are the tastiest.

Rodents will be nesting soon. To force them to nest elsewhere, *delay* renewing the mulch under shrubs until after the ground freezes. Pull ground cover plantings away from shrub stems. If rodents are a chronic problem, set up wire cages around shrubs to protect the bases of the stems from their gnawing.

Pest insect populations will diminish as the month progresses. Do not worry about those on deciduous shrubs, which are about to lose their leaves anyway. *Pluck off* any bagworm cases dangling on needled evergreens.

Planning

While you are outdoors doing yard chores, be sure to take time to notice the shrubs in your yard and the neighborhood. Note which ones are developing wonderful fall foliage color and, perhaps, berries. A trip to a nearby arboretum or an illustrated book on shrubs will help you identify them. If you would like to add them to your landscape, look for them at the garden center now, or plan to check for them next spring. Shrubs such as **Viburnums** are especially wonderful because they have both fall color and berries.

Shopping List: anti-desiccant spray, burlap or other windscreen material, hardware cloth, animal-repellent spray, birdseed

Planting

This month is a great time for planting or transplanting shrubs in many areas of Pennsylvania. They accept the move more easily than trees usually do—the smaller the shrub, the faster it will adjust.

Transplanting requires the extra planting step of first digging up the shrub. Use a good long-handled shovel, and wait until the ground has softened a bit from a recent rain.

1 *Moisten* the soil the day before. Loosely tie the stems of the shrub together to enable you to see the ground to dig.

2 *Dig* around the roots as far out as you can and still have a manageable rootball. The larger the better, so that fewer roots are cut or disturbed, making an easier transition for the shrub. However, you need to be able to lift the shrub without ruining your back.

3 When the shovel can go completely under the shrub, the roots are free. *Shove* a piece of burlap under the rootball from one side, then tip it to the other side to allow you to pull the burlap completely under it. (A helper makes this job a lot easier.)

4 Use the burlap to *lift* the shrub out of its hole, then wrap it around the rootball to hold the soil on the roots while you dig a saucer-shaped hole at the new site.

5 Follow the steps for planting balled-and-burlapped shrubs (see April).

Care for Your Shrubs

Plant some tiny hardy bulbs under your newly transplanted shrubs before spreading winter mulch. **Crocus, Snowdrops, Squill,** and others go only an inch or two into the soil, so this will not disturb the shrub roots. You'll be glad you took the time when spring comes.

To prevent pest eggs or spores from overwintering and causing problems again next year, clean up fallen leaves and fruits from under shrubs that have suffered from disease or pest problems. Put them in the trash, not the compost. Then *spread* fresh mulch.

Collect the leaves that fall from deciduous trees this month for free mulch.

- *Mow* over them with the mulching mower when you cut the lawn the final few times, and collect them in a bagging attachment;

- OR use the mower side discharge to *blow* them toward the center of the lawn as you make passes, then collect the pile after you cut the final swath of lawn;

- OR *rake* the leaves and chop them with an electric leaf-shredder, or string-trimmer or mower.

Set up protection for shrubs that are either newly planted or are in sites exposed to harsh winter sun and wind. Erect burlap screens to block prevailing winds, or snow fencing if drifting snow is a problem. Do not use plastic.

Watering

Water all recently planted shrubs and established evergreens, which continue to lose moisture through their foliage all winter. They need as much moisture as they can absorb before the ground freezes.

Fertilizing

Spring-planted shrubs and those that went in last fall but have not yet been fertilized will benefit from some granular slow-acting fall-season fertilizer formulated for nursery stock. After deciduous shrubs drop leaves and enter dormancy, their roots will grow actively until the ground freezes hard later in the fall. Follow package directions.

Pruning

As a precaution, *cut back* extremely long branches of shrubs if they are

Growing Smarter

The backbone of any backyard bird habitat is its shrubs. They provide all-important shelter and, in many cases, nuts and berries for food. Attract a variety of bird species to your yard to help you with pest insect problems.

1 **Learn about birds.** The more you know about their lifestyles and food preferences, the easier it will be to please them.

2 **Plant for diversity.** Choose a variety of shrubs of different types (evergreens and deciduous), sizes, and site preferences (woods, sun, wet).

3 **Provide a source of fresh water** year 'round for birds to drink and bathe in. Use a heater, dripper, or other device to keep it thawed in winter.

4 **Let part of the property go a bit wild.** Birds need brush and the food sources that hide there. Let flowers develop seeds at the end of the season.

5 **Avoid general use of chemical insecticides.** Spot-treat problems with selective botanical or biological products.

6 **Set up bird feeders.** Birdseed supplements natural food sources as they become depleted.

likely to whip in winter wind. Reduce their length to that of the rest of the branches.

Cut and bring indoors some berry laden branches for harvest season arrangements. **Viburnums, Beautyberry,** and **Winterberry Holly** are real standouts in vases, with silvery plumes of ornamental grass and other gleanings from the yard and garden.

Problem Solving

The condition of **no or few berries** on a **Holly** may have several causes. The plant may be male. It may be too young. It may be too far from a male consort. It may have been so rainy and chilly last spring that the bee pollinators were unable to visit the flowers. Wait until next year.

NOVEMBER

Planning

November is a transition month in much of Pennsylvania. It bridges a possible Indian Summer and the first real snow in some parts of the state. Plan to have shrubs set for the winter by Thanksgiving so they will be prepared for any eventuality.

Get out the binoculars and a notebook so you can watch the birds that visit the bird feeder and the berry laden shrubs in the yard. Mockingbirds will be very interested in **Holly** berries. Keeping fresh water available for birds in freezing weather is a challenge. Site a birdbath in the sun so the water will melt for parts of some days. Float a table tennis ball in it to keep some movement to retard freezing. There are birdbath heaters if all else fails.

Shopping List: suet for birds, birdbath heater, bark mulch

Planting

Last call for planting and transplanting shrubs in areas where the ground has not frozen. *Store* balled-and-burlapped shrubs safely while they wait for planting day. Keep the rootball moist. Even though their branches or evergreen foliage can withstand the considerable cold,

their roots cannot. They are accustomed to being safely in the ground by now. *Plant* as soon as possible.

If the ground is already frozen hard, it is too late to plant. Store the shrub in a cool space that does not freeze in the winter, such as an unheated garage. Keep the rootball moist. An alternative is to *dig* a hole in the compost pile or a mulch pile and temporarily bury it there, its pot or burlapped rootball well covered with organic material as insulation.

Care for Your Shrubs

Once the ground has frozen hard, *spread* mulch over shrub root zones to insulate the soil during the winter season. The layer of organic material can be a bit thicker than it is in summer—3 or 4 inches—but it must not rest against the bark of shrub stems. It will buffer temperature fluctuations in the soil that may disturb roots.

Winter protection measures may be necessary for some broadleaf evergreens that must endure direct winter sun and wind where they are located. *Spray* foliage surfaces and undersides with anti-desiccant spray (Wilt-Pruf™ or similar product) to minimize moisture loss. Use this

spray on your living or live-cut Christmas tree as well, to prevent it from drying out while it waits to come indoors.

Watering

If there is not much rain, continue to monitor soil moisture under evergreens as long as the ground is not frozen. *Water* where the soil is dry. *Check* shrubs that are not mulched for some reason, because their soil will dry out faster if there is minimal rainfall. Keep the hose handy until serious cold arrives.

Fertilizing

By now shrubs are dormant. If you haven't done so yet, sprinkle some granular, slow-acting fall/winter fertilizer for nursery stock over their root zones for the snow or rain to soak in through the mulch. Use the amount indicated on the product label. If you fertilize this fall, you will not have to do it in the spring.

Pruning

Unless there is some damage to shrub branches, there is no reason to prune this month. If you have not already done so, you can cut some boughs from conifers such as **Fir, Spruce, Juniper,** or **Pine** to lay over bulb beds to protect the soil. Cut carefully to preserve the nice shape of the shrub.

You might want to take the pruners out to cut some shrub branches for an arrangement for the Thanksgiving table. This is also a good time to clean and sharpen the pruners.

Problem Solving

Deer-hunting season notwithstanding, deer still dare to visit a lot of yards in Pennsylvania as fall becomes winter. Prepare according to the seriousness of the problem. Experiment with repellent sprays, bars of soap, and other measures if deer are a minor nuisance. Up the ante with wire cages around individual shrubs and maybe even electric fencing if they threaten nice ornamentals such as **Rhododendrons.** If deer are constant intruders, consider installing black-mesh polynetting fencing around the perimeter of your yard (and across the driveway) to deter them. The ultimate defense is to wrap your property in 10-foot-high wire or polynetting with electrified wires running through it about 4 feet off the ground.

Rodents such as mice and voles like to chew on the tender bark of shrub stems. When they chew enough to girdle its stems, a shrub will die. If you detect rodent damage on plants, *protect* them by surrounding the shrub or individual stems with cages of hardware cloth (wire mesh) or with commercial tree-guard products. Make sure they are high enough so that a few feet of snow under a mouse or chipmunk will not boost it high enough to reach its target.

Growing Smarter

The ultimate shrub in the eyes of many homeowners and gardeners is the one that is attractive almost year 'round. Sound impossible? There are some shrubs that actually fit this description. Here are some shrubs with multiseason interest—flowers, berries, colorful foliage, great bark, and interesting shape.

- **Aucuba**
- **Crape Myrtle**
- **Oakleaf Hydrangea**
- **Oregon Grape**
- **Red Twig Dogwood**
- **Southern Magnolia**
- **Viburnum**
- **Virginia Sweetspire**
- Most needled evergreens

DECEMBER

Planning

The catalogs that arrive in the mail this month will remind you to think about the new gardening year coming up. Spend some time at your windows—front, side, back—and notice whether there are shrubs in view. Notice places where new shrubs might be attractive.

This is a good time to bring your gardening journal or notebook up to date. *Record* the names and planting times of new shrubs, weather highlights, fertilizing times, and major pruning efforts. It is helpful to note which shrubs have performed particularly well and which had problems. Since pest insects arrive at nearly the same time each season, a record of when they arrived last year will give you early warning next summer.

This is the traditional time to make New Year's resolutions. A good one is to resolve to be sure that the soil under shrubs is mulched with a layer of organic matter year 'round. Another is to resolve to sharpen your pruners and loppers at least once each season. See how many resolutions you can come up with.

Holiday List: a good forged-steel, long-handled shovel, an indoor-outdoor thermometer, a good pair of pruners, a gift certificate for a new shrub

Planting

If you plan to have a living Christmas tree, select its site and dig the hole where you intend to plant it, so you can do so immediately after the holidays even if the ground has frozen by then. *Cover* and store the loose soil in pails where it will not freeze.

Care for Your Shrubs

If you haven't already set up protection for shrubs against sun, wind, snow, critters, and desiccation, do so now. Evergreen shrubs with flexible branches that might flop or break off in a heavy snowfall may benefit from tying. Loosely gather the branches against the stems, and loop some twine around the entire bundle. Tie them so that air and light can penetrate the interior of the shrub.

Low-wattage outdoor holiday lights will not harm shrubs. Wrap or drape the strings of lights loosely. Be sure they are UL approved for outdoors.

Watering

There is always a possibility that a fall drought will endanger evergreens. *Check* soil moisture under the mulch layer if three weeks passes without rain or snow.

Pruning

Cut a few branches from shrubs for use as holiday decorations. Try some new ones in addition to the traditional **Holly** and needled evergreens. Add color with the gold-and-green-speckled foliage from **Aucuba.** Various shrub **Dogwoods** offer bright red and yellow bare twigs. Leafless **Winterberry** branches are literally crusted with red berries. The corky stems of **Burning Bush** and the kinky ones of **Curly Willow** will add interest. Various **Junipers** have blue, silver, or yellow foliage. Don't forget that **Yew, Rhododendron, Cherry-laurel, Mountain Laurel,** and **Skimmia** are great additions to wreaths and bouquets.

Problem Solving

Critters: Toward the end of the month, check for signs of rabbits, voles, chipmunks, and mice. Look for deer hoofprints in the snow or mud and gnawed bark on shrub stems and low-hanging branches. Reinforce barriers or other protections you installed last month.

Trees

William Penn was so moved by the sight of the eastern hardwood forest that thickly carpeted the lands granted to him by a charter from King Charles II of England that he named his colony Pennsylvania, or Penn's Woods. How appropriate this was. From the beginning, trees have been an integral part of life in Pennsylvania, their silhouettes forming a backdrop to the lives of the generations that have lived among them for centuries. From the era of the Lenni Lenape Indians, to the time of the early Dutch and English farmers, then the Quakers, and then through successive waves of immigrants that pushed west into the mountains and on to Pittsburgh, tall trees have been a fact of life in this state.

Today, trees are so much a part of our sense of the place that they are still everywhere, despite urbanization and suburban sprawl. Remnants of the great forest that resides in our cultural memory preside over municipal parks, corporate campuses, schools, and churchyards. Trees line the streets of our cities. And, of course, it is the rare home landscape that does not feature at least one tree. When I was growing up in suburban Philadelphia during the post-war housing boom, the local builder who was most respected was the one who took the trouble to save the trees on the lots where he put houses. The other builders scrambled to plant a tree or two on each of their lots in an attempt to make their houses as desirable.

Trees in the Home Landscape

As much as we love our trees, we do tend to take them for granted. Partly that is because they have always been part of the scene. Partly it is because they have been, until recent times, quite self-reliant. Mostly, I think, it is because we do not know enough about them to understand that they need care, and we do not know how to give that care. Trees in a landscape situation have a far different experience from that of their counterparts in the forest. They do not benefit from living in a community of trees. They must compete with turfgrasses for water and nutrition in the soil. They must cope with air pollution, damage from yard-care equipment, compacted soil, and utility company pruning. The list of insults goes on. The net result is that these trees live shorter, more stressful lives.

It takes only one experience of having to cut down a large shade tree in the yard to realize the significant role trees play in a landscape. After the sound of huge lengths of trunk and limbs falling with concussive thumps onto the ground, then the noise and commotion of the chainsaws and chipper, then possibly the whine of a stump grinder . . . there is a profound silence. There is also a huge hole to the sky, and the familiar is forever changed.

Large shade trees form a vertical framework for your outdoor living space. They establish and define its scale and create a balance for its overall design. Trees link the sky with the ground, roofing it with their canopies. Smaller trees soften the edges of the yard and its buildings. They provide ornamental features such as colorful flowers, berries, fruit, and bark. Their wonderful variation in foliage color, texture, and shape is appealing over all the seasons.

Trees

And that is just the beginning. Trees have practical as well as aesthetic functions in the landscape. Judiciously sited trees can moderate the climate indoors. The leafy canopy of a tree on the south side of a house will block the hot sun in the summer, and a row of sturdy needled evergreens planted to the north or west will block prevailing winds in the winter. Trees also protect other plants. Large ones shelter smaller shade-loving understory trees, flowers, and shrubs from exposure to harsh winds and heavy rain. Their leaf canopies create microclimates by transposing light, filtering it, or blocking it to create textured shade. An assortment of both large and smaller trees provides the diversity in a landscape that attracts a diverse population of beneficial insects and other wildlife. This fosters a healthy balance of prey and predator, thus a healthy environment for everyone.

Trees increase the monetary value of your property. Ask anyone who has put a house on the market recently, or who has suffered fire or hurricane damage to his or her property. While the value of shade trees varies with their location, age, and species, realtors estimate that each healthy specimen on a property can add $1000 or more to its value. It is worth the time to inventory and photograph your trees every few years. Store the information in a safe place so it will be available to insurance adjustors if necessary.

A Tree Care Plan

Trees are not demanding, but they need attention from time to time. Considering their value, it is worth the money to hire a professional consulting arborist to inventory and evaluate your trees. A tree-care service will also do this for you; bear in mind that they will have an understandable expectation that they will be doing any work they recommend.

Knowing the answers to the following questions will help you plan a care program for your trees:

- What is the name of this tree (common and scientific)?

- How old is this tree?

- What is its life expectancy?

- Is it a desirable tree species?

- Is this tree in a good location for light, air circulation, and soil?

- Does this tree need pruning? Why?

- Are the roots girdled or on the soil surface?

- Are there signs of injury, pest infestation, or disease?

The recent summers of drought remind us that trees in a residential landscape cannot go it alone indefinitely. A basic-care step from the minute they are planted and throughout their lives is to make sure trees have sufficient water. They lose an enormous amount through their foliage daily, especially on a hot day.

Another step is to make sure they have adequate nutrition. This is largely a function of the health of the soil they are growing in. If the soil is full of organic matter from decomposing organic mulch, then supplemental fertilizing is necessary only when trees are very young. If trees receive adequate light and have room to grow, then they avoid common causes of stress and will be able to resist most common pest and disease problems.

Finally, do no harm. Do not pile soil on tree roots, do not compact the soil over their roots, and do not injure the tender bark with weed-trimmers and mowers.

Trees for Pennsylvania

Small Trees (up to 30 feet at maturity)

Common Name (Botanical Name)	Zones	Ornamental Qualities	Uses	Comments
Crape Myrtle (*Lagerstroemia indica* and cultivars)	7 to 10	Mid-July to frost: crinkly blooms in pinks, white, reds, lilac. Fall foliage color; patchy colorful bark.	Street or garden tree; hedge, shrub.	Takes hard pruning; dwarf versions available. Indian-named cultivars are more cold hardy.
Eastern Redbud (*Cercis canadensis*)	4 to 9 (Native)	Deep-pink flowers along bare stems in spring, then pods. Heart-shaped leaves turn yellow in fall.	Specimen, accent. Shade tree.	Older plants dislike being moved. Susceptible to canker. **'Forest Pansy'** has purple foliage.
Flowering Crab Apple (*Malus* cultivars)	4 to 8	April blooms in white or pink. Small red or yellow fruits in fall.	Specimen, fence line, shrub border.	Choose cultivars carefully for disease resistance.
Flowering Dogwood (*Cornus florida*)	5 to 8 (Native)	White or pink flowers in early May. Hard red berries and rich reddish leaf color in fall.	Specimen, garden bed, woodland edge. Shade tree.	Full sun stresses this understory tree. Prone to disease problems.
Hawthorn (*Crataegus viridis* 'Winter King')	5 to 7 (Native)	White flowers in May, red fall foliage, good bark; orange-red fruits.	Specimen, hedge, streetside. Shade tree.	This cultivar is disease-resistant, smaller, has fewer thorns.
Japanese Lilac Tree (*Syringa reticulata*)	4 to 7	White "lilac" flowers in early summer. Glossy cherrylike bark when young.	Specimen, shade tree.	Neat, conical habit. Disease-resistant.
Japanese Snowball (*Styrax japonica*)	6 to 8	Tiny, white bell flowers drip along branch undersides under the foliage in mid-spring.	Specimen, accent.	Some have pink flowers. Site on a hill for viewing up into the canopy.
Kousa Dogwood (*Cornus kousa* and hybrids)	5 to 8	White flowers in June, rich fall color, and red dangling fruits. Patchy bark visible in winter.	Specimen, property line, shade woodland.	Blooms later than **Flowering Dogwood**. More disease-resistant.

Trees for Pennsylvania

Small Trees (up to 30 feet at maturity)

Common Name (Botanical Name)	Zones	Ornamental Qualities	Uses	Comments
Magnolia (*Magnolia* sp. and hybrids)	4 to 9 (Some are native)	**Southern** (*M. grandiflora*) has evergreen foliage; large, creamy white flowers. **Saucer** (*M. soulangiana*) has cupped pink-blushed flowers before foliage.	Specimen, accent.	Only in warmest regions of PA. Blossoms are vulnerable to early spring frosts. Some have fragrant flowers.
Maple, Japanese (*Acer palmatum*)	5 to 8	Finely cut foliage in reds, greens.	Specimen, accent, pond side. Shade tree.	A huge variety of foliage colors and types.
Maple, Paperbark (*Acer griseum*)	5 to 7	Green foliage turns orange, red in fall. Peeling russet bark.	Specimen, accent. Anchor flower bed.	Slow-growing. Something for every season.
Sweetbay Magnolia (*Magnolia virginiana*)	6 to 9 (Native)	Creamy flowers in June. Semi-evergreen.	Specimen, flower border.	Takes wet soils. Flowers are fragrant.

Medium Trees (up to 30 to 50 feet at maturity)

Common Name (Botanical Name)	Zones	Ornamental Qualities	Uses	Comments
Catalpa, Northern (*Catalpa bignoides*)	5 to 7 (Native)	White flowers in June. Large, dramatic leaves, showy beanlike pods.	Shade tree; specimen or accent.	Fast-growing, coarse, tough. Irregular canopy. Cut back annually for larger-foliaged shrub.
Cherry, Ornamental (*Prunus* sp. and hybrids)	6 to 8	White or pale- or deep-pink flowers April to June, depending on variety.	Specimen, groves. Line drives. Shade tree.	Decorative. Attracts pollinators, birds. Some weeping types.
Eastern Redcedar (*Juniperus virginiana* sp. and cultivars)	3 to 9 (Native)	Needled evergreen foliage.	Screen, accent, hedge.	Tough, versatile. Available in many sizes.

Trees for Pennsylvania

Medium Trees (up to 30 to 50 feet at maturity)

Common Name (Botanical Name)	Zones	Ornamental Qualities	Uses	Comments
Goldenrain Tree (*Koelreuteria paniculata*)	6 to 9	Yellow flowers in July; interesting dried capsules.	Small yards, patios, street.	Handles urban conditions.
Holly, American (*Ilex opaca* sp. and hybrids)	5 to 9 (Native)	Glossy, spined leaves, pyramidal shape. Red or yellow berries on female.	Specimen.	Tolerates coastal conditions; deer favorite. PHS Gold Medal winner.
Honeylocust (*Gleditsia tricanthos inermis*)	3 to 7 (Native)	Fine foliage leaflets, long seedpods; yellow fall color.	Patio and streetside; shade tree.	Buy thornless and podless types. Attracts butterflies.
Parrotia (*Parrotia persica*)	5 to 8	Small red spring flowers. Spring to fall leaf color.	Specimen and shade tree.	Tough and lovely.
Pear, Ornamental (*Pyrus calleryana*)	5 to 9	White spring flowers; fall foliage color in some.	Specimen and shade tree.	Fast grower. Handsome shape. Newer cultivars do not split.
River Birch (Heritage® *Betula nigra*)	4 to 9 (Native)	Yellow fall foliage; pale peeling bark.	Specimen and shade tree.	Resists borers, tolerates clay soils and summer heat. Likes moist soil.
Sourwood (*Oxydendron arboreum*)	5 to 9 (Native)	July, white flowers; deep red fall color.	Shade, specimen.	Flowers make great honey. Multi-season interest.
Yellowwood (*Cladastris kentukea*)	4 to 8 (Native)	Fragrant June flowers; yellow fall foliage; smooth gray bark.	Shade, specimen.	Blooms heavily every other year.

Trees for Pennsylvania

Large Trees (50 feet or taller at maturity)

Common Name (Botanical Name)	Zones	Ornamental Qualities	Uses	Comments
American Arborvitae (*Thuja occidentalis*)	3 to 7 (Native)	Evergreen conifer. Green or yellow-green foliage in flat sprays.	Screen, hedge, windbreak.	Available in dwarf forms. Adaptable. Deer favorite.
Atlas Cedar, Blue (*Cedrus atlantica* 'Glauca')	6 to 9	Blue-needled evergreen conifer. Sculptural habit; decorative cones.	Accent, espalier, container.	Long-lived, elegant.
Baldcypress (*Taxodium distichum*)	5 to 10 (Native)	Soft green needled foliage is deciduous; turns to russet in fall.	Accent, screen.	Likes wet soil, but does fine in regular. "Knees" are novelty. Stately.
Ginkgo Maidenhair (*Ginkgo biloba*)	3 to 8	Interesting foliage, turns golden in fall.	Street tree, shade tree.	No pests. Female bears smelly fruits.
Japanese Zelkova (*Zelkova serrata*)	5 to 8	Pleasing vase shape, great fall foliage color.	Specimen, street, and shade tree.	Tough, nearly pest-free. Substitute for **Elms.**
Katsura Tree (*Cercidiphyllum japonicum*)	4 to 6	Small reddish flowers in March. Blue-green foliage.	Specimen and shade tree.	Drought-sensitive. Fall foliage smells like chocolate.
Kentucky Coffeetree (*Gymnocladus dioicus*)	5 to 8 (Native)	Large leaves composed of small leaflets. Lima bean–like fruits on female.	Shade tree.	Bold, coarse winter silhouette.
Lacebark Elm (*Ulmus parvifolia*)	5 to 9	Blooms in fall. Glossy, late June. Yellow fall foliage.	Street and shade tree.	Peeling bark creates colorful mottled effect.
Linden, Littleleaf (*Tilia cordata*)	4 to 8 (Native)	Fragrant creamy flowers in late June. Yellow fall foliage.	Specimen, street, and shade tree.	Tolerates urban conditions. Nice shape. Flowers attract bees. A Japanese beetle favorite.

Trees for Pennsylvania

Large Trees (50 feet or taller at maturity)

Common Name (Botanical Name)	Zones	Ornamental Qualities	Uses	Comments
Maple, Sugar (*Acer saccharum*)	3 to 8 (Native)	Rich red, orange, yellow fall foliage color.	Shade tree.	Source of maple syrup.
Maple, Swamp Red (*Acer rubrum*)	4 to 9 (Native)	Blooms in March. Rich red and gold fall foliage color.	Specimen or shade tree.	Fast grower. Likes moist soil. Copius spring seeds feed wildlife.
Oak, Red or White (*Quercus* sp.)	3 to 8 (Native)	Statuesque forms; rich red fall foliage color.	Shade or specimen tree.	Acorns for wildlife; handles urban sites; extremely long-lived.
Pine, Eastern White (*Pinus strobus*)	3 to 7 (Native)	Graceful, aromatic, 5-inch needles.	Screens, borders, hedges.	Food (cones) and shelter for wildlife. Brittle in storms.
Planetree (*Platanus* × *acerifolia*)	5 to 8	Large leaves, colorful, peeling, patchy bark. Fuzzy seed capsules in pairs dangle from twigs.	Shade tree.	**Sycamore** hybrid; less prone to anthracnose; handles urban sites. Moist soils best.
Sweetgum (*Liquidambar styraciflua*)	5 to 9 (Native)	Prickly seed capsules, handlike ornaments, red or yellow fall foliage.	Shade or specimen tree.	Fast-growing, likes moisture; **'Rotundiloba'** has rounded leaves, is fruitless.
Tuliptree (*Liriodendron tulipifera*)	4 to 9 (Native)	Tulip-shaped flowers in May; yellow fall foliage. Straight, stately trunks.	Shade woodland.	Attracts honeybees, hummingbirds, butterfly larvae. Drought indicator.

Planning

Trees stand out in bold relief in the bleak days of winter. The evergreens soften the landscape and offer shelter to birds and other wildlife. The varied bark patterns and branching architecture of leafless deciduous trees have a beauty that is obscured other times of year. Observe the trees on your property closely this month. Look for:

- broken branches that have not yet fallen through the canopy to the ground (a potential hazard to pedestrians below).

- ragged stubs where branches have broken off and need a smooth cut to heal.

- dry, cracking bark that is located low on the trunk and exposes the wood beneath.

- a trunk flat on one side above signs that roots are curling around it under the soil.

- trees or limbs where the leaves are brown but have not fallen as usual.

- holes bored in limbs or trunk, and sawdust visible nearby.

- fans of fungus growing from the trunk or base of the tree.

Have a certified arborist examine trees that have these problems, older trees, or those that suffered serious pest, drought, or disease problems last season. Make a date for followup care, if necessary.

Rather than throw it away just yet, set up your live-cut Christmas tree out in the yard, and redecorate it with goodies for the birds. Adorn this alternate feeder with pieces of citrus fruit, strings of cranberries and raisins, and pine cones stuffed with suet.

Shopping List: bird seed, anti-desiccant (also called anti-transpirant) spray, gasoline for the chain-saw

Planting

Plant your living Christmas tree in the ground as soon as possible.

1 *Remove* the tree from the heated house as soon as possible, and store it in a cool, protected area such as a closed-in porch or unheated garage. (The longer it stays indoors in the warmth, the less chance it will have of surviving life outdoors.)

2 *Allow* the tree several days of transition time to acclimate to cold weather at the sheltered, unheated location. Keep its soilball moist and protected from freezing. Roots above ground are very vulnerable and will freeze quickly without protection.

3 *Dig* the hole if the soil is still unfrozen, or pull off the tarp and mulch from the hole you dug last month in case the soil might freeze. On a relatively mild day, set the tree's rootball in the empty hole. Check to be sure it is level with—or slightly higher—than the surrounding ground. Fill in the hole with plain loose soil, and firm it around the rootball.

4 *Water* the planting area thoroughly. Then *spread* 3 or 4 inches of organic mulch such as chopped leaves, pine needles, straw, or wood chips over the soil out beyond the branches. This will insulate the soil from extreme temperature fluctuations that may harm the tree roots. *Do not fertilize* at this time.

Care for Your Trees

Check the mulch layer under trees planted this fall for signs of rodent nests or chewing damage on their trunks. Do not spread mulch or plant ground cover within a foot or two of their trunks.

Take the opportunity during a "January thaw" period when temperatures moderate somewhat to spray anti-desiccant on the foliage of evergreens that are exposed to harsh winter sun and wind. A product such as Wilt-Pruf™ coats the leaves to reduce moisture loss but does not harm the tree.

Watering

If the ground is not frozen and there has been little rain or snow, check to see if the soil around newly planted trees is still moist. *Insert* the probe of a houseplant water meter into the soil of each tree about 6 inches deep, sticking it into the rootball about a foot or two out from the trunk. Evergreens lose moisture into the air from their foliage all winter.

Pruning

Cut injured or dead limbs from trees with a smooth cut just past the ridge of branch collar tissue where they attach to the trunk (see February for detailed instructions). If a pruning job requires a ladder and/or a chain-saw, consider hiring a professional arborist to do the job quickly and safely.

Cut down old and injured trees, and cut them up for firewood. *Cut up* fallen limbs that are lying around. Let the wood dry out for a year.

Growing Smarter

Increasingly, deer are at the top of homeowners' lists of yard and garden problems. You may notice their damage before you actually see deer on your property. These are the most obvious signs of deer visitors.

- Tender new growth at tips of small, young trees and shrubs are nibbled off.
- The lower stems of shrubs and trees are stripped of foliage.
- The bark of small trees is torn and abraded by bucks rubbing the velvety covering off their antlers in the fall.
- Lower limbs of small shrubs and saplings are broken or trampled by young bucks who are rehearsing fierce combat as rutting season approaches.
- Tall weeds are crushed where the deer have bedded down.

When you see these signs, it is time to think about barriers or other controls.

Wood that has dried enough for the stove or fireplace will have visible cracks at each sawed end.

- *Stack* logs away from the house to prevent bug and rodent problems. Lay them bark side up so that air can circulate around them.

- *Cover* just the top of the pile with a tarp to keep rain and snow off it.

Problem Solving

Heavy snow and ice are potentially damaging to trees. *Knock* snow from evergreen boughs, starting with the lower branches. Use a broom to gently push up the branches to dislodge the snow. Repeat the action, moving upward until the upper branches are snow-free. Then redo the bottom branches where snow has accumulated again during this process. Do not try to remove ice from tree branches or to free trees that are bent over to the ground (such as **Birches**) with ice and snow. Allow it to melt on its own.

Deer and rodents may nibble on bark and tender shoots of young trees. *Wrap* tree trunks in hardware cloth (wire mesh) or other protective material. Make sure it is high enough to protect the trees even if there is a layer of snow for the critters to stand on.

Planning

One of the toughest things to decide is that a large tree should be taken down. Evaluate your trees and resolve to **remove and replace** any that are not doing well. Candidates are those that are old, diseased, too big for their location, disturbing sidewalks, or maimed from repeated severe pruning by utility companies or injury from passing cars or lawn-care equipment. The sooner you put them out of their misery, the sooner a new young, vital replacement can start to grow in that spot. Consult books and visit your local arboretum for ideas. Check mature size to be sure possible choices are appropriate to the space.

Do not plant or replace a street tree in the area between the curb and the sidewalk, called a "tree lawn." In the early days of suburbs, new developments all had tree-lined streets. Sixty or eighty years later, those trees are aging prematurely because of compacted soil, surface roots that bulge in the confined space, and injury from passing trucks. Now, many communities have ordinances forbidding planting trees in tree lawns.

This is the time of year to order a fruit tree from a mail-order catalog if you have always wanted an **Apple** or **Pear** tree in the yard. Some **Apple** trees are small enough for hedges, screens, and container growing.

Check pruning equipment, and *sharpen* loppers and saws for the new season.

Shopping List: tree fertilizer, tree-staking kits

Care for Your Trees

Spray horticultural oil on fruit trees to smother overwintering eggs and larvae of insect pests. Heavy **dormant** (Volck) oil is traditionally used early this month while trees are bare. If you do not have a chance to spray before leaf buds start to swell, use **light** (superior) horticultural oil. This coats the bark and foliage as well, and is safe for use on foliage and flower buds.

Check any trees that were staked when planted last year. Sometimes alternately freezing and thawing soil heaves and shifts soil, disturbing the supporting stakes. Make sure the ties are not rubbing the tender young tree bark.

Watering

Check the soil under the mulch of newly planted trees and evergreens if snow cover or rainfall has been limited. Broadleaf and nee-dled evergreens continue to lose moisture through their foliage during the winter, and those in containers are in particular danger of drying out. *Water* them if necessary.

Fertilizing

If you did not get around to fertilizing trees in the fall, do so this month or next. Not all trees need fertilizer. Wait for a year or two before fertilizing recently planted or transplanted trees. *Fertilize* them and other relatively young ones every couple of years until they are fully established and about ten years old. After that, there is no need to fertilize unless there is a specific problem that fertilizer can help correct. By this time, their roots should be well extended for many feet out into the surrounding soil where they can access sufficient nutrition.

Use a slow-acting, granular product formulated for trees and other woody plants. It may say "nursery stock" on the label. There are also products labeled for acid-loving evergreens—**Hollies, Camellias, Pines, Oaks,** and others—if you have lots of them. *Sprinkle* it on the mulched soil out somewhat beyond the branch dripline. Eventually snow or rain will soak it in. Follow package instructions for the amount.

Pruning

If there is a lot of major tree pruning to be done this year, begin it this month while deciduous trees are still dormant. *Cut away* branches that rub against one another. If a young tree has a double trunk, cut away the less dominant one. This will establish a single strong trunk and avoid splitting later.

Problem Solving

Root problems compromise the health and vigor of trees. One problem is confined roots due to poor planting technique. Failure to remove the burlap wrapping or a sufficient amount of the wire cage from the rootball can cause problems several years in the future. Roots can become so large that they are constricted by the wire, reducing the flow of water and nutrients. Others are inclined to grow in circles within the wrappings (some burlap is synthetic and does not break down) and become girdled, with the same result. (See April Planting for instructions on planting balled-and-burlapped trees.)

Growing Smarter

Proper pruning contributes greatly to a tree's health and welfare. That is never more true than when cutting off a good-sized limb. It takes three separate cuts in different places to do it properly.

Limb Removal

1 First, cut partially into the underside of the branch to be removed about a foot or so out from where it attaches to the limb or trunk. This will assure that when the limb is cut through from the top, it will not strip off bark as it falls.

2 Next, cut entirely through the limb from the top a foot or two beyond the undercut. By removing the bulk of the limb, you will reduce the weight at the place where you will make the final smooth cut near the trunk.

3 Finally, locate the ridge or collar of bark tissue where the limb joins the main trunk or larger limb from which is being removed. Make a smooth cut just on the outside of this branch collar, so that it remains around the cut. The specialized callus tissue there will grow around and over the exposed wound to heal it.

Rodents are a real nuisance. Watch for signs of voles, mice, chipmunks, or rabbits near young trees. Stamp down the snow around the tree to collapse voles' burrows near the tender bark on tree stems. (See September for rodent controls.)

Deer activity will increase, especially if there is constant snow cover. Erect fencing or wire cages if you have not already done so.

Planning

As important as their beauty is, trees are not just beautiful. They are also useful to indoor and outdoor environments. Think about how a new tree might provide shade for a patio area, or screen the noise and eyes of the street to create family privacy. A large deciduous tree located on the south-facing side of a house cools it with its leaf canopy in the summer. Then in the winter, its bare branches allow the sun to shine on the house to warm it. A row or grove of tall evergreens on the north side blocks the cold wind in the winter.

Choose a new tree carefully, for it will last a long time. Look for specific cultivars and varieties of trees that are known to do well in Pennsylvania and are known to be more disease-resistant or problem-free than others.

- For a more disease-resistant **Dogwood,** choose a **Kousa** (*Cornus kousa*) or hybrid, instead of our native **Flowering Dogwood** (*Cornus florida*).

- For an **Ornamental Pear** (*Pyrus calleryana*) that lasts longer than ten or twelve years, choose 'Aristocrat' rather than 'Bradford', whose limbs tend to split when mature.

- Choose fruit trees and **Crabapples** that are noted as disease-resistant.

Shopping List: new tree, tree-staking kit, shovel, organic mulch, all-purpose spray for fruit trees

Planting

It is okay to *plant* trees now where the soil is no longer frozen. They come from the nursery either in containers, or with their roots in a ball of soil wrapped in burlap and sometimes a wire cage. If ordered by mail, they will likely arrive as small whips that are bare-root and nestled in damp sawdust, wood chips, or newspaper. Keep young trees cool and their soil moist until you can get them into the ground. **To plant bare-root trees:**

1. *Dig* a hole with sloping sides, wide enough to accommodate the root system on the young tree. Make it about as deep as the roots measure from their tips to the crown of the tree where they join its main stem.

2. Take some loose soil, and *build* a cone of packed soil in the middle of the bottom of the hole.

3. *Set* the tree in the hole so that its crown rests on top of the mounded soil and the roots fall down along its sides.

4. *Fill* the hole with soil, periodically firming it around the roots with your hand. (Stamping on it may break off fragile root fibers.) Form a ridge of soil just beyond the edge of the planting area on firm soil to make a water-holding reservoir. Then *water* well to eliminate air pockets.

5. *Check* that the tree crown is level with, or slightly above, the surface of the surrounding ground. If it is not, tug it upward, and firm the soil around and under where the roots are so it is at the correct level. *Spread* a 2- or 3-inch layer of organic mulch over the planting area. Do not pile the mulch against the tree stem.

Care for Your Trees

Sometimes, but not always, newly planted trees require staking for their first season. Insert sturdy posts equidistant around the tree, just beyond the planting hole. Loop soft rope from each stake to about $1/3$ of the way up the tree stem and back to each stake. Allow some flex in the ties to allow the tree stem to move a bit so it gains strength. Make sure the ties do not abrade the tender bark. Plan to *remove* the stakes and ties within six to nine months.

Staking

Spray fruit trees with light horticultural oil if you missed the dormant oil spraying last month.

Watering

Water newly planted trees well if rainfall is sparse. Don't forget those that were planted last fall. Established trees that are well mulched can manage for several months without rain, especially in cool weather.

Fertilizing

While this a good time to fertilize established trees, do not fertilize newly planted trees until they have been in place for at least a year. It is not necessary to fertilize trees over eight or ten years old if they

are growing well. Too much fertilizer promotes excessive growth of tender stems and leaves, which attract aphids and other pests. The organic material in mulch improves soil texture and fertility as it decomposes over time, and trees continue to benefit from that.

Pruning

Continue winter pruning jobs. This is a good time to *saw off* lower limbs of the larger shade trees that obstruct pedestrians or the view of traffic. The younger and smaller they are when cut, the faster the wounds will close over. Raising the canopy a bit this way allows more light to reach ground cover plants below.

Problem Solving

Birds are great allies in the campaign against **pest insects** in trees. Woodpeckers, flickers, and others dig borers and bugs from tree bark. Robins feed on tent caterpillars; wrens eat tons of tiny bugs. Even seed-eating birds hunt for bugs to feed their babies in the spring. Invite birds to set up housekeeping in your yard by putting up birdhouses (nesting boxes) for those that prefer houses. Those that prefer open-air living will build nests in the branches of your trees, and will be on the job when the pest insects begin to appear.

Planning

Pennsylvania celebrates Arbor Day this month. Observe this occasion by planting a tree and/or visiting your local arboretum for festivities. Spend some time looking at a book about trees to become acquainted with some of the wonderful ones that are ideal for home landscapes.

When choosing a tree to plant in the yard, consider its size. While it may not begin to fill the space where a mature tree once stood for quite a while, a youngster with a $2^1/_2$-inch-diameter trunk will grow faster and overtake a larger, 4-inch one. The larger tree takes longer to recover from the transplanting ordeal, and it grows more slowly when it does.

Shopping List: more light horticultural oil, mulch, a good pruning saw

Planting

Most nurseries and garden centers will plant trees that you purchase from them and guarantee them for a period of time. Choose from freshly dug trees whose soilballs are wrapped in burlap, twine, and maybe a wire cage, or select from those growing in containers (see planting steps in May). Certain trees, such as **Oaks** and **Birches,** prefer spring planting.

Recommended tree-planting techniques encourage the roots to grow laterally into the soil surrounding the planting hole as soon as possible. If the surrounding soil is not the greatest, this will come as a bit of a shock to the tree. The sooner it accepts and adapts, the better off it will be. **To plant balled-and-burlapped trees:**

1 *Dig* a saucer-shaped hole about twice as wide as the rootball and as deep as it is high. Keep the rootball moist prior to planting.

2 *Set* the tree in the empty hole, oriented as you wish. Take care not to damage the tender bark on the trunk while moving it. *Cut away* as much of the burlap wrapping as you can reach. If there is a wire cage, *remove* as many rows of wire as you can. Brush off the soil at the top of the rootball until the root flare at the base of the trunk is exposed.

3 *Adjust* the rootball so that its surface is level or slightly above ground level. Fill the hole with plain soil, and firm it snugly around the rootball. Fashion a rim of soil beyond its edge to create a water-holding reservoir.

4 *Spread* a 2- or 3-inch layer of organic material such as chopped leaves, pine needles, wood chips, or commercial bark product over and slightly beyond the planting area.

5 *Water* the planting area well so that the soil is moist down at least 10 inches. If your soil is mostly clay, *water* for a while, then stop. Resume in about a half-hour for a while longer. *Do not fertilize* for at least a year.

Care for Your Trees

Wrap the trunk of the new tree with tree wrap or hardware cloth to protect its tender bark from deer and rodents. The bark will toughen up as it ages, and the wrapping will not be necessary every year.

Stake a newly planted or transplanted tree only if it is vulnerable to windstorms or other harsh weather (see March).

Remove any staking from trees planted last spring. Check others to see if the ties are too tight for the growing tree.

Take care not to damage tree trunks with lawnmowers and weed-trimmers. A ring of mulch or ground cover plants over the tree roots will protect them.

Watering

April showers will probably take care of watering your trees this month. Keep an eye on newly planted ones, and *check* their soil if there is no rain for two weeks.

Fertilizing

Finish any fertilizing you intended to do last month but did not get to. Spring is the peak growth time for plants of all kinds, so they need the nutrition boost now.

Pruning

Prune out vertical suckers and water sprouts from along the branches of fruit trees, **Magnolias, Crab-apples,** and others that tend to produce them. In cases where you remove a diseased branch, disinfect your tools after each cut and before using them on another tree (dip them in a 10:1 solution of household bleach and hot water).

Growing Smarter

Lightning is attracted to tall, isolated targets such as telephone poles, tall buildings, and, of course, trees. Big old, valued specimen trees are frequent victims, especially those whose branches overhang buildings. The wiring and plumbing in buildings are good conductors of electricity. Trees protrude into the air and are better conductors than air, so they are sitting ducks. Since wood resists conducting the charge, tree tissues can suffer severely as their sap boils and becomes steam, bursting apart the bark and stems. As it dissipates, the electric charge will rupture cell tissues, scorching them. Lightning protection cables are intended to conduct lightning to the ground where a metal rod is buried. Professional arborists will install and check these systems.

Most needled evergreen trees have symmetrical natural habits, so pruning for shape is not needed. Occasionally the brittle branches of **Pines** break in a storm and must be removed. *Cut away* jagged stubs where breakage occurred as soon as possible. A smooth cut near the branch collar heals best.

Problem Solving

Aphids may cluster at the tips of tree branches where tender new leaves emerge. Spraying them with a forceful stream of water from the hose every couple of days will probably solve the problem. *Spray* those on small trees where it is easy to reach the infested areas with insecticidal soap as directed on the label.

To avoid harming pollinating bees, *delay* spraying aphids on fruit trees until after blooming has ended.

Tent caterpillar nests are visible in tree branches by the end of the month. Either *cut off* the branches they are attached to and put them in a plastic bag in the trash, or poke the tents open with a long stick so the eggs or young worms are exposed for birds to eat.

Weeds begin to grow now. Use mulch to discourage them around trees. Wait until the soil is moist, and *pull* gently to get the entire root when they are young. If you suspect poison ivy, put a plastic bag over your hand and arm, pull the plant, then pull the plastic bag down so the plant ends up inside, never touching your skin.

Planning

In addition to their orna-mental value, trees have signifi-cant economic value. At selling time, a mature, healthy tree may add as much as $1000 to the purchase price of a residential property, and trees certainly add to the property's curb appeal. Keep records of when you buy and plant new trees, and record the names and approximate ages of the ones that are already on your property as you learn their identities. Photograph them over the years, and note any special care that they have required, such as major pruning, cabling, or spraying. This documentation is also useful for insurance purposes if trees are damaged by storms.

A young tree makes a nice gift for a special family event. Give a tree (and a gift certificate to have it planted) to commemorate the arrival of a new baby, a marriage, a death, an anniversary, or holiday. Make planting it the centerpiece of a family reunion.

Shopping List: ground cover plants, tree wrap to protect trunks

Planting

Many trees are raised and sold in containers. Container trees are eas-ier to handle and can be planted almost any time of the year except during severe heat and drought or when the ground is frozen. Planting them is slightly different from plant-ing bare-root (see March) or balled-and-burlapped (see April) trees. **To plant a containerized tree:**

1 *Dig* a hole with sloping sides, making it twice as wide and just as deep as the tree's container.

2 *Remove* the tree from its con-tainer, and gently knock or brush off excess potting medium from around the roots and on top of the rootball.

3 *Set* the rootball in the hole, positioned as you prefer, and level with or slightly above the surrounding soil. Make sure the root flare at the base of the trunk is visible at the top of the rootball now and after the tree is planted.

4 *Mix* the excess potting medium from the container with some of the dirt dug from the hole, then put it in the hole to fill in around the rootball. This soil mixture provides a transition for the roots from the "ideal" potting mix to the real soil in your yard as they grow outward.

5 *Firm* the soil over the rootball, using the excess to make a ridge beyond the filled hole to create a water-holding reservoir. *Spread* a 2-inch layer of mulch over the planting area up to—but not on top of—the root flare, and *water* well. Repeat watering weekly until it rains generously.

Many trees grow well outdoors in decorative planters year 'round, especially on narrow city streets and in malls. Plant a tree that seems too small for the yard in a container for a few years before putting it in the ground. If you are not sure where to plant a new tree, or if you plan to move to a new property in a year or so, plant it in a decorative container for the interim.

Bonsai specimens are trees that have been miniaturized by means of spe-cial branch and root pruning. Except for those species that are not cold hardy in Pennsylvania, **Bonsai** plants grow outdoors year 'round, too.

By month's end it should be safe to move outdoors the tender trees that lived as houseplants all winter, so they can enjoy the summer. Give them a few hours outdoors in the shade over a week or two, gradually increasing their exposure until they can stay out all night. **Ficus** and **Citrus** like sun, but do not put them in direct sun immediately or their foliage will scorch.

Care for Your Trees

Renew the mulch layer to 2 or 3 inches under trees where it has begun to decompose and has become too thin to deter weeds and hold moisture. Spread it up to, but not over, the root flare at the base of the trunk.

Successful pollination of fruit trees may burden their branches with excessive numbers of fruits. Over the next six weeks *thin* crowded apples, peaches, and pears so that fruits are 4 to 6 inches apart for larger, healthier fruits.

Watering

In the absence of rain, water *young* mulched trees when their soil is dry down several inches. Water slowly and deeply with a dripping hose, soaker hose irrigation, or sprinkler.

Pruning

When spring-flowering trees bloom this month, notice any flowering branches that do not resemble the majority of those on the tree. On grafted trees, the rootstock sometimes sends up branches that flower among those of the desirable tree variety grafted on top of it. Look for branches growing from below the graft union (the swollen knob on the trunk) and that have flowers of different color or type (single rather than double, for example). *Cut off* the rootstock interlopers at the trunk.

Cut some flowering tree branches for display inside the house. Make the cuts so that the profile of the tree is not affected.

While it is still okay to do major pruning this late in the spring, some trees "bleed" sap so profusely that it is better to do it earlier or later. **Maples, Yellowwood, Styrax, Birch,** and **Elm** have this tendency. Bleeding does not harm them—after all, certain **Maples** are purposely tapped to make **Maple** syrup—but it is messy and easy to avoid.

Fertilizing

Do not fertilize newly planted trees.

Problem Solving

Wooly adelgid is a serious pest of the **Canadian Hemlock,** our state tree. It attacks those in the wild as well as those planted in yards and gardens. The insects appear as soft, white dots at the base of the narrow-needled foliage on the undersides of branches. Infested branches start to look brownish and thin, and eventually, the entire tree will die. The best control for this problem is not to purchase a **Hemlock.** If you already have one in your yard that is worth saving, resign yourself to twice-yearly spraying of light horticultural oil. Since the spray must thoroughly cover all the foliage and stems, it is best to have professionals do this, especially if the tree is large.

Bacterial Leaf Scorch is endangering **Red Oaks** and **Pin Oaks** in Pennsylvania and nearby states. Insects carry the bacterium which has been around since the 1800s. Once injected into twigs, it clogs the veins that carry nutrients from the tree's roots to its leaves. First the leaves turn brown and wither, then the infected limbs die. Eventually the entire tree succumbs and must be taken down.

JUNE

Planning

Part of the fun of moving to a new home is getting acquainted with the plants in the yard. When you agree to purchase a property, ask the current owners to provide a list of the names of the trees, as best they can. Enjoy observing and learning about them. Keep track of the history of the largest or most valuable trees during the time you live in the house. Record information about:

- name and approximate age

- when a tree leafs out

- ornamental features (flowers, bark, fruit, or nuts)

- major pruning events

- major pest problems and outcome of treatments

- wildlife that depend on the tree

- service the tree has rendered (held a swing, treehouse)

Most of the deciduous trees will have leafed out by mid-month. **London Plane** trees and **Crape Myrtles** are notoriously late; do not be alarmed if they are still leafless. Other trees that are slow to leaf out are **Mimosa, Kentucky Coffeetree, Black Locust,** and **Honeylocust.**

Shopping List: wettable sulfur for fungal disease protection, insecticidal soap

Planting

It is okay to *plant* containerized trees this month as long as it is not too hot and dry (see May).

Have some fun rooting a tree yourself. Insert a freshly cut stem from a willow tree into moist soil, first removing its leaves. It will root in a few weeks.

Care for Your Trees

- *Remove* support stakes from trees planted a year ago. Their roots have had time to grow and can support them now.

- *Protect* trees from lawnmower and trimmer injury.

- *Forbid* parking of any vehicles or heavy construction equipment within several feet of the outer edge of the branch canopy of any tree. They will compact the soil and stress tree roots.

- Avoid fastening anything to a tree— birdhouse, child's swing, fencing, clothesline, or treehouse that would cause a major wound. When in doubt, consult a tree expert.

Watering

This may be the year to address the water needs of your trees. They need about 2 inches of water a week in the heat of summer.

- *Install* soaker hose drip irrigation under small, medium, or young trees.

- *Mulch* the soil under the trees to retard evaporation of moisture from the soil and prevent runoff of excess water from hard rains.

- *Aerate* the soil over the root zone of trees so that it can absorb and hold water well.

- *Water* slowly and deeply by dripping hose, drip irrigation, or low sprinkler.

Newly planted trees will need lots of moisture to compensate for the normal loss through their foliage to help them cope with the stress of transplanting. If rainfall is scarce, *check* soil moisture for mulched trees every ten days or so. Do not overdo and drown roots. Puddling water will compact the soil and deprive tree roots of oxygen.

Fertilizing

Limit routine maintenance fertilizing to spring or fall. Never fertilize trees and other plants when they are stressed by heat, drought, or pest and disease problems. Granular slow-acting products release nutrients consistently and gradually over the season as the trees need them, so the fertilizing you did in spring will sustain the younger ones just fine. Older trees are able to manage on their own under normal conditions.

Pruning

Some tree branches are still bare. Do not assume they are dead and prune them off. To determine whether a bare branch or young tree is still alive, bend some twigs or branches to see if they are flexible. Scrape the bark with a fingernail to see if there is moist, green tissue beneath. Brittle, browned twigs are dead—*prune* them back to where wood shows signs of life.

Problem Solving

Trees that drop bark, fruit, and leaves this early in the season may or may not be in trouble. Some trees are just messy and constantly drop twigs, fuzzy balls, seeds, flower bracts, last year's leaves, or excess fruit set. Many routinely slough off strips or patches of bark.

Growing Smarter

Not all trees are equally desirable in a home landscape. Certain ones are real problems because they are breakage-prone, messy, smelly, or weedy.

The **Norway Maple** is an example of a weedy tree. It is listed on the Pennsylvania Department of Conservation and Resources list as an invasive pest that is degrading the environment. **Norways** seed prolifically. Landscape bullies, they quickly develop wide-ranging root systems that insinuate themselves into areas where moisture is available, and monopolize them. Because they are able to handle poor soil, crowding, and drought, they compete successfully against other woody plants, even natives that are well adapted to local conditions. Their seedlings turn up in the middle of otherwise civilized hedges, ground cover patches, and shrub borders. Do not be charmed by their gorgeous late-fall yellow foliage (they are the last of the **Maples** to display color). They thrive at the expense of other trees and shrubs.

How can you be sure a seedling is a **Norway Maple?** Pluck a leaf, and break off its stem. If you squeeze the tissue at the base of the leaf where the stem was attached and a milky sap appears, it is a **Norway.** Pull up seedlings when they are young and will pull fairly easily. Wait too long, and you will have to use a herbicide.

Evergreens are constantly shedding older leaves and needles to make way for fresh ones to maintain their green foliage year 'round.

Anthracnose and wilt diseases cause dropping leaves. **Sycamores** and their **Planetree** cousins may be infected with anthracnose, a fungal disease. Older trees live with this and just produce a second flush of foliage. Trees infected with wilt diseases may lose leaves from a branch or side of the tree permanently. When trees shed leaves from the tips of branches only, that is a sign they are stressed by something. Make every effort to keep your trees happy. *Plant* them in the right place, *water* them in drought, *mulch* their soil, and *protect* them from injury by lawn-care equipment and competition from turfgrass over their roots.

Planning

Nice shade trees make the yard a pleasant family retreat in the summer. Even family pets are grateful for their cool shade. As you watch the birds and butterflies and hear the bees busy at their honey-gathering (**Black Locust, Sourwood, Tupelo,** and **Linden** flowers make great honey), think about how adding more and different kinds of trees might create an even more inviting habitat for everyone.

Environments that are healthy for all—humans, plants, pets, and visiting creatures—always have lots of different kinds of plants. A diversity of trees, shrubs, flowers, vegetables, and herbs feeds and shelters a diversity of insects and animals. This assures that populations of pests and predators stay pretty much in balance. A healthy yard is easier to take care of. Take an informal inventory:

- Does your yard have some conifers such as **Pines** and **Spruces** that will provide shelter to birds in storms, and cones to feed them and the squirrels?

- Does it have some small flowering trees to attract pollinators and add fragrance to the scene over the season?

- Does it have some fruit- or nut-bearing trees such as **Crabapple, Kousa Dogwood,** and **Buckeye** that support birds and squirrels?

Shopping List: netting for fruit trees, drip irrigation hoses and fasteners

Planting

Delay planting trees, if possible, until fall. Container-grown trees can manage, but it is very stressful for them to endure transplant shock during the hot months, even though their roots suffer minimal disturbance. With its foliage canopy that emits moisture in the heat, a tree newly planted this month must also begin generating root cells in unfamiliar soil. This takes an enormous amount of energy, which would otherwise be devoted to maintaining its vigor and growth. **To minimize summer transplant shock:**

- *Plant* when several days of overcast, relatively cool weather are predicted, OR erect a shade cloth awning to shield the transplanted tree from the sun for a while.

- *Water* generously, but do not drown the rootball. *Mulch* the soil to keep it cool.

If trees are threatened by damage from construction or other unavoidable hazardous situations, *transplant* them rather than leave them in place. *Dig* them up, and temporarily plant them in containers in the shade, or bury their roots in a pile of compost or organic mulch until the conditions change. Removing some of their foliage will reduce moisture loss and stress during this time.

Care for Your Trees

Certain backyard fruit trees may be about to produce fruit. Check frequently, and *pick* the fruit as it ripens. Do not allow overripe fruit to fall on the ground and rot. It will attract bees and pest animals, and possibly spread fungal disease to the trees.

Watering

If rainfall is scarce, *check* soil moisture under mulch around young and newly planted trees weekly. Mulch will effectively cool the soil and deter runoff of valuable moisture when it does rain.

Eliminate the grass over tree root zones. Turfgrass roots grow in the same top 6 to 12 inches of the soil that tree roots do. Guess which grabs most of the moisture? Chances are the grass is struggling anyway because the tree shades it too much.

- *Let* the area go to moss, if moss is starting in the area;

- OR *plant* a nice ground cover such as **Pachysandra, Liriope,** or **Vinca** over tree roots (this will protect the tree and the soil while providing more plant diversity in the landscape);

- OR at least *replace* the turfgrass with a ring of organic mulch, about 2 or 3 inches thick, which will protect the roots and trunk from damage from yard-care equipment. It will also improve the soil as it decomposes over the summer.

Trees in containers dry out quickly, so *check* them daily. They, too, should have a layer of mulch over the soil.

Fertilizing

If you did not mix a complete granular, slow-acting fertilizer into the potting mix in the containers for potted trees, be sure to *water-in* dilute, fast-acting fertilizer containing minor nutrients periodically. Potting mixes are usually soilless, so they have no nutrients in them.

Pruning

Clip off water sprouts and suckers along branch surfaces of **Crab-apples, Magnolias,** and others. Except for removing broken or diseased branches, delay other pruning until trees are dormant to avoid stimulating yet more growth.

Watch for "widow-makers." These are dead branches in the canopies of older trees. Often summer storms break them off. They may get caught in the tree for a while and then drop on unsuspecting passersby below. *Prune off* these dangerous limbs as soon as you notice them.

If new growth on nearby trees shades a flower or vegetable garden, prune off lower limbs or thin some branches from the canopy to permit more light to reach the garden. This is best done in the spring or fall rather than the summer, but sometimes the problem is not obvious until the middle of the growing season. Follow the steps for cutting off a tree limb carefully (see February).

Problem Solving

Japanese beetles arrive in many parts of Pennsylvania in early July. Although they prefer roses and other flowering plants, they may be attracted to the foliage of young, new trees. They particularly like **Linden** trees. Look for them, and knock any you can reach into a jar of soapy water. Do not put out pheromone bag traps. They will attract beetles into your yard from elsewhere, and there is no guarantee that the beetles will all end up in the bag. For long-term control of Japanese beetles, control their white grub larvae in your lawn (see Pest Control Chart in Appendix).

Noxious weeds really take off this month. Wild grape, poison ivy, bittersweet, and wild honeysuckle will climb up trees right before your eyes. They eventually spread over leafy canopies, blocking foliage access to the sun. Cut main stems to deprive them of support from their roots, and they will die up in the tree. *Dig* or pull up stems only if you are sure you can get all of the roots. Otherwise, paint the stems and lower foliage with a herbicide such as Roundup®, which will also kill the roots.

Birds and squirrels can be pests when cherries and pears ripen. Throw netting over fruit trees to foil the pests.

Planning

As back-to-school time draws closer, thoughts eventually turn to cooler weather and fall yardwork. Those trees that did not survive transplanting, injury, or the cumulative effects of insults such as drought, poor pruning, or compacted soil will need to be replaced, and there are probably other places on the property where new trees might be attractive, too.

Studies show that patterns of family outdoor life change every seven years or so as children grow up, dogs are acquired or die, and adults develop new interests. Sandboxes, swing sets, and wading pools give way to patios, outdoor grills, and expanded gardens or a putting green. Perhaps it is about time to rethink your backyard's suitability as an outdoor room. Think about how the addition of some trees would contribute to the diversity and functionality of your yard. How would they affect both the outdoor and indoor climate by shading the sun and blocking the wind?

If you are tempted to cut down a large, attractive tree to make room for new construction or reduce shade or for some other practical reason, think twice. Good, mature trees are in demand for large properties, and you may be able to sell it. Call local arborists and nurseries, and tell them about it. Professionals have equipment called a tree spade which enables them to dig up a large tree and its rootball, load it on a truck, and deliver it to a new home.

Plan to plant and transplant trees starting in September.

Shopping List: commercial bark mulch

Planting

Delay purchase of balled-and-burlapped trees for several more weeks. As the weather cools, growers dig and wrap new ones to sell at the nursery this fall. They are likely to withstand transplanting better than those that have stood around above ground all summer with their rootballs wrapped in burlap, at risk for drying out.

Meanwhile, research the tree species you are interested in to determine their requirements for light, soil, and moisture. Learn about their growth habits, and their mature sizes and shapes. This way you can make sure there is an appropriate site on your property for a tree's mature height and spread.

Care for Your Trees

Trees cultivated in a landscape typically experience more stress during their lives than those growing in the wild. Therefore, they usually have a shorter life. This is especially true of street trees and trees in urban environments. In the wild, they grow in communities; their soil is not compacted, and is constantly renewed by decomposing organic debris on the forest floor; and they do not have to compete with grass for water and nutrients. To lengthen the life of your trees, try as much as possible to reproduce similar conditions for trees on your property.

Harvest apples, pears, and peaches from backyard fruit trees as soon as they ripen. Keep them off the ground to avoid rotting, which promotes disease and attracts yellowjackets.

Watering

If it is a droughty summer, there may be water-use restrictions. If there are, implement a triage system for watering plants in your yard:

AUGUST

1 Water trees first since they are the most expensive, most permanent, most difficult to plant and to replace, and contribute more to the value of your property.

2 Water newly planted trees, then older trees.

3 Water recently planted shrubs and any unmulched shrubs.

4 Water perennial flowers, then annuals which are less expensive and easier to replace.

5 Finally, water lawns.

Of course if you have food crops, they will go to the head of the list, especially since it is likely to be harvest time.

Fertilizing

Hold off fertilizing any trees until late September or October when the deciduous ones have lost their leaves. While evergreens do not go as dormant, they too will slow down. The nutrition will support the vigorous root growth that trees experience in the fall and spring.

Pruning

Leave most pruning until fall or winter—the exceptions are certain fruit trees. Seasonal pruning of fruit trees requires special knowledge, so it is important to read a good book on their care.

Pruning landscape trees in summer helps maintain their shape, especially of dwarf trees. *Prune out* water sprouts from along branches and any suckers that grow from below the knobby place where a tree may have been grafted to special rootstock.

Problem Solving

Fall webworm tents are often quite visible at the branch tips of trees near the edges of highways. If they appear on your own trees, either *clip off* the branches to which they are attached, or poke open the tents with a stick. The birds will eat the young caterpillars once they are exposed to view.

Bagworm infestations on needled evergreens such as **Spruce, Juniper,** and **Arborvitae** show up as dangling, twiggy bags that hang like Christmas tree ornaments. The bags shelter the bagworms, which venture out of the bags to feed on tree foliage, then withdraw into them for protection. *Pull off or cut off* the

Growing Smarter

Some trees that tolerate wet soil:

- **Alder (***Alnus* **sp.)**
- **Baldcypress (***Taxodium distichum***)**
- **Swamp Red Maple (***Acer rubrum***)**
- **Sweetbay Magnolia (***Magnolia virginiana***)**
- **Sweetgum (***Liquidambar styraciflua***)**
- **Willow (***Salix* **sp.)**

bags you can reach. *Spray* the foliage where they are feeding with a product containing *Bt* (*Bacillus thuringiensis*). When the caterpillars ingest the bacteria they will sicken, stop eating, and die in a few days.

Weeds are a problem in the disturbed soil around recently planted trees. If grown from seeds surfaced in the tree-planting process, they will become tougher and more belligerent. Watch out for poison ivy climbing up tree trunks. All parts of it are toxic—leaves, berries, stems. Use a herbicide such as Roundup® on it.

Planning

Prepare for this year's leaf fall. Leaves are a wonderful source of free organic mulch for use under trees and shrubs. If you do not already have a **compost pile,** use the leaves to start one.

Designate an out-of-the-way spot on the property as a collection area for organic debris from planted beds, pruning, and leaf fall (leave the grass clippings on the lawn). Even if you do nothing more than pile it all in a heap and let it sit and decompose, you will get wonderful compost next season. Eventually you may want to neaten the pile by enclosing it with fencing or wooden pallets. There are a few ways to speed up decomposition of organic yard waste:

- *Shred or chop* materials into small pieces.

- *Turn* the pile frequently—as soon as it heats up inside to 130 to 150 degrees F.

- *Add* special composting worms called "red wigglers."

In the colder areas of the state, homeowners might get a frost at the end of this month. It is time to clean up, repair, and refill the bird feeders.

Shopping List: new rake, compost fork, compost thermometer, chipper/shredder or shredder-vac, fertilizer, hardware cloth, birdseed

Planting

In the colder parts of Pennsylvania, tree-planting time begins just after Labor Day. Elsewhere, wait until deciduous trees lose their leaves and go dormant.

Check the willow branches you stuck in the ground a couple of months ago. If they have developed roots, plan to transplant next spring.

If you plan to plant a new tree this fall, consider hiring the local nursery staff or a landscape contractor to plant it for you. It is worth the money to have it done quickly and properly. It is certainly easier on your back! Professionally planted trees are often covered by warranty for a year or two. Read the tree-planting instructions (April) to be sure it is done correctly.

Care for Your Trees

It's time to spray light horticultural oil on **Hemlocks** again. Twice-a-year sprays will control the wooly adelgid insect that plagues them.

Plant some spring-flowering bulbs under deciduous trees, either in the soil under the mulch or among green ground cover plantings. Because minor bulbs such as **Crocus, Squill, Glory of the Snow,** and **Snowdrops** are planted shallowly, they do not disturb tree roots, and they look lovely against the dark tree trunks in early spring. They get enough sun when they need it before the trees leaf out. When the leafy canopy has fully emerged and blocks their sun, they are ready for dormancy.

Check the ties on staked spring-planted trees to make sure they are still lax but firmly fastened around the expanding tree trunk. *Remove* supports from trees planted last fall if you have not already done so.

Watering

Continue to monitor soil moisture under the mulch of spring planted trees. *Water* them if the soil is dry.

Fertilizing

Fertilize young trees that have been in the ground for a season. Granular, slow-acting fertilizer needs a few weeks to soak into the soil and be available to their roots by the time they lose their leaves. *Sprinkle* a granular slow-acting product formulated for foliage or flowering trees and shrubs on the soil out at least as far as the dripline. Use just the amount suggested on the package label, and let rain or snow soak it in.

Trees that are over eight or ten years old and are growing perfectly well do not need fertilizing every year. Their root systems have spread sufficiently wide to access the nutrients they need. Decomposing organic mulch improves the soil over their roots and provides some nutrition throughout the year.

Pruning

Delay most pruning until late fall or winter when deciduous trees are leafless. Delay pruning **Oaks** until spring. An exception is when some strange-looking foliage alerts you to the presence of a reversion or a witches' broom.

1 *Reversions* are situations when a branch of a plant develops foliage of a different color or texture than the rest of the plant. Something triggers it to produce branches that resemble one of its parents. Although a reversion does not harm the tree, if left alone it may eventually take over the entire plant. *Prune it out* to maintain the uniform appearance of the tree.

2 A *witches' broom* develops when a branch produces a tangle of immature-looking suckers covered with stunted, congested foliage. This is a mutation caused by trauma, disease, insect attack, or unknown factor that derails normal branch development in this one place. Arborists and horticulturists often try to start new varieties from this altered tissue, but homeowners usually prune them from the tree because they are unsightly.

Problem Solving

Fall webworm nests may still be around. Open them up, or prune them out of trees promptly.

Rodents such as mice and voles are also getting ready for colder weather. *Delay* renewing thin mulch around trees until after the ground freezes to force rodents to make their cozy nests elsewhere. *Remove* ground cover plantings within a foot or so of the trunk. Protect trunks of young trees by encasing them in hardware cloth or commercial tree-wrap products.

Growing Smarter

Pennsylvania residents are treated to a gorgeous show every fall as the stands of forest that cover so much of our state are ablaze with color. Many of the trees that carpet our mountains will also grow in our home landscapes, so it is possible to enjoy a show in our own backyards. Some trees that offer richly colored fall foliage are:

- **Aspen**
- **Birch**
- **Dogwood, Flowering**
- **Linden**
- **Maples—Sugar, Red**
- **Nyssa (Tupelo)**
- **Oaks**
- **Sourwood**
- **Sweetgum**

A couple of needled evergreens are deciduous, and their foliage turns color before it drops:

- **Baldcypress**
- **Larch**

Planning

Frost arrives in Pennsylvania yards this month, signaling the beginning of dormancy, winter resting time for trees. But first the trees will put on a show. As the foliage of various deciduous trees turns color over the next few weeks, visit your local arboretum or take a drive in the countryside, and enjoy the glorious color. Make a note of which trees might look good in your yard.

Season's end is a good time to update your tree records. Note major pruning, problems, and observations for each tree. Jot down flowering or fruiting dates as well. This information and a brief summary of the weather over the season may be helpful in the future.

If you do not have room in your own yard for trees, you can still plant one. Arboretums, botanic gardens, and many communities have memorial tree programs through which you can donate a tree in the name of a loved one. You pay for the tree and (usually) a sign or plaque with the name of the tree, the person, and other information. The staff plants and cares for it.

Shopping List: animal repellent, deer fencing

Planting

This is a good time to *plant* many tree species, as this is their best root-growing time. The ground is still soft, and there is no heat to stress them. Since the deciduous trees are dormant and have no leaves, they can devote their energy to producing a good root system to get a head start on next season. Many kinds of trees are freshly dug this time of year and are available in nurseries. Others are a bargain because they have not sold all season and are marked down in price. Examine them carefully before buying.

The planting techniques previously outlined (see April) are designed to encourage trees to send their roots out into the soil beyond the hole as soon as possible.

- *Cut off* most of the burlap and string wrappings, because they may be synthetic and refuse to biodegrade.

- *Cut off* as much of the wire basket as possible, because most tree roots grow laterally rather than downward.

- *Give* the hole sloping sides to encourage outward root growth. Otherwise, the roots might prefer to stay in the hole, which feels like a container.

- To be sure the rootball does not sink below level, *do not* put loose soil at the bottom of the hole under the rootball. The roots must grow outward at the right depth.

- To force the tree to accept the new soil environment, *use* only plain soil when filling the hole (unless the soil is thick, thick clay).

- *Remove* any excess soil at the top of the rootball to expose the root flare (collar) so you can judge exactly how deeply to plant the tree.

Care for Your Trees

Wrap or otherwise *protect* the tender bark of young trees from possible damage by rodents and deer. If you have chronic rodent problems, hold off on winter mulching until the ground is frozen. By then the critters will have nested elsewhere.

Mulch newly planted trees of all kinds through the winter. *Spread* a 3- to 4-inch layer of organic material such as chopped leaves, pine needles, wood chips, or commercial bark product on the soil over the root zone. Mulch is not intended to prevent the ground from freezing. It insulates it once it is frozen, so that fluctuating winter temperatures do not alternately thaw and then refreeze the ground and disturb tree roots. As it slowly breaks down, organic mulch also improves the fertility, texture, and aeration of the soil. Trees that have evergreen ground cover plants growing over their root zones already enjoy a "living mulch."

To avoid drainage problems on the property, clean fallen leaves from roof gutters.

roots are within a foot of the soil surface. Injecting fertilizer is for special situations that a certified arborist will determine.

Healthy mature trees do not need routine fertilization. They are not growing so fast, and their root systems are so widely spread that they can access nutrients they need. (They benefit indirectly from a winter-type fertilizer spread over areas of the lawn that cover some of their roots.)

saturated soil. *Thin* the canopy of densely branched trees to reduce "sail" resistance. Professional arborists will evaluate special trees for you. They may recommend cabling to support heavy, extended limbs, or install ground wires to protect against lightning.

Weeds like fall weather. Take advantage of any mild weather to deal with stubborn perennial weeds and invasive vines around trees. *Spray* them with a herbicide such as Roundup®, as directed on the label.

Brown needles fall from evergreens such as **White Pine** this time of year, as replacement new green growth appears. This is normal. Pine needles make great mulch!

Watering

Evergreens of all kinds need good, moist soil going into winter. If rainfall is scarce, *water* the trees before the ground freezes and they can't access moisture in the soil anymore. They will continue to transpire and lose moisture through their foliage all winter.

Pruning

Remove any limb that is rubbing against another, and raise the branching scaffold if lower branches obstruct foot traffic or the view. Take care of injured or diseased branches on all trees as soon as possible.

Fertilizing

Fertilize any young trees that you did not fertilize last month. Skip those newly planted last spring and this fall. There is no need to inject fertilizer deep into the soil around trees, because most of their

Problem Solving

Hurricanes, heavy thunderstorms, and the occasional tornado that visit some regions of Pennsylvania pose enormous threats to trees. Even large, well-established specimens can lose limbs or literally fall over, their rootballs torn from over-

Planning

In many parts of Pennsylvania, the Norway Maples *still show golden foliage.* Since they are about the last trees to lose their leaves, they are easy to identify. Take action, and root out their pesky, weedy seedlings before they take over your entire yard!

Roosting boxes shelter small birds when winter really closes in. Designed to be mounted on poles or trees, they are open at the bottom, their inside walls lined with pegs for perches. Many birds will seek refuge in them in severe winter weather; their collective body heat keeps a box warm and snug.

Plan to purchase a live-cut or living Christmas tree that has been shipped in from a distance as soon as it is available for sale. The sooner you get it off the sales lot and home, the better. Since it may have been cut weeks ago, it is already drying out.

- Immediately *cut off* an inch or two from the base of the trunk of a **live-cut tree,** and set the tree in a pail of water outdoors in a sheltered spot. *Check* it often, and refill the pail when the water gets low. It is surprising how much water a tree will quickly take up.

- Set the soilball of a **living tree** in a large container such as a galvanized metal tub or sturdy kiddie pool, and pour water over it to moisten the soil. Lay damp burlap or some other covering over the top and sides of the rootball in its container to keep the rootball moist. Do not let it sit in water; just keep the soil moist.

Shopping List: bird food, new feeder, Christmas tree stand that has a large water reservoir, hardware cloth or commercial tree trunk protectors

Planning

You can still *plant* a tree if the soil is not frozen. If you acquire one, it is better to plant it than to try to store it over the winter.

Overwinter small trees in pots, one of three ways:

1 in a cold frame or unheated garage or porch if the ground is frozen

2 buried in the ground, pot and all, and mulched

3 semi-buried in a sheltered place in the yard with wood chips, bark mulch, or other organic material piled over the pot

Water if it is a dry winter.

Care for Your Trees

Spray anti-desiccant on the tops and undersides of the foliage of evergreens that are exposed to harsh winter sun and wind. A product such as Wilt-Pruf™ coats the needles on conifers and broader leaves on **Hollies** and **Rhododendrons** to reduce the amount of moisture they lose from transpiration. This coating does not harm the tree. It will eventually wear off, so a second spray will be necessary during the January thaw. Follow the directions on the product label.

Watering

Water needled and broadleaf evergreens if there is no rain after two or three weeks.

Fertilizing

If you did not fertilize young trees over a year or two old in October, do so now. Use a slow-acting, granular product formulated for trees and other woody plants. There are also products labeled for acid-loving evergreens—**Hollies, Camellias, Pines, Oaks,** and others—if you have lots of them. (They will also do fine with the same fer-

...tilizer you use on other trees and shrubs.) Follow package instructions to determine the amounts.

Pruning

The only pruning to do now until year's end is to remove broken or diseased branches. Anytime the protective bark covering of a tree is cracked or broken open, there is a potential for disease spores or insects to penetrate its interior. By promptly removing injured or diseased branches with a smooth cut through healthy tissue just beyond the branch collar, you will remove a source of further infection and help the tree begin to heal itself.

Problem Solving

Troubleshooting pre-winter checklist:

___Any bagworms on needled evergreens?

___Any **Norway Maple** seedlings in hedges and garden beds?

___Any "widow-maker" branches visible now that leaves have fallen from trees?

Growing Smarter

A LIVING CHRISTMAS TREE:

The time to decide on which kind of Christmas tree you will have is this month, when trees go on sale. The idea of a living tree is very appealing. Rather than presiding over the inevitable gradual desiccation, decline, and death of this lovely plant during the holidays, why not have one that can be planted outdoors in the yard to grow and prosper for years to come?

The reality of a living Christmas tree is something quite different. The fact that you must keep the tree healthy during the holidays dominates the entire experience. That boils down to preventing it from drying out.

- Because it is alive and transpiring, a living tree needs constant moisture—more so the minute it is brought indoors.
- A living tree has a heavy rootball. The more soil it has, the better for the tree, but the harder it is to move and maneuver in the house.
- Provide a large container for the rootball.
- To minimize stress on the tree, keep it in a heated room no more than three or four days.
- Acclimate it gradually by carrying it inside in steps over several days: first to an unheated porch, then to a cool indoor room, finally to the main display area.
- Keep the soil in the rootball and the wrappings moist at all times.
- Light the lights as little as possible.
- Reverse the acclimating process so it can be back outdoors where it is most happy in just a few days.

___All trunks of young trees protected against rodents and deer?

___Any weedy vines climbing trees?

___Any ragged stubs where branches have broken off?

___Any trees that do not have a protective winter mulch or ground cover planting?

___Gutters free of late-falling **Norway Maple, Oak,** and **Beech** leaves?

Planning

If you decide to have a living Christmas tree this year, make arrangements ahead of time for planting it. Choose a sunny site that is roomy enough for the tree at maturity. Plan carefully to assure it will survive the indoor experience in good health.

Have your camera ready to record fresh snowfalls on evergreen boughs out in the yard. Take pictures of the lovely branching patterns of deciduous trees now that the leaves have fallen. Photographs are a great way to enjoy the season in your yard and consider how you might improve it.

Shopping List: tub to hold rootball of living Christmas tree, anti-desiccant spray, animal-repellent spray

Planting

Dig a hole for transplanting a living Christmas tree before the holidays if the soil is likely to be frozen at planting time. Make a saucer-shaped hole, twice as wide as the rootball on the tree and exactly as deep as the rootball is high. *Cover* the hole and the fill soil nearby with straw or insulating mulch to keep the soil from freezing. Throw a tarp over the hole and soil to keep them relatively dry.

If the ground is not frozen, any balled-and-burlapped trees can be planted this month.

Care for Your Trees

To ensure that a living Christmas tree does not dry out, set it up for display in the heated house for a maximum of only three or four days. (See November, Growing Smarter.)

Watering

Mulch or snow cover should keep the soil over tree root zones moist even if rain is scarce. Deciduous trees do not use much moisture when they are dormant. *Check* evergreens. Soaker hoses covered with mulch are not affected by winter weather.

Pruning

Although this is not official pruning time, it is a great time to *lightly trim* **Hollies, Pines,** and other evergreens to acquire boughs and cones for holiday decorations. Put the cut ends in tepid water immedi-

ately so that they take up moisture. Keep them in water until it is time to use them.

Spray wreaths and other live greens with anti-desiccant to prevent their drying out during the festivities. Do not use live greens around fireplaces, lighted candles, and other potential fire hazards.

Problem Solving

Critters are attracted to the thin tender bark and stems of young trees when their normal food sources are under snow or out of season. Tall wire cages may be necessary to protect young trees if deer are a major concern. Stamping down the snow around tree stems reduces access by burrowing voles or by deer and rabbits standing on a foot or two of snow. Try sprays that repel by taste or odor too. Respray as recommended on the product label. Alternate products to maintain effectiveness.

Strong winter winds threaten young and newly planted trees in exposed sites. Either *stake* them or erect wind barriers of burlap or other material to block the worst of its force. Do not use plastic.

Vines, Ground Covers, & Grasses

Beyond their individual beauty, beyond even their collective beauty in a garden design, plants contribute many things to residential landscapes. This is why even non-gardening homeowners value and enjoy plants in their yards. Plants play a practical as well as an aesthetic role, as they improve a yard's comfort, health, and value. They can also make a yard easier to care for—and no plants do this better than those that function as ground covers, especially those that climb or crawl. Vines, grasses, and other plants that grow well planted in large masses are enormously useful for solving common landscape problems that make yard care difficult or even unsafe.

Solving Yard Problems

Too much lawn to care for? A patch of evergreen ground cover is ideal for reducing lawn size, yet retaining the green look. Plant **Liriope, Pachysandra, Vinca,** or something similar in generous islands out in the existing lawn to reduce the overall turf area. Create groves of ferns or ornamental grasses in turf areas, or fill in remote or undeveloped areas of a large property with naturalized plantings of wildflowers. Add a wide border of colorful **Verbena, Petunias, Portulaca,** or herbs around an existing patio or poolside to eliminate some turfgrass areas.

Tough terrain? Steep slopes or uneven grades on properties make mowing lawns difficult and dangerous, and the unevenness promotes soil erosion wherever turf breaks down. Replace the turfgrass with a self-reliant perennial ground cover plant with a deep root system that holds the soil. Use smaller, finer-textured plants such as **Liriope, Lilies-of-the-valley,** or **Creeping Phlox** in small areas. Use larger plants such as **Daylilies** or ornamental grasses in broader areas. Often low-growing shrubs such as carpet-type **Junipers, Azaleas, Dwarf Deutzia,** or **Clumping Bamboo** are effective on hillsides. Choose sun-lovers for a sunny bank, shade-tolerant plants for slopes that face north or for those under trees.

Tree surface roots? **Beeches** and certain other trees typically have surface roots. Others develop them because the soil is so compacted their roots must gravitate to its surface to obtain oxygen. Piling soil on them endangers the tree. Instead, plant **Ivy,** minor bulbs, or **Tiarella** among the roots to obscure them, yet allow them the air they need. Shallow-rooted plants minimize disturbance to the tree roots.

Too much shade? Trying to grow turfgrass in shade is an exercise in futility. Plant instead a ground cover plant that tolerates shade. Use annuals such as **Impatiens, Begonias,** or **Coleus** for a colorful and different summer look in that spot every year, then mulch the area with chopped leaves in the winter. Or go with a more permanent perennial plant such as evergreen **Hellebores.** Try **Moss** if the soil is both compacted and acidic.

Tree and shrubs dry out quickly? Only recently has it been understood how shallow the root systems of most trees and shrubs really are—typically only 8 to 12 inches deep. Those in poor soil are at constant risk of drying out whenever rainfall is scarce. A living mulch of ground cover plants is even better than a traditional mulch of wood chips or chopped leaves at helping the soil absorb and retain moisture. Use evergreen, perennial plants such as **Liriope, Lamium, Vinca,** or **Pachysandra,** which do not need much moisture for themselves.

Vines, Ground Covers, & Grasses

Difficult soil? The typical residential property has soil that is less than ideal. Some areas may be too sandy, others too clayey. Some may have that special mix called builder's fill, which features construction debris. Low parts of the yard may be chronically damp and boggy. Again, ground cover plants can come to the rescue. Carpet these areas with plants that appreciate the unique soil conditions, making a virtue of necessity. Use ornamental grasses, **Potentilla,** and **Yucca** in sandy soil. Use **Red Twig Dogwood, Astilbe, Iris, Virginia Sweetspire,** or **Forget-me-nots** in the low-lying wet areas.

Unsightly ripening bulb foliage in spring? The gradually ripening foliage of **Tulips, Daffodils, Hyacinths,** and others always presents a problem. Many plants used as ground covers are effective at obscuring the unsightly foliage until it is time to clean it up. Evergreen **Ivy** or **Pachysandra** foliage will complement the bulbs during their bloom period and then cover their dying foliage. Herbaceous plants such as **Hosta, Ferns,** or **Sweet Woodruff** emerge just in time to cover the bulb foliage as it dies back.

Stem or trunk damage on woody plants? Landscapes are easier to maintain with power tools, but more and more trees and shrubs are sustaining injury from string-trimmers and mowers. A simple nick in tender bark allows insects and disease to invade and cause plant stress, which reduces the plant's life expectancy. Replace the turf around the stems of trees and shrubs with a ground cover planting to create a barrier so that passing equipment cannot get close enough to harm them.

Compacted soil? Unless soil is aerated periodically, it gradually becomes compacted from the weight of pounding rain, foot traffic, or construction equipment. Areas between stepping stones, paths where the kids or the mail carrier take shortcuts, and edges of walks and driveways where traffic strays from the pavement are chronically compacted. Carpet these areas with low-growing plants or ornamental grasses that cope with compacted soil better than turfgrasses do.

Unsightly areas? Every property has its eyesores—both temporary and permanent. Once again, ground cover plants and grasses can save the day. Let vining plants crawl over crumbling walls or fences, decaying stumps, and rock piles. Send them up drainpipes and over utility boxes. Use foliage plants to obscure drains, septic zones, and air-conditioner compressors.

Limited growing space? Many newer homes are located on smaller properties, and many older ones have lost their sunny expanses as trees have matured. The best way to take maximum advantage of limited growing space is to grow plants vertically. Use flowering vines to provide color for the landscape, as well as vertical interest.

Yard lacks interest? The absence of traditional garden beds does not mean a yard must have boring green grass and a few ho-hum shrubs. Planting ground covers, vines, and grasses are another way to add color, texture, and variety to a property. They are, in most cases, relatively care-free. Many are essentially the same plants found in a mixed flower border, or even a vegetable garden. Climbing up or covering the ground to solve landscape problems, they still attract birds, butterflies, and beneficial insects and enhance the entire property.

Vines for Pennsylvania

Common Name (Botanical Name)	Type	Habit / Size	Ornamental Qualities	Comments
Boston Ivy (*Parthenocissus tricuspidata*)	Woody perennial	Clinger / 50 feet plus	Three-lobed shiny leaves turn scarlet in fall. Mid-June flowers become blue-black berries.	Attracts birds.
Climbing Hydrangea (*Hydrangea petiolaris*)	Woody perennial	Clinger / over 60 feet	Deciduous, textured dark-green leaves. Flat clusters of scented white florets in late May.	Hosts beneficial insects. Attractive rough bark. Slow to eastablish.
English Ivy (*Hedera helix*)	Woody perennial	Clinger / to 90 feet	Glossy dark-green foliage with three lobes. Mature foliage is rounder, has green-globe flowers in fall.	Lots of interesting variegated types. Also a ground cover.
Hardy Kiwi (*Actinidia kolomikta*)	Woody perennial	Twiner / to 30 feet	Deciduous foliage blotched with pink and white. May flowers yield edible fruits in fall.	Not the best **Kiwi** for eating. Primarily an ornamental.
Hyacinth Bean (*Dolichos lablab*)	Herbaceous annual	Twiner / to 10 feet	Dark-green leaves on purple stems, pink pealike flowers and decorative purple pods July through fall.	Loves heat. Interesting black seeds with white line. A great plant.
Hybrid Clematis (*Clematis* hybrids)	Woody perennial	Grabber / to 15 feet	May / June bloom, then intermittently in purple, pinks, white. Dedicuous foliage. Fluffy, whorled seedheads.	Hybrids have large, flowers. Prune hard in spring, then again after major bloom period.
Moonflower (*Ipomoea alba*)	Herbaceous annual	Twiner / to 15 feet	Rich-green leaves showcase luminous, scented, white funnel flowers.	Good for evening garden; attracts lovely moths. Slow to germinate but worth the wait.
Morning Glory (*Ipomoea purpurea*)	Herbaceous annual	Twiner / to 20 feet	Light-green foliage; pink, blue, white funnel flowers until frost.	Do not confuse this with the invasive **Wild Morning Glory.**
Scarlet Honeysuckle (*Lonicera sempervirens*)	Woody perennial	Twiner / to 15 feet	Semi-evergreen, bluish green leaves. Bright red tubular flowers May to frost.	Native. Attracts hummingbirds.
Sweet Pea (*Lathyrus ordoratus*)	Herbaceous annual	Clinger / to 6 feet	Charming pea flowers in shades of pink. Fragrant.	Plant early; cool weather–lover.
Wisteria (*Wisteria* sp.)	Woody perennial	Twiner / to 40 feet	Deciduous foliage, divided in leaflets. May flowers of lilac, pink, or white. Pods and yellow leaves in fall.	Can be pruned as a shrub. Slow to flower—maybe 10 years.

Perennial Ground Covers for Pennsylvania

Common Name (Botanical Name)	Type / Zones	Height	Ornamental Qualities	Comments
Allegheny Spurge Pachysandra (*Pachysandra terminalis*)	Perennial runners to zone 5	6 to 10 inches	Terminal whorls of medium-green, smooth foliage are evergreen. White, scented flowers in April.	Versatile, neat, and tough. Takes shade or sun, mediocre soil.
Ajuga Bugleweed (*Ajuga reptans*)	Perennial zone 3	3 to 6 inches	Dark-green or purplish semi-evergreen foliage. Spikes of purple florets in May.	Some have white flowers; some have variegated or bronze foliage.
Barrenwort (*Epimedium* sp.)	Perennial to zone 5	8 to 12 inches	Small heart-shaped, green foliage. Dainty spurred yellow, pink, white, red florets early to mid-spring.	Foliage sometimes red-tinged. Dried stems for winter interest. Takes dry shade.
Bearberry Cotoneaster (*Cotoneaster dammeri*)	Woody shrub zone 5	To 12 inches	Evergreen foliage; tiny white flowers, red berries.	Trailing stems may root when they touch the ground.
Bellflower (*Campanula poscharkyana*)	Perennial to zone 4	4 to 6 inches	Semi-evergreen, heart-shaped foliage; lilac-blue starry flowers late May or early June.	Dainty but vigorous. Great for stone walls or garden edge.
Bergenia (*Bergenia cordifolia*)	Perennial zones 3 to 8	8 to 12 inches	Heart-shaped, glossy reddish-tinted leaves. Rose-pink flowers on stems in late winter, early spring.	Woodland, or moist sites; sun or part shade. Tolerates poor soil.
Creeping Juniper (*Juniperus horizontalis*)	Woody evergreen shrub to zone 3	1 to 2 feet	Dense horizontal stems of blue-green scale-like foliage; purplish winter tinge. Female's cones become berries in winter.	Tolerates urban sites—heat, drought, salt. Attracts songbirds. Native.
Creeping Phlox (*Phlox stolonifera*)	Perennial to zone 4	2 inches	Smooth, tidy, dark-green evergreen foliage hugs ground. Blue, pink, or white flowers on 10-inch spikes in May.	Likes partial shade, sun-to-shade transition. No mildew problems. Native.
Deadnettle (*Lamium maculatum*)	Perennial to zone 4	8 to 12 inches	Semi-evergreen variegated foliage. Pink or white florets on upright leafy stems in May and June.	Variegated white with green or golden foliage brightens partial-shade areas.
Foamflower (*Tiarella cordifolia*)	Perennial runner to zone 5	6 to 12 inches	Semi-evergreen, maple leaf–type foliage. Fuzzy bottlebrush flowers in May.	Spreads by runners but easy to control. Native.
Ginger (*Asarum europaeum*)	Perennial to zone 5	6 to 8 inches	Neat, glossy, kidney-shaped evergreen leaves are rich green.	Handsome clumps spread slowly.
Green and Gold (*Chrysoganum virginianum*)	Perennial to zone 5	4 to 10 inches	Small, single yellow flowers bloom spring into summer amid dense green foliage.	Likes partial shade, good drainage, decent soil. Clumps.
Japanese Painted Fern (*Anthyrium nipponicum* 'Pictum')	Perennial to zone 3	12 to 18 inches	Handsome fronds are multi-colored reddish, silver, and silvery-green.	Slow-growing clumps brighten shade. Likes dappled light.
Lamb's Ears (*Stachys byzantina*)	Perennial to zone 5	6 inches	Woolly, silvery green or white foliage; 15-inch spikes with pink florets in June.	Melts out in winter, then regenerates. Takes heat; few deer problems.

Perennial Ground Covers for Pennsylvania

Common Name (Botanical Name)	Type / Zones	Height	Ornamental Qualities	Comments
Lily-of-the-Valley (*Convallaria majalis*)	Herbaceous bulb to zone 4	6 to 8 inches	Deep-green narrow foliage; stems of fragrant tiny white nodding "bells" in May.	All plant parts are poisonous. Foliage dies back late summer.
Lilyturf (*Liriope* sp.)	Perennial clump or runner to zone 6	8 to 12 inches	Semi-evergreen, narrow, green grasslike foliage. Spikes of lavender florets in August, late winter.	Some have leaves of yellow or silver variegation. Cut back in spring for new growth.
Moneywort (*Lysimachia nummularia* 'Aurea')	Perennial runner to zone 4	1 to 2 inches	Tiny, rounded, greenish yellow-gold foliage is evergreen. Small yellow flowers July to August.	More sun makes yellower foliage. Will grow in water. Takes some foot traffic.
Sweet Woodruff (*Galium ordoratum*)	Perennial to zone 5	6 to 8 inches	Foliage whorls deeply cut, fine-textured, pale green. Flat clusters of tiny white florets in May.	Shallow, fibrous roots spread rapidly. Likes woodsy soil. Deer-resistant.
Vinca Periwinkle (*Vinca minor*)	Perennial to zone 5	6 to 8 inches	Lustrous, dark-green, oval foliage along wiry stems. Lilac, purple, or white flowers April into May.	Low arching stems root as plant spreads. Some have variegated foliage.
Wintercreeper (*Euonymus fortunei*)	Trailing shrub to zone 5	8 to 12 inches	Evergreen foliage is all green or variegated with silver or yellow.	Tough and versatile. Also used as a vine. Long-lived.

Grasses for Pennsylvania

Common Name (Botanical Name)	Type	Size	Ornamental Qualities	Comments
Blue Fescue (*Festuca glauca*)	Clumper	6 to 12 inches tall (12 inches wide)	Wiry, blue-gray foliage; thick clumps resemble mopheads.	Good for ground cover duty, edging, between stones in walk.
Feather Reed Grass (*Calamagrostis acutiflora*)	Clumper	4 to 5 feet tall and wide	Upright habit. Deep-green, lustrous foliage. Flowers appear early summer, then turn beige and attractive through fall.	'Karl Foerster' is PPA winner for 2001. Usually massed for vertical accent.
Little Blue Stem (*Schizachyrium scoparium*)	Clumper	24 to 36 inches tall	Very narrow, strong blue foliage. Turns copper-orange in fall. Late summer blooms.	'The Blues' has startlingly blue foliage.
Maiden Grass (*Miscanthus sinensis*)	Clumper	3 to 12 feet tall (spreads as permitted)	Widely arching leaves. Great foliage pattern variability. Blooms August to October.	'Strictus' has yellow-banded, upright leaves. Less likely to flop.
Northern Sea Oats (*Chasmanthium latifolium*)	Clumper	3 to 5 feet tall	Graceful, nodding flowers produce oatlike seeds. Yellow-brown fall color.	Self-sows its seeds prolifically. Lovely into winter.
Ravenna Grass Hardy Pampas Grass (*Saccharum ravennae*)	Clumper	To 12 feet tall	Upright, gray-green leaves. September plumes bloom at 14-feet plus.	Drought-tolerant. One of the tallest hardy grasses.
Switch Grass (*Panicum virgatum*)	Clumper	To 8 feet tall (3 feet wide)	Variously green to bright-blue foliage, golden to burgundy in fall. Airy flowers start late July.	'Heavy Metal' has upright narrow form, gray foliage.

Planning

After the activities of the December holidays, it is time to relax and get some reading done. The pile of catalogs that has been accumulating for weeks beckons, so why not indulge? Among the featured goodies are lots of perennial and annual plants of all kinds that can be used as ground covers or vines. Think about how interesting it might be to use plants that you routinely use in a mixed flower border, massed instead as a ground cover. The plants will look striking while they protect the soil.

Study your winter landscape from windows in various rooms in your house.

- Is there some vertical interest in the form of tall grasses or woody vine stems wrapped around arbors or posts?

- Is there some foliage color and texture on the ground, relieving the ho-hum expanse of lawn?

- Is there the sound and movement of the wind stirring brittle grass stems?

Take some photographs of the yard to help you see it more objectively. Save the pictures in your garden notebook or journal, and compare them to those you will take in future years to document the development of your garden.

Vines are popular these days, exceedingly adaptable, and lovely for smaller properties where horizontal growing space is limited. They can offer architectural interest, foliage color, flowers, berries, pods, food and shelter for birds, screening for privacy, and lots more. Why not make a New Year's resolution to grow at least one new vine this year?

Care for Your Plants

One of the great things about ornamental grasses and other perennial plants that are suitable for use as ground covers is that they are self-reliant. If they are hardy for where you live in Pennsylvania (check the zone number on the plant label or in a book on garden and landscape plants), they can fend for themselves in the cold and frost.

It is a good idea to *mulch* the soil in beds where ground cover plants (or bulbs) were planted last season and have not yet knitted together. A 3- or 4-inch (maximum) layer of organic material such as chopped leaves, pine needles, or wood chips will buffer extreme temperature fluctuations, which sometimes cause the soil to heave plants to the surface. Do not pile mulch against vine and shrub stems—it can encourage rot.

Make sure vines are securely attached to their supports. If you planted **Pansies** in the fall to make a head-start ground cover, mulch or snow cover will protect the **Pansies,** too.

Spray anti-desiccant spray on evergreen ground covers such as **Carpet Junipers, Skimmia,** and **English Ivy** that are exposed to harsh, bright winter sun and wind. This will help them retain moisture and prevent their foliage from drying and turning brown. In areas where there is dependable snow cover, this is not necessary.

Watering

If the late fall and early winter have been dry, recently planted evergreen vining plants, as well as evergreen perennials and shrubs that serve as ground covers, will need watering. This is especially true if they are not mulched. They are still transpiring through their leaves, which causes them to lose moisture and dry out. Take advantage of a winter thaw, and run the hose on the soil for a while.

Pruning

Pruning time does not officially begin until next month, but be sure to *clip off* broken branches any time you discover them. Clean cuts prevent further tears on the bark and will heal faster. *Cut back* any branches of vines that are whipping around in winter wind because they are too long or will not stay attached to their support. They are a danger to themselves and others.

Ornamental grasses still look attractive in the winter landscape. *Delay* cutting them back for a few more weeks.

Problem Solving

Rodents are always a potential problem during the winter. They nest in ground cover plantings or in the mulch at the base of woody vines. Their chewing on the tender bark of woody vines and ground covers can girdle stems and kill the plants. To forestall the problem, delay mulching until the ground freezes hard, forcing them to nest elsewhere. Install wire wraps around

Growing Smarter

Because they are naturally vertically oriented, vining plants need little encouragement to climb on anything handy. The trick to growing them successfully is to match each vine to a support that displays it attractively yet is sturdy enough to hold it securely until season's end, when many vines are heavily burdened with multitudes of branching stems weighted with blooms and/or seeds. As a rule, annual vines such as **Morning Glory** develop less weight than perennials such as **Wisteria.** Make sure the support is sited where light conditions are correct for the particular vines you plant. Here are some suggestions for supports:

- arbor
- downspout
- fence
- light post
- wall
- mailbox post
- pergola
- shrub
- teepee
- utility pole
- tree stump
- trellis
- tuteur

vulnerable stems, or *spray* them with repellent.

Deer are the other big problem. If they are in the area, they are on the lookout for tender leaves, berries, and shoots to sustain them during the cold, harsh weather. *Spray* vulnerable patches of ground cover with repellent spray. Alternating products that repel by smell or by taste every two weeks is more effective than using the same one repeatedly. Follow the directions on the product labels. Lay chicken wire over beds of ground cover, or use it to fashion temporary fencing around vines and low shrubs.

If they are starving, deer will go to any lengths to eat. If they are just passing by, the fencing may discourage them. In many areas deer avoid plants with fuzzy or silver leaves and aromatic twigs. Try **Lamb's Ears, Dusty Miller, Lavender,** and **Artemisias** as ground covers next year.

Planning

The depths of winter is a good time to read up on gardening topics that you are too busy to research during the season. Make notes in your journal for later reference. You may need to learn more about deer; maybe a fence is in your future. If a review of your garden notebook indicates deer problems in several previous seasons, it is time to address the situation before you lose too many more plants.

Barriers are the only truly effective way to control deer. Some work by simply screening the view so deer are not aware of the menu in your yard. Others are so tall that deer cannot jump them. In the face of heavy pressure by starving deer, the most effective fences are polynetting around the perimeter of your entire property, or electrified fences. A combination is the best.

If there is not much snow, late winter is a good time to put up deer fencing. The leaves are off the trees and plants have died back, so access is easier, and it is easier to see where to erect the poles or fasten netting to existing trees. Remember to gate the driveway, too.

Visit a local arboretum or botanic garden, and get acquainted with winter-blooming vines and ground cover plants such as **Winterhazel** (*Corylopsis pauciflora*), **Winter Jasmine** (*Jasminum nudiflorum*), **Windflower Anemone** (*Anemone blanda*), and **Christmas** and **Lenten Rose** (*Helleborus* sp.).

Planting

The only planting that might go on this month will occur indoors toward month's end. Get a jump on the season by starting annual vines from seed under lights, rather than waiting to direct-sow them outdoors in April or May. A head start is not necessary for many annuals, because they germinate quickly once the soil is warm outdoors. Others, such as **Moonflower,** seem to take forever to germinate outdoors, so it helps to get them going early. To raise sturdy, healthy seedlings you will need some special equipment:

- seeds

- peat pots or other containers

- soilless potting medium

- adjustable fluorescent lights

- heat mat (optional)

- some counter space or a seed-starting table (see Annuals, January)

Steps:

1 *Fill* each peat pot with moistened soilless potting mix.

2 *Drop* one or two seeds in each pot, and cover with more mix. (There is no obligation to use all the seeds in the packet. In fact, extras will keep, and they will come in handy if your seedlings do not flourish.)

3 *Water* each pot, then set all of them on a tray for easy transport.

4 *Cover* the peat pots with plastic wrap or a plastic bag to prevent the mix from drying out.

5 *Give* the pots warmth from a heat mat, radiator top, or incandescent light until they sprout.

6 *Remove* the plastic, and set the tray of peat pots under fluorescent lights that can be adjusted so they are consistently about 2 inches above the seedlings as they grow.

7 *Snip off* the second, less vigorous seedling so there is just one per pot.

8 *Water* when the potting mix seems dry.

Also by month's end, **Pansies** will start to appear at garden centers. Pick some up if you didn't plant them last fall. *Plant* them as soon as you can work the soil. They can go into pots sooner.

Another cool-weather ground cover plant, **Forget-me-not,** probably seeded in last year. Because it is a biennial, its clumps of narrow green foliage have survived the winter and are visible as the snow melts. Do not mistake them for weeds. Before they begin to send up flower stems, *transplant* randomly scattered **Forget-me-not** clumps to bulb beds or other sites where they can serve as a spring ground cover.

Care for Your Plants

Look closely to see if bulbs are beginning to emerge in patches of **Ivy, Vinca,** or **Pachysandra** as the month progresses. They add welcome color to the yard, and later the ground cover plants will hide their ripening, collapsing foliage. *Remove* any large fallen leaves from last fall that may threaten to smother their progress.

Check **Pansies** planted last fall to be sure they are not smothered by mulch. They will be raring to go.

Fertilizing

Late winter is a good time to fertilize *woody* vines and ground cover plantings, if you did not do so last fall. Use a granular, slow-acting product labeled "nursery" or "for trees and shrubs." *Sprinkle* it on the soil over each plant's roots as directed on the label for the rain or snow to soak in. Well-established vines and shrubby ground covers such as **Junipers** do not need regular annual fertilizing. By all means, *do not* encourage **Wisteria!** It overgrows automatically and does not need more nutrition.

Pruning

If you did not cut back your ornamental grasses last fall or during the winter, do so in the next few weeks. If left alone, the tall stems will flop over and provide a self-mulch as new shoots push their way up from the clump to form this season's plant. Cutting them back will make for a neater plant in a garden setting. If you wait too long, you risk inadvertently cutting the tops of the new shoots as well.

Problem Solving

Deer will continue to visit. If your defenses are not in place, refer to January. If they do damage, take notes. *Record* which plants seem to be their favorites and which ones they ignore. Note their location in the yard. *Spray* repellent on remaining targets.

Rabbits do their share of damage to a winter landscape, too. They might nibble the tender bark of a young shrub or vine all the way around the stem. They strip fleshier-stemmed plants apart, sometimes nibbling off the tender tips. Wrap exposed stems in chicken wire, or *spray* them with repellent, as directed on the product label.

Planning

Now is the time to choose plants to cover those areas in the yard where grass won't grow or where you do not want to mow. Traditional choices are the low-growing, tough, permanent evergreen standbys such as **English Ivy, Liriope,** or **Pachysandra,** which are great for under trees where there is shade and frequent replanting of annuals may disturb roots. There are also lots of other kinds of plants that, planted *en masse,* can make great ground covers:

- *Annuals* are your best bet for sunny sites where flowering plants thrive. They bloom with gusto all season, providing color and sometimes fragrance. They attract butterflies and other wildlife, as well. **Purple Wave Petunias** and trailing **Nasturtiums** are examples of trailing annuals, particularly effective for covering the ground.

- *Moss* is great for shade areas with chronically acidic, compacted soil. Rather than fight **Moss** where it has appears on your property, encourage it to spread.

- Many *herbs* are great at spreading and blocking weeds. They smell good where you step on them. **Creeping Thyme, Oregano,** and **Globe Basil** are good choices.

- Sometimes *food plants* are good ground cover choices. Ornamental and edible plants such as **Alpine Strawberries, Low-bush Blueberries,** and **Lettuce** need sun.

- *Shrubs* do a great job covering the ground with foliage, berries, and flowers. They hold the soil and prevent erosion on slopes. Consider **Carpet Junipers, Cotoneaster, Dwarf Deutzia,** and a host of others.

Planting

Plant **Pansies** as soon as possible. They love chilly weather. If the soil is not hopelessly soggy and frosty, plant them about 6 inches apart in the sunny area you want to have them cover. Set them closer for rapid coverage.

Sweet Peas prefer chilly weather, just as their edible cousins do. *Plant* these vines at the same time you plant **Peas** in the food garden—near the end of the month.

Shrubs that come by mail are likely to be bare-root. Keep them moist until the soil is workable, then *plant* them over the area they are intended to cover. Follow the steps for planting shrubs (see Shrubs, March).

Care for Your Plants

Mulch newly planted ground cover plantings to discourage weeds until the plants have a chance to knit together and cover the soil. *Spread* a 2- or 3-inch layer of chopped leaves, pine needles, or wood chips over the soil between the plants.

Dig up and divide overgrown clumps of ornamental grasses as their new shoots begin to appear. First *cut back* last year's stems if you haven't done so already. Then, EITHER:

1 *Dig* down in the soil around the grass clump until you dislodge it from the soil.

2 *Lift* the entire rootball out of the ground.

3 *Cut* it into manageable rooted chunks by slicing down through it with a sharp spade.

4 *Replant* one, then give away the extra chunks.

OR:

1 Use a sharp spade to *slice* down into the rootball while it is still planted.

2 *Cut* chunks or wedges free (as when cutting a piece of pie).

3 *Remove* them by digging under and around them, leaving the main rootball in place.

4 *Fill* in the hole with soil.

5 *Replant* or give away the extra chunks.

Perennial vines wake up from dormancy soon. *Check* trellises and other supports to be sure they are ready to meet the challenge of vigorous vines. Be forewarned: the first year perennial vines *sleep*, the second year they *creep*, and the third year they *leap!*

Watering

It is more than likely that the soil on your property will be too wet rather than too dry this month. If it is dry, *water* newly planted **Pansies** and **Sweet Peas**, as well as any biennials and plants planted last fall. Mulched plants will survive a bit of dry weather just fine.

Fertilizing

Well-established beds of evergreen ground covers do not require annual fertilizing. Compared to turfgrasses, they are light

feeders, and the leaves that fall down among the foliage of the planting provide some nutrition when they decompose.

Pruning

Mow beds of **Liriope** to cut off the evergreen foliage that is shabby and winterworn. Set the mower at its highest setting to avoid inadvertently cutting new **Liriope** shoots or the emerging foliage of bulbs that may also be planted in the bed. Mulching-type mowers cut the **Liriope** foliage into small pieces that fall back down on the bed to serve as a mulch and a source of nitrogen for new growth. Mowing also renews **Vinca, Ivy,** and **Pachysandra** every few years.

Problem Solving

Rot diseases are common in certain low-growing ground covers that grow in soil that does not drain well. **Ajuga** is an example. Every so often, patches of it will "melt" away. Usually enough remains to spread and fill in again with time. Organic matter or fine gravel added to clay soil at planting time helps soil drain better and forestalls rot.

Growing Smarter

To get rapid ground coverage:

1 Plant annuals. Perennials take at least one season to get established before they start to spread.

2 Plant large plants—either shrubs or more-mature plants in larger pots from the garden center.

3 Plant lots of plants—small plants close together cover the ground well.

4 Plant aggressive spreaders. This is a calculated risk, because most do not know when to put on the brakes.

Slugs become active before we expect them. The trick to controlling them is to put out traps early to catch the first arrivals on the scene. They overwinter in moist, acidic organic debris in shady areas in the yard. Set out a shallow pie plate or a commercial slug "bar" trap filled with beer (they are attracted by the yeast) in the area where vulnerable ground cover plants such as **Hostas** will be emerging. *Check* it daily for slug bodies to pinpoint when they start feeding. Set out more traps (a slight distance from vulnerable plants) to lure more slugs once you know they are active.

Planning

Lawn-mowing season begins this month. Think about reducing the size of your lawn and the amount of time, energy, and money it costs. *Replace* some of the turf-grasses with other ground cover plants. Patches of different plants provide texture and color variety to the landscape. By adding to the plant diversity in your yard, you will create shelter and support for more beneficial insects for a healthier, lower-maintenance environment.

One area where a permanent ground cover planting rather than turfgrass makes sense is on a steep slope. It is dangerous and difficult to mow such sites. Another area is under trees and shrubs. When planted in a ring over their root zones, ground covers fend off injurious mowers and weed trimmers. Ground cover plants do not compete with the trees for soil moisture and nutrients the way turfgrass does.

As the songbird nesting season approaches, think about hanging a wren house from your arbor or pergola before the vines leaf out and access becomes more difficult.

Planting

Before the month is too far along, *plant* ornamental grasses in beds, borders, or areas where they are to serve as ground covers. They are easiest to manage when their new shoots are just starting to emerge:

1 *Remove* weeds, then aerate the soil by digging and turning over shovelsful to break it up.

2 *Add* some organic matter to the soil if it is clayey to help it drain well. There's no need to add fertilizer, as ornamental grasses (unlike turfgrasses) do not like a rich diet.

3 Rake the soil smooth, and *mark* where each grass plant will go. In ground cover plantings, make sure they are equidistant from each other, spaced to allow for their mature spread as indicated on the plant label.

4 *Dig* a hole for each plant as deep as its pot is tall. If the area is sloped, dig the hole straight up and down so the plant will sit vertically.

5 *Slide* the plant from its nursery pot after a tap on its bottom. Set the plant in the hole, and fill in with plain soil dug from the hole.

6 *Water* well for good root-to-soil contact. *Mulch* between plantings to discourage weeds until the grass foliage grows and shades the soil between the plants.

Care for Your Plants

Well-established evergreen ground cover plantings of **Ivy, Pachy-sandra, Liriope,** and **Vinca** need very little routine care, but periodically they will need renovation. Mow them every six or eight years—more often if the plants lack their customary vigor and color.

1 *Set* the mulching mower at its highest setting, and mow to cut off the bulk of the ground cover foliage.

2 *Topdress* the exposed tangle of soil, bare stems, and chopped foliage with some organic matter. Compost, chopped leaves, topsoil, or mushroom soil will do fine.

3 While it is not essential, you might also *sprinkle* a small amount of granular, slow-acting, all-purpose fertilizer (not lawn fertilizer) over the area.

4 *Water* if it does not rain within a day or two.

In a few weeks the ground cover plants will generate fresh new foliage and look terrific.

Watering

This is the month that is famous for its showers, so it is tempting to assume there will be no need to drag around the hose yet. But if it has been an unusually dry winter, your plants are not mulched, or you have newly planted areas—and two weeks pass without significant rainfall—*water* ground covers and vines in dry soil.

Fertilizing

As planting season gets underway, incorporate some granular, slow-acting fertilizer into the soil each time you plant new vines and ground cover plants. This will provide consistent, uniform nutrition over many weeks.

Pruning

Before you are quite ready, leaves will start to emerge along the woody stems of your **Hybrid Clematis.** Use them as an indication of how healthy the old wood is.

Growing Smarter

As a group, ornamental plants are superior to turfgrasses as ground covers. Ornamental plants:

- are more disease-resistant.
- need less fertilizer and water.
- are available for every situation—sun, shade, wet, dry.
- provide a variety of textures, colors, and habits.
- shelter more kinds of beneficial insects.
- prevent soil compaction.
- discourage weeds.
- protect trees and shrubs from injury by mowers and trimmers.

Cut back the stems as low to the ground as you can and still have some leaves sprouting. This will stimulate vigorous growth and flowering in another month or two.

Thin out dead and injured stems and branches from perennial vines that have endured winter. **Kiwi, Autumn Clematis,** and others respond with vigor to late-winter pruning.

This month begins the **Wisteria** pruning season. For this first pruning, just remove excess growth along the main stems—*cut back* to the already formed flower buds on the spurs on last year's wood.

Problem Solving

Shade presents a problem sometimes because it seems as if most plants prefer sun, or at least significant light. Increase available light under trees by limbing them up or thinning their branch canopy. This will allow more light to reach the soil.

Yellowed or dead patches in evergreen ground cover plantings, especially at the edges or corners near sidewalks, is often due to visits by local dogs. Their urine, which is high in nitrogen, burns plant foliage. *Spray* those areas with repellent, or put up decorative, low fences to signal "keep off!"

Weeds emerge as enthusiastically this month as do desirable plants. Pull them when they are young after a rain moistens the soil. It is impossible to get the entire root of taprooted dandelions and thistle. *Spot-treat* them with a herbicide such as RoundUp®, which kills roots in the ground.

Planning

Vines add a new dimension to the yard. They also represent an opportunity to try new plants without taking up a lot of space. Many perennial and annual flowering plants are willing climbers. Annual vines grow fast and bloom steadily all season, but they have to be replaced each year. Perennial vines survive winters and grow thicker and stronger every year. Typically, they bloom for a short time, then produce fruit or berries later in the season. Think about how you can use their advantages to your advantage:

- screening a view or noise
- creating shade for a shade garden
- disguising a drainpipe or other eyesore
- attracting hummingbirds and butterflies
- adding drama and four-season interest to the yard

Plan ahead. Any plant raised or kept indoors will need a period of gradual adjustment to the outdoors before planting. The acclimating process takes a week or ten days because the weather is still likely to be erratic. Take flats or trays of plants outdoors for increasing lengths of time during mild days, returning them to the house at night. Then leave them out all night for a few nights. Introduce them to direct sun gradually, or their foliage will scorch.

Planting

The appearance of young transplants at the garden center signals that planting time is near. By mid-month, seedlings you start indoors are also ready to be planted outdoors. Once the danger of frost has passed and the soil has dried out and warmed a bit, start preparing the soil for planting. *Plant* annuals intended for ground covers as you would any annual (see Annuals, May), taking care to site and space them so they will quickly grow together to shade the soil.

Perennial vines and shrubs will probably be in sizable containers (although sometimes **Clematis** and **Climbing Roses** are sold bare-root), in which their roots have become accustomed to soilless mix and lots of fertilizer. Plunking them into ordinary soil will offend them, and their roots may be inclined to stay put rather than grow outward as they must. To prevent this and ease their transition, *loosen* the roots when you remove each plant from its container. Mix any potting medium that falls away with the regular soil. After setting the plants in their holes, fill them in with this soil combination, and firm it around each plant before watering (see Perennials, May).

Most annual vines are best grown by seed, directly sown onto the ground where they are to grow. Follow the instructions on the seed packet. It does not take long or take many seeds to start some **Morning Glories** or **Hyacinth** (**Lablab**) **Beans.** Certain favorites such as **Moonflower** seem to take forever to germinate, but be patient—it is worth it.

Care for Your Plants

Mulch newly planted plants over 6 inches tall with a 2- to 3-inch layer of organic material such as chopped leaves.

Make sure trellises are fastened out from walls several inches to allow air circulation behind the vine. This will protect wall surfaces from mildew and marks from the vine. Trellises should be detachable to allow for painting or repairing the supporting wall surface.

Large clumps of **Hostas** and **Daylilies** used as ground covers do not need dividing unless they become so crowded that their health is compromised.

Watering

Water all newly planted plants if it does not rain regularly. If the plants are mulched, the soil will not dry out so fast. Use a house-plant moisture meter probe to check the soil down about 3 inches for annuals and 6 inches for larger perennial transplants.

Fertilizing

If you did not add some granular, slow-acting, all-purpose fertilizer to the soil when you prepared it before transplanting new plants, *sprinkle* a little on the mulch around them now for the rain to soak in. Established ground cover plantings and ornamental grasses do not need supplemental feeding.

Pruning

Perennial vines will already be off and running. *Prune off* dead stems and twig tips injured in winter dieback. *Clip off* unruly stems to train the development of the vine and encourage fullness.

Trailing ground cover plants such as **Vinca** and **English Ivy** enjoy a growth spurt now, also. *Cut back*

HOW VINES CLIMB:

- Clingers attach with sticky rootlets from stems to surfaces. They will damage mortar if it is soft or old.
- Grabbers latch on to the nearest support with special tendrils they produce from their leaf stems. They like relatively thin supports such as wire or netting.
- Sprawlers lean against or lie across whatever is handy. Stems must be fastened with twine or woven between rungs of a support.
- Twiners wrap themselves around supports. They need very substantial, sturdy structures.

any stems that venture out into the lawn or up a nearby tree, to keep them in bounds. If **Ivy** is growing on the house, trim it so that it does not encroach on chimneys, windows, or gutters at the roofline.

Problem Solving

Aphids show up pretty early in the season. They fancy the tender flowerbuds and the succulent new growth at the tips of plant stems and vine tendrils. Until beneficial insects arrive to deal with them, *pinch off* aphid-infested plant tips, or wash off the pests with a strong water spray from the hose. Insecticidal soap sprayed directly on them is effective, but some plants, such as **Honeysuckle,** can't handle the soap spray—test it on one part of the plant first.

Tent caterpillar nests in trees shelter tiny caterpillars. These larvae will soon leave the tough, weblike nests to feed on vine and ground cover plant foliage. *Clip* the supporting branches of the nests to remove them, and put them in the trash. Poke those that are out of reach with a long, sharp stick to tear them open and expose the caterpillars to the birds.

Division of Grasses

Planning

As newly planted vines begin to stretch and show their stuff, some pre-planning will save a lot of grief later.

- *Ensure* that a supporting structure is in place and is appropriate for the type of vine you have.

- *Examine* the bolts, eye hooks, or other type of fasteners that you use to hold a wire matrix or wooden trellis out from the wall. Make sure they are secure.

- *Check* the footings on arbors and pergolas that must bear the weight of a heavy **Wisteria** or **Climbing Hydrangea.**

- *Have* soft twine or cloth ties handy for tying the stems of any vine that leans to its support as soon as it reaches it. Proper training now saves time and trouble later.

Strange as it may seem, this is a good time to order hardy bulbs for fall planting. Pre-season discounts from mail-order companies really add up if you are buying in bulk for a seasonal ground cover planting. Companies will ship in late summer or early fall at planting time.

As spring segues into summer, record when your new plants bloom, and add that information to the notes you have on your other plants. It is easier to remember when something blooms if you notice what else is blooming at the same time.

Planting

By now it is safe to bring tender annual or tropical vines outdoors to spend the summer. Acclimate them gradually to the fresh air and sunshine. *Plant* **Mandevilla, Plumbago,** or **Bougainvillea** in the ground next to a mailbox post or other structure it can climb or cover. If you intend to keep a plant in a pot, remove it to check the roots. If the roots are winding around the base of the soilball, it's time for repotting.

- Choose a somewhat larger pot—but no more than 2 inches wider—with a drainage hole.

- Fill it with fresh soilless mix, and add some complete granular, slow-acting fertilizer.

- Set the plant in the pot at the same depth it was in its previous pot.

- Fill in with mix, and *water* well.

If you do not intend to position the pot near a post or fixture for it to climb, insert a stake into the pot (be careful not to damage plant roots) to make a free-standing vine.

Here's a different idea. Try setting a potted vine on top of a sunny wall or deck edge and letting it fall downward instead of climb upward. **Sweet Potato Vine, Jasmine,** and others look quite lovely when displayed this way.

Care for Your Plants

Expect young vine stems to take a while to grow up to the bottom of their supporting structure and grab hold. Temporarily *stake* them to train them in the right direction until they are able to grab on or you can tie them on.

Some ground cover plants are valued more for their foliage than for their flowers. To maintain foliage production and a fresh look, routinely *pinch off* the incipient flowers of **Coleus, Lamb's Ears, Artemisias,** and similar plants.

Pull up any **Pansies** that did ground cover duty early in the season. As the heat arrives, they become lank and leggy. *Replace* them with heat-loving annuals such as **Creeping Zinnias, Nasturtiums, Portulaca,** or **Salvias.**

Watering

If rain is scarce, newly planted ground covers and vines may need some extra water—especially if they are not mulched. Established plants and ornamental grasses should be fine for at least two weeks between rains or watering. Vines in pots and planters will need checking frequently because soilless potting medium dries out quickly in the hot sun.

Fertilizing

The dose of granular, slow-acting fertilizer mixed into their soil or added to their containers during repotting provides sufficient nutrition to vines and ground cover plants for the season. It releases nutrients gradually over the number of weeks indicated on the package label. Resist the temptation to fertilize more, which will stimulate rampant foliage growth at the expense of flowers. More pruning and maintenance will be necessary, and the risk of attack by pest insects will be greater.

Pruning

After the **Wisteria** finishes blooming, it will generate leafy stems with gusto. In no time it will engulf its

Growing Smarter

Ground cover plants need not be trailing and low growing. Almost any plant will cover the soil when planted *en masse.* Whether it is annual or perennial, evergreen or deciduous, shrub, herb, wildflower, or bulb, a good ground cover plant has certain attributes:

1 It grows and spreads fairly rapidly, but in a disciplined manner.

2 It is easily removed if it oversteps its bounds.

3 It does not need constant grooming, watering, and feeding.

4 It holds up over many years (or, as an annual, over the entire season) with minimum care.

5 It is ornamental in one or more ways—foliage, flowers, fruits.

support and anything in its vicinity. *Prune* this excess greenery back before the buds for next year start to form in July so that you do not unwittingly cut them off, too. Try to shape and control the size and direction of the vine until the next pruning in late summer.

Regularly *deadhead* faded **Daylily** blossoms to improve their appearance and promote rebloom over the season. Pull or cut drying stems.

Problem Solving

Slugs are out in force by now in the moist, shady parts of your yard. Use traps (see March) to catch as many as you can. *Sprinkle* diatomaceous earth (DE) powder over the soil in a circle around vulnerable plants. Slugs will be injured if they try to slither over these sharp microscopic particles.

Aphids are everywhere, but in a healthy landscape, beneficial insect populations are sufficient to control them. *Pick off* infested leaves and flowers to reduce their numbers.

Weeds, too, are ubiquitous. A mulch layer on bare soil between ground cover plants and around vines and grasses discourages most weeds. Pull stubborn ones, or *spot-treat* them with herbicide (on still days, to prevent dangerous drift onto valuable nearby plants).

Planning

This month the areas turned over to attractive, relatively low-maintenance ground cover plantings are beginning to come into their own. You will appreciate having less lawn to mow.

Where annual vines have stretched to several feet tall, they define and enclose spaces for quiet and privacy. Those covering light-colored walls are reducing the reflected light and heat to help keep things cool around the pool or patio. Watch for hummingbirds around the **Mandevilla, Morning Glory, Honeysuckle,** and **Trumpet Creepers** that flaunt tubular, brightly colored blossoms.

Remember to take some photographs of the early-summer landscape, and *record* what's abloom in your garden notebook, calendar, or journal.

Planting

Soon it will be too hot to plant perennial vines and ground cover shrubs or ornamental grasses without risk. Although they are available in containers at the garden center or nursery all summer, they will have difficulty establishing new roots and topgrowth in the heat and possible drought. If you do not have them in the ground shortly after the Fourth of July weekend, it is best to wait until fall.

Annuals planted for ground cover duty this month will have to play catch-up. Shade them from the sun for a few days after planting, and *mulch* them well. Those planted in late May are already knitting together.

Care for Your Plants

Certain ground cover plants have difficulty with heat. After flowering and by mid-month, cool shade–lovers such as **Lily-of-the-valley, Deadnettle,** and **Sweet Woodruff** begin to look shabby and may collapse and give up. **Tiarella,** or **Foamflower,** may melt away in patches. Clean up dead leaves, and *cut back* limp stems to help them regenerate fresh foliage or wait out the weather in dormancy. Fortunately, annual plants such as **Madagascar Vinca, Impatiens, Nasturtiums,** and **Trailing Petunias** love this weather.

Keep an eye on the vines. *Tie or wrap* rapidly extending stems to their supports before they reach out and embrace some neighboring plants. **Moonflower** vines and tropicals such as **Mandevilla** need major heat before they are interested in growing and blooming.

Watering

New, mulched ground cover patches and those that are well established in decent soil can go a week to ten days without rain before they need watering. Ornamental grasses can go longer. If it is terribly hot, *check* soil moisture every few days with a houseplant water meter probe. Even plants in shaded areas, such as **Ferns,** may dry out because nearby trees take most of the soil moisture and their leaf canopies block light rains. Check them, too.

Pruning

After large-flowered **Clematis** blooms in June, cut back the stems at least halfway to stimulate possible repeat bloom later in the summer. Alternatively, just a light clipping of rampant stems will neaten its appearance and leave some of the interesting seedpods to enjoy.

Climbing Hydrangea takes many years to start producing flowers.

Once it does, prune it each year just after it blooms. *Cut back* branching stems that extend outward more than 15 inches from the main stem. Otherwise, they will become so heavy that their collective weight may pull the vine from its support altogether. *Clip* these branching stems individually back to a point where some leaves emerge.

Pinch back Impatiens stems that may be growing leggy. This will keep the plants bushy and compact so they do a better job of covering the ground. They will resume blooming soon.

 ## Problem Solving

Japanese beetles typically arrive early this month. Since they are so punctual, if you record the date, you will know when to expect them in your yard every year. In no time it will be clear what their favorite plants are, so patrol that area frequently with a jar of soapy water. Knock them from the foliage into the jar. They do not bother ornamental grasses.

Heat and humidity stress plants. Those that are already unhappy because they have the wrong soil, light, or diet are prime candidates for pest or disease problems. Take the trouble to site plants properly, and keep them watered.

Scale is likely to appear on certain **Hollies** and **Euonymus** species. Watch for the waxy or whitish bumps under the leaves and along the stems. *Spray* all surfaces of affected plants thoroughly with light horticultural oil to smother the insects hiding under the bumps.

Spider mites thrive in hot, dry weather. They zero in on stressed plants such as **Ivy, Azaleas,** and **Junipers.** They cause pale stippling on leaves, and sometimes their fine webbing is visible among the twigs and branchlets. *Spray* infested foliage with a strong water spray every other day to disrupt the mites' life cycle. If that doesn't work over the long term, *spray* them with insecticidal soap as directed on the product label. Think about why the plant is so stressed and how you can remedy that underlying condition.

Weeds mar the appearance of a patch of ground cover. They also steal soil moisture and nutrients from the desirable plants, so keep after them.

Growing Smarter

People assume that **English Ivy** strangles and kills the trees when it climbs up their trunks. So many dead trees are covered with ropes of **Ivy** stems, it seems like a logical conclusion—but **Ivy** is not the culprit. Typically, the trees are already dead before the **Ivy** adopts them as a convenient place to climb.

English Ivy is not a twiner. It does not climb by wrapping itself around the trunks; it crawls up tree bark by means of its sticky rootlets. The only time **Ivy** might threaten harm to a tree is if it climbs into its foliage canopy and spreads over it thickly. By denying it essential sunlight, the **Ivy** could conceivably harm the tree's fruits. Since **Ivy** prefers partial shade, it is not likely to do this either.

Planning

August is grass, vine, and ground cover appreciation month. A landscape that has ground covers, vines, and ornamental grasses is more self-reliant than most. This is a particular advantage when it is too hot to take much pleasure in working outdoors, and when it is time to go away on vacation. If you plan to sit by the pool or patio, you will appreciate the way vines create cool seclusion.

Like turfgrasses, ornamental grasses may be cool-season or warm-season types.

- Because they do not mind spring chill, *cool-season* grasses mature faster and bloom earlier. Look for their flowerheads now.

- Typically, *warm-season* grasses start later because they wait for warmer weather. Consequently, they take a bit longer to reach their mature height and to flower. Look for their flowers late this month and next month.

Grasses produce stems tipped with feathery flowers that resemble nodding bottlebrushes, plumes, or sheaves. Flowers eventually mature into bristly seedheads and feathery tassels that capture the late summer sunlight. Bring some indoors to add to flower arrangements.

Planting

It is too hot to plant this month. Wait a few weeks until after Labor Day. Hold plants in containers in the shade, and water them well while they wait.

Care for Your Plants

Check vines to be sure they are securely fastened to their supports. The pounding rain and gusty winds from our classic late summer thunderstorms might break long stems or even whip a vine off its trellis or wall.

You may discover some ripening fruits on the **Kiwi** vine. Wait until they are very soft before picking and eating them. **Lablab** vines develop shiny, reddish-purple pods that dangle attractively near clusters of small purplish flowers. Allow the pods to remain on the vine until they dry out. Then *pick* them, pop them, and save the interesting seeds you find inside for next year.

Weed ground cover beds to reduce plant stress. Plants should not have to compete with interlopers for water and nutrients in the soil, and because insects that spread diseases often live in weeds, removing them also keeps disease pathogens at bay.

Watering

Do not worry if the **Moss** you have started as a ground cover seems to dry up. It will revive as soon as it gets moisture from your sprinkler or the next rain.

Be aware that many **Ferns** prefer cool, moist conditions, so they will have a particularly difficult time during heat and drought. Their ideal soil has lots of organic material in it to keep moisture available to **Fern** roots even if there is no rain. If possible, *water* them every four or five days if rainfall is scarce. Make sure the moisture soaks in several inches each time.

Pruning

Impatiens will bloom well into October if there is no frost. Give them a new lease on life by pinching them back, watering them, and feeding them lightly with a very dilute liquid fertilizer if you have not done so already.

Keep after aggressive vines to direct their growth and control their spread. If known invasives are growing on your property and you do not want to abolish them altogether, prevent their escape into the wild by cutting off their flowers before they make seeds.

Porcelainberry, Oriental Bittersweet, and Akebia are notorious for spreading rampantly and driving out native species in our parks and open spaces. While their berries may be desirable as ornamental features, they are a menace. Birds will distribute them everywhere.

Japanese Honeysuckle is a major invader also.

Problem Solving

Wilting foliage may mean a plant is hot, rather than sick or thirsty. To confirm this, *check* wilted plants after the sun and heat of the day have passed. If the foliage has recovered, the problem is heat. If it has not perked up, chances are that dryness is the problem. If it does not perk up within a half-hour after a good watering, then look for signs of disease. Pull infected plants immediately and discard them in the trash.

Phomopsis twig blight sometimes afflicts carpet-type Junipers and other needled evergreens. The fungus attacks branch tips in the spring, eventually killing them. *Prune out* the dead, gray-brown branches to get rid of fungal spores that remain, before they spread to healthy branches. Consider spraying a commercial fungicide if shrubs are severely affected.

Fungal diseases are in their heyday this month because plants are often under stress from heat and humidity. Mostly they cause spots, blotches, or cankers on plant foliage, killing the tissues and threatening the stems with dieback. *Clip off* any affected leaves or stems, and put them in the trash to prevent the spread of the disease. Clean up old mulch under infected plants to remove a source of repeat infection. To protect surrounding healthy perennial plants in ground covers where air circulation may be limited, *spray* their foliage with a sulfur-based, general garden fungicide as directed on the product label. Repeat the spray as new foliage emerges. If annuals are infected, it is probably easiest to pull them all up and discard them in the trash. They are temporary anyway. Clean up the mulch, and plant fall annuals there with fresh mulch.

Slugs, mites, lacebugs, the usual suspects, are still potential problems for plants. See details on controlling them in the entries for previous months. For more information on pest control, see the troubleshooting chart in the Appendix.

Growing Smarter

When is an ivy not an true **Ivy?** When it is poison ivy. This plant masquerades as a shrub, a ground cover, or a vine, so it is often hard to identify. Its resemblance to **Boston Ivy** confuses the issue even further. Both have three-lobed leaves, fall berries, and lovely fall color. Look closely at **Boston Ivy.** You will see that its leaves are actually a single leaf with three pointed lobes rather than a group of the telltale three separate leaflets of poison ivy. Remember: "Leaves of three, let it be."

Planning

"Fall is for Planting" signs are up at the garden center. Fall begins right after Labor Day for gardeners. Think ground covers:

- This perfect time for renewing and renovating lawns is also a perfect time to consider if more lawn area might be devoted to ground covers instead of high-maintenance turfgrasses.

- Areas under trees where grass struggles mightily are good candidates for alternatives such as **Moss, Pachysandra, Liriope,** or other shade-loving plants.

- Planting new trees and shrubs? This is the perfect time to start a ground cover planting in the soil over their root zone.

- In cases where shrubs have spread wider, allow the ground cover planting under them to expand outward apace.

Flowering continues. Enjoy **Mums, Asters, Black-eyed Susans, Celosia,** and other fall bloomers planted as ground covers. **Autumn Clematis** will spill over everything. **Autumn Crocus, Colchicum,** and **Sternbergia** bulbs will appear.

Coming up: Keep the binoculars handy to enjoy the visits of birds to the plants with seedheads and berries. (Goldfinches love the seeds of **Black-eyed Susans.**) Keep your garden journal and camera handy, too, to record the change of colors in the yard.

Planting

Most woody plants—including perennial vines and shrubs suitable for ground covers—prefer fall planting. *Plant* low-growing shrubs that will cover and hold the soil on slopes. Some, such as **Cotoneaster** and **Beautyberry,** produce berries and foliage color in the fall. While you are planting, pop dozens of small **Crocus** or **Snowdrop** bulbs in the ground for a great spring ground cover show.

Moss is a great ground cover alternative. The many different plants that belong to this plant category like the type of environment that is common in Pennsylvania—shade, acidic soil, coolness, and humidity. Some kinds will take a fair amount of sun if there is humidity. If you already have some **Moss** growing on your property, you can assume that the conditions are right, at least where it has made itself at home. Properly prepared ground invites transient **Moss** spores to stop by and settle in:

1 *Clear* the area of weeds, and rake debris off the soil. Firm the soil with a roller or footsteps to smooth and compact it.

2 *Sprinkle* powdered sulfur to increase the acidity of the soil to the ideal pH of 5.5 (skimmed-milk powder or **Rhododendron** fertilizer are alternatives to the sulfur). The rain or your sprinkler will soak it in.

3 Keep the soil weed-free because **Mosses** like barren soil, then see what spores drop by to colonize the area.

Another way to introduce **Mosses** is to invite them to expand from where they are already growing in a sickly lawn or elsewhere in your yard by preparing adjacent soil as above.

Yet another way is to plant small patches of **Moss** as **Moss** "sod," in prepared soil. *Transplant* these from other parts of the yard or from property where you have permission to harvest it. If you can find several different types, they will make an interesting tapestry. *Plant* them with space between, and let them knit together.

Care for Your Plants

Bring in the potted tropical vines that you intend to overwinter indoors as houseplants. They need warmth, and there is the possibility of a light frost upstate before the month is over.

1 **Clip** the longest climbing stems back to about 2 feet.

2 **Dig** the plant out of the soil, disturbing the roots as little as possible, and put it in a pot filled with soilless potting mix. Wash off the plant with a forceful water spray when you water it in the pot.

3 Leave the plant outdoors while it adjusts to its pot. **Spray** it with insecticidal soap or hot pepper spray to eliminate pests.

4 Bring it indoors gradually—for increasingly longer times over a week or two—so it can adjust to stressful indoor conditions. Set it where it will receive bright sunshine until the shorter days of fall will trigger its rest time.

5 Reduce watering, and do not fertilize. Locate the plant where nighttime temperatures are 60 to 65 degrees F, until late winter when growth will begin again.

Growing Smarter

Many vines and ground cover plants end the growing season aglow with brilliantly colored foliage and berries. Two outstanding vines are **Boston Ivy (*Parthenocissus tricuspidata*)** and **Virginia Creeper (*Parthenocissus quinquefolia*)**.

Many shrubs suitable for ground cover also feature colorful berries:

- **Bayberry**
- **Beautyberry**
- **Chokeberry**
- **Cotoneaster**
- **Dwarf Barberry**
- **Nandina**
- **Skimmia**

Watering

If rainfall is limited, **water** all newly planted ground cover shrubs and vines. Well-mulched, established plantings can manage several weeks between rainfalls.

Fertilizing

When planting woody shrubs and vines, delay fertilizing until at least next spring.

Pruning

To prevent their self-sowing all over the yard, cut seedheads from **Northern Oat Grass** before they release seeds. **Cut off** maturing berries on **Porcelainberry, Akebia,** and other vines that are known invasives before birds spread them into the wild.

Discipline the **Wisteria** one more time. Cut back wildly rampant stems, taking care not to clip off buds that formed in July for next year's flowers.

Ornamental grasses will begin to lose their color and turn beige or pale yellow, their seedheads bursting into fluffy plumes as they release their seeds. Wait to cut them back until late winter.

Problem Solving

Insect problems should be about over, since they, too, are getting ready for winter. Many leave behind eggs or larvae safely secreted in organic debris around the yard. The good news is that beneficial insects are doing the same thing.

Weeds persist. Take advantage of warm days to **spray** the tough perennial ones with herbicide to prevent their return in the spring. Continue to **pull** annual ones before they release their seeds.

Planning

First frost signals a slow-down out in the garden. Annual ground cover plants are likely to succumb to the brief chill and die, leaving a bare expanse of ground that will need a protective winter mulch of straw or chopped leaves. Perennial grasses, vines, and ground covers put on their final show of the year with an explosion of foliage color, late flowering, and/or berry production.

Get out the camera again to capture the changing scene as golden light backdrops the show. *Record* any sightings of new birds that may stop off during migration to sample the berries growing in your yard.

Cooler weather makes this month an ideal time for accomplishing major landscape projects that require a fair amount of physical labor.

- Repair walls and re-attach trellis supports.

- Reinforce trellises and fences that support heavy vines.

- Build or repair arbors.

- Build a pergola.

- Set stepping stones for a walkway with spaces between for ground cover plants.

- Expand ground cover beds.

- Terrace slopes with landscape timbers.

Planting

This is a good time to *plant* bulbs intended for ground cover. Either naturalize them by casting them freely over the intended site and then planting them where they fall, or insert them among established ground cover plants such as **Ivy, Vinca, Hosta,** or **Liriope.** Various kinds of **Daffodils** or minor bulbs such as **Crocus, Snowdrops,** or **Woods Hyacinth** are best suited for this use. Over the years they will spread to form large patches of color in the spring.

Plant shrubs like **Juniper** for ground cover. Choose containerized plants, making sure they are all the same variety and color and roughly the same size. Clear the area of weeds, rocks, and debris, and dig into the soil some organic material such as chopped leaves, compost, or mushroom soil to improve drainage and moisture retention. Set the potted shrubs over the area to determine desirable spacing, then *dig* saucer-shaped holes at the exact spots that are as deep as the pots and a bit wider as the pots. *Plant* as described in the May Planting section in the Shrubs chapter.

Care for Your Plants

Remove frost-blackened annual vines from trellises and other supports.

Lay netting or garden fleece over **Moss** and other ground covers to catch leaves that might mat and block moisture and smother the plants over the winter. After leaf fall is over, roll up the leaf laden netting, carry it to the compost area, and dump its contents on the pile. Store the netting until it is time to protect berry patches from birds next summer.

Spray needled evergreen shrubs that are exposed to drying from harsh winter wind and sunshine. Use an anti-desiccant spray according to label directions.

Watering

Install a drip irrigation system in certain areas that are difficult to water or where plants depend on regular moisture. There is better access to the open soil now that plants have died back. Snake "leaky pipe"–type soaker hoses through ground cover plantings. Emitter-type hoses are better for shrub and vine plantings that are less closely planted. Mechanical or digital timers are useful but not necessary. **Cover** the hoses with winter mulch. Ornamental grasses do not need much water, so they do not need an irrigation system.

Drip irrigation is ideal for shallow-rooted plants that dry out quickly during hot, dry summers. It delivers water directly to the soil so that none is lost to evaporation. The water enters the soil slowly for maximum absorption so none will be wasted in runoff. Plant foliage stays dry, thus less at risk from mildew diseases.

Fertilizing

After established deciduous trees and shrubs lose their leaves, it is okay to **spread** over vine and ground cover soil some winter-type fertilizer formulated for woody or nursery plants. It will help with root growth during the time when the ground has not yet frozen, and will be there to start off next season. Wait until next year to fertilize recently planted plants.

Pruning

Unless vines and ground cover plants are a danger to themselves or others, delay pruning until late winter or early spring. You do not want to risk stimulating new growth during a possible period of Indian Summer, as the growth would be killed back immediately, come hard frost. Clipping off the occasional overlong, errant, or injured branch is okay.

Problem Solving

Rodents are scouting for winter nesting sites. Although your summer mulch is probably pretty thin by now, wait until the ground freezes before spreading a fresh winter layer. Mice, chipmunks, voles, and others will have already nested elsewhere.

Poison ivy gives itself away at this time of year. If you have not noticed it in the yard all summer, you will now. Deal with it before birds carry its berries away to start even more plants. All parts of the plant are poisonous. **Pull up** small plants with a long plastic bag covering your hand and lower arm. Once the plant is out of the ground, pull the plastic bag off

your arm over the plant as you hold it, effectively turning the bag inside out with the plant ending up inside, never touching your skin. **Discard** in the trash. **Spray** larger vines with a herbicide such as RoundUp®. When the vines have died, cover your legs, hands, and arms, cut up the dead vines into pieces, and put the pieces in a plastic bag for the trash.

Growing Smarter

If certain varieties of annuals such as **Geraniums, Wax Begonias,** or **Impatiens** became ground cover favorites over the summer, bring them in to overwinter indoors. Either **dig up** existing plants and pot them in soilless planting mix to serve as houseplants, or take stem cuttings from them to root and make new plants (see Annuals, October).

Planning

Take harvest season indoors with berry laden branches from vines and ground cover plants. Dried pods and bleached stems of ornamental grasses topped with airy, spent seedheads also make wonderful floral displays for Thanksgiving.

Outdoors there is much to enjoy. After **Boston Ivy** and **Virginia Creeper** drop their leaves, the delicate tracings of their dried stems stand out on walls and tree trunks. Grasses grow blowzy and carefree, their stems flexing in the increasingly chilly wind, adding movement and sound to the autumn landscape.

Take a few moments to record in your notebook or journal the dates of first frost and hard frost, what continues to bloom in November, and things you would like to do with vines, grasses, and ground covers next year.

Planting

Dig into unfrozen ground to plant minor bulbs for ground cover duty under trees and shrubs, between stepping stones, and elsewhere. It is better to plant them at the last minute than to store them over the winter.

If you have not yet planted **Pansies,** put some in where the ground is still workable, and they will have a head start for spring. In and around areas where **Forget-me-nots** bloomed last year, tufts of narrow dark-green leaves will persist through the winter and bloom next spring. If you want to relocate them to a better place, *transplant* them now if the ground is still soft. *Water* well.

Care for Your Plants

Leave small leaves that fall between **Pachysandra, Ivy,** and beds of similar evergreen plants as a natural mulch. They will decompose and add nutrients to the soil so you do not need to routinely fertilize these ground covers. *Remove* larger leaves (**Sycamore** leaves are the size of dinner plates!) to prevent their matting and blocking moisture from penetrating the soil beneath the ground cover. Either capture them in netting spread over the top of the ground cover planting, or *dislodge and remove* them with a powered blower/vac. Most vacuums simultaneously shred the leaves into a bag so that you have instant mulch to return to the plantings or to spread elsewhere.

This is a good time for final fall cleanup in the yard to prevent over-wintering of pest insects and disease pathogens.

- *Cut back* dead plant stems, and discard them on the compost pile.

- *Pull up* stakes, remove temporary fencing, and bring in any ornaments that may crack in cold weather to be stored in a warm place.

- *Set up* a winterproof container to hold water for birds. Locate it in the sun so its water will be melted at least part of the day when temperatures really drop and winter closes in.

Fasten the thick, woody stems of long-established perennial vines such as **Kiwi, Wisteria,** and **Climbing Hydrangea** securely to their supports. *Check* ties to be sure that they are not too tight around stems after a season's growth.

Watering

Only if it has been a dry fall is it necessary to water plants this month. Lack of rainfall will most affect recently planted shrubs and vines, or those that are not mulched. Do not let evergreen shrubs—either broadleaf or needled—go into the winter in dry soil. Before the ground freezes, soak it well so that these plants can take up the moisture they need for the winter. Because they are never entirely dormant, they continue to transpire and lose moisture through their leaves.

Fertilizing

While it is okay to sprinkle a granular, slow-acting product labeled for woody or nursery plants around *established* shrubs and vines now, delay this job until late winter or early spring for *recently planted* ones.

Pruning

Cut back the tall stems of ornamental grasses now if you want to—but if left in full-blown majesty, the larger ones can be a real asset to an otherwise bleak winter landscape. Snow sets off their subtle beige, golden, or parchment foliage and fluffy seedheads.

Limit any pruning to repair of injured or dead branches on vines or shrubby ground cover plants. In a couple of months you can prune for shape and to renovate plants.

Growing Smarter

Throughout this book fertilizer recommendations are for slow-acting rather than fast-acting products. The difference is primarily in the form of nitrogen they contain. In slow-acting products, the nitrogen is water-insoluble. Whether its source is natural or chemical (synthesized in a laboratory then coated), nitrogen dissolves gradually over time. In fast-acting products—either liquid, granular, or powdered to be dissolved in water—the nitrogen is water-soluble and is immediately available to plant roots.

While there are many situations when immediate availability is desirable, in most landscape situations plants are neither in a hurry for their nitrogen nor are they comfortable rapidly absorbing intermittent large doses. Perennial plants and woody plants like vines and shrubs are in it for the long haul. They need consistent, uniform nutrition available all season. Slow-acting fertilizer provides this steady, long-term nutrition, saving you the time and energy required for repeat-fertilizing with fast-acting products. Slow-acting fertilizer is gentle on the plant and the microlife that lives in the soil.

Problem Solving

Deer will continue to be a problem through the winter. If they are desperate for food, they may go to great lengths and risk to reach the plants in your yard. Occasional casual visitors can usually be thwarted by wire used as cages around individual plants or laid over patches of ground cover. Various repellents sprayed on their foliage may work. Desperate or regular visitors can only be deterred by an effective high fence. Use 10-foot-high black polymesh mounted on trees or posts around the perimeter of your property, or string electrified wire.

Planning

As winter closes in and holiday activities monopolize time and energy, take a moment to reflect on the year's gardening successes and failures. Jot down some ideas for acquiring and planting more grasses, vines, and ground covers next year.

Drop daily catalog arrivals in a designated box until you have time to look through them. Their many color photographs and great descriptions are really helpful for learning to identify plants. Good ones have lots of information about suitable planting locations and how to grow and care for the plants.

Think about what to put on your **holiday gift list.** Perhaps a good book on vines and ground covers? How about an arbor for the garden? Gift certificates to garden centers and nurseries are great to give and receive.

Planting

If the ground is still soft, get any leftover unplanted bulbs into the ground. They will cover the ground with color in just a few months.

Care for Your Plants

Cover bare soil in the yard with a 3- to 4-inch layer of organic material such as chopped leaves, wood chips, evergreen boughs, or pine needles to maintain an even soil temperature, even though the air temperature varies in winter. Plants do better if the soil stays at about the same temperature rather than repeatedly freezing and thawing.

Watering

It seems as if there is not as much snow during Pennsylvania winters as there used to be. It has always been a source of moisture during winter thaws and in the spring. If it neither snows nor rains for an extended period of time, *water* evergreen vines and ground cover plantings.

Pruning

Occasionally the weight of wet snow or ice snaps off branches from vines and ground cover shrubs. Saw or cut off the branch cleanly back where it joins another one.

Problem Solving

Critters of various kinds may try to nibble on the tender bark of young shrubs and vines during the winter. If you anticipate problems, wrap hardware cloth or a commercial tree-wrap product around vulnerable stems. Remember, rabbits, deer, mice, and voles can reach pretty high when standing on a foot or two of snow.

Road salt pushed by passing snowplows with snow onto ground cover plantings near the street causes them to desiccate and turn brown. The salt absorbs the moisture in the soil and plant roots dry out. Pour pails of water on areas where salt has been deposited to dilute it and wash it deeply into the soil past plant roots.

Growing Smarter

Nothing improves a nighttime winter landscape more than holiday lights. Low-wattage lights that are rated for outdoor use do not harm shrubs and vines, but the way they are attached may cause problems if they are left up for several months. Never wrap the light wires snugly around shrub and vine stems and branches. Drape, rather than wrap, the strands of lights over and among the branches. It is okay to wrap them around a trellis or arbor that a vine is climbing.

Water & Bog Plants

It is no surprise that the popularity of water gardening—growing aquatic and bog plants in ponds or containers—grows and grows each year. Of course long-time gardeners are going to enthusiastically embrace the opportunity to learn about and acquire a whole category of new plants. For them, water gardening is a natural extension of terrestrial gardening, and they welcome the opportunity to extend the skills they have into a new arena. It is a wonderful way for admitted plant nuts to indulge themselves even more in their favorite pastime.

The surprise is the popularity of water gardening among those who are not experienced with plants and who have not learned the basic skills of growing and nurturing them. Often it is the very people who announce they have brown thumbs when the conversation turns to gardening who are not at all shy about putting a pond in the yard. Many take confidence from recollections of childhood adventures with aquariums. Others draw on memories of languid summer vacations at the lake. They may start with only fish in the pond, then they add a few plants, then they add some more plants. Perhaps water seems more forgiving than soil—maybe growing plants in water seems less permanent, so it is less daunting.

Water Gardening

I think the best explanation for the appeal of water gardening to everyone, gardener or not, is that the activity has to do with water as much as it has to do with plants. Water is our earliest life experience, even before conscious memory. It cradles our gestation and nurtures our earliest growth. Our bodies are 98 percent water. In ways long forgotten, water is our element. Those who garden in water often talk about the serenity they feel when they work near their ponds and containers, caring for their water plants and the wildlife this environment attracts. Literally and figuratively, a water garden is an oasis.

In nature, an oasis is an armistice zone. It is a place that all creatures come to, depend on—prey and predator alike. A water garden oasis is also a zone of peace in our residential landscapes. The surface of the water offers a visual tranquilizer, the ripples from the bobbing foliage of water plants and the darting of fish providing constantly changing patterns in the light. The sound of a trickle from a fountain or waterfall or a gurgle from a bubbler is restful. Here is an opportunity to play. Permission is granted to get wet and muddy. Add to that the sense of well-being gained from creative expression in designing the water garden and the sense of physical well-being gained from the exercise while planting and lifting pots and tending plants. Certainly gardening in water is a powerful antidote to the daily stress that attends contemporary life.

Water Gardens

Not too long ago, only wealthy people grew **Water Lilies, Lotus,** and other exotic water plants. Only they could afford to buy large properties with natural ponds or to build swimming pool–like water gardens. Aquatic plants were not commonly available for sale, and there were not many kinds to choose from.

These days, water gardening is within the reach of everyone. Modern technology has provided inexpensive materials and equipment for building ponds. There are now several types of sturdy, flexible poly liner materials, as well as stiff, preformed fiberglass liners that will

Water & Bog Plants

last for years and years. One can buy PVC tubing, efficient sealed pumps, easy-to-handle filters, netting, lighting, and a host of other products that homeowners can afford and install themselves.

And the plants. The choices seem infinite. Driven by the upsurge in consumer interest, hybridizers and growers have produced myriad colors and forms of **Water Lilies** and **Lotus.** Plant explorers have searched out interesting new aquatic plants from all over the world. Closer to home, many plants that grow in local lakes, creeks, and wetlands have been given a second look and a new appreciation. Now they are part of a rich selection of native water plants available to homeowners. Most recently, the trend has been to discover terrestrial plants that double as aquatic plants. Both professional growers and home gardeners are identifying certain **Hibiscus, Canna, Hostas,** ornamental grasses, ferns, **Lysimachia, Lobelias,** and others that do not just tolerate wet soil but will actually grow in water. The possibilities seem endless.

There is no denying that water gardening is strenuous at times. This is especially true if you garden in an inground pond. Fortunately, more and more landscape service companies are offering to do pond design, construction, repair, and maintenance for homeowners. If your enthusiasm for water gardening gets out of control (not uncommon!), there is help at hand to build a second pond, or to clean the ponds. Companies that specialize in these services sometimes offer to board your tender plants in their greenhouses for the winter, or take your extra or overlarge fish off your hands. They also troubleshoot for you when problems develop.

There is no excuse for putting off trying this wonderful kind of gardening. Start small with just one or two plants and a large decorative jar or half-barrel of water. Experiment, play, learn, find peace.

Water Plants in a Pond

Water Garden Plants for Pennsylvania

Common Name (Botanical Name)	Type Hardiness	Function	Size	Comments
Anacharis (*Egeria densa*)	Submerged Hardy to zone 6	Oxygenator	To 3 feet tall	Floating, evergreen, branched stems bear male white flowers in summer at water surface.
Arrowhead (*Sagittaria latifolia*)	Marginal Hardy	Ornamental	1 to 1½ feet tall	Spikes of white flowers over arrow-shaped leaves in summer. Triangular stems.
Canna (*Canna glauca*)	Marginal Tender	Ornamental	6 feet tall (dwarf, 3 to 4 feet)	Blooms all summer in many bright colors. Broad leaves of many types are variegated.
Cardinal Flower (*Lobelia cardinalis*)	Bog Hardy	Ornamental; transition	30 to 36 inches tall	Bright-red flowers attract hummingbirds.
Carolina Water Shield (*Cabomba caroliniana*)	Submerged Hardy to zone 6	Oxygenator	Indefinite spread	Fan-shaped, ferny leaves. Small white or purple flowers in summer just at water level.
Cattail (*Typha* sp.)	Marginal Hardy	Four-season interest	To 7 feet tall	Beige floret spikes in late summer.
Chameleon Plant (*Houttuynia cordata*)	Bog Hardy to zone 6	Ground cover	6 to 12 inches tall	Can be invasive. Also grows in pot in 2 inches of water.
Duckweed (*Lemna minor*)	Floater Hardy	Water cover	Indefinite spread	Multiplies rapidly. Difficult to eradicate. Fish eat it.
Fairy Moss (*Azolla* sp.)	Floater Tender	Water cover	Indefinite spread	A true **Fern,** so no flowers. Tiny leaves have fall color.
Iris, Japanese (*Iris ensata*)	Bog or marginal Hardy	Ornamental	24 to 30 inches tall	Deep-purple summer blooms; narrow foliage.
Lotus, American (*Nelumbo lutea*)	Immersed Hardy	Specimen	2 to 3 feet tall	Blue-green foliage; yellow flowers bloom in summer. Native to U.S.
Lotus, Sacred (*Nelumbo nucifera*)	Immersed Hardy	Specimen; accent	1 to 7 feet tall	Needs warm weather to bloom. Seedpods, fragrant flowers. Grow in container to control vigorous spread.
Papyrus, Dwarf (*Cyperus isocladus*)	Marginal Tender	Novelty	To 30 inches tall	Spikes topped with radiating leaves. Use indoors in pot in winter.
Parrot's Feather (*Myriophyllum aquaticum*)	Submerged Tender	Oxygenating and ornamental; water cover	6-foot trailing stems	Sparse foliage on submerged stems; soft foliate tips show above water.

Water Garden Plants for Pennsylvania

Common Name (Botanical Name)	Type Hardiness	Function	Size	Comments
Pickerel Rush (*Pontederia cordata*)	Immersed Hardy	Ornamental	24 to 36 inches tall	Native plant. Blue flowers mid- to late summer. Restrict to pot; a pest in the South.
Snowflake (*Nymphoides indica*)	Floater Tender	Water cover	Indefinite spread	Heart-shaped leaves, green marked with reddish brown; small white or yellow summer flowers.
Taro (*Colocasia esculenta*)	Marginal Tender	Specimen	2 to 4 feet	Dramatic leaves in green, purple, or both; likes some shade.
Variegated Sweet Flag (*Acorus calamus* 'Variegata')	Marginal Hardy	Ornamental	Up to 5 feet	Aromatic, green strap leaves with cream or white stripes.
Water Hyacinth (*Eichhornia crassipes*)	Floater Tender	Cleans water	10 to 12 inches	Blue flowers in late summer. Unique roots. Multiplies rapidly.
Water Lettuce (*Pistia stratiotes*)	Floater Tender	Cleans water; novelty	To 8 inches tall; indefinite spread	Rosettes of wedge-shaped, ribbed leaves. Troubled by aphids.
Water Lily, Hardy (*Nymphea* sp.)	Immersed Hardy	Specimen; accent	Typically spreads 2 to 5 feet	Summer blooms of many colors close at night. Good cut flower.
Water Lily, Tropical (*Nymphea* sp.)	Immersed Tender	Specimen; accent	Spreads 2 to 5 feet or more	Usually fragrant. Some bloom at night. Interesting colored blooms held above foliage.
Yellow Flag (*Iris pseudacorus*)	Marginal Hardy	Ornamental	1 foot	Gray-green strap leaves. Stems bear 4 to 10 yellow flowers in summer.

Marginal = potted, feet in water at edge of pond
Bog = planted directly in wet soil (with or without pond)
Immersed = in pot with roots, crown, and stems completely in water, foliage above
Submerged = covered completely with water
Floater = bobs on surface
Transition = essentially a land plant but likes moist soil at pond edge

Planning

Even in winter, a water garden has a special appeal. The surface shimmers in the cold light of winter, threatening at times to ice over completely when temperatures drop very low. Beneath the surface rest dormant perennial aquatic plants, safely below the frost line, waiting for the lengthening hours of sunlight that will signal the return of spring. Like their counterparts in the soil, they are poised to send up tender new shoots in just a few weeks. Fish are dormant too, their cold-blooded systems responding to the low water temperature, their metabolisms virtually stalled.

If you have not gardened in water, this month is a good time to think about starting. If digging a pond seems too big an undertaking, plan to experiment with growing some aquatic plants in ornamental containers aboveground on a porch or patio this coming season. After testing the waters, so to speak, you may decide to create an entire garden in water.

Seasoned water gardeners can review last year's experiences in their journals this month. Consider how nice the pond might look on winter nights with landscape lighting.

Shopping List: a de-icer or heater for water garden ponds, *My Pennsylvania Garden,* a journal for recording this year's events in the water garden

Planting

This is a good time to divide or take cuttings from tender aquatic plants that are overwintering indoors under lights as houseplants.

- Cut sections of stem from plants such **Parrot's Feather, Water Mint,** or **Snowflake** that are in pots in water or in an aquarium. Put them in water to root, then *pot* them in soil, and *immerse* the pots in water.

  OR

- Slip **Taro** (or other plants that have developed rooted runners) from its pot, and separate the tiny rooted offshoots from the main plant. Take care to preserve as much root as possible. Plant the offshoots in small pots, and immerse them in water again.

Care for Your Water Garden

Check those tender water garden plants that are stored indoors in a cool, dark space. Make sure the potted ones are still wet and that the wrappings of tubers and rhizomes of **Water Lilies** are still damp. If they have dried out, *remoisten* them, then slip them into a plastic bag. Leave it open at one end, or puncture some holes in it to allow air circulation.

Pruning

To provide winter interest, the attractive leaves or stems of grasses, **Cattails,** and other hardy perennials planted near the edge of the water garden can be left unpruned. If snow or ice makes them flop into the water, however, cut them back.

Problem Solving

Frozen pond surfaces cut off gas exchange between the air and water, threatening fish and plants at the bottom of the pond. Install a de-icer device, or melt a portion of the ice by gradually pouring boiling water over it. Keep a bubbler or waterfall running. Never chop a hole in the ice. The concussion will hurt fish.

Electricity for pond lighting or pump may fail because of damage to the wiring. *Check* for signs of rodent gnawing or loose connections.

Planning

Aquatic nursery catalogs are wonderful sources of information about aquatic plants and how to grow them. They offer color photographs and descriptions of each species. The best catalogs also offer detailed instructions for creating a water garden—digging a pond or setting up ornamental containers such as half-barrels. Experienced water gardeners will want to spend time looking at this year's crop of catalogs because so many new plants are available. Dwarf versions of traditional favorites make water gardening in containers even easier and more fun.

It is not too soon to plan an inground water garden or to think about purchasing a new container for aboveground water gardening. Spring is just around the corner.

Shopping List: pots and heavy soil for potting plant divisions, fertilizer tabs, plants from mail-order aquatic plant nurseries

Planting

Check stored, tender aquatic plants to be sure their soil or wrappings are still moist and that the temperature in their storage space is between 40 and 50 degrees F. They must not freeze.

By the end of the month, tender plants that have overwintered in a greenhouse or as houseplants—their pots in water and under lights—may start to send up new shoots. If they begin to crowd their pots, *transplant* them into larger containers. If a plant is already large, divide the plant and repot the divisions. While large immersed plants are nice, remember that they are heavier to raise and lower into the water; and **Papyrus, Taro, Lotus,** and others that are allowed to grow too large may be out of scale in a typical backyard pond. Either *divide* them, or put them in an ornamental jar or tub of their own for display aboveground.

Care for Your Water Garden

Brush any accumulated snow from the surface of the water garden pond. It blocks sunlight from penetrating the water.

Birds and other wildlife need a source of fresh water, and water gardens are a perfect source. Prevent the pond surface from freezing over entirely by:

- installing a de-icer or heater designed for use in water garden ponds.

- running the pump to power a bubbler or waterfall to maintain water movement.

- floating table tennis balls or other inflated objects on the water surface.

- gradually melting one area by pouring boiling water over it each day.

If any debris from trees has fallen onto the pond surface, *clean* it up so it does not sink to the bottom and foul the water later. Leaving the netting from last fall across the pond will prevent wind-blown debris from falling in the water.

Water plants that are growing indoors under lights for the winter; they will need just a bit of fertilizer to keep their foliage healthy. If you included some granular, slow-acting product or fertilizer tabs in the soil when you last potted them, that should be sufficient. If you did not, *sprinkle* just a trace of water-soluble fertilizer into their water.

Pruning

As snow and frost begin to recede toward the end of the month, *tidy up* the planted areas around the edge of the water garden pond or containers. If you have not already clipped off dead stems from marginal plants and cut back nearby ornamental grasses,

Growing Smarter

A healthy, attractive water garden is a diverse ecological niche where various kinds of water plants function in concert with wildlife to maintain a desirable growing environment. The more diverse the plants, the better the balance between beneficial and pest insects, and the better the water quality for plants and the fish, snails, frogs, snakes, and other creatures that require an aquatic environment. Each plant contributes toward a balanced, self-sustaining system.

Some plants reduce algae in the water, others attract beneficial insects, others provide shelter for fish. All this, and they look attractive, too! When planning a water garden, plan to have many types of plants. Just as when you garden in soil, you will need tall ones at the back or edge of the pond, others to be specimens or accents, and others to act as fillers and ground (water) covers. You will need the following kinds of plants:

Submerged plants are barely visible under the water. They do the behind-the-scenes work of generating and maintaining oxygen in the water. (Ex: **Anacharis, Cabomba**)

Floating plants bob, untethered, on the water surface. As carefree as they look, they are also at work, shading and filtering the water to discourage bright-green algae. (Ex: **Water Hyacinth, Azolla, Duckweed, Snowflake, Water Clover**)

Immersed plants have their roots, crowns, and part of their stems in water. Their main job is to look (and smell) gorgeous to attract insects. (Ex: **Lotus, Water Lilies**)

Marginal plants prefer their roots and crowns just at the water surface. They hold the soil in natural ponds, shelter wildlife, and provide a transition from water to soil. (Ex: **Canna, Papyrus, Pickerel Weed**)

Bog plants need soggy mud around their roots to thrive. They are not actually in the water—in fact, they may be in a separate boggy place of their own. They attract insects and wildlife, and hold the soil. (Ex: **Iris, Taro, Lobelia, grasses, Marsh Marigold, Japanese Primrose, sedges, Pitcher Plant, ferns**)

do that soon. Minor bulbs such as **Crocus** and **Snowdrop** will be appearing soon nearby.

Problem Solving

Pest insects may attack tender water plants overwintering indoors under lights. Like other houseplants, they are vulnerable to problems with scale or aphids because they are stressed by the less-than-ideal conditions indoors. Wash plant stems and foliage as often as it takes to keep the pests at bay. *Avoid* overfertilizing.

Children playing in the snow may fail to detect the water garden pond if it is semi-frozen and/or covered with snow. To prevent accidents, put up a low fence, or *ring* the pond with flower pots or something similar to indicate the area is out of bounds.

Planning

Anytime after the ground thaws is a good time to dig a pond for an inground water garden. Growing aquatic plants aboveground in large ornamental containers is a way to garden in water in a small yard, balcony, or patio near the house. It is also a good way to expand the water garden without having to dig another pond. Aboveground water gardens are easier to work with, especially for gardeners with bad backs.

Shopping List: ornamental containers for **aboveground water gardening,** water-conditioning crystals or "tonic" for the water and the fish; **for a new inground pond,** flexible or preformed liner, pump, edging material

Planting

Soon it will be time to pot up plants that have recently arrived mail-order or that have been stored since last fall and need dividing. In cultivated water gardens, aquatic plants are planted in soil in plastic pans, baskets, or nursery pots. Even if the water garden pond has a natural soil bottom, gardening with potted plants is easier.

- They are not able to spread beyond their designated spot.

- They are easier to move and remove from the garden for maintenance.

- Their height can be adjusted to assure correct water depth over their roots.

- They facilitate cleaning the water garden pond.

Care for Your Water Garden

Examine and repair, if necessary, the edges of the water garden pond if the winter freeze thaw cycles have disturbed the soil there.

To dig a new water garden pond:

1 Clear the area of plants, rocks, and debris. *Check* to be sure there are no utility wires or pipes underground in the area. The ground must be level. **For a flexible liner:** outline the pond's dimensions with a hose, rope, or line to guide the digging. **For a preformed liner:** position the liner in the desired spot, then trace its outline on the soil to guide the digging.

2 *Dig* from the edges toward the center. Excavated soil goes into a cart to be deposited at a pre-

determined spot. Dig the sides fairly straight (unless the soil is silty or sandy) to a depth of at least 2 feet if you plan to have fish. Preformed liners need holes that are 2 inches deeper and 3 or 4 inches wider around the sides than the form measures. *Preformed ponds are usually not deep enough to allow overwintering fish in Pennsylvania.*

3 Create a shelf for marginal plants along one side (usually the back, because plants may be tall). Make it about 12 inches deep and 15 or 20 inches wide, then dig down to the main depth. **Preformed liners** will have a built-in shelf.

4 *Line* the bottom of the hole with 2 inches of damp sand, old carpet, or carpet padding to protect flexible or preformed liners from punctures by sharp stones that may gravitate toward the soil surface under them. Make sure the **preformed liner** is level in the soil, its rim just above soil level.

Fill the preformed pond with water once the liner is settled in the soil.

5 Spread the **flexible liner** on the ground to soften in the sun to make it easier to work with. Then, EITHER

(a) Center it over the excavated hole, anchoring its corners temporarily with rocks or vigilant friends. Run the hose onto its center, and allow the gradual weight of the water to carry the liner down into the hole, while you monitor and release the corners. As the pond fills, the weight of the water coaxes the liner to conform to its shape.

OR

(b) Center the liner over the hole to loosely droop into the space. Step into the hole, and fit the liner to its shelf and sides, pleating excess material where they curve.

6 *Trim* the edges of the liner, but leave a generous 4 feet to allow for laying it under the first row of edging stones or whatever, then folding it over them and laying a second course of edging. It must bear your weight when you haul heavy pots out of the water.

Growing Smarter

DETERMINING POND LINER SIZE:

1 Measure the width and length of your pond, and draw a sketch to scale of its general outline with those two dimensions. Then draw a rectangle that encloses the pond outline.

2 Determine the length and width measurements of that rectangle.

3 Determine the depth of the pond at its deepest point

4 Calculate liner length as: Pond Length + twice its depth + 2 feet for edging.

5 Calculate liner width as: Pond width + twice its depth + 2 feet for edging.

OR

Take the pond measurements to the garden center, and ask someone on staff to figure it out.

Pruning

Cut back ornamental grasses at the water garden's edge to make way for their new sprouts. *Dig up and divide* overlarge clumps. *Prune* other perennials and shrubs which may have winter injury to twigs.

Problem Solving

Water quality. When a pond is new, the water will look dirty and clouded for several weeks while it achieves biological balance. *Resist* the temptation to drain and refill the pond. Time will solve the problem.

Algae of various kinds is always present in water gardens. Early in the season, the stringy bright-green type may appear because the sun has unrestricted access to nutrients in the water. Murky "blooms" will clear up as a biological balance is achieved over time. Meanwhile, *do not feed* fish until the water is warmer, and pull out accessible strands of stringy algae with a stick or net.

Predator birds may investigate the new pond. Great blue herons or others may go after the fish in new or established ponds that have little or no plant foliage to shelter them. Keep last fall's leaf netting over the pond, or set up a matrix of unobtrusive fishing line over the water to foil the birds until plant foliage covers the water surface.

Planning

Maintenance of a water garden is similar to maintenance of a terrestrial garden. The goal is to provide plants with an environment that keeps them happy and to avoid disease and insect problems.

When properly in balance, the pond life does most of the work to maintain water quality. Fish eat mosquito larvae, and oxygenating plants offer food, shelter, and oxygen for fish as well as aid gas exchange for plant roots. Snails and other scavengers eat algae and debris from the bottom of the pond.

Of course a water garden is not a totally natural environment. A certain amount of maintenance is necessary to keep everything balanced, particularly important if you have a few ornamental fish. Storms, floods, spills, or other environmental events may foul the water. Wildlife predators may upset containers, eat fish, or disturb the edge. The pond will need cleaning periodically because organic debris that has accumulated at the bottom will become anaerobic and deplete the oxygen in the water. Cleaning is usually done in the fall (see October), but it can be done in spring if necessary.

Water gardens are a *potential danger*: While they are a marvelous Nature lesson for kids, children have a great affinity for water and are attracted by fountains or waterfalls and colorful fish. Consider some sort of decorative fencing around the water garden to alert visitors they are near the edge. Local municipal ordinances may require more substantial fencing.

Shopping List: pots for divided plants, water thermometer, new plants, decorative fencing, snails

Planting

Divide and repot hardy water garden plants that have overwintered at the bottom of the pond. Pot up plants ordered by mail. Wait another month before dividing and potting up stored tender plants.

Plant Water Lily rhizomes in heavy soil. The soil should be either clay or heavy garden soil or commercial aquatic planting medium to assure that particles do not float from the pot into the water. A mulch of rinsed gravel on top also helps.

1 *Use* a wide, relatively shallow container such as a rectangular, plastic dishpan that will comfortably accommodate the narrow, rooted rhizome set horizontally (like an **Iris**). The container should be 7 to 9 inches deep.

2 *Fill* the dishpan about 1/3 to 1/2 with damp soil. Insert fertilizer tablet(s) into the soil according to package directions.

3 *Orient* the rhizome at a 45 degrees angle, its crown where new leaves may be sprouting pointing upward. Spread its roots over the soil.

4 *Add* soil so there is at least an inch or two over the rhizome's cut end (if it has just been divided) and its roots. Allow its growing tip and crown to protrude from the soil, which should reach to within an inch or two of the container rim.

5 *Firm* the soil gently over the rhizome, and water it in. Then *immerse* the pot in the pond or container gradually so that air bubbles have a chance to escape. Be aware that it will be quite heavy until it is under water.

6 Set **Water Lily** pans on the bottom of the pond if it is no deeper than 18 inches. Set them on bricks, overturned pots, or other supports in deeper water.

Divide and repot marginal plants as they begin to show new growth. Divisions of **Iris, Papyrus, Pickerel Rush,** grasses, **Thalia,** and others should go into standard nursery pots in heavy soil at the same depth as they were in their previous pots. Remember to include a little granular, slow-acting fertilizer, but do not overdo, or you will be repotting again in the middle of the season. Set them on the shallow shelf at the edge of the water garden or on supports so they are at the proper depth.

Care for Your Water Garden

If you have not already removed the fall/winter netting over the water garden pond, do so. You will need access to the water to set newly potted plants in place and to check the fish. This is a good time to add some water-conditioning crystals to help the water quality and the fish.

As the water warms, the fish will become more active and will be interested in eating. In established water garden ponds there is vegetation for them to nibble on, so they do not need to be fed. A new pond will have very little plant life for a while, so they will appreciate some fish food from you. Once the season is underway, fish can fend for themselves. Feeding them every so often provides an opportunity to check their health. Watch for babies in established ponds, because some fish spawn in the fall.

Pruning

If submerged plants were not thinned and tamed last fall, haul out matted bunches from the pond, and throw them on the compost pile. Leave enough in the water to oxygenate it and shelter fish while other plants get established. **Anacharis, Cabomba,** and others will regenerate enthusiastically as soon as the water temperature rises.

Problem Solving

Water quality will be less than ideal as the water temperature rises and biological interactions adjust accordingly. In new ponds, the helpful, furry brown algae will develop to cover liner surfaces. It promotes desirable bacterial activity. The water is temporarily murky because of dirt from newly potted plants, pollen in the air from trees that are flowering, seeds from **Maple** trees, and other debris.

Overfeeding fish fouls the water. Do not offer more than they can eat in three minutes. A filter attached to a pump that circulates the water in the pond helps establish and maintain water clarity. A **submersed filter** lies at the bottom of the pond and needs weekly, then several-times-a-week, cleaning as summer

Growing Smarter

Potted water garden plants, like their terrestrial cousins, are happy in lots of types of pots as long as they have drainage holes and are roomy enough for growing root systems. Because plants are either partly or entirely in water, it helps if the pots are substantial—clay, high-grade plastic, or poly material. Round or rectangular plastic dishpans, plastic clothesbaskets, and broad but shallow standard pots are least likely to tip over. Set pots securely on cinder blocks or other supports that can maintain them at the correct depth. Line those that have lots of openings with landscape fabric or white polyspun garden fleece to prevent dirt from leaking out, while allowing water to flow in and out.

heat develops. A **biological filter** stands nearby outside the pond; it requires less-frequent cleaning.

Planning

A water garden pond cleaned or built last fall is ready to go as soon as new plants arrive from the store or those from last season are repotted. The nice thing about having them in pots is that they can be easily rearranged. Take advantage of the wide variety of foliage colors, textures, and shapes to coordinate a pleasing design. Locate the vertical plants to form a backdrop for the flowers of specimen **Water Lilies.**

Consult your notes or photos for reminders of how you placed the immersed and marginal plants last year. Do not crowd the plants. If you plan to have a fountain, do not put **Water Lilies** near it; the falling water will batter their foliage.

If you are interested in having a bog garden and do not have a naturally boggy spot in the yard, create one just beyond the edge of the water garden pond.

1 **Excavate** a shallow hole or trench in the soil about 2 feet deep and as wide as you want the bog to be. Slope the sides.

2 **Lay** a piece of flexible pond liner or heavy-duty plastic over the hole, conforming to the hole's bottom and reaching up its sides. **Anchor** its corners to keep it in place.

3 **Cover** the liner with soil to within a few inches of the level of the surrounding ground, gradually reducing its depth as it reaches and covers the liner edges.

4 **Soak** the soil with a hose if there is no rain, and let the moisture saturate the soil for a day or two. Then plant.

Shopping List: long-handled net, fish, fish food, water dechlorinator, more plants

Planting

It is time to plant the water garden.

1 Position the specimens (**Water Lilies**) in the water first, allowing generous space between them to allow for their foliage spread over the water surface. (Gently nudge away floating stems of submerged plants from last year as you sink the pots of **Water Lilies** and set them on

supports or the bottom of the pond.) Leave a place of honor for the **Lotus,** a focal point, if you intend to have one. Leave space for tender **Water Lilies** to go in when it is warm enough.

2 Set pots of potted, new submerged plants such as **Anacharis** on the bottom of the pond between the pots of **Water Lilies.**

3 Put floating plants such as **Water Clover** or **Snowflake** in next to serve as "ground cover" and to provide foliage color and texture contrast. **Water Hyacinths** will probably not be available for another month, unless you wintered some over from last season. Add them when you acquire them.

4 **Arrange** marginal plants in groups at their preferred depths in the shallow water on the pond shelf. Factor in their various heights and foliage shapes, colors, and textures (**Canna,**

Iris, **Taro**, grasses, **Cattails**, and others) as you place them.

5 Add fish to new water garden pond after the plants are set up and the chlorine in the water has dissipated. (It is not safe to put fish in most container water gardens.)

Care for Your Water Garden

Hardy Water Lily foliage will open and spread over the water surface. Adjust the position of the pots slightly to prevent crowding.

Check to see that pots have not shifted or fallen over in the water garden. Sometimes fish, a critter visitor, or water currents from a pump or waterfall disturb things.

If it has not rained, check to see if the bog plants in the soil at the edge of the garden have enough moisture. If they are in a garden area that depends on pond overflow, you may have to water it until the next rain. *Check* the marginal plants on the shelf in the water garden pond to be sure the water level is correct for them.

Growing Smarter

WATER LILIES:

- **Hardy/Perennial Water Lilies** are tougher, requiring less care.

Foliage: leaves from April to October, have smooth edges, some may have purple markings.

Flowers: appear earlier, more abundantly than **Tenders/Tropicals,** bloom June through early fall, bloom in sun–mid-morning to 5 p.m. Blossoms are white, and shades of pink, red, and yellow; last about 5 days; sit on the water surface; don't open on cloudy days; some are scented.

Site: can be immersed to 18 inches or more; needs still water.

- **Tender/Tropical Water Lilies** must be stored indoors over the winter.

Foliage: sharp serrations on leaf edges; variegated with purple.

Flowers: pinks, reds, white, blues, lilacs—intense flower color; flowers tend to be larger-sized (up to 12 inches diameter), bloom almost twice as often as Hardies; **day bloomers** 10 till 5; flowers last about three days; some are **night bloomers,** sunset to 9 a.m.; fragrance much sweeter, stronger than Hardies; rise above water on stems.

Site: needs water 68 degrees F or above, needs 10 to 12 inches of still water over soil surface in pot.

Problem Solving

Chemicals in treated municipal water will kill fish. If you use municipal water to fill the pond or to top it off when water levels drop, wait until the chlorine or chloramine dissipates (a day) before adding fish. Add drops of a de-chlorinating product as directed on its package label if fish are already resident in the water garden.

Cloudy water may persist for a few weeks because biological activity in the pond accelerates as the water warms up. *Wait it out.* Do not worry about the presence of brown, furry algae on pot and liner surfaces. That is a *good* sign.

Planning

This is the month that water gardens come into their own. Whether they are in an inground pond or aboveground ornamental containers, aquatic plants respond to the warm weather. Submerged plants and little floating plants may show tiny pale flowers in late spring.

Think about installing a pump and filter in the pond, if you have not already done so. While neither is necessary if you do not have fish, they are essential if you originally stocked the recommended 1 inch of goldfish per 5 gallons of water. Eventually, even these few little fish will grow and generate nutrient-dense waste that compromises water clarity.

For attachment to a **submersible filter,** choose a pump powerful enough to move up to $1/2$ the total volume of water in your pond each hour. If coupled with a **biological filter,** which is outside the pond, the pump needs to move from $1/6$ to $1/4$ the total volume of the pond per hour.

Besides powering the filter, a pump will power a fountain or waterfall and circulate the water throughout the garden to keep oxygen levels high. Like a fan does with air, the pump creates a more uniform temperature by blending cool deep water with warmer shallow water.

In half-barrels, kettles, and other large water garden containers, use a bubbler to circulate the water and make a soothing, soft trickling sound that attracts birds.

Plan to install an electrical outlet near the water garden. Because it is near water, be sure it meets code and has a ground fault interrupter.

Shopping List: fertilizer tabs, mosquito dunks, film for camera

Planting

It's time to pot up **Tender Water Lilies.** "Tropicals" need water to be over 70 degrees F before they really start to grow. (They go out into the pond about the same time that young **Tomato** plants go out into the vegetable garden.) Keep the tubers (that have arrived mail-order or that were stored dormant all winter in the garage or cellar) moist until potting time.

1 Select wide dishpan-type pots, about 5-gallon capacity, similar to those suitable for **Hardy Water Lilies.** *Drill* drainage holes if they do not have them. Fill each pot $1/3$ full with moist, heavy garden soil, and insert fertilizer tabs in the soil according to instructions on the label.

2 Add a bit more soil, then lay the horizontal tuber on its surface, its roots splayed out over the soil and its growing tip aimed upward. *Cover* it with soil up to its crown where some greenish buds might be visible at the growing tip. There is a pale line or ridge there. The soil should be an inch or two below the rim of the container after you press it gently over the tuber and water it so it settles.

3 Gravel mulch is optional. It helps prevent soil from fouling the water as you lower the plant into the water garden. But clay soil, gradual immersion, and tipping the pot at an angle to allow air bubbles to escape usually minimizes the problem anyway.

Care for Your Water Garden

Fertilize both types of **Water Lilies** with tabs once a month when the water temperature rises above 70 degrees F. Lean over the pond's edge, and poke them into the soil in each **Water Lily's** pot, then pinch soil back over the hole to assure the tab does not float out.

Remove, rinse, and replace the pad from a submersed filter every few days. As the weather gets warmer and the water gets warmer, you will have to do it more often.

Tall bog plants in soil on the edge of the water garden pond or tall marginal plants in the shallow water occasionally get floppy. *Stake* these plants as you would plants in a regular garden to improve their appearance and prevent them from fouling the water.

Pruning

Prune off injured or dying **Water Lily** foliage and spent blossoms. A pole pruner is useful for reaching and clipping leaves out in the center of the water garden pond. Do not let the prunings fall down in the water. Clip off dried or bent stems from marginal plants to keep them attractive.

Hardy Water Lily blooms are wonderful to enjoy indoors. Cut one, and float it in a crystal bowl of water on the dining room table.

Growing Smarter

LOTUS PLANTS:

- **Sacred (Asian) Lotus (*Nelumbo nucifera*)**

  Not reliably hardy in Pennsylvania, needs deep water, heights vary from 2 to 7 feet out of the water, needs large pond for scale and room. Large leaves 2 feet across, stems up to 6 feet tall. Aerial leaves unfurl after initial floating ones. Large blooms in white, pink, yellow, rose; heady fragrance; blooms six to eight weeks in midsummer. Funnel-shaped seedpods. Dwarf type is **'Momo Botan'**; Miniature is **'Mrs. Perry D. Slocum'**.

- **American (Native) Lotus/Water Chinquapin (*Nelumbo lutea*)**

  Hardy in Pennsylvania. Plants usually 5 feet tall. 2-foot-wide bowl-shaped leaves on 2-foot-tall stems above water. Large creamy-yellow flowers; single, 5 to 7 inches across. Round seeds rather than oval Asian ones.

Problem Solving

Algae bloom should be receding now as the water settles after the plants are positioned. Their foliage will shade the water surface by the end of the month, inhibiting algae growth. In new ponds, the new submerged plants are slower to take over their sheltering and oxygenating duties.

Predator birds will find it more difficult to go after fish which now have some hiding places. If foliage is slow to cover the water garden pond, tip a plastic milk crate upside down on the bottom to shelter fish. They can swim through the open sides and hide. Set pots of water plants on the crate.

Uprooted plants may be caused by visiting ducks, geese, or turtles, and sometimes racoons are responsible. Large koi fish are capable of disturbing plants and causing them to come out of their pots. *Cover* plants with netting until they are well established.

Planning

For an inspiration in water gardening, visit the pools of exotic **Tropical Water Lilies** *at Longwood Gardens in Kennett Square, Pennsylvania.* Many botanic gardens also have display water gardens that are great sources of information on various plants and designs.

As the summer heat closes in, the water garden becomes an oasis for your family and the resident wildlife in the yard. The sound of fresh water attracts birds and insects as well as local pets, squirrels, and other visitors. The new ecological niche you have created now teems with less-visible residents as well—dragonflies, toads, frogs, tadpoles, spiders, and possibly a snake. The aquatic plants provide greater plant diversity in the yard. They host a greater diversity of beneficial creatures, which makes a healthier environment for all.

Consider installing night lights and in-pond lights which can greatly extend and enhance your enjoyment of your water garden.

Take some photographs of the water garden at its peak to savor this winter. The photos will also be useful next spring.

Shopping List: statuary for the water garden area, a fountain, more plants

Planting

Add plants to the water garden pond or ornamental containers anytime during the season. If over 60 percent of the pond's water surface is not yet covered by foliage, add more—this will prevent algae problems. Conversely, if the garden is overcrowded now that the plants are growing vigorously, **remove** some of them, and put them in barrels or pots filled with water.

The small delicate foliage of many floating plants provides nice texture, size, and color contrast to the large, broad leaves of **Water Lilies** and **Lotus.** The foliage provides shade and takes up nutrients to discourage algae. Some floaters are hardy and can stay in the pond over the winter; they are slower to bulk up. The tender types such as **Water Hyacinths** behave like annuals in a regular garden. They take off with the advent of warm weather and go strong all season.

Lotus will start blooming three to four weeks after air temperatures are consistently above 80 degrees F, usually this month in Pennsylvania. They may not bloom their first season after transplanting, but their foliage is great.

Care for Your Water Garden

If plants are growing too fast or stems are weak and floppy, *cut back* on fertilization. Plants receive some nutrients from the water, especially if you have fish in the water garden pond.

Do not let the water level in the pond or container drop more than an inch or two. The liner should not be exposed to sunshine. If it does not rain and water is evaporating, top-off the garden with a hose. (Be sure to add de-chlorinating drops if you have fish.) *Check* the bog garden to be sure the soil is wet just below the surface. Wet it down with the hose if there is any doubt.

The water will be clear now, indicating that all elements are in balance. There are several things you can do if stringy green (filamentous) algae appears, or the water begins to look like pea soup because it is too rich with nutrients:

1 *Limit* food for fish.

2 *Reduce* the number of fish in the pond.

3 *Stop* fertilizing plants.

4 *Add* more submerged plants.

5 *Shade* more of the water surface from the sun.

Pruning

Hardy Water Lily blossoms will last five days or so, then begin to deteriorate. Clip them off before they get soggy and disintegrate in the water; this will keep the water cleaner and encourage new blossoms.

Prune off excess or unsightly foliage of plants both in and around the water garden.

Thin **Parrot's Feather** and other submerged plants that become really thick. Check for snails and baby fish before tossing prunings on the compost pile.

Problem Solving

Invasive plants are a problem in water gardens and bogs, just as in regular garden beds. Certain marginal and bog plants such as **Horsetails** and **Lotus** send out root runners and rapidly overstep their bounds. Make sure they are in sturdy pots to control their spread. **Duckweed,** a floater, is less easy to restrict. Scoop it out in sections of the water garden as it threatens to cover the water surface completely. **Water Hyacinths** will choke any open water if they are not thinned periodically.

Growing Smarter

AMAZING WATER HYACINTHS:

Research continues to reveal the virtues of plants—even those that sometimes act as pests. Although **Water Hyacinths** are a problem in the South, where they survive winters to choke lakes and streams, they are redeeming themselves in freshwater research laboratories. So effective are their roots at filtering water that they have been demonstrated to convert black (not just gray) water into potable water. This has enormous implications for the future, when fresh water will become scarcer.

In your own water garden, a single **Water Hyacinth** plant does the job of about six bunches of submerged plants. Its bizarre feathery roots dangle underwater as deep as 12 to 14 inches, drawing nutrients and impurities out of the water as they flow by the tiny root filaments. On the surface of the water, these plants bob along with the current, their rich, glossy green foliage supported by bulbous stems filled with air. They rapidly develop offshoots at the ends of horizontal stems. After midsummer they begin to produce showy, upright, pale lilac-blue flowers that open with light and close end of day. They bloom best when plants are crowded in water that contains lots of nutrients.

Mosquitoes can be a problem in water gardens if there is neither moving water nor fish. To avoid breeding them, kill larvae with *Bt* (*Bacillus thuringiensis*) in the form of a floating donut called Mosquito Dunks™. Follow package directions for use and storage.

Aphids and other pest insects might appear when plants are stressed by heat and crowding. Dip mildly affected leaves into the water, or rinse them with a hose to wash off the pests. (Beware of municipal water if you have fish in the water garden.) *Clip off* leaves that are badly marred.

Planning

If you plan to have your water garden pond cleaned by landscape contractors or pond specialists this fall, make a date before the month is over. October is a good time to schedule this project. Most plants are ready for dormancy, and tender plants need to be taken indoors for winter storage. The service should include the installation of netting to prevent falling leaves from fouling the fresh water. Have them service your pump and check the tubing.

Make sure your water garden pond is filled to the maximum with water before you go away on vacation. There will be some evaporation in the heat, and rain is likely to be scarce this month. If there are small children in your neighborhood, consider covering the pond with temporary netting or screening, or surround it with fencing while you are gone to prevent a possible accident. The plants and fish should be able to take care of themselves for several weeks.

Shopping List: leaf netting, another ornamental container for aboveground water gardening

Planting

It is okay to *divide and repot* pot-bound plants in midseason. Some plants may have outgrown their containers to the point where their flowering and health is compromised. Sometimes bulging tubers and restricted matted roots actually split thin plastic nursery liner-type pots.

1 *Remove* the plant from its pot, and lay it on a rock or other hard surface.

2 *Use* a sharp knife or a spade to slice through the crown and stems to make rooted halves or quarters, depending on its size.

3 *Trim* excessively long roots from each chunk, and *plant* each one in heavy garden soil in its own pot.

4 *Return* one newly potted division to the water garden. The other(s) can go into an aboveground auxiliary water garden or become a gift for a friend.

Care for Your Water Garden

Continue to check water levels in the bog areas as well as in the water garden pond itself. A certain amount of evaporation takes place from fountains and waterfalls, so check often to be sure that the liner around the edge of the pond is not exposed to the sunlight any longer than can be helped. If you have fish, remember to add de-chlorinating drops when you add municipal water from the hose. Protect the fish by adding the water gradually if the temperature differential is great (if you are adding colder water from a well, for example).

This is the last month to *fertilize* **Water Lilies.** As the number of daylight hours begins to shrink noticeably, the plants will reduce flowering somewhat, and there are probably enough nutrients in the water to keep them going. If the water garden has become overcrowded with **Water Lily** foliage and floating plants, remove a pot or two of plants and set them in a separate ornamental container of water for the rest of the season.

Pull out some of the trailing stems of submerged plants and some of the floaters to open up space in the overgrown garden. Submerged oxygenating plants should take up only about $1/3$ the total volume of water in the pond.

Pruning

If **Hardy Water Lily** blossoms and foliage are rising out of the water, they are too crowded. If there is no room to correct the problem by repositioning their pots, prune off some foliage to thin it and prevent disease.

Prune off yellowed, dried, or torn foliage promptly from bog and marginal plants, too, to improve their appearance and maintain good air circulation. Do not let stems flop into the water garden.

Do not deadhead Lotus pods, because they are part of the ornamental appeal of this plant. When they are dried and the plant goes dormant, cut the stems and use the pods for floral crafts and flower arrangements.

Problem Solving

Pots of plants tipped over can be caused by several things. Often excessive growth of plant roots squeezes through the drainage holes and develops matted clumps. They can disturb the balance of pots positioned on overturned pots or bricks and cause them to fall over. Trim back roots, or *repot* into a larger pot. Visiting critters who come to

Growing Smarter

In both land and water gardening, certain plants prove to be poor citizens. While they may be attractive, they are too undisciplined to fit in the garden design, and their rampant growth requires much too much maintenance. Even though they are in pots in or at the edge of a water garden, these plants grow so fast that they are constantly needing dividing or larger pots. If you grow these *aquatica non grata,* give them a container of their own aboveground. When discarding divisions or prunings from these plants, take care not to let them escape into the wild in local streams or lakes. Throw them into the trash rather than onto a compost pile. Some invasive water plants:

- **Bamboo** ("running" varieties)
- **Duckweed (*Lemna minor*)**
- **Horsetail (*Equisetum hymale*)**
- **Purple Loosestrife (*Lythrum salicaria*)**
- Certain varieties of **Milfoil**

drink at the water garden pond will occasionally knock pots from their perches on the pond shelf or edge.

Weeds are a problem both in pots of marginal plants in the water and in the boggy soil areas. Pull them before they set and sow their seeds.

Raccoons are a problem in water gardens in some areas. Signs of their visits are disturbed edges of ponds. There may be loosened stones and/or a wet, slippery slope in the soil from the edge into the water in natural ponds where they access the water.

Woodchucks may feed on bulbs and tubers of plants such as **Iris** and **Thalia** at the edge of water garden ponds. The plants will suddenly disappear. A single woodchuck can do a tremendous amount of damage there, just as in vegetable gardens. Serious fencing will be necessary to discourage this critter.

Planning

Although the weather may still be warm, the daylight hours are shrinking, and water plants react to this just as all the other plants in the yard do. Now is a good time to photograph this year's pond at its peak, because foliage will begin to brown soon, and flowering will slow down. Make some notes in your garden notebook or journal about the season. Which plants did best? What were the problems, disappointments? Note major weather events.

It is time to confront the big decision—whether to try to overwinter the **Tropical Water Lilies** and other tender water plants, or to treat them as annuals and allow them to die when frost arrives. You can always buy new ones next year. Because they are literally tropical, they cannot survive the winter cold outdoors, even in the deepest part of the pond. They will require storage space such as a cellar or garage that is unheated but in no danger of freezing. Any water plants (hardy or tender) growing in large, decorative containers in aboveground water gardens will eventually need to be stored as well.

Shopping List: water thermometer, pond de-icer or heater

Planting

Dividing and repotting overgrown water garden plants is normally done in the spring when they are about to emerge from dormancy—but it may be more convenient to do it in the fall after they enter dormancy, prior to storing them for the winter. If this is not a year for a major pond-cleaning project, there may be time to divide some and give them away to save storage space. Follow the directions for repotting water plants (see April). *Do not fertilize* them, because they will not be growing for several months. Add fertilizer tabs next spring when you get them out of storage.

Fall presents an opportunity to plant up the outside edge of the water garden with ground cover plants and hardy bulbs that will bloom attractively early in the spring. Most hardy bulbs like good drainage, so do not try to plant **Narcissus** and **Tulips** if the area around the pond's edge is a bog.

Delay this planting if pond cleaning is on the agenda. The sides of the pond may be trampled a bit. Good additions to a damp area at pond's edge are:

- **Japanese Primrose** (*Primula japonica*)
- **Marsh Marigold** (*Caltha* sp.)
- **Ornamental Skunk Cabbage** (*Lysichiton* sp.)
- Various sedges and rushes
- Certain ferns

Care for Your Water Garden

Allow plants to begin to die back. The perennials will behave just like those in your soil garden. Marginals on the pond shelf and bog plants along the edge will start to form seedpods, and their stems will dry and bleach to straw color. Some, especially any ornamental grasses, may be decorative enough to allow them to remain over the next several months. Let them soften the edge of the winter pond. Eventually they will need cutting back.

Do not fertilize any water garden plants until next spring.

Feed the fish. While the weather is still mild, they feed voraciously, loading up on food to help them last over the winter. Feed them a bit more often, a bit more at each feeding. Do not feed more than they can collectively devour within five minutes. More than that will just be wasted and will dissolve and foul the water.

If frost is due in your region of Pennsylvania before the month ends, begin to dismantle ornamental containers that hold water plants. Lift the plants and cut them back for storage at the bottom of a water garden pond (if you have one) or in the unheated area where you will store tender water plants. Drain the water from the large containers, and bring indoors those that may crack in the cold.

Pruning

In expectation of first frost and plant dormancy, *clip off* dead and dying stems from marginal and bog plants to prevent their flopping into the water. Treat them as you would any perennial, and cut them all the way back after frost.

In anticipation of leaf fall from deciduous trees, *cover* the water garden pond with leaf netting. If this is the year for a major cleaning, there is no need to set up netting until that job is done.

Growing Smarter

Flexible pond liners occasionally develop leaks. A drop in the water level for no reason is usually a clue, although the water loss might be caused by other things. First rule out other causes of the water loss. **Checklist:**

____1. Has a fountain device tipped against the edge of the pond so it is spraying the water outside of the pond?

____2. When the pump is disconnected from the fountain or waterfall, does the water level stop dropping? The leak must be in the re-circulating system somewhere.

____3. Are the edges of the liner properly secured under the edging?

____4. Has some of the edging material come loose so there is a low spot?

____5. Are all tube connections to devices outside of the pond, such as a waterfall or biofilter, tight?

If the water level has fallen and remained at a certain point even after a rain, this suggests the leak is in the liner. There are kits to patch liners.

Problem Solving

Insect and disease problems can be reduced next year by cutting back plants as they go dormant. This will deny pest eggs and disease spores a place to overwinter.

Predator birds will be able to get at the fish when plant foliage no longer covers the water surface to provide shelter. Set up leaf netting early, or string monofilament fishing line over the pond surface to foil blue heron and other opportunistic passersby.

Planning

This is water garden pond–cleaning month in most regions of Pennsylvania. Do this project either before or during leaf fall time, but schedule it as plants are going dormant and can be cut back. Whether you are doing it yourself or hiring someone to do it, clean the pond at least every year or two before the ground freezes. In alternate years, it is usually sufficient to gently scoop out accumulated organic gunk from the bottom of the pond with a net.

Fall is also a good time to make improvements in the water garden:

- Install a waterfall to help aerate the water year 'round.

- Add a pump or a filter.

- Add low-voltage lighting around the pond to reflect softly off the water surface.

Bring any statuary and containers indoors if they are likely to crack in the winter weather.

Empty aboveground water gardens in jars and barrels, and store the plants, because they will freeze aboveground.

Shopping List: landscape lighting kit, hardy bulbs, mulch

Planting

Pull any remaining plants out of the water garden pond, if they have not already been removed because of cleaning. Store tender ones in their pots of wet soil in plastic bags with air holes punched in them. Tubers of **Lotus** or **Water Lily** can be stored wrapped in damp newspaper in the plastic bags. Make sure they are in a place that does not freeze during the winter.

Care for Your Water Garden

Stop feeding fish completely when they fail to eat what you dispense within two or three minutes. Because they are cold-blooded, their metabolism slows as the water temperature drops. Do not feed them even if it warms up during some days, lest the food becomes stuck in their systems when returning cold slows them down again.

Water garden ponds that have pre-formed or flexible liners rather than natural soil bottoms need cleaning so the decaying organic matter that accumulates at the bottom does not suck up all the oxygen in the water. This will degrade the water quality and kill the fish. It is not difficult to clean a pond, but it does take time.

1 *Drain* most of the water by disconnecting the tube that pumps water to the waterfall or fountain and directing it to pump water out of the pond instead.

(This nutrient-rich water is great for the regular garden.) Fill two or three pails for use during the cleaning. When the water level drops to a foot or so in the deepest part of the pond, turn off the pump temporarily.

2 *Remove* all potted marginal plants from the shelf. Inspect them to be sure that tiny fish, snails, or other creatures are not caught in them. Set them aside in an out-of-the-way place.

3 *Net* the fish, and temporarily put them in one of the pails filled with pond water. *Pull up* the trailing stems of submerged plants and floating plants, and save cuttings from them in other pails.

4 *Lift* the pots of **Hardy Water Lilies,** and set them aside in the shade. If it is a sunny, warm day, cover them with wet newspaper.

5 *Restart* the pump, and drain the pond completely so that the layer of mud (it may be pretty smelly if you have delayed this job too long) is exposed. With a plastic shovel, net, or other tool with rounded edges (to

prevent puncturing the liner), scrape up the mud, and put it in a garden cart or pail. *Check* for wiggling creatures that may have burrowed into it, and remove them to a safe temporary place.

6 *Rinse* the sides of the pond with the hose, gently dislodging any dirt with a soft broom. It is not necessary to get every bit of matter from the sides and bottom. Pump the rinse water from the bottom where it collects.

7 Stop and *inspect* the liner for tears or cracks, and *repair* it if necessary. Then return to the bottom of the pond a small amount of the mud you removed to provide the microbial life necessary to promote healthy water.

8 *Prune back* the stems and foliage of **Hardy Water Lilies** and other plants that will be overwintering deep in the water, and set their pots on the bottom at the pond's deepest point.

9 Begin to *refill* the pond with fresh water from the hose. Add de-chlorinating and water- and fish-conditioning treatment crystals to the water as it fills.

Growing Smarter

There are water plants, and there are plants that will grow in water. Those in the first group, true aquatic plants, require a water environment to grow and thrive. Those in the second group are plants typically grown in soil—but do not mind some water over their feet and ankles. Among these are **Hostas** such as **'Gold Standard'** and **'Frances Williams',** certain ornamental grasses, **Canna, Creeping Jenny (***Lysimachia nummularia***'Aurea'), Chameleon Plant,** sedges, and some **Hibiscus.**

10 *Return* the fish to the pond if the temperature of the water in the fish-holding pail is not much different from that of the new water in the pond. If the new water is very cold, allow it to stand for a while to avoid shocking the fish.

11 When the pond is full, *lay* narrow-gauge netting over it. It will prevent falling leaves and debris from trees from fouling the clean water, yet it will let light through.

Pruning

As they go dormant, *cut back* withered plants in the boggy garden area. Leave ornamental grasses to enhance the winter landscape.

Problem Solving

Frogs and toads need to burrow in the mud for the winter. In ponds with preformed or flexible liners, they do it in the soil near the edge. When fastening the leaf netting over the water, leave a can that is open at both ends or a piece of pipe under one edge to allow frogs and toads to move from the soil to the water and back. Also leave a place for birds and other wildlife to access the water to drink when unfrozen fresh water is at a premium during the winter.

Rodents may try to nest in mulch over bog plants and other beds near the water garden pond, and they may attempt to chew on the wiring for the pump and landscape lighting. *Delay* spreading a fresh layer of mulch on soil beds until after the ground freezes.

Planning

If your water garden pond is over 2 feet deep, it is possible to overwinter the fish as well as the hardy plants in it in most areas of Pennsylvania. (The typical pre-formed, molded water garden ponds are not deep enough to assure that some of the water will be below the frost line.) As long as it is not frozen solid, the water can supply necessary oxygen for the fish. Some gardeners install a water heater or de-icer device to prevent the water surface from freezing at all. Others keep their pump running to keep the water moving. A waterfall may freeze over periodically, but underneath the ice crust the water may keep moving and aerating the pond.

Think about expanding your water garden next year with the installation of a preformed pool or setting up several decorative jars or half-barrels at different sites on the property.

Shopping List: ornamental jars or pans for growing and displaying water plants indoors

Planting

An alternative to overwintering **Tender Water Lilies** in their dormant state in a cool place is to bring them into the warm house and grow them as houseplants. *Use dwarf or miniature* Water Lily *varieties for this.*

Lift them from the outdoor water garden before they go completely dormant. *Cut back* dead and limp foliage, and trim excessive matting roots. *Divide* overgrown tubers by cutting them into pieces with growing points on each. *Repot* one piece of tuber (or more) in soil in a pot. Set the pot in an attractive cache pot that holds water and place it in a sunny window. Store as dormant or *discard* the rest of the tuber pieces.

Care for Your Water Garden

As hard frost threatens this month, be sure all tender water plants are properly stored in an unheated area that will not freeze. An old refrigerator in the basement set at 45 degrees F or a cool cellar is suitable. Last call for winterizing water gardens:

- After removing all plants, *drain,* clean, and cover shallow preformed ponds so they will not collect debris and water over the winter.

- *Cut back* and set hardy plants at the deepest part of a deep pond with a flexible liner. The filter will not be necessary during the winter. *Optional:* Install a heater or de-icer.

- *Cover* the pond with netting to keep the water clean and protect the fish from predators.

- *Remove* and store plants, then drain, rinse out, and overturn wooden half-barrels and other ornamental containers that will winter outdoors.

- *Bring* terracotta, plastic, and ceramic jars indoors to prevent them from cracking in the cold.

- *Spread* a 3- to 4-inch layer of organic material over bog and soil beds as a winter mulch to buffer extreme fluctuations in soil temperature.

Problem Solving

Blowing leaves and falling twigs from trees are a problem all winter. Stretch netting with a UV inhibitor across the pond, and fasten it securely to keep the water from being fouled. It will allow light into the pond for the fish.

Drying out of stored dormant water plants is sometimes a problem if there is low humidity where they are stored. Make sure those in pots of wet soil are covered with plastic with air holes. Wrap divisions or cuttings from tubers and roots in layers of wet newspaper in a similar plastic bag.

Planning

It's never too soon to start your list of New Year's resolutions. Put "keep a garden journal" at the top, and resolve to try at least one new kind of water plant next year. Year's end is the perfect time to reflect on the past season of water gardening:

- Take a few minutes to catch up on this year's journal or notebook, and record the triumphs and the defeats in the water garden over the last twelve months.

- Try to find all the labels from the plants you acquired this past season, and store them in an envelope in the back of the journal.

- Take some photographs before and after the first snow to remind you of how the water garden looks off-season.

Bask in the glow of the holiday lights shimmering on the water garden surface this month.

Shopping List/Christmas List: a book on aquatic plants, membership in a water garden society, subscription to a water gardening magazine, an aquarium set up for overwintering tender aquatic plants

Care for Your Water Garden

If it has been a dry fall and early winter, it may be necessary to raise the water level of the water garden pond. Maximum depth protects the liner and the plants at the bottom. Add de-chlorinating drops if there are fish in the pond.

Pruning

Pots of hardy plants should be at least 2 feet deep in the water at the bottom of the pond.

No plant stems or foliage of overwintering hardy water plants should protrude above the water surface. If some have started to send up shoots because of a mild fall, cut them back to the soil level in their pots.

Problem Solving

Unsatisfactory plants are invasive and/or obviously out of scale with the garden area, surrounding plants, or your yard. This is often true of varieties of **Lotus, Cattails,** and certain marginal plants such as **Petasites.** *Remove* them from your water garden, and plant other plants

Growing Smarter

A celebrity in any bog garden is the **Pitcher Plant,** and the **Common Pitcher Plant** (*Sarracenia purpurea*) will grow in Pennsylvania. These exotic plants, with their thick, hollow green- or purple-veined stems topped with hoods to trap insects, are interesting year 'round. In the spring they send up narrow stems topped with nodding purplish flowers with five petals. Try growing one.

instead. **Lotus** and **Cattails** come in dwarf versions that may be more suitable.

A **frozen pond surface** is not a problem as long as there is oxygen in the water. Sometimes portions of the ice will thaw when the sun comes out later in the day or the next day. Use a de-icer, or run the pump to circulate the water in the pond and aerate it.

Appendix

TROUBLESHOOTING PESTS AND DISEASES

Pest Name	Common Targets	Appearance	Damage	Some Control Methods
Aphids (aka Plant Lice)	Houseplants; trees; shrubs; flowers; vegetables; water plants.	Soft, pear-shaped; spindly legs. May be green, yellow, pink, black, or white.	Clusters on stems and foliage of tender new growth cause wilted, curling foliage and sap plant vigor.	Pinch infested tips and discard. Wash with water spray, insecticidal soap, or pepper wax spray. Green lacewings and ladybugs eat aphids.
Bagworms	Needled evergreens.	Bags of fine twigs dangle from branches.	Worms feed on foliage, then retreat to protective bag.	Pick off reachable bags. Spray *Bt* on foliage while worms feed.
Bean Beetles, Mexican	**Green Beans, Limas; Summer** and **Winter Squash.**	Round, copper-colored beetle, rows of black dots on its back. Yellow eggs under leaves. Striped small beetle adult.	They chew on leaves, skeletonize them.	Handpick beetles and squish eggs. Use neem, pyrethrum spray on beetles. Soldier bugs.
Borers	Shrubs, (especially roses, **Lilac**); trees (especially fruit trees); **Squash.**	Larvae of beetles and moths; small worms burrow into plant stems.	Leaves wilt; holes in woody stems, sawdust nearby.	Prune off affected stems below holes. Predatory nematodes. Spray *Bt* on stem surfaces.
Cabbage Worms	**Cabbage, Broccoli, Cauliflower, Kale, Brussels Sprouts, Radishes, Turnip.**	Larvae of small white butterfly.	They rasp large holes in leaves.	Spray *Bt* on foliage. Soldier bugs.
Caterpillars (Parsleyworm, Tomato Hornworm, et al.)	Trees, shrubs, vegetables, flowers.	Worm larvae of moths, butterflies.	They chew holes in edges of foliage; may leave only veins.	Handpick. Spray *Bt* on foliage. Trichogramma wasps.
Chlorosis	Acid-loving trees and shrubs such as **Holly, Azalea, Mountain Laurel.**	Foliage becomes yellowish, green veins stand out.	Disease indicates iron not available in soil for plant.	Acidify soil by sprinkling garden sulfur over root zone.
Damping-off	Seedlings.	Black streaks on lower stem.	Young seedlings flop over and die.	Use sterile seed-starting medium; water from below.

Appendix

TROUBLESHOOTING PESTS AND DISEASES

Pest Name	Common Targets	Appearance	Damage	Some Control Methods
Fall Webworms, Tent Caterpillars, Gypsy Moth Caterpillars	Trees, especially **Oak;** trees and shrubs at roadsides and other stressful sites.	Nests resemble webbed tents in twigs.	Caterpillars feed on tree foliage, chewing large holes, possibly skeltonizing it.	Prune out nests. Poke open unreachable nests with a stick. Spray foliage with **Bt** when worms hatch and begin to eat. Parasitic wasps will prey on some.
Fungal Disease	Turfgrasses.	Blackish or gray coating on foliage; spots, circles of mold or fungi.	Gray or dark streaks on foliage. Tattered or matted blades. Dead patches.	Mow grass dry. Do not walk on wet or frosty grass. Water early in day. Spray fungicide on healthy grass.
Japanese Beetles	Roses, annuals, perennials, shrubs and trees, some vegetables.	Metallic green-and-copper beetle.	They leave ragged holes in buds and leaves; will skeltonize roses' foliage.	Handpick. Spray neem or pyrethrum as directed.
Lacebugs	Broadleaf shrubs, such as **Azalea, Rhododendron, Pieris,** that are stressed by too much sun.	Tiny squarish dots with netted wings; leave specks of excrement under leaves.	They suck leaf juices until leaves are pale and stippled. Leaves become dry and bleached-out.	Move plant to shadier location. Spray with insecticidal soap.
Powdery Mildew	Roses, annuals, perennials, vegetables, houseplants.	Grayish blotching or coating on foliage.	Lower leaves dry, curl, and drop. Unsightly, but not fatal to mature plants.	Improve air circulation. Spray garden (sulfur) fungicide on healthy and new foliage to prevent infection.
Scale	Trees, shrubs, perennials, houseplants, **Asparagus.**	Raised, waxy bumps on leaf undersides and stems.	Insects feed on juices of plant tissues; foliage looks pale.	Scrape off gently with fingernail. Spray horticultural oil to smother. Green lacewings.
Slugs, Snails	Plants in moist, acidic soil in shade (ex., **Hosta**).	Soft-bodied, 1 to 4 inches long; leave a trail of mucous as they travel.	At night, they chew large ragged holes in leaves.	Handpick from under debris. Trap with yeast/beer bait. Sprinkle DE on soil around plants.
Spider Mites	Ivy, houseplants; foliage of stressed plants in dry conditions.	Resemble tiny spiders; they suck juices from foliage.	Pale strippling on leaves; fine webbing on stems. Leaves curl, turn brown.	Wash with forceful water spray; repeat. Insecticidal soap. Spray horticultural oil to smother.

Appendix

TROUBLESHOOTING PESTS AND DISEASES

Pest Name	Common Targets	Appearance	Damage	Some Control Methods
Thrips	Roses (especially red, white, yellow); citrus, **Dahlias, Foxgloves, Daylily, Iris, Gladioli, Mums, Privet.**	Tiny yellowish-brown insects with narrow feathery wings; they burrow into buds, suck juices.	Flowers distorted, droop. Buds fail to open, dry out.	Clip off infested flowers. Use Merit insecticide. Encourage beneficial insects.
Whiteflies	**Tomatoes** and some other vegetables; houseplants.	Tiny white specks fly off when disturbed. Note black dots of excrement under foliage.	They suck juices from foliage, which turns pale. Not life-threatening to most mature healthy plants.	Insecticidal soap; green lacewing larvae.
White Grubs	Turfgrass roots.	Japanese beetle larvae; fat, curled worms with brown heads; they overwinter in soil.	Grass dies, sod lifts easily because roots are destroyed.	Starlings, skunks, moles prey on grubs. Cut grass tall to discourage beetles from laying eggs. Spray with predatory nematodes. Spread milky spore disease.

PEST CONTROL GUIDELINES

- Maintain a diversity of plants to encourage natural controls by beneficials.
- Purchase pest- and disease-resistant plant varieties.
- Keep plants happy and as stress-free as possible with good care.
- Observe plants regularly to catch a problem at its earliest stage.
- Identify the problem accurately before starting control measures.
- Use the least-toxic control measure first.
- Read product labels carefully and follow instructions exactly.
- Treat only the particular plant or lawn area that exhibits the problem.
- After treating the problem, think about the underlying cause and address that.
- Store and dispose of all pesticides safely.

AUTHOR'S CAUTION

From time to time in this book, I recommend the use of pesticides. The use of such pest controls, however, must remain the choice of each individual gardener. It may not always be necessary to use pesticides to control insects or diseases. A particular pest or disease may not be harmful to your particular plants.

If pest control does become a problem, you should consider the use of alternative means. These include the use of resistant varieties, the use of botanical and microbial insecticides or soaps, encouraging predators and parasites, mechanical means such as screening, hand picking, and improving botanical practices.

If you do find it necessary to use traditional chemical pest controls, first consult your local authorities such as your extension office for correct pest identification and control recommendations. Once you have decides to use a specific pest control product, you must read and follow label directions carefully.

USDA Cold Hardiness Map

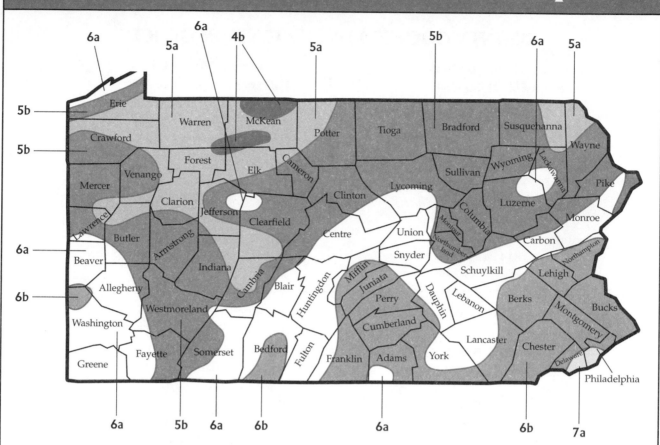

PENNSYLVANIA QUICK FACTS

Frost Dates

Zone 5
First expected frost: on or about September 30th
First hard frost: on or about October 10th
Last hard frost: May 5th
Last expected frost: May 20th

Zone 6
First expected frost: on or about October 10th
First hard frost: on or about October 31st
Last hard frost : April 20th
Last expected frost: May 10th

Zone 7
First expected frost: on or about October 20th
First hard frost: on or about November 10th
Last hard frost: March 31
Last expected frost: April 20

Precipitation
Average annual total precipitation statewide is about 42 inches.

Soil
pH typically 6.3
Type: clay/loam
Test kits are available from the office of your county extension agent.

Avg Annual Min. Temp.		Zone
-20° F	to -25° F	4b
-15° F	to -20° F	5a
-10° F	to -15° F	5b
-5° F	to -10° F	6a
0° F	to -5° F	6b
5° F	to 0° F	7a

Appendix

COUNTY COOPERATIVE EXTENSION OFFICES

Adams (717) 334-6271
Allegheny (412) 473-2540
Armstrong (724) 548-3447
Beaver (724) 774-3003
Bedford (814) 623-4800
Berks (610) 378-1327
Blair (814) 693-3265
Bradford (717) 265-2896
Bucks (215) 345-3283
Butler (724) 287-4761
Cambria (814) 472-7986
Cameron (814) 486-3350
Carbon (717) 325-2788
Centre (814) 355-4897
Chester (610) 696-3500
Clarion (814) 226-4956
Clearfield (814) 765-7878
Clinton (717) 726-0022
Columbia (717) 784-6660
Crawford (814) 333-7460
Cumberland (717) 240-6500
Dauphin (717) 921-8803
Delaware (610) 690-2655
Elk (814) 776-5331
Erie (814) 825-0900
Fayette (724) 438-0111
Forest (814) 755-3544
Franklin (717) 263-9226
Fulton (717) 485-4111
Greene (724) 627-3745
Huntingdon (814) 643-1660
Indiana (724) 465-3880
Jefferson (814) 849-7361,
    (814)849-8297
Juniata (717) 436-7744

Lackawana (570) 963-4761
Lancaster (717) 394-6851
Lawrence (724) 654-8370,
    (724) 654-2741
Lebanon (717) 270-4391
Lehigh (610) 391-9840
Luzerne (570) 825-1701,
    (570) 602-0600
Lycoming (570) 433-3040
Mckean (814) 887-5613
Mercer (724) 662-314
Mifflin (717) 248-9618
Monroe (717) 421-6430
Montgomery (610) 489-4315
Montour (570) 275-3731
Northampton (610)746-1970
Northumberland (717) 644-4455
Perry (717) 582-2131
Philadelphia (215) 471-2200
Pike (717) 296-3400
Potter (814) 274-8540
Schuykill (717) 622-4225
Snyder (717) 837-4252
Somerset (814) 445-8911
Sullivan (717) 928-8941
Susquehanna (717) 278-1158
Tioga (717) 724-9120
Union (717) 524-8721
Venango (814) 437-7607
Warren (814) 563-9388
Washington (724) 228-6881
Wayne (717) 253-5970
Westmorland (724) 837-1402
Wyoming (717) 836-3196
York (717) 840-7408

Appendix

THE PENNSYLVANIA HORTICULTURAL SOCIETY'S
GOLD MEDAL PLANT AWARD

Since 1988 the Pennsylvania Horticultural Society's Gold Medal Plant Award program has honored little-known and underused woody plants of exceptional merit for gardens. They are chosen for their beauty, superior performance, and hardiness in zones 5 through 7. Each year a distinguished committee of the Philadelphia area's most knowledgeable horticulturists from local arboreta, public or private gardens, and allied industries evaluate plants that have been nominated for the Gold Medal. Some plants are familiar, others new, and they may be native or introduced. For additional information, contact the Pennsylvania Horticultural Society at 215-988-8800.

Arborvitae: *Thuja* 'Green Giant' 1998
Beautyberry: *Callicarpa dichotoma* 1989
Birch: *Betula nigra* 'Heritage' 1990
Boxwood: *Buxus* 'Green Velvet' 1995
Buckeye: *Aesculus pavia* 1995
  Aesculus parviflora 1998
Cherry: *Prunus* 'Okame' 1998
  Prunus 'Hally Jolivette' 1994
Clematis: *Clematis* 'Betty Corning' 1992
Crabapple: *Malus* 'Donald Wyman' 1989
  Malus 'Jewelberry' 1989
Cryptomeria: *Cryptomeria japonica* 'Yoshino' 1993
Daphne: *Daphne caucasica* 1990
Dawn Redwood: *Metasequoia glyptostroboides* 1999
Deutzia: *Deutzia gracilis* 'Nikko' 1989
Dogwood: *Cornus kousa* (*C. florida* 'Rutban' Aurora™) 1993
  Cornus kousa (*C. florida* 'Rutlan' Ruth Ellen™) 1993
  Cornus mas 'Golden Glory' 2001
  Cornus sericea 'Silver and Gold' 1990
English Ivy: *Hedera helix* 'Buttercup' 1998
Enkianthus: *Enkianthus perulatus* 'J. L. Pennock' 1999
Fir: *Abies nordmanniana* 1992
Fothergilla: *Fothergilla gardenii* 'Blue Mist' 1990
Goldenraintree: *Koelreuteria paniculata* 'September' 1997
Hawthorn: *Crataegus viridis* 'Winter King' 1992
Heptacodium: *Heptacodium miconioides* 1995
Holly: *Ilex* 'Harvest Red' 1991
  Ilex glabra 'Densa' 1994
  Ilex × meserveae 'Mesid' Blue Maid™ 1996
  Ilex opaca ('Jersey Princess', 'Old Heavy Berry', 'Satyr Hill') 2001
  Ilex 'Sparkleberry' 1998
  Ilex verticillata 'Scarlett O'Hara' 1996
  Ilex verticillata 'Winter Red' 1995
Hydrangea: *Hydrangea macrophylla* 'Blue Billow' 1990
  Hydrangea arborescens 'Annabelle' 2001
  Hydrangea quercifolia 'Snow Queen' 1989

Juniper: *Juniperus virginiana* 'Corcorcor' Emerald Sentinel 1997
Lilac: *Syringa meyeri* 'Palibin' 2000
  Syringa reticulata 'Ivory Silk' 1996
Magnolia: *Magnolia* 'Elizabeth' 1988
  Magnolia 'Galaxy' 1992
  Magnolia grandiflora 'Edith Bogue' 1992
  Magnolia kobe's var. *stellata* 'Centennial' 1997
Mahonia: *Mahonia bealei* 1998
Maple: *Acer buergerianum* 2000
  Acer griseum 1993
  Acer palmatum 'Tamukeyama' 1997
  Acer palmatum 'Waterfall' 1999
  Acer triflorum 1996
Oak: *Quercus alba* 2000
Parrotia: *Parrotia persica* 2000
Plum Yew: *Cephalotaxus harringtonia* 'Prostrata' 1994
Red Chokeberry: *Aronia arbutifolia* 'Brilliantissima' 2000
Rose of Sharon: *Hibiscus syriacus* 'Diana' 1991
Schizophragma: *Schizophragma hydrangeoides* 'Moonlight' 1998
Spruce: *Picea orientalis* 1992
Stewartia: *Stewartia pseudocammellia* var. *koreana* 1990
Summersweet: *Clethra alnifolia* 'Hummingbird' 1994
  Clethra alnifolia 'Ruby Spice' 1998
Umbrella Pine: *Sciadopitys verticillata* 1991
Viburnum: *Viburnum × burkwoodii* 'Conoy' 1997
  Viburnum × burkwoodii 'Mohawk' 1993
  Viburnum dilatatum 'Erie' 1993
  Viburnum 'Eskimo' 1992
  Viburnum nudum 'Winterthur' 1991
  Viburnum plicatum f. *tomentosum* 'Shasta' 1991
Virginia Sweetspire: *Itea virginica* 'Henry's Garnet' 1998
Weigela: *Weigela florida* Wine and Roses™ 2000
Witchhazel: *Hamamelis × intermedia* 'Diane' 1991
  Hamamelis mollis 'Pallida' 1989
Yellowwood: *Cladrastis kentukea* 1994
Zelkova: *Zelkova serrata* 'Green Vase' 1998

Appendix

INFORMATION RESOURCES

Pennsylvania Horticultural Society
100 N. 20th Street, 5th Floor
Philadelphia, PA 19103-1495
(215) 988-8800
www.libertynet.org/phs

National Audubon Society
700 Broadway
New York, NY 10003
(212) 979-3000
www.audubon.org

National Wildlife Federation
Backyard Wildlife Habitat
   Program
8925 Leesburg Pike
Vienna, VA 22184-0001
(703) 790-4434
www.carskaddan@nwf.org

American Rose Society
P. O. Box 30,000
Shreveport, LA 71130-0030
(318) 938-5402
www.ars.org

All-America Selections
Nona Wolfram-Koivula
1311 Butterfield Road, Suite 310
Downer's Grove, IL 60515
(630) 963-0770

International Society of
   Arboriculture
Derek Vannice
P.O. Box 3129
Champaign, IL 61826
(217) 355-9411
E-mail: isa@isa-arbor.com

Netherlands Flower Bulb
   Information Center
Sally Ferguson
30 Milwood Street
Brooklyn, NY 11225
(718) 693-5400
www.bulb.com

Turfgrass Producers International
Douglas H. Fender
1855-A Hicks Road
Rolling Meadows, IL 60008
(800) 405-TURF

MAIL-ORDER SOURCES OF SEEDS, PLANTS, AND EQUIPMENT

Burpee Seed Company
300 Park Avenue
Warminster, PA 18974
(800) 888-1447
www.burpee.com
Seeds, flowering plants

Brent & Becky's Bulbs
7463 Heath Trail
Gloucester, VA 23601
(877) 661-2852
www.brentandbeckybulbs.com
Bulbs

The Conard-Pyle Company
372 Rose Hill Road
West Grove, pA 19390-0904
(800) 458-6559
www.starroses.com
Roses

Duncraft
102 Fisherville Road
Concord, NH 03303-2086
(800) 593-5656
www.duncraft.com
Bird supplies

Forestfarm
990 Tetherow Road
Williams, OR 97544-9599
(541) 846-7269
www.forestfarm.com
Trees, shrubs, perennials

Gardener's Supply Company
128 Intervale Road
Burlington, VT 05401
(802) 863-1700
www.gardeners.com
Tools and supplies

Jackson & Perkins
1 Rose Lane
Medford, OR 97501-0702
www.jackson-perkins.com
Roses

Lilypons Water Gardens
6800 Lilypons Road
P.O. Box 10
Buckeystown, MD 21717-0010
(800) 999-5459
www.lilypons.com
Water lilies, bog plants

Musser Trees
P.O. Box S-91M
Indiana, PA 15701
(412) 465-5685
www.musserforests.com
Trees, shrubs, ground covers

Park Seed Company
P.O. Box 31
Greenwood, SC 29647
(800) 845-3369
www.parkseed.com
Seeds, perennials

Plow & Hearth
560 Main Street
Madison, VA 22727
(800) 627-1712
www.plowhearth.com
Tools and supplies

Renee's Garden
(888) 880-7228
www.reneesgarden.com
*Gourmet vegetables, kitchen herbs,
   cottage garden flowers*

MAIL-ORDER SOURCES OF SEEDS, PLANTS, AND EQUIPMENT

Seeds of Change
P.O. Box 15700
Santa Fe, NM 87506-5700
(888) 762-7333
www.seedsofchange.com
Organically grown vegetable and flower seeds

Wayside Gardens
1 Garden Lane
Hodges, SC 29695-0001
(800) 845-1124
www.waysidegardens.com
Perennials, shrubs, roses, bulbs

We-Du Nurseries
Route 5, Box 724
Marion, NC 28752-9338
Perennials, wildflowers

White Flower Farm
P.O. Box 50
Litchfield, CT 06759-0050
(800) 503-9624
www.whiteflowerfarm.com
Perennials, shrubs, roses, bulbs

PLANT SOCIETIES IN PENNSYLVANIA

African Violet Society of Central
   Pennsylvania
Susan Reis
1181 Williams Street
State College, PA 16801
(814) 238-4436

American Conifer Society
Central Region Chapter
Frank Goodhart
27 Oak Knoll Road
Mendham, NJ 07945
(908) 879-4788

American Hosta Society
Regional Director
Carol Brasher
16 McKay Farm Road
Woodbury, CT 06798
(203) 266-4268

American Rhododendron Society
Greater Philadelphia Chapter
Tom Conover
505 E. Wynnewood Road
Wynnewood, PA 19096
(610) 896-7584

American Rhododendron Society
Valley Forge Chapter
Winfield Howe
7 Surrey Lane
Downingtown, PA 19335-1507
(610) 458-5291

American Rose Society (PA & NJ)
Gustave R. Banks
117 Farmdale Road
Mt. Holly, NJ 08060-3296
e-mail: jrsyrose@bellatlantic.nct

Azalea Society of America
P.O. Box 34536
West Bethesda, MD 20087-0536

Bio-Dynamic Farming and
   Gardening Association
P. O. Box 550
Kimerton, PA 19442

Botanical Society of
   Western Pennsylvania
401 Clearview Avenue
Pittsburgh, PA 15205

Central Pennsylvania
   Orchid Society
Dr. John H. Dollar
P.O. Box 116
Tyrone, PA 16686
(814) 684-3886

Chrysanthemum Society
   of Pittsburgh
Miss Barbara Plutnicki, President
(412) 521-1389

Penn West
   Chrysanthemum Society
Greensburg
Mr. Richard Fleming, President
(724) 836-1629

Delaware Valley
   Chrysanthemum Society
Ralph B. Parks
821 Meredith Drive
Media, PA 19063-1740
(610) 566-5644

Delaware Valley Daffodil Society
Ann M. Howe
7 Surrey Lane
Downingtown, PA 19335-1507
(610) 458-5291

Delaware Valley Daylily Society
Beth Creveling
980 Bypass Road
Perkasie, PA 18944
(215) 249-0682
Cathy Tomlinson
(610) 458-0177

Delaware Valley Fern &
   Wildflower Society
c/o Alice-Blake Simonson,
   Treasurer
1030 Lime Kiln Pike
Maple Glen, PA 19002

Appendix

PLANT SOCIETIES IN PENNSYLVANIA

Delaware Valley Hosta Society
Warren Pollock
202 Hackney Circle
Surrey Park
Wilmington, DE 19803-1911
(302) 478-2610

Delaware Valley Iris Society
Charles and Betsy Conklin
91 Duncan Lane
Springfield, PA 19064
(610) 544-3984

Delaware Valley Water
   Garden Society
Fred Weiss
339 Valley Road
Merion Station, PA 19066
(610) 667-7545

Greater Philadelphia
   Dahlia Society
Steve Thomas
566 Sugartown Road
Malvern, PA 19355
(610) 644-4581

Greater Pittsburgh Cactus &
   Succulent Society
President: Paul J. Hoffman
10176 Sudberry Drive
Wexford, PA 15090

Hardy Plant Society/
Mid-Atlantic Group
Sylvia Cooperman
20 Crown Oak Drive
Chester Springs, PA 19425

Herb Society of America
Philadelphia Unit
Kathy Bepler
1515 Ridley Creek Road
Media, PA 19063
(610) 566-6261

Ivy Society
Hedera Etc.
Lionsville, PA 19353-0461
(610) 970-9175

Mid-Atlantic Lily Society
Ellen Ressler
510 E. Conestoga St.
New Holland, PA 17557
(717) 354-9556

National Rhododendron Society
11 Pinecrest Dr.
Fortuna, CA 95540

Native Plant Society
P.O. Box 281
State College, PA 16804
(814) 238-8879

North American Rock
   Garden Society
Delaware Valley Chapter
Ann Rosenberg
5 Westview Drive
Bryn Mawr, PA 19010
(610) 525-8683

North American Rock
   Garden Society
Pittsburgh, PA
Patty McGuire
(412) 366-8364

Northeastern Pennsylvania
   Orchid Society
Jack Buziuk
62 South Fulton Street
Wilkes Barre, PA 18702-6402
(570) 824-2961

Orchid Society of Northwestern
   Pennsylvania
Jean Metcalf
2553 Main Street
Lake City, PA 16423
(814) 774-4932
ejmet@ncinter.net

Orchid Society of Western
   Pennsylvania
Barbara Tisherman
5145 Beeler Street
Pittsburgh, PA 15217
(412) 683-0207
btisherman@aol.com

Pennsylvania Iris Society
Vincent Lewonski
509 S. Bishop Avenue
Secane, PA 19018-2903
(610) 623-3921
VinceLewonski@yahoo.com

Pennsylvania Native Plant Society
P.O. Box 281
State College, PA 16804-0281

Philadelphia Botanical Club
David Lauer
Academy of Natural Sciences
1900 Benjamin Franklin Parkway
Philadelphia, PA 19103-1195
(215)-357-2646
DML100@aol.com

Philadelphia Rose Society
Pat Pitkin
923 Springfield Drive
West Chester, PA 19382
(610) 692-4076

The Pittsburgh Violet &
   Gesneriad Society
Northland Public Library
300 Cumberland Road
Pittsburgh, PA 15237

Susquehanna Orchid Society
Bruce Johnson
131 Maple Lane
Lebanon, PA 17042
(717) 274-1542

Appendix

GLOSSARY

acclimate. To become accustomed to a different environment.

aerate (aeration). To introduce (introducing) oxygen into the soil to improve it. This is commonly done by digging into the soil in gardens or using equipment to pull up cores of soil and open holes in turf. Air in the soil supports the microbial life that makes it fertile.

alkaline soil. Soil that has a pH greater than 7.0. It lacks acidity, often because it has limestone in it. Certain plants prefer soil that is somewhat alkaline.

all-purpose fertilizer. Either powdered, liquid, or granular, it contains a balanced proportion of the three key nutrients—nitrogen (N), phosphorus (P), potassium (K)—and it is suitable for maintenance nutrition for most plants. It is also called balanced or general-purpose fertilizer.

annual. A plant that lives its entire life in one season. It is genetically determined to germinate, grow, flower, set seed, and die the same year.

anti-transpirant/anti-desiccant. A product that reduces a plant's moisture loss through its foliage (transpiration) by coating the foliage with a thin film.

arborist. A person who is trained to care for trees.

***Bacillus thuringiensis* (Bt).** A bacterium that kills larval worms or caterpillars by attacking the digestive system. Available as a dust or a powder to be mixed in water and sprayed on plant foliage when the caterpillars are actively eating.

balled-and-burlapped. Describes trees and shrubs grown in the field whose roots are wrapped with protective burlap and twine when they are dug up to be sold or transplanted.

bare-root. Describes the packaging of certain plants sold without any soil around their roots. Often young shrubs and trees purchased through the mail arrive with their exposed roots covered with moist peat or sphagnum moss, sawdust, or similar material and wrapped in plastic.

barrier plant. A plant that has intimidating thorns or spines and is sited purposely to block foot traffic or other access to the home or yard.

basal. At the base, growing closest to its point of origin. Basal leaves are those that grow at the base of the stem, at the crown of the plant.

beneficial insects. Insects or their larvae that prey on pest organisms and their eggs. They may be flying insects such as ladybugs, parasitic wasps, praying mantids, and soldier bugs; or soil dwellers such as predatory nematodes, spiders, and ants.

biennial. A plant that is genetically programmed to grow over two seasons before setting seed and dying.

bolting. The tendency of a leafy plant such as lettuce or spinach to to to seed prematurely. Often in response to very hot weather, such a plant sends up tall stalks that bear flowers, then seeds; this usually affects the quality and flavor of the foliage crop.

bract. A petal-like modified leaf structure on a plant stem near its flower. Often it is more colorful and visible than the actual flower, as in **Dogwood.**

broadcasting. Sowing seed by casting out handfuls over a prepared seedbed. This method is used to sow turfgrass or wildflower seed.

Bt. *See Bacillus thuringiensis.*

bud union. *See* **graft.**

canopy. The overhead branching area of a tree, usually referring to its extent, including foliage.

chlorosis. A nutritional deficiency in plants indicated by yellowed foliage with green veins. Most common in plants that require acidic soil (such as **Holly** and **Azalea**), it signals that they are not able to take up sufficient iron from the soil.

climber. A plant that grows vertically by means of elongating stems. It may twist, cling, or use holdfasts to climb vertical surfaces or supports.

cold hardiness. The ability of a perennial plant to survive the winter cold in a particular area. Plants that are listed as cold hardy to -10 degrees F do well in the Philadelphia area.

Appendix

GLOSSARY

composite. A flower that is actually composed of many tiny flowers. Typically they are flat clusters of tiny, tight florets, sometimes surrounded by wider-petaled florets like a **Daisy** or **Sunflower.** Composite flowers are highly attractive to bees and beneficial insects.

compost. Organic matter that has undergone progressive decomposition by microbial and macrobial activity until it is reduced to a spongy, fluffy texture. Added to soil of any type, it improves its ability to hold air and water and to drain well.

corm. The swollen, energy-storing structure, analogous to a bulb, under the soil at the base of the stem of plants such as **Crocus** or **Gladiolus.**

county agent/extension agent. An employee of the state university who is trained to provide information and assistance to farmers and homeowners about agricultural and horticultural techniques, soil analysis, and pest control. There is an office in every county. *See* page 340 for list of phone numbers.

crown. The base of a plant at, or just beneath, the surface of the soil where its roots meet its stems. This term is also used sometimes to describe the branching area of a tree.

cultivar. A CULTIvated VARiety. A naturally occurring form of a plant that has been identified as special or superior and is specifically selected for propagation and production.

damping off. A fungal disease that targets young seedlings. Spores in the soil cause their stems to blacken and collapse. Using sterile potting medium helps prevent this problem.

deadhead. To remove faded flowerheads from plants to improve their appearance, abort seed production, and stimulate further flowering.

deciduous. The opposite of evergreen; describes trees and shrubs that lose their leaves in the fall.

desiccation. Drying out of foliage tissues, usually due to drought or wind.

diatomaceous earth (DE). Finely ground shells of a tiny algae. This natural pesticide is an effective barrier against slugs; when sprinkled on the soil around vulnerable plants, the sharp edges of the powder cut their bodies.

direct-sow. To sow seeds directly into the garden rather than starting them in small pots for later transplanting.

division. Splitting apart perennial plants to create several smaller rooted segments. Useful for controlling a plant's size and for acquiring more plants, it is also essential to the health and continued flowering of certain species.

dormancy (dormant). The period, usually winter, when perennial plants temporarily cease active growth, and rest. Some plants, such as spring-blooming bulbs, **go dormant** in the summer.

drip irrigation. An efficient water delivery system through special lines, or hoses, laid through planted beds. Water either soaks through the hoses or leaks through special emitters inserted in them to go directly to plant roots.

dripline. (a) The outer reaches of a tree's branching canopy where rainfall drips from branch tips. (b) A line, or hose, that is part of a drip irrigation system.

establishment. The time at which a newly planted tree, shrub, or flower begins to produce new growth, either foliage or stems. This is an indication that the roots have recovered from transplant shock and have begun to grow and spread.

evergreen. Perennial plants that do not lose their foliage annually with the onset of winter. Describes needled or broadleaf foliage that persists and continues to function on a plant through one or more winters, aging and dropping unobtrusively in cycles of three, four, or more years.

fertilizer. Any material that, when added to the soil, contributes one or more nutrients required by plants. Fertilizers called "complete" or "balanced" offer the major nutrients nitrogen, potassium, and phosphorus plus an assortment of minor nutrients.

foliar. Of or about foliage. Usually refers to the practice of spraying foliage, as in fertilizing or treating with insecticide. With a foliar spray, leaf tissues absorb liquid directly for much faster results, and the soil is not affected.

Appendix

GLOSSARY

flexible liner. A waterproof barrier made from PVC, butyl, or other flexible material in a pond, bog, or pool dug into the ground.

floret. A tiny flower, usually one of many forming a cluster that comprises a single blossom such as a **Lilac** or **Spider Flower.**

fungicide, garden. Any product that acts to prevent, control, or eradicate plant diseases caused by fungi.

germinate. To sprout; to enter a fertile seed's first stage of development.

girdling roots. Roots that circle around the root flare at the base of a tree or shrub rather than growing outward into the soil.

graft (union). The point on the stem of a sturdy-rooted woody plant to which a stem from a highly ornamental plant is joined. Roses are commonly grafted.

habitat. The natural environment of a plant. A plant removed from its habitat and brought into cultivation in a residential landscape does best when the new conditions are similar to those of its native habitat.

handpick. To eliminate pest insects or slugs and caterpillars by plucking them from plant foliage or knocking them into a plastic bag or jar of soapy water to kill them.

hardening-off. The process of gradually acclimating indoor plants—houseplants or seedlings raised under lights—to outdoor weather.

hardiness. *See* **cold hardiness.**

hardscape. The permanent, structural, nonplant part of a landscape such as walls, sheds, pools, patios, arbors, and walkways.

herbaceous. Describes plants that have fleshy or soft stems that die back with frost; the opposite of woody.

herbicide. Any product or chemical agent that kills plants. Some act on foliage and stem tissues, some act on seeds.

hills. Raised mounds of soil created for planting seeds of certain crops such as **Corn** or **Squash.** There are several seeds in each hill.

hybrid. A plant that is the result of either intentional or natural cross-pollination between two or more plants of the same species or genus. This pedigree is expressed by the multiplication symbol × in between the two words in its botanical (scientific) name.

insecticide. Any product, compound, or garden aid formulated specifically to kill insects.

intensive planting. The practice of planting food crops closer together than recommended to utilize garden space most efficiently and maximize production. This technique is most successful in raised beds where the soil is exceptionally fertile and aerated.

irrigation. *See* **drip irrigation.**

larva(e). An insect in its immature stage, after it hatches from an egg. Typically a worm or caterpillar form of a butterfly, moth, or beetle, larvae are voraciously hungry; this is the stage at which insects are most destructive to plants.

lime. Limestone processed as granules, pellets, or powder for use in adding calcium to soils. Spread on lawns and growing beds, it raises the pH of the soil (reduces its acidity) and provides calcium to plants. Dolomite limestone also contributes magnesium.

liner, pond. Either a molded fiberglass form or a flexible butyl or poly fabric that creates an artificial pond for the purpose of water gardening.

low water demand. Describes the moisture needs of plants that tolerate dry soil for varying periods of time. Typically they have succulent, hairy, or silvery-gray foliage and tuberous or taproots. **Xeriscape plants** have low water demand.

melting out. The tendency of certain plants to die out in midseason; they collapse, wither, or rot for no apparent reason.

mulch. A layer of material over bare soil that protects the soil from erosion and compaction by rain, and also discourages weeds. It may be inorganic (gravel, fabric) or organic (wood chips, bark, pine needles, chopped leaves).

native. Indigenous. Native plants are those determined to have been growing in their wild habitat in a particular region or state before the arrival of European settlers.

Appendix

GLOSSARY

naturalize. (a) To plant seeds, bulbs, or plants in a random, informal pattern as they would appear in their natural habitat. (b) The tendency of some non-native plants to adapt to and spread throughout their adopted habitats.

nectar. The sweet fluid produced by glands on flowers that attracts pollinators such as hummingbirds and honeybees, for whom the fluid is a source of energy.

organic material, matter. Any material or debris that is derived from plants. Carbon-based material that is capable of undergoing decomposition and decay.

peat moss. Organic matter from peat sedges (United States) or sphagnum mosses (Canada), often used to improve soil texture. The acidity of sphagnum peat moss makes it ideal for boosting or maintaining soil acidity while also improving its drainage.

perennial. A flowering plant that lives over three or more seasons. Many die back with frost, but their roots survive the winter and generate new shoots in spring.

pesticide. Any product, compound, or device that kills pest insects, disease pathogens, pest animals, or weeds.

pH. A measurement of the relative acidity (low pH) or alkalinity (high pH) of soil or water based on a scale of 1 to 14, with 7 being neutral. Individual plants require soil within a certain pH range in order for nutrients to dissolve in moisture and become available to plant roots.

pinch. To remove tender stems and/or leaves by pressing them between thumb and forefinger. This is a pruning technique that is used to encourage branching, compactness, and flowering in plants or to remove aphids clustered at growing tips.

photosynthesis. The process by which plants, collecting energy from the sun by means of the chlorophyll in their foliage, transform carbon dioxide in the air and water from the soil into carbohydrates that fuel their growth.

pollen. The yellow, powdery grains in the center of a flower. A plant's male sex cells, they are transferred to the female plant parts by means of wind, insects or animal pollinators, to fertilize them and create seeds.

potbound. *See* rootbound.

pre-emergent. Acting prior to the germination of a seed. A product, compound, or chemical that inhibits the sprouting of a fertile seed (as in pre-emergent herbicide).

pre-formed liner. A mold available in many sizes and shapes for setting into the ground to make a water garden pond; usually made of molded fiberglass or a similar material.

reversion. The appearance on a cultivar of a tree or shrub of one or more branches with foliage that is characteristic of the species.

rhizome. A swollen energy-storing stem structure, similar to a bulb, that lies horizontally in the soil, with roots emerging from its lower surface and growth shoots from a growing point at or near its tip (as in Bearded Iris).

rootbound (or potbound). The condition of a plant that has been confined to a container too long, its roots having been forced to wrap around themselves and even swell out of the container. Successful transplanting or repotting requires untangling and trimming away some of the matted roots.

root flare. The transition at the base of a tree trunk where the bark tissue begins to differentiate and roots to form just prior to entering the soil. This area should not be covered with soil when planting a tree.

rootstock. *See* understock.

root zone. The area that the roots of a given plant currently occupy or can be expected to spread to when mature. Water, fertilizer, and mulch are most effectively applied to the soil surface over the root zone.

scion. The ornamental, desirable part of a grafted plant. Usually refers to a cutting, shoot, or bud that is to be grafted onto the understock, which supplies the root system.

self-seeding. Describes the tendency of some plants to sow their seeds freely around the yard. This creates many seedlings the following season, which may or may not be welcome.

Appendix

GLOSSARY

shearing. The pruning technique whereby plant stems and branches are cut uniformly with long-bladed pruning shears (hedge shears) or powered hedge trimmers. Used in creating and maintaining hedges and topiary.

slow-acting fertilizer. Fertilizer that is water-insoluble and therefore releases its nutrients gradually as a function of soil temperature, moisture, and related microbial activity. Typically granular, it may be either organic or synthetic.

sod. Pieces of soil in which turfgrass plants are already growing.

soil test. Chemical analysis of soil to determine its fertility, pH, and nutrients. This is usually done by private laboratories or state university facilities. Less sophisticated tests can be done by gardeners using inexpensive kits available at garden centers.

sooty mold. A gray or black fungus on the foliage of plants infested with pest insects. It is fostered by the sticky, sweet juices that leak from plant tissues as insects suck on them. Its presence signals that a plant has an insect problem.

succession planting. The practice of promptly replacing food crops that have passed peak production with new transplants of another crop. Most effective in raised beds where the soil is rich enough to support several crops over a season, it maximizes production in a limited space.

sucker. A new growing shoot. Underground plant roots produce suckers to form new stems and spread by means of these suckering roots to form large plantings, or colonies. Some plants produce root suckers or branch suckers as a result of pruning or wounding.

sulfur. An element and nutrient that is useful in the garden. Sprinkled on the soil, it lowers the pH to make it more acid. Mixed with water, it is used as a fungicide.

thinning. The process of removing selected sprouts from a crowded row of newly germinated seedlings to create sufficient space for the remaining ones to grow and mature.

transplant. A young plant that is mature enough to be planted outdoors in a garden bed or decorative container.

true leaves. The second set of leaves that appear on a young seedling. They resemble the leaves of the species.

tuber. A type of underground storage structure in a plant stem, analogous to a bulb. It generates roots below and stems aboveground (examples: **Dahlias, Taro, Potatoes**).

understock (also rootstock). The plant that provides a sturdy root system onto which a desirable species is grafted to create an ornamental plant (examples: **Hybrid Tea** rose, **Cherry** tree).

variegated. Having various colors or color patterns. Usually refers to plant foliage that is streaked, edged, blotched, or mottled with a contrasting color, often green with cream or white.

water sprout (also sucker). A tender branch shoot growing vertically from a tree limb. While some trees tend to produce water sprouts routinely, it is often a sign of tree stress.

white grubs. Fat, off-white, wormlike larvae of Japanese beetles. They reside in the soil and feed on plant (especially grass) roots until summer, when they emerge as beetles to feed on plant foliage.

wings. (a) The corky tissue that forms edges along the twigs of some woody plants such as **Winged Euonymus.** (b) The flat, dried extensions of tissue on some seeds, such as **Maple,** that catch the wind and aid seed dissemination.

witches' broom. A mass of small sprouts that bristle from a tree or shrub branch bearing otherwise normal-sized leaves and twigs. Often a response to an injury or infection of some sort, witches' brooms may provide a source for the propagation of new and unusual versions of a species.

xeriscape. Describes plants that tolerate dry soil for varying periods of time. *See* **low water demand.**

Appendix

BIBLIOGRAPHY

American Horticultural Society. *A–Z Encyclopedia of Garden Plants*. Ed. Christopher Brickell. New York: Dorling Kindersley, 1997.

Bagust, Harold. *The Gardener's Dictionary of Horticultural Terms*. Strand, London: Cassell Publishers, 1992.

Ball, Jeffrey N. and Liz Ball. *Smart Yard: 60 Minute Lawn Care*. Golden, CO: Fulcrum Publishing,1994.

Ball, Jeffrey N. *The 60 Minute Vegetable Garden*. New York: Macmillan, 1985.

Ball, Jeffrey N. with Liz Ball. *Yardening*. New York: Macmillan, 1991.

Barash, Cathy Wilkinson. *Edible Flowers from Garden to Palate*. Golden, CO: Fulcrum, 1993.

——. *Evening Gardens*. Shelburne, VT: Chapters Publishing, 1993.

Coggiatti, Selvio. *Simon and Schuster's Guide to Roses*. New York: Simon & Schuster, 1986.

Cresson, Charles O. *Charles Cresson on the American Flower Garden*. New York: Prentice Hall, 1993.

Dennis, John V. and Mathew Tekulsky. *How to Attract Hummingbirds and Butterflies*. San Ramon, CA: Ortho Books, 1991.

Dirr, Michael A. *A Manual of Woody Landscape Plants*. Champaign, IL: Stipes Publishing, 1998.

DiSabato-Aust, Tracy. *The Well-Tended Perennial Garden*. Portland, OR: Timber Press, 1998.

Fell, Derek. *The Pennsylvania Gardener*. Philadelphia: Camino Books, 1995.

Greenlee, John. *The Encyclopedia of Ornamental Grasses*. New York: Michael Friedman Publishing Group, 1992.

Fizzell, James A. *Month-by-Month Gardening in Michigan*. Franklin, TN: Cool Springs Press, 1999.

Hart, Ronda Massingham. *Deer-Proofing Your Yard and Garden*. Pownal, VT: Storey Communications, 1997.

Hedrick, U. P. *A History of Horticulture in America to 1860*. Portland, OR: Timber Press, 1988.

Heriteau, Jacqueline and Charles Thomas. *Water Gardens*. NewYork: Houghton-Mifflin, 1994.

Herwig, Rob. *Growing Beautiful Houseplants*. New York: Facts on File, 1987.

Klein, William M., Jr. *Gardens of Philadelphia and the Delaware Valley*. Philadelphia: Temple University Press, 1995.

Lammers, Susan M. *All About Houseplants*. California: Ortho Books, 1982.

McKeon, Judith C. *The Encyclopedia of Roses*. Michael Friedman Publishing Group, Inc., Emmaus, PA: Rodale Press, 1995.

M'Mahon, Bernard. *The American Gardener's Calendar*, 11th edition. Philadelphia: J.P. Lippincott and Company, 1857.

Polomski, Bob. *Month by Month Gardening in the Carolinas*. Franklin, TN: Cool Springs Press, 2000.

Ray, Richard and Michael MacCaskey. *Roses: How to Select, Grow, and Enjoy*. Horticultural Publishing Company, Inc. Tucson, AZ: H.P. Books, Inc., 1985.

Seitz, Ruth Hoover. *Philadelphia and Its Countryside*. Harrisburg, PA: RB Books, 1994.

Shaudys, Phyllis. *The Pleasure of Herbs*. Pownel, VT: Storey Communications, 1986.

Smith, Edward C. *Vegetable Gardener's Bible*. Pownel, VT: Storey Communications, 2000.

Solit, Karen with Jim Solit. *Keeping Your Gift Plants Thriving: A Complete Guide to Plant Survival*. Pownel, VT: Storey Communications, 1985.

Sunset editors. *How to Grow Herbs*. Menlo Park, CA: Sunset Books, 1984.

Tomlinson, Timothy R. and Barbara Klaczynska. *Paradise Presented*. Philadelphia: The Morris Arboretum of the University of Pennsylvania, 1996.

Index

Index

Index

Index

Index

Index

Index

Index

Index

Index

Index

Index

Index

Index

Index

About the Author

Liz Ball

Liz Ball is a horticultural writer, photographer, researcher, and teacher whose articles and photographs have appeared in numerous catalogs, magazines, and books. An occasional contributor to *Green Scene,* the magazine of the Pennsylvania Horticultural Society, and *Pennsylvania Heritage* magazine, she writes regularly for the National Garden Bureau and Burpee's web site. Her weekly "Yardening" column has appeared in her local newspaper for over eight years.

Liz has co-authored nine books on plant and landscape care. She is the sole author of *Composting* (Smith & Hawken, 1997), *The Philadelphia Garden Book: A Gardener's Guide for The Delaware Valley* (Cool Springs Press, 1999), *Step by Step Yard Care and Step by Step Garden Basics* (Better Homes & Gardens, Meredith, 1999), and *My Pennsylvania Garden: A Gardener's Journal* (Cool Springs Press, 2000).

Liz writes about a wide range of gardening topics for gardeners, but specializes in addressing issues that concern non-gardening homeowners who have lawns and plants to care for but limited time and interest in working in the yard. She has researched and written over 200 plant- and yard-care tip sheets for these "Yardeners."

A long-time gardener herself, Liz gave up a 25-year career teaching writing, literature, and history at the secondary level to focus on horticulture. She has since taught courses on gardening at local community adult and arboretum programs and on garden writing for the Arboretum School of the Barnes Foundation and the Department of Special Programs at Temple University, Ambler Campus. She is currently teaching writing to Professional Gardening students at Longwood Gardens. She speaks often to garden clubs, horticultural societies, and civic groups, and at the Philadelphia Flower Show.

Liz serves on the education committee of Scott Arboretum at Swarthmore College and is a recording secretary for the local chapter of the North American Rock Garden Society. She is a national director of the Garden Writers Association of America. Liz manages her own photography business, Garden Portraits, maintaining a small slide library of images of plants and residential yards and gardens that she licenses to publishers of books and magazines.

In her spare time, Liz presides over a suburban yard that serves as an informal laboratory and demonstration garden for ongoing plant and equipment testing, research, workshop presentations, and occasional TV/video spots. It features vegetable and ornamental beds, small fruit trees, various turfgrass areas, a composting operation, and, lately, deer fencing.

More Books by Liz Ball

My Pennsylvania Garden: A Gardener's Journal

My Pennsylvania Garden is a beautifully illustrated garden journal spanning a year in the life of your garden. Two pages per each week allow ample space to record notes, comments, and observations. The journal is packed with tips, hints, full-color photographs and original illustrations to brighten your gardening day. In addition to the weekly journal pages, an introduction explains more about gardening in Pennsylvania, how to start and maintain a journal, and provides lists of recommended plants. Also, several pages are devoted to recording your own plant inventory, for notes and photographs, and to list resources and suppliers.

ISBN #1-930604-06-8
Retail Price: $19.95

The Philadelphia Garden Book: A Gardener's Guide For The Delaware Valley

The first book by Liz Ball for Cool Springs Press was written for the Philadelphia-area gardener who wants clear, sound information from an experienced gardener. Liz carefully selected 175 plants that thrive in the gardener's heaven known as the Delaware Valley. Full-color photographs for easy plant identification accompany concise, accurate information in an easy-to-use format.

Written as a practical how-to book both for beginning and experienced gardeners, *The Philadelphia Garden Book* is an excellent resource for people who want more information on recommended plants for their area. It is also an ideal reference for those who want to learn more about their local nurseries, arboreta, and public gardens and who want a taste of the unparallel horticultural history of the Delaware Valley. It is a wonderful resource and a great companion book to *Month-by-Month Gardening in Pennsylvania*.

ISBN #1-888608-46-3
Retail Price: $24.95

Look for them both at your local bookstore, or visit our website, **www.coolspringspress.com.** If you cannot find the books locally, you may order both by phoning Cool Springs Press directly at 888-591-5117.